Sacred Vessel of the Mysteries

Sacred Vessel of the Mysteries:

The Great Invocation — Word of Power, Gift of Love

John Berges

PLANETWORK PRESS

 Published in the United States by Planetwork Press, P.O. Box 180, Northfield, NJ 08225. All inquiries should be addressed to Planetwork Press.

ISBN 0-9641549-2-7

First Edition, September, 1997

Printed in the United States of America

Inquiries about other Planetwork publications may be sent to the above address.

Permissions

I would like to thank Dover Publications, Destiny Books, David Fideler, author of: *Jesus Christ, Sun of God: Ancient Cosmology and Early Christian Symbolism,* Lucis Publishing Co., Quest Books, and U.S. Games, Inc. for permission to quote from previously published material.

Credits:

Although I have not quoted directly from it, I want to credit the book *Numbers Facts, Figures and Fiction* by Richard Philips, published by Cambridge University Press, Cambridge, Great Britain, 1994. This book has been instructive and helpful in my research linking the fascinating world of numbers to esoteric numerology.

Dedicated with
Love, Respect, and Humility
to
The Tibetan
Master Djwhal Khul

Contents

List of Illustrations

List of Tables

About the Author

John Berges, M.Th. is a student and teacher of the ageless wisdom. He lives in Egg Harbor Twp, New Jersey, where he and his wife teach and minister at the Farmington Community Church and Wisdom Center. He is also the creator of the *Seven Ray Energy Cards,* an intuitive counseling system based on the seven rays. He and his wife, Darlene, are also the authors of *The Daily Seven Ray Energy Journal*, a journaling accessory to the *Seven Ray Energy Cards.*

Preface

Sometime during the first three or four months of 1993, I felt a curious urge to convert the Great Invocation to numbers using the standard numerological method found in most popular books on the subject. Now, more than four years later, I find myself writing a preface to a book on the esoteric numerology of the Great Invocation.

During that time in 1993, I was studying for a master's degree in theology at Sancta Sophia Seminary, a non-traditional school of Esoteric Christianity. My work at Sancta Sophia was part of an ongoing process of spiritual study in esoteric philosophy which began in my teenage years. In 1993 the Great Invocation was not new to me, for I had discovered it in a book by Alice A. Bailey when I was seventeen years old, so this world prayer had been a part of my life for almost thirty years.

That night in 1993 was not unusual. I was simply waiting for my wife, Darlene, to finish using the computer, so I could write a report for school. It was while I sat waiting that I got the idea to write down the Great Invocation and convert each letter to a number. After about an hour of writing and adding, I knew the Great Invocation held a value of 5. This did not impress me all that much at the time, but by the time I met my advisor at graduate school in May, I told her that an investigation and analysis of the Great Invocation using numbers might be an interesting project for my trimester work. She gave her approval, and I eagerly began what has turned out to be the most fascinating and profound experience of my life.

In August of 1993, I delivered my reports to school. Three months of research and investigation had yielded some very interesting results which led me to believe the Great Invocation might contain esoteric information hidden beneath the "outer surface" of its words. When graduate school met in February of 1994, I submitted a proposal to write my master's thesis on the esoteric numerology of the Great Invocation. My proposal was approved and I delivered my thesis, both oral and written, in September of 1994. At that point in my study, I could already see there was enough material to convert that thesis into a book.

Now, almost three years later, the results of that endeavor are a reality. I can honestly say this study, investigation, and experience has changed my life immeasurably. If nothing more develops from this work, I still consider it a relative success because it has allowed me to penetrate more deeply into the meaning and significance of life on this small planet. Nevertheless, the success and reward of any work is questionable if it fails to contribute to the spiritual growth and understanding of those it touches. Therefore, if this book opens you to new ideas, a new vision of the world, a wider, more inclusive view of the cosmos and your place in it, then I will consider it a success.

This study has answered some questions, while at the same time it has generated many new ones. This is good, since truth is relative, leading us from questions to answers, to more questions. Thus, I make no claim for understanding everything within these pages. I have deliberately pushed the envelope on the ideas touched upon here in an effort to widen the horizon of our worldview. I have made every effort to be objective regarding the number relationships and correspondences discussed within these pages. I have recorded the very best of what I have discovered concerning the Great Invocation. I have discarded questionable material as well as many insignificant items only loosely related to this amazing world prayer.

Every letter/number relationship in this book can be reproduced with a pencil, paper, and ordinary calculator. I have worked with the numbers and calculations in this book many times, checking for errors. To the best of my knowledge every calculation is correct. As you read these pages, I invite you to review the numbers for yourself. This will not only help you understand the material more clearly, but it will prove a powerful experience. Realization of the intimate connections between the spiritual symbolism of numbers and the Great Invocation is mind expanding. This, in turn, triggers further associations with other profoundly spiritual concepts which, on the surface, would appear to have no relation to the Great Invocation. It is this sudden recognition of deep connectivity which I hope you can experience firsthand. Then you will know the transforming power of the Great Invocation and receive the powerful gift of Love which this Sacred Vessel carries within its words.

The Question of Language

The Great Invocation is a prayer. It is humanity's prayer. It doesn't belong to any particular religion and no one can claim it as their personal creation. Alice A. Bailey never claimed to have written it; she received it from a Tibetan Teacher of the ageless wisdom. He never claimed its authorship, and in fact stated that no one is aware of its age. This Tibetan teacher simply translated it into modern English, so that people could use it to invoke the help of God to make the world a better place in which to live.

Essentially, I wrote this book to clarify one point—the profundity of the Great Invocation. I am the first to admit that I did not realize the magnitude of the hidden meaning of its words. Through the years, I, like many others around the world, have repeated the Great Invocation thousands of times. Like many others, I have struggled at times to keep this from becoming a mechanical process. One thing, however, I have not done is change the words of the Great Invocation. Why not? Is it because I am dogmatic about them? No. It is simply because I understand the meaning of the philosophy and terminology which determined those words. This is not such a big deal. Thousands of people all over the world know this about the Great Invocation, but because it is used daily by millions of people worldwide, there are always those who think they can "improve" it by changing the words. From the esoteric standpoint, when the words of any prayer (or mantram) are changed, so too, is the subjective energy upon which it is based. Technically speaking, it no longer remains the same prayer or energy pattern.

I don't question the sincerity of such people, and I believe I understand their motivations in most cases. But at the same time, it means they are not saying the Great Invocation as it was originally intended, and thus not activating and releasing the optimal spiritual forces required to accelerate planetary spiritual evolution. I don't say people are not contributing, but I do say relative to the Great Invocation and its original planned effect, they are not employing the most powerful prayer ever given to humanity for bringing about optimal spiritual growth worldwide. Why take a less effective medicine when a more potent cure is readily available?

I believe most people can use the Great Invocation without reservation once they understand the significance behind the words. These people may not agree with all the concepts involved, but at least they will know the choice of words was intentional and carefully planned.

For the most part, four areas of irritation exist within the Great Invocation which often prevent people from using it with full effectiveness. These words are "men," "Christ," "little wills of men," and "evil."

Many people are offended by the use of the word "men" because of the disparities within society between men and women. The ageless wisdom is ageless because it transcends time. It also transcends physical space and the forms which inhabit that space—including the genders of physical bodies. The teachers of the ageless wisdom are interested in the psychological and spiritual development of the souls that incarnate in these bodies, regardless of gender.

To the ageless wisdom, MAN is a free-willed, self-conscious, intelligent spiritual entity capable of creativity through the use of mind at many levels of existence, most of which are beyond our present knowledge. The human soul is MAN, the thinker and doer. The souls that incarnate in female body types are certainly MAN as described by the ageless wisdom. The injustice which exists against women should be fought against the correct enemy. That enemy is not the Great Invocation, nor those who use it according to its original intent.

The presence of the word "Christ" in the Great Invocation also offends some people. The esoteric meaning of the Christ will be explained in more detail later; for now I will only say that the ageless wisdom recognizes Christ as the Teacher and Savior of all humanity; not Christians alone. The Christ transcends all religious organizations, institutions, and structures. These are simply forms or vehicles for carrying a message. The Christ represents the Life and Quality within the forms. When the forms become old, brittle, and unable to change (as all forms do), the Christ employs new and better forms for carrying His message to humanity.

When the Great Invocation addresses the Christ, it summons the return of a World Teacher Who loves and cares for every human being on Earth. The invocative call is for spiritual guidance from the most advanced human being on our planet today. When using the Great Invocation we are inviting the World Teacher to come forth and help us help ourselves. Whether He is called the Messiah, the Imam Mahdi, the Bodhisattva, the Maitreya Buddha, the Kalki

Avatar, or the Christ is less important than the healing and teaching He brings.

Some people are offended because of the phrase "little wills of men." Again, an understanding of the philosophy of the ageless wisdom is necessary to properly understand this phrasing. The ageless wisdom teaches that all entities in the universe are evolving in a great chain of being. Human beings are above animals, plants, and minerals in their evolution, but below the development of the superhuman kingdoms. Our Creators are solar Deities Who were at the human stage billions of years ago in cycles long since ended. In terms of will and its use, the wills of men are naturally (and logically) "little" in comparison to such advanced Lives. Some day the wills of human beings will be prodigious, but at this stage in the great chain of being, our wills are small relative to Those advanced Lives ahead of us on the evolutionary scale.

Finally, we come to the word "evil." This word might be offensive to some people; nevertheless, the ageless wisdom recognizes the existence of evil in the universe. Evil is that which stands at odds to the prevailing direction of evolution. In terms of our planet, evolution is the Purpose, Intent, and Plan of a cosmic Entity in Whom we live and move and have our being, as St. Paul expressed it. There is little we as humans can do about cosmic evil except "seal the door where evil dwells." This phrase from the Great Invocation means that we have the power to seal the Earth from evil's influence in our world. We are told that separatism and materialism are the two forces of evil on our planet. The qualities of brotherhood, cooperation, love, compassion, respect, equality, freedom and goodwill are all building blocks in right human relations. These qualities will seal the door where evil dwells.

These words—men, Christ, the little wills of men, and evil—were not written into the Great Invocation to offend people. There are no hidden religious or political agendas; no wish to bruise anyone's ego, or degrade women. At the simplest, most direct level these are the words of a prayer; a prayer which asks for Light, Love, and Power to restore God's Plan on Earth.

As you will soon discover, these words were carefully chosen for another reason as well, for in the numeric symbolism of their letters, the words of the Great Invocation carry some of the most profound secrets of Man's origin, purpose, and destiny. The fundamental teachings of the ageless wisdom are hidden in the very structure of the words and phrases of this world prayer.

There is one more important point to be made, and this concerns the question of language translation. For whatever reasons, the Great Invocation was given to the world in English, and as this book demonstrates, the English words used in this world prayer were carefully chosen and arranged. Various individuals whose first language is not English have asked me how the Great Invocation is affected when it is translated into other languages. This is a good question and it raises an important point—the Great Invocation has *already* been translated into English from the seven original symbols of which it is constituted. Because some of the original meaning is always lost in translation, the Tibetan Teacher, Djwhal Khul, took great care to choose the most accurate words possible to represent those seven original symbols. Therefore, I believe some meaning or energy is definitely lost when the Great Invocation is translated *a second time* into a language other than English.

Despite the unavoidable use of language translation, I do not feel this detracts from the Great Invocation's effectiveness. This might appear as a contradiction, since I have just explained why I think the words of the Great Invocation should not be altered. This is not the case, however, because it is a matter of intent. Is the Great Invocation being translated as accurately as possible, based on the original, or is it being translated to suit someone's personal point of view? This applies to translations between languages and alterations within languages. After all, the Tibetan has already translated the Great Invocation into English, and what was his intent? We return to our previous point about the presence of particular words in the Great Invocation which offend people. Anyone who changes the Great Invocation (or anything for that matter) needs to examine their intent, the motivation behind the action.

In this sense, translation is almost beside the point. It is really a matter of motive. What is occurring mentally, emotionally, and spiritually when we are reciting the Great Invocation? What are we invoking, and why? Does it really matter what language we are using when our hearts and minds are focused on bringing the Light, Love, and Power of God to suffering humanity? I think not.

The Great Invocation is not directed at any one particular group of people, organization, religion, or nation—it is for everyone. Therefore, its use is least effective when directed to any one sector of society to the exclusion of another.

The Great Invocation is least effective when its words are modified in any language for personal reasons such as political and social agendas. Such reasons are inherently exclusive and separative in nature.

The Great Invocation is still effective when used with selfless intent for the good of all people everywhere on the Earth—no matter what language is used. This is spiritual service; this fulfills the goal of using the Great Invocation.

However, the Great Invocation is *most* effective when used as described above *and* in English, *but* only if one understands the meaning and significance of the words. This pertains to English speaking people as well as to those who don't speak English. What good is reciting the words of the Great Invocation without understanding the meaning behind them? This is where this book begins, and this is one reason why so many people want to change its words—they do not understand the philosophy behind the words. This is no one's fault; it is a symptom of the Great Invocation's popularity and wide appeal to people across a wide spectrum of spiritual belief. In other words, because the Great Invocation has been printed, published, and copied by so many people in so many different circumstances, it is likely that thousands of people have no idea the Great Invocation originated with Alice Bailey and the Tibetan Teacher, Djwhal Khul. Consequently, they have no concept of the extensive and profound philosophy on which its words are based.

This brings us to the esoteric aspect of the Great Invocation. Much of the coding and symbolism embedded within its words is lost when the Great Invocation is translated into other languages, just as that same coding is lost when other English words are substituted for the originals. This is why I believe the original version, as published by Lucis Trust, should not be altered for any reason. The original English version contains hidden information vital to our understanding of man's purpose on Earth.

It is most important for everyone to use the Great Invocation with sincerity, focussed awareness, and a spirit of goodwill. We should be fully present when we say the Great Invocation. We must realize we are summoning powerful and compassionate spiritual Forces to enter our lives and help us make this a better world. When we sound the Great Invocation we are taking responsibility for engaging a global process of spiritualization which transcends any one religion, political bloc, nation, or individual.

Acknowledgments

I want to thank the following organizations and individuals for their contributions to this work: the Dean and Governors of Sancta Sophia Seminary, where the initial reports and thesis were presented; the President and Vice President of the University of the Seven Rays, where I have been given the opportunity to present these findings to a wider audience; the officers of Lucis Trust of which Lucis Publishing and the Arcane School are vital components. The generous permission granted by Lucis Publishing to quote extensively from the books of Alice A. Bailey and Djwhal Khul is deeply appreciated. I thank the Arcane School because it represents the foundation upon which I have been able to build my lighted house. Special thanks must also be given to Lucis Trust for allowing me to publish material which addresses the important subject of the Great Invocation in the manner I have chosen.

Closer to home, the love and support of the members of Farmington Community Church and Wisdom Center have been enormous throughout this entire project. The encouragement and feedback of my spiritual family as they sat through many an unpolished presentation of raw ideas about the Great Invocation is to be commended and I thank them all.

In addition, I also thank the MSE class of USR, which meets at Farmington, for their supportive energy, with a very special great Big Bear hug to O. T. W. who has done so much behind the scenes.

Last, but not least, I thank the editing and production group commandeered to help assemble the Sacred Vessel. Heartfelt thanks to the Master of Cover Art and Esoteric Typography, Lord of Comma, Ms. Vocabulary, and Ladies "That," "Which," and "But." (T.S., K.S., A. B., D. B., P. J., and S. C.) Also, thanks to T. C., R. S., A. L., P. V., J. L., K. C., B. M., M. A. R., J. A., and T. G.

I must explain that that "That" named above has become "that" sensitive in the process and is my loving and faithful wife, friend, and companion on the Way, Darlene. She has been part of this work from its inception. Her constant support and sacrifice have contributed immeasurably to the successful completion of this project.

Author's Note

Djwhal Khul is also referred to as DK and the Tibetan.
Alice A. Bailey is also referred to as AAB.
Helena P. Blavatsky is also referred to as HPB.
These persons are found in the index according to their full names.
Hermes Trismegistus is sometimes referred to as Hermes and is found in the index under Hermes.

In addition, I have taken the liberty of capitalizing terms which I find significant according to the context of the material.

1

Laying the Foundation

"It is the most stupendous utterance of all time. I do not hesitate to use the most extreme superlatives I can find."[1] These words of Foster Bailey, the husband of Alice A. Bailey (AAB), describe the Great Invocation in an article appearing in *The Beacon* magazine in 1951. Foster Bailey continues:

> I well remember the strain of the days before the morning when, as the sun rose, Mrs. Bailey brought me the words of this Invocation as she had written them to the exact dictation of the Tibetan.[2] It was an occasion of the most complete at-one-ment with him that she had probably ever achieved.[3]

Most people seeing the Great Invocation for the first time experience it as a beautiful prayer dedicated to all humanity. It calls for the restoration of God's Plan on Earth through the invoking of spiritual Light, Love, and Power. However, behind this selfless world prayer is a fascinating story and history. The Great Invocation did not simply appear out of a vacuum, but like most things was born through crisis—a crisis of worldwide proportions involving the basic freedom of humanity. The Great Invocation carries a simple message with which all people can identify—no matter what their background may be. The power of these words lies in their simplicity.

Yet, these seemingly simple words carry a potency and a message that reaches to the very depths of our planetary existence. There are hidden layers to these words that await discovery. In order to appreciate this world prayer at its deeper levels we must first explore some of the background of Alice A. Bailey and her relationship to Djwhal Khul (DK), also known as the Tibetan. We will also need to learn some of the fundamental aspects of the ageless wisdom philosophy recorded by AAB. First we begin with the two persons who collaborated in bringing the Great Invocation to humanity.

Alice A. Bailey

Alice Bailey was born in Manchester, England in 1880, as Alice La Trobe-Bateman. Both her parents died by the time she was eight years old, and as a result Alice and her sister lived with their grandparents in Moor Park, Surrey, England. In her autobiography, AAB describes the first twenty years of her life as "completely disciplined by people or by the social conventions of the time."[4] Indeed, Alice and her sister were educated by various governesses and were later sent to a finishing school in London.

After her schooling, Alice worked as an evangelist for the British army in Ireland and India. During this period of her life she describes herself as "forcefully preaching the old-time religion."[5] It was in India that she met her first husband, Walter Evans. Eventually they married and settled in America where Walter studied theology and was ordained in the Episcopal Church. When Walter was assigned his first church, Alice soon found herself teaching Bible classes and performing all the necessary duties of a minister's wife.

By 1915, however, Alice and Walter Evans separated due to Walter's uncontrollable temper and abusive behavior. By then they were living in California, and Alice was supporting her three daughters by working in a sardine factory. It was at this point in her life that Alice, now thirty-five, came into contact with Theosophy through two English women who befriended her. Alice spent the next several years working hard at the factory while studying the many new ideas of Theosophy, which she struggled to integrate with the strict Christian ideas of her upbringing.

As she tells the story, it was not long before she was studying *The Secret Doctrine* of Helena P. Blavatsky (HPB) with the help of two other women who had been Blavatsky's personal students. Before long Alice joined the Theosophical Lodge in Pacific Grove, California where she began teaching classes in Theosophy.

At this point in the story we must mention that from the time Alice Bailey was a teenager she had been under the guidance of a mysterious man who visited her on at least two occasions—once in England in 1895 and again in India in 1906. Although he offered guidance and advice, he never demanded Alice's obedience. It was in 1918 that Alice learned the identity of this mysterious man, for she saw his portrait hanging in the shrine room of the Theosophical Lodge to which she had just been admitted after several years of study. He was known as the Master Koot Humi (KH) and the fact that Alice Bailey claimed to have been under His guidance since adolescence created an uproar in the lodge. After all, Alice was only a neophyte and why would such a great Teacher as KH contact such a new student of the Ageless Wisdom? As AAB explains:

> Believing that they would be pleased and not intending in the very least to be boastful I said, in all innocence, "Oh, then, He must be my Master, for I've talked with Him and been under His guidance ever since." This person looked at me and said, with rather a withering inflection, "Am I to understand that you believe yourself to be a disciple?"[6]

This incident initiated Alice into the glamours and controversies which so often surround the subject of guides and gurus. Mrs. Bailey never used her association with any Master of the Wisdom to inflate her own ego; on the contrary, she did her utmost to downplay such relationships, because they only hindered her service activities. (I recommend reading *The Unfinished Autobiography* in order to get a complete picture of AAB's attitudes concerning such matters.) As we shall see, this entire issue soon became critical in Alice's life.

The year 1919 proved to be quite momentous for AAB for several reasons. First she met Foster Bailey who she eventually married after being granted a divorce from Walter Evans. Alice and Foster became quite active in the Theosophical Society and their work together was the beginning of a partnership which would eventually lead them to New York City and the founding of Lucis Trust and the Arcane School. The other important event that year was Alice's contact with the Tibetan Teacher Djwhal Khul. As AAB explains:

I now come to a happening in my life about which I hesitate to speak. It concerns the work which I have done for the past twenty-seven years. This work has received world-wide recognition and has evoked world-wide curiosity. It has also brought me some ridicule and suspicion, but surprisingly little, and I have been quite able to understand it because I started by being very suspicious myself.[7]

It was in November 1919 that I made my first contact with The Tibetan. I had sent the children off to school and thought I would snatch a few minutes to myself and went out on to the hill close to the house. I sat down and began thinking and then suddenly I sat startled and attentive. I heard what I thought was a clear note of music which sounded from the sky, through the hill and in me. Then I heard a voice which said, "There are some books which it is desired should be written for the public. You can write them. Will you do so?" Without a moment's notice I said, "Certainly not. I'm not a darned psychic and I don't want to be drawn into anything like that."[8]

Despite her wariness, and after much soul searching AAB agreed to work with the Tibetan, serving as His amanuensis and secretary. Although AAB was a student of the ageless wisdom, she never claimed authorship for eighteen of the twenty-four books that bear her name. As she explains:

Today, as the result of twenty-seven years work with the Tibetan I can snap into telepathic relation with Him without the slightest trouble. I can and do preserve my own mental integrity all the time and I can always argue with Him if it seems to me, at times, that—as an Occidental—I may know better than He does as regards points of presentation. When we have an argument along any line I invariably write as He wants the text written, though He is apt to modify His presentation after discussion with me. If He does not change His wording and point of view, I do not change what He had said in any way.[9]

Their work together lasted for thirty years until Alice A. Bailey died in 1949. By the time of her transition AAB had accomplished a great deal in the field of spiritual and esoteric study beyond the work she did with DK. Along with Foster and other dedicated co-workers Alice Bailey created the Lucis Trust, the Arcane School, World Goodwill, the Triangles network, and other service activities.[10]

Djwhal Khul and the Hierarchy

Undoubtedly, the most controversial aspect of Alice Bailey's work was her claim that the majority of the books she wrote were actually dictated to her by a Tibetan Master of Wisdom named Djwhal Khul. It is not the intention of this book to debate the existence or non-existence of Djwhal Khul. Such matters are best left to the personal feelings of each individual. However, in order to put the Great Invocation into the proper perspective it is important to relate some of the background of the Tibetan Teacher.

In brief, H. P. Blavatsky, founder of the Theosophical Society, introduced the idea of a spiritual brotherhood which guides the evolution of humanity from behind the scenes of world events. These guides are known as the spiritual Hierarchy, or simply the Hierarchy. Much has been written about this brotherhood, both positive and negative. Members of this band of spiritual guides are known as the Masters of Wisdom or Lords of Compassion.[11] Two of the most well known Masters of the Theosophical movement are the Masters Morya and Koot Humi. All of these advanced souls have lived as human beings but have evolved beyond the physical plane of existence. According to the ageless wisdom, They exist at a level of expanded awareness beyond the normal range of human activity. The spiritual Hierarchy can be thought of as the Kingdom of God. The function of the Hierarchy in general is to oversee the evolution of life on the planet; in particular it guides the evolution of human consciousness according to the Plan of God.

Almost invariably when students of the ageless wisdom discuss evolution they are talking about the growth of consciousness, not about evolution in the Darwinian sense. They are talking about the evolution of consciousness, not bodies. The form is ready and only awaits spirit to bring it to completeness. This is the message of Christ, Buddha, Mohammed, Moses, Krishna, Lao Tse, and many other teachers sent forth from the Hierarchy. Hierarchy is non-sectarian; Hierarchy transcends religious forms. The kingdoms which the Hierarchy guides are the mineral, vegetable, animal, and human. Humanity represents the fourth kingdom in nature and Hierarchy is the fifth.

The most advanced member of this Hierarchy is the Christ. According to the ageless wisdom, the term "Christ" or anointed one is a position indicating the leader of Hierarchy. This idea is the same as the office of president in a government or corporation, in that different individuals hold the office at various times. The Master Jesus sacrificed His life so that the One now called the Christ could work through Him in Palestine 2,000 years ago. The Master Jesus is the leader of all Christianity, while the Christ as head of the spiritual Hierarchy presides over all worldwide activities (including religions) that work toward human betterment.

According to the books written by Alice Bailey, the Tibetan Master Djwhal Khul is also a member of this spiritual Hierarchy. One aspect of His role in the immediate Plan is to bridge the religious and philosophical beliefs of the East and West in order to prepare the world for a global civilization which respects the rights of the individual while at the same time provides for the overall needs of society. At this point it is best to let DK speak for himself from an extract first published in August of 1914, which appears in each of his books written through AAB:

> Suffice it to say, that I am a Tibetan disciple of a certain degree, and this tells you but little, for all are disciples from the humblest aspirant up to, and beyond, the Christ Himself. I live in a physical body like other men, on the borders of Tibet, and at times (from the exoteric standpoint) preside over a large group of Tibetan lamas, when my other duties permit. It is this fact that has caused it to be reported that I am an abbot of this particular lamasery. Those associated with me in the work of the Hierarchy (and all true disciples are associated in this work) know me by still another name and office. A.A.B. knows who I am and recognises me by two of my names.
>
> I am a brother of yours, who has travelled a little longer upon the Path than has the average student, and has therefore incurred greater responsibilities. I am one who has wrestled and fought his way into a greater measure of light than has the aspirant who will read this article, and I must therefore act as a transmitter of the light, no matter what the cost. I am not an old man, as age counts among the teachers, yet I am not young or inexperienced. My work is to teach and spread the knowledge of the Ageless Wisdom wherever I can find response, and I have been doing this for many years. I seek also to help the Master M. and the Master K.H. whenever opportunity offers, for I have been long connected with Them and with Their work. In all the above, I have told you much; yet at the same time I have told you nothing which would lead you to offer me that blind obedience and the foolish devotion which the emotional aspirant offers to the Guru and Master Whom he is as yet unable to contact. Nor will he make that desired contact until he has transmuted emotional devotion into unselfish service to humanity,—not to the Master.

> The books that I have written are sent out with no claim for their acceptance. They may, or may not, be correct, true and useful. It is for you to ascertain their truth by right practice and by the exercise of the intuition. Neither I nor A.A.B. is the least interested in having them acclaimed as inspired writings, or in having anyone speak of them (with bated breath) as being the work of one of the Masters. If they present truth in such a way that it follows sequentially upon that already offered in the world teachings, if the information given raises the aspiration and the will-to-serve from the plane of the emotions to that of the mind (the plane whereon the Masters can be found) then they will have served their purpose. If the teaching conveyed calls forth a response from the illumined mind of the worker in the world, and brings a flashing forth of his intuition, then let that teaching be accepted. But not otherwise. If the statements meet with eventual corroboration, or are deemed true under the test of the Law of Correspondences, then that is well and good. But should this not be so, let not the student accept what is said.[12]

The subject matter covered in the eighteen books on which AAB and DK collaborated is vast, but one of the most important themes covered in their work together concerned the reappearance of a World Teacher, called the Christ. It should be noted that the Christ does not represent any one religion, but serves all humanity. According to DK, the reappearance of the Christ will inaugurate the new age of Aquarius and represent a major evolutionary advance in consciousness for humanity. The Great Invocation plays a central role in this coming event.

The Great Invocation was given to humanity in order to aid in the return of the World Teacher. The Tibetan asked those who felt dedicated to His work to:

> Prepare men for the reappearance of the Christ. This is your first and greatest duty. The most important part of that work is teaching men—on a large scale—to use the Invocation so that it becomes a world prayer and focuses the invocative demand of humanity.[13]

Alice Bailey was completely dedicated to the work of preparing humanity for the coming of a World Teacher through promoting right human relations and goodwill throughout the world via the service activities of the Lucis Trust. Although she died before commenting on the Great Invocation in her autobiography, she was well aware of the importance of the Great Invocation relative to the spiritual preparation of humanity prior to the coming of the Christ.

This was implicit through her thirty years of close work with the Tibetan. During this time He dictated much material to her concerning the critical world events of the twentieth century. (Details of the events leading up to the public release of the Great Invocation will be covered fully as we proceed.)

The primary aim of this book is to show that the Great Invocation is much more than a prayer of great vision and hope for a better world (as if this were not enough); for underlying the outer structure of the words are clues and codes revealing an even larger vision, a vision of a vast intelligent Life of superhuman dimensions in which we human beings find ourselves living—St. Paul's "One in Whom we live and move and have our being." Through the use of esoteric numerology we will demonstrate how the ideas and mysteries of the ageless wisdom are woven into the very word fabric of the Great Invocation.

The Ageless Wisdom View of God

> Each form, from that of the tiniest atom to that of a vast constellation, is an embodiment of a life, which expresses itself as consciousness, awareness, and responsive sentiency through the medium of some type of response mechanism. Thus we have the establishing of a universe of lives, interacting and interrelated, all of them conscious, some of them self-conscious, and others group-conscious, but all grounded in the universal mind, all possessing souls, and all presenting aspects of the divine Life.[14]

The teachings presented by the Tibetan in the Alice Bailey books describe all life in the universe as being conscious at some level, whether it is the consciousness of an atom or a galaxy, a plant or a human, an animal or a planet. The term "God" is relative in this model of reality. At the universal level, the ageless wisdom recognizes the existence of an intelligent, loving, and purposeful Being Who created and sustains the universe. If the universe is thought of as the singular expression of God universal, then the next step in understanding this concept is to think of the galaxies as sub-systems operating within the corporate body of the universal God.

Modern astronomy now knows there are many billions of galaxies contained within the universe. The ageless wisdom concept views galaxies as integrated life systems having the same fundamental characteristics as the original universal Creator, namely will, love, and intelligence. This threefold aspect is an integral part of all the components of the universe, and corresponds to the trinity concept of Christianity—Father, Son, and Holy Spirit.

Table 1. Basic Triplicities.

First Aspect	Second Aspect	Third Aspect
Father	Son	Mother
Will	Love	Holy Spirit
Spirit	Soul	Body
Life	Consciousness	Form

In effect, the ageless wisdom recognizes galaxies as whole living conscious life forms operating on a scale beyond any human being's power to comprehend. An entity expressing itself through a galactic body structure composed of stars, planets, and other celestial objects is literally alive and functioning at its own level of consciousness and intelligent purposes. What these may be we have no way of knowing. An important point to understand at this stage is that relative to us humans, a galaxy is a God. It is not the supreme universal God, but it is Godlike relative to our level of evolution.

The next level of organization in this model of reality pertains to related groups of stars within the galaxies themselves.[15] The Tibetan mentions in his writings that our solar system, along with six other solar systems, comprise part of the "body" of a cosmic entity He calls the "One About Whom Naught May Be Said." In addition to these seven solar systems, Djwhal Khul frequently discusses three other star groups of primary importance to our tiny Earth and solar system. These are the seven stars of the Big Dipper within Ursa Major (which DK simply refers to as the Great Bear), the Pleiades, and the star Sirius. These three star systems are said to govern and control the seven solar systems. To this vast array of cosmic solar Lives we must add one more celestial group, the twelve constellations of the zodiac. Our solar system, along with the six others in our local system, are governed by the Great Bear, the Pleiades, and Sirius via the twelve star groupings known as the zodiacal constellations. These act as cosmic filters between the seven solar systems and the three governing constellations. All of these make up the celestial system known as the "One About

Whom Naught May Be Said."

Relatively speaking, this collection of star systems (three transmitting, twelve intermediate, and seven receiving solar systems) is the ruling Intelligence or God in which we, on our tiny planet Earth, live and have our being. It is very important to remember, however, that each one of these celestial units is an independent, Self-conscious, Intelligent Life living within the corporate sphere of influence of a greater Life. These, including ourselves, are all systems and sub-systems existing as part of an infinite Hierarchy of Universal Life.

Djwhal Khul has revealed a wondrous and mind-reeling description of our place in the universal scheme of things. Although He has revealed much about the One About Whom Naught May Be Said (a cosmic Logos), there are many unknowns, plenty of unanswered questions, and a mind-boggling array of complex relationships existing between the various parts of this celestial Mystery. Despite these daunting complexities, the presented vision is undeniably awe-inspiring and beautiful when approached with an open mind and a willingness to examine it in depth.

Descending this dizzying cosmic scale of life we finally arrive at our own solar system. Our solar system is also a living conscious Entity of cosmic proportions relative to human existence. This Being is called the solar Logos. Sometimes the Tibetan refers to the solar Logos as "The Grand Man of the Heavens." We live within the body of this Being and come under Its laws. Within the living structure of the solar Logos are other cosmic Beings called "planetary Logoi" (sometimes referred to as "Heavenly Men"). Our Earth is one of these Logoi. Our planetary Logos is a conscious, living, loving intelligence who is OUR GOD. Some names given to our planetary Logos are the Ancient of Days, Melchizedek, and Sanat Kumara, a Sanskrit name that will be discussed in greater detail later on.

Our Earth, like all the other cosmic entities discussed to this point, is a consciously evolving Being living in cooperative group relationship with the other planetary Beings in our solar system. We are given to believe that definite communication goes on between the planetary Logoi and the solar Logos. Communication goes on at higher levels as well—at stellar levels and beyond. The entire universe is alive and conscious at innumerable levels of awareness and evolution. Philosophically considered, this model is called Hylozoism and is explained by DK as follows:

> This posits a living substance, composed of a multiplicity of sentient lives which are continuously swept into expression by the "breath of the divine Life." This theory recognises not so-called inorganic matter anywhere in the universe, and emphasizes the fact that all forms are built up of infinitesimal lives, which in their totality—great or small—constitute a Life, and that these composite lives, in their turn, are a corporate part of a still greater Life. Thus eventually we have that great scale of lives, manifesting in greater expression and reaching all the way from the tiny life called the atom (with which science deals) up to that vast atomic life which we call a solar system.[16]

A brief definition of Hylozoism states:

> From the Greek *Hyle* ("matter") and *zoe* ("life"). A doctrine predicating life of all matter. Held by many early philosophers, among them Thales, (Q.V.), suggestions of the view are to be found in most philosophies which find the world to be teleologically ordered. If all living forms are sentient to some degree, Hylozoism becomes a subclass of Panpsychism.[17]

Pursuing Panpsychism we find:

> From the Greek *pan* and *psyche* meaning that everything is possessed of soul. The doctrine that everything is possessed of life is termed Hylozoism....Although Panpsychism makes a stronger claim, the distinction between possessing soul (or sentience) and possessing life is difficult to maintain in practice.[18]

I am going into some detail here because the ageless wisdom stresses the fundamental importance of life, consciousness, and form as the basis of all existence. When it is said that a galaxy or solar system is an integrated life form this does not simply mean that these are random collections of dead matter that just happened to become organized into orbiting whirlpools of new stars and planets. No, the theory suggests that the form of a solar system, for instance, is only the outer visible manifestation—the physical body so to speak. This solar system is also conscious. It experiences the cosmos as a distinct living Entity and furthermore, this Entity is evolving in ways beyond our ability to comprehend.

The same holds true for our Earth. All these celestial systems are living, evolving souls with physically manifested "bodies," whether they are planetary, solar, or cosmic. This idea relates to the world soul of Plato (428-348 BCE) and the Neoplatonic school of Plotinus (205-270 CE):

> In Plotinus, who in his own way systematized the Platonic themes, the world soul is an emanation from God, the One, by way of the Nous or intelligible world, and contains the physical world as its body.[19]

Earth-Who's In Charge?

Up to this point we have seen that the ageless wisdom describes a hierarchical organization to the universe. Apparently, the cosmos contains vast centers of unique and distinct intelligent life forms most of which exist in dimensions beyond the physical universe. This hierarchical organization is reflected on our own planet Earth in the form of centers of consciousness. These centers comprise intelligent, purposeful Entities living at various levels or planes of consciousness. There are three primary centers which directly relate to the Great Invocation. These three centers are Shamballa, Hierarchy, and Humanity. The ageless wisdom teaches that each of these centers represents a definite aspect of the planetary Logos of the Earth, Who is referred to as Sanat Kumara, the Lord of the World. It is important to remember that every whole system (center) is composed of sub-systems which are also conscious and evolving within the greater system. Therefore, Shamballa, Hierarchy, and Humanity are specific centers of existence containing living beings at various levels of evolutionary development. Relative to each other Shamballa is the most advanced, the Hierarchy is intermediate and Humanity is least evolved. As already mentioned, the Hierarchy is made up of Masters and Teachers Who were once humans that evolved beyond the human center, so we will briefly describe Shamballa and Humanity.

Shamballa

The center called Shamballa is the directing agency of the Earth's purpose within the solar system. The Beings who live within the consciousness sphere of Shamballa are very highly evolved, and most of them have gone through the human experience in bodily form millions of years ago, before the Earth existed in its present form. The Beings who exist in Shamballa work closely with Sanat Kumara—they work intimately with the purposes and will of God. The will and purpose of Sanat Kumara include all the kingdoms of nature on Earth including humanity. Certain of the

Masters in the Hierarchy work specifically with that part of Sanat Kumara's purpose which concerns human evolution. This purpose is transmitted to the Hierarchy from Shamballa where it is developed into an immediate Plan for humanity. The Plan is then worked out through various Masters and their groups within the Hierarchy, and also groups of human beings living in the outer world.

Humanity

The third major center of importance in the life expression of Sanat Kumara is humanity itself. Humanity is the key to the success of the present evolutionary plan of Earth. According to the ageless wisdom the human center is just now coming into its real operational phase relative to the other two centers of Shamballa and Hierarchy. The human center is the first kingdom of nature in which consciousness of individual self is said to manifest. Apparently humanity is needed to help fulfill the plans and purposes of Sanat Kumara, and Hierarchy is assigned to guide us through this critical stage of human evolution.

The human center undergoes psychological development that is assessed by Hierarchy and Shamballa in terms of groups. Generally speaking, humanity is phasing between adolescence and young adulthood. We are in a transition phase, and at a crisis point in our group development, which is obvious to many people everywhere at this time. Chapter 2 will focus on this crisis in relation to the Great Invocation.

Initiation

The subject of initiation is another key factor of the ageless wisdom. It is vital to have a basic understanding of initiation in order to appreciate the enormous implications of the Great Invocation in relation to the current world crisis facing humanity.

Simply put, initiation means entering into something new. Often initiation is the beginning of a new life experience. It can be likened to a rite of passage, such as when an adolescent becomes an adult by reaching a symbolic age in a given culture, or when particular religious sacraments are performed signifying an entering into some sacred spiritual commitment, such as baptism or communion.

Another example might be joining a secret society in which the individual is initiated by having to undergo some form of discipline in order to be accepted and given knowledge only known by the members. All these examples and many others can be applied to the term initiation; however, the Master DK places initiation on an entirely different level of understanding.

> Initiation might be defined in two ways. It is first of all the entering into a new and wider dimensional world by the expansion of a man's consciousness so that he can include and encompass that which he now excludes, and from which he normally separates himself in his thinking and acts. It is, secondly, the entering into man of those energies which are distinctive of the soul and of the soul alone,—the forces of intelligent love, and of spiritual will. These are dynamic energies, and they actuate all who are liberated souls.[20]

When we think of initiation our minds tend to create elaborate scenes of dramatic ceremony and ritual, perhaps drawing images from Hollywood. And although ceremony and ritual play a large role in religion and Masonic work, the Tibetan downplays the importance of the dramatic enactment involved with initiation.

> Initiation has been so frequently presented as being a ceremony that I have felt it necessary to offset strenuously that erroneous significance.
>
> Initiation is only a ceremony in so far that there comes a climaxing point in the initiatory process in which the disciple's consciousness becomes dramatically aware of the personnel of the Hierarchy and of his own position in relation to it. This realisation he symbolises to himself—successively and on an increasingly large scale—as a great rhythmic ceremonial of progressive revelation in which he, as a candidate, is the centre of the hierarchical stage....I am not here saying that the teachings given in the past by various occult groups, or in my book *Initiation, Human and Solar*, are not correct or do not recount accurately what the candidate *believes* has taken place. The point I seek to make is that the ceremonial aspect is due to the thoughtform-making capacity of the disciple.[21]

The names given to the five initiations closely follow the five main events in the life of Jesus as presented in the Gospels. The Tibetan alluded to the relationship between the initiations and the events in the life of Jesus in the book *Initiation, Human and Solar*. In 1937 Alice Bailey wrote her own book entitled *From Bethlehem to Calvary* which clearly defines each one of the five initiations in relation to the Gospel story. In the introduction to her book, Alice Bailey describes each initiation succinctly:

> 1. The Birth at Bethlehem, to which Christ called Nicodemus, saying, "Except a man be born again, he cannot see the kingdom of God."
> 2. The Baptism in Jordan. This is the baptism to which John the Baptist referred us, telling us that the baptism of the Holy Spirit and of fire must be administered to us by Christ.
> 3. The Transfiguration. There perfection is for the first time demonstrated, and there the divine possibility of such perfection is proven to the disciples. The command goes forth to us, "Be ye therefore perfect even as your Father which is in heaven is perfect."
> 4. The Crucifixion. This is called the Great Renunciation, in the Orient, with its lesson of sacrifice and its call to the death of the lower nature. This was the lesson which St. Paul knew and the goal towards which he strove. "I die daily," he said, for only in the practice of death daily undergone can the final Death be met and endured.
> 5. The Resurrection and Ascension,[22] the final triumph which enables the initiate to sing and to know the meaning of the words: "Oh death, where is thy sting? Oh grave, where is thy victory?"[23]

Following is a table showing the five initiations with their names as given by Djwhal Khul.

Table 2. The Five Initiations.

Initiation	Name	Stage
First	Birth	Aspirant
Second	Baptism	Probationer
Third	Transfiguration	Disciple
Fourth	Renunciation	Adept
Fifth	Revelation	Master

One of the objectives of Djwhal Khul's writing project with Alice Bailey was to clarify the subject of initiation and remove many distorted ideas surrounding this important and sacred spiritual topic. Unfortunately, much of the glamour, claim making, and misinformation arose through basic misunderstanding of spiritual, theosophical, and occult literature that was easily becoming available to thousands of people at the turn of the twentieth century. Most of this increased interest was due to rapid advances in education and technology which allowed anyone with the time, money, and education to access esoteric literature at an unprecedented speed and volume. In fact, this is even more so today.

We can hardly scratch the surface of initiation here except to give a general idea of this topic according to Djwhal Khul's books and in relation to the Great Invocation. From the Tibetan's viewpoint, initiation concerns a fundamental and realized expansion of consciousness resulting in an unmistakable altering of the initiate's comprehension and attitude to life. The emphasis is on service to humanity and the greater Whole and any changes in the material aspect of the initiate's life are secondary. In other words, what we commonly hold to be initiations are dim reflections in the outer world of a deep and profound transformation of the soul within the form. The initiate now sees the world with new eyes and can no longer return to the person he or she was before initiation occurred.

This concept is amply illustrated in Christianity, the Mystery Religions of the Greco-Roman world, and by a good number of ancient philosophers who understood the process of spiritual rebirth. Rebirth into the new life was part of the ancient Mysteries even before Christianity officially proclaimed this sacred process of being born again (into the kingdom of God), as described in the Gospel story. In his book *The Ancient Mysteries, A Sourcebook*, editor Marvin W. Meyer offers several fine examples of the power of initiation.

> Just how the initiates into the mysteries appropriated this power we do not know, but they may have understood themselves to have experienced an immediate or mystical encounter with the divine. At times this experience seems to have entailed an approach to death and a return to life. Sometimes, as in the Eleusinian and Egyptian mysteries, the *mystai* underwent dramatic rituals of darkness and death and emerged afterward into new light and life. In several texts the initiates are specifically declared to be reborn....
>
> In a literary fragment attributed to Plutarch (in Stobaeus, *Anthology* [*Anthologion*] 4.52.49), the experience of death is compared with initiation into great mysteries. Plutarch initially notes the similarity of the Greek verbs *teleutan* (to die) and *teleisthai* (to be initiated) and then observes that people who die and people who are initiated go through comparable transformations.[24]

Djwhal Khul uses similar language when He describes the experience and results of the first initiation called the "Birth at Bethlehem."

> The "new man" who has come to birth at the first initiation must and will tread the occult or scientific way, which inevitably leads him out of the world of mysticism into the scientific and assured perception of God as life or energy.
>
> The first initiation marks the beginning of a totally new life and mode of living; it marks the commencement of a new manner of thinking and of conscious perception.[25]

Beyond the individual level of experience, initiation plays an important role in the spiritual evolution of our planet in terms of the group experience. The human race is very significant in relation to the plans and purposes of Sanat Kumara, the planetary Logos, and His position relative to the greater purpose of the solar Logos. As difficult and far-fetched as this may sound to many people, the ageless wisdom stresses the importance of the human role in the Plan of God. Initiation is important in this regard because it is the process by which the conscious awareness of the individual initiate is expanded. As more human beings take initiation there is a cumulative effect in the mass of humanity. This process of initiation builds slowly in the early phase of human spiritual evolution and gradually accelerates as the cumulative effect of more advanced humans begins to radiate into the mass population of the Earth.

Each one of these expansions *reveals* more knowledge of the true nature, meaning, and purpose of life on our planet. These revelations are gradual and cumulative, as each initiation is undergone by the initiate.

> You have to bear in mind that each initiation enables the initiate to "see ahead" a little further, for revelation is always a constant factor in human experience.[26]

The first three initiations are meant to purify and integrate the individual so that their lives become transformed and filled with light and understanding or wisdom. Increasingly, more is revealed about the nature and purpose of the planetary Life we call God and which DK calls Sanat Kumara, and Jesus called the "Father." The third initiation is really considered the first initiation by the Hierarchy because the first two are considered as preparations for the third. The third initiation marks the initiate's entrance into the spiritual kingdom of God or the Hierarchy—the fifth kingdom of nature. It is the beginning of a transition between the human kingdom and the spiritual kingdom which is consummated at the fourth initiation.

The fourth initiation is in the words of the Master DK, "a culminating experience and a point of entrance into a new life for which all the past has been a preparation."[27] This initiation of Renunciation marks the point of renouncing all contact with the world of human living because the initiate has mastered all that the human world has to offer. The initiate has nothing more to learn in this world and thus, is liberated into a new realm of experience. In the life of Jesus the fourth initiation was the crucifixion.

At the fifth great expansion of consciousness the initiate experiences what is called the "Revelation" initiation. Djwhal Khul says little about this initiation except:

> It is not possible for me here to indicate the nature of the revelation which is accorded to the initiate of the fifth initiation. It is too closely related to Shamballa, and I have not myself done more this life than take the fifth initiation and climb the Mount of Ascension. The revelation for me is not completed and—in any case—my lips are sealed.[28]

According to DK, our modern civilization is on the brink of a major spiritual rejuvenation which will once again restore initiation to a prominent role in the spiritual life of humanity.

> In the era which lies ahead, after the reappearance of the Christ, hundreds of thousands of men and women everywhere will pass through some one or other of the great expansions of consciousness.[29]

In other words, after the Christ returns as the World Teacher, a heightened spiritual atmosphere will exist in the world that will allow many more people to advance in their spiritual lives than is now possible. Alice Bailey describes this process of mass initiation in this way:

> Humanity stands today upon the path of probation. The way of purification is being trodden by the masses, and we are in process of purging ourselves from evil and materialism. When this process is

> completed, many will find themselves ready to make preparation for the first of the initiations, and to undergo the new Birth.[30]

Alice Bailey wrote those words in 1937. Today, as we approach the year 2000, humanity is closer to a time of great spiritual transformation. Crisis is always a part of the process of initiation. Initiation is a time of intense catharsis, turmoil, and upheaval. The Great Invocation is an important link in the spiritual development of humanity because it invokes the spiritual forces of Light, Love, and Will, which lead to liberation from the thralldom of materialism and separatism. The human family is deeply and profoundly involved in an evolutionary process of cosmic proportions. As we will discover later on, the process of initiation is a forcing process and an experiment that extends far beyond our planet. Sanat Kumara and Shamballa, the Christ and the Hierarchy, Humanity and the Great Invocation are all connected by the common golden thread of initiation. We are all being subjected to a loving but forced process of accelerated growth and expansion of consciousness that will transform our lives dramatically if successful. The Great Invocation is an extraordinary gift of power given to us now in our hour of trial, to aid our passage through the dangerous waters of rapid global change.

The Seven Rays

The subject of the seven rays forms a major part of the teaching offered by the Tibetan in his work with AAB. These rays are simply distinct qualities of energy that permeate our entire solar system and which are said to emanate from the constellation of Ursa Major (the Great Bear). The seven rays originate from the seven stars making up the Big Dipper. The Big Dipper is actually a group of stars contained within Ursa Major. An interesting fact related to this idea comes from Robert Burnham Jr. in his *Burnham's Celestial Handbook*.[31] Mr. Burnham describes the Big Dipper as a moving cluster of stars (more than seven) which are all related as a group, and not simply a pattern of totally unrelated stars as seen from Earth. Further, as of 1978—the publication date—Burnham points out that the Ursa Major cluster is the closest known star cluster to the Earth.

Having said all that, DK ascribes tremendous importance to

these seven rays of energy. He says:

> I wonder sometimes if any of you realise the epoch-making importance of the teaching which I have given out anent the seven rays as manifesting energies...With all that I have given you concerning the seven rays and the seven Ray Lords, much more can be discovered; these seven great Lives can be seen and known as the informing essences and the active energies in all that is manifested and tangible upon the physical plane, as well as on all the planes of divine expression.[32]

The seven rays are:

Ray 1–Will or Power
Ray 2–Love-Wisdom
Ray 3–Active Intelligence
Ray 4–Harmony Through Conflict and Beauty
Ray 5–Concrete Knowledge and Science
Ray 6–Devotion and Idealism
Ray 7–Ceremonial Order

The subject of the seven rays is large and complex and we will limit our discussion of the seven rays to their connection with the Great Invocation. Humanity comes under the influence of various ray energies according to cycles existing beyond our current level of understanding, but governed by universal laws and principles. Djwhal Khul indicates some of these cyclic periods in relation to the twentieth century crisis in which the Great Invocation appeared. The relationship between the seven rays and the Great Invocation is important because it gives us a broader understanding of recent historical events. This more inclusive perspective adds meaning to the dizzying swirl of crises which has characterized the twentieth century.

With these basic principles and terms set in place, we are now ready to put the Great Invocation into historical perspective.

Notes

1. Foster Bailey, "The Great Invocation," *The Beacon* Vol. XXX No. 3-4 (June-July 1951): 86. Note: The Beacon is a bi-monthly magazine containing articles of esoteric and spiritual topics published by Lucis Publishing.
2. Another name used by AAB for the Master Djwhal Khul.
3. Ibid., 87.
4. Alice A. Bailey, *The Unfinished Autobiography*, 26.
5. Ibid., 80.
6. Ibid., 155.
7. Ibid., 161.
8. Ibid., 162-63.
9. Ibid., 167-68.
10. Further information concerning these services can be obtained by writing to Lucis Trust, 120 Wall St., 24th floor, New York, NY 10005.
11. The term "Masters of Wisdom" also denotes those spiritual teachers of the Hierarchy who are more developed on the mental side, while the "Lords of Compassion" are those Masters who have developed more on the feeling side. Naturally, this is all relative to human understanding, and words are poor substitutes for explaining levels of growth beyond the current range of human evolution. It might be said that some souls evolve more toward the heart and others develop more toward the head, but all exist as wise and loving teachers and guides.
12. Alice A. Bailey, *The Externalisation of the Hierarchy*, vii-viii.
13. Ibid., 641.
14. Alice A. Bailey, *Esoteric Psychology*, vol. I, 136.
15. It should be noted that astronomers recognize the fact that galaxies tend to exist in group formation. I mention this because the wisdom teachings given by DK emphasize the concept of group living and interrelationships at all levels of existence.
16. Ibid., 149.
17. W.L. Reese, *Dictionary of Philosophy and Religion*, s.v. "Hylozoism."
18. Ibid., s.v. "Panpsychism."
19. Ibid., s.v. "World Soul."
20. Alice A. Bailey, *Esoteric Psychology*, vol. II, 12.
21. Alice A. Bailey, *The Rays and the Initiations*, 530-31.
22. DK calls this fifth stage of initiation the Revelation.
23. Bailey, *From Bethlehem to Calvary,* 22-23.
24. Marvin W. Meyer, ed. *The Ancient Mysteries, A Sourcebook*, 8.
25. Bailey, *The Rays and the Initiations,* 666-67.
26. Ibid., 703.

27. Ibid., 697.
28. Ibid., 707.
29. Alice A. Bailey, *The Reappearance of the Christ*, 127.
30. Alice A. Bailey, *From Bethlehem to Calvary*, 23.
31. Robert Burnham Jr., *Burnham's Celestial Handbook,* vol. 3, 1947.
32. Alice A. Bailey, *Esoteric Healing*, 583.

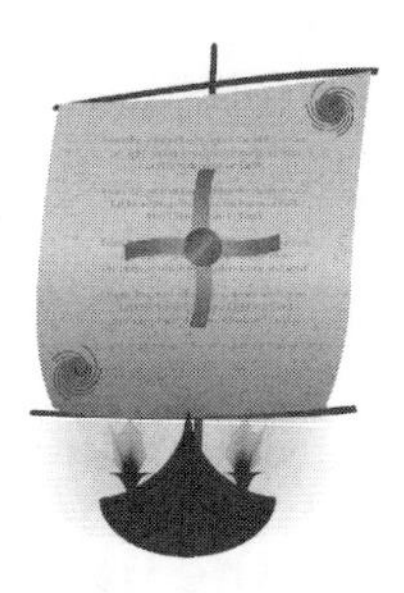

2

Historical Overview

The Invocation for Power and Light Stanzas One and Two

The Great Invocation consists of three different and distinct prayers or invocations given by the Master Djwhal Khul over a ten year period, from 1935 to 1945. What is known today as the Great Invocation is referred to by DK as "the final stanza of the 'Invocation for Power and Light...' "[1] The Tibetan's use of the word "stanza" may cause some confusion because we often use the word stanza to refer to a specific part of one poem, prayer or song. But DK's use of "stanza" refers to the three parts He gave to Alice Bailey in 1935, 1940, and 1945. From His standpoint, the three parts or stanzas are one invocation. Most people today are only familiar with the (third) part currently used, which is widely known as the Great Invocation, and this third part is the subject of this book. The third stanza of the Invocation for Power and Light follows:

From the point of Light within the Mind of God
Let light stream forth into the minds of men.
Let Light descend on Earth.

From the point of Love within the Heart of God
Let love stream forth into the hearts of men.
May Christ return to Earth.

From the centre where the Will of God is known
Let purpose guide the little wills of men—
The purpose which the Masters know and serve.

From the centre which we call the race of men
Let the Plan of Love and Light work out
And may it seal the door where evil dwells.

Let Light and Love and Power restore the Plan on Earth.

This world prayer, now spoken by millions of people all over the world, was given to Alice A. Bailey by Djwhal Khul on April 17, 1945 (the date appearing in *Externalisation of the Hierarchy*, p. 488). From that time until November 1949 when AAB made her transition, DK provided some analysis and interpretation of the Great Invocation, along with suggestions for its use and distribution.

Before discussing the third stanza, however, a historical overview of the extreme and profound circumstances surrounding its release is necessary because, according to the Tibetan, humanity had reached the most critical point in its evolution. An ancient conflict, which originated in Atlantis between material and spiritual forces, was re-emerging in the twentieth century. As explained by DK, in the ancient conflict the spiritual forces "won," but only by destroying Atlantis, and not because of humanity's spiritual strength.[2] After this intervention by the higher spiritual Guides of the planet, the Hierarchy withdrew from open contact with humanity leaving it free to work out its own destiny with only occasional appearances by spiritual teachers who came into the world to guide and teach through religion, philosophy or other means.

The First World War was part of this karmic reaction, and by 1935 the Hierarchy was hopeful that humanity had matured enough to choose the spiritual way over materialism. It was under these circumstances that the first stanza of the Great Invocation was made available for humanity's use. But according to DK, by 1939 the situation was as follows:

> The test to which humanity was to be subjected and which is today the controlling factor was whether—it would consecrate that knowledge and its scientific and mental attainment to group good or to selfish ends, to material issues or to spiritual incentives and impulses. This ancient conflict has now been carried through into another field of human expression, that of the mind and—as the race has progressed and the personalities of human beings have reached a high stage of integration and achievement—the conflict has become acute, the issues clearer and the ranging of the opponents into two clearly defined groups is now so complete that the final struggle has become possible.[3]

With this brief background setting the stage, following are the first two stanzas:

Let the Forces of Light bring illumination to mankind.
Let the Spirit of Peace be spread abroad.
May men of goodwill everywhere meet in a spirit of cooperation.
May forgiveness on the part of all men be the keynote at this time.
Let power attend the efforts of the Great Ones.
So let it be, and help us to do our part. Stanza One 1935

* * * * *

Let the Lords of Liberation issue forth.
Let Them bring succour to the sons of men.
Let the Rider from the Secret Place come forth,
And coming, save.
Come forth, O Mighty One.

Let the souls of men awaken to the Light,
And may they stand with massed intent.
Let the fiat of the Lord go forth:
The end of woe has come!
Come forth, O Mighty One.
The hour of service of the Saving Force has now arrived.
Let it be spread abroad, O Mighty One.

Let Light and Love and Power and Death
Fulfil the purpose of the Coming One.
The WILL to save is here.
The LOVE to carry forth the work is widely spread abroad.
The ACTIVE AID of all who know the truth is also here.
Come forth, O Mighty One and blend these three.
Construct a great defending wall.
The rule of evil *now* must end. Stanza Two 1940[4]

When DK communicated the first stanza in 1935, there was great opportunity and hope on the part of the Hierarchy that humanity was ready for a spiritual renaissance that would result in international cooperation and world peace. In a message to AAB on October 10, 1934 DK wrote:

> Esoterically speaking, a point of contact, a moment of "spiritual intercourse," is imminent, and *out of that moment a new world can be born....*
>
> If this spiritual contact can be brought about, it means that the Hierarchy will no longer be hidden and unknown, but will be recognised as present upon the physical plane. This would at first be necessarily on a small scale.[5]

This communication was followed by the April, 1935 message entitled "A Challenging Opportunity" in which the first stanza was given. This invocation "...will set up a rhythm and a momentum of great potency."[6]

Apparently, humanity was not responding to calls for goodwill, international cooperation, and world peace. In September of 1939 Djwhal Khul wrote that powerful spiritual energy involving the will of God had been directly released upon the world by certain advanced Beings in Shamballa. Although this energy was having some positive effects on humanity, it was also stimulating the aggressive forces within some very powerful personalities. DK names such men as Mussolini, Hitler, Lenin, Stalin, and Franco as "...expressions of the Shamballa force."[7] The main point to bear in mind is that humanity was being greatly stimulated by powerful energies. Unfortunately, humanity was not responding as well as had been expected or hoped by the spiritual guides of the planet in Hierarchy and Shamballa, for much ancient karma of humanity was being worked out. In other words, humanity was being subjected to increased pressure to face the mistakes and injustices of the past and move forward spiritually as one human family. The stress of this "accelerated growth process" was apparently too much to handle for many people. To make matters worse, certain aggressive personalities who DK claimed were being influenced by evil forces soon took advantage of the situation.

By November of 1939 the world crisis was at a boiling point.

> The situation is serious. Sea and air and land are arrayed against the Forces of Light; they are the agents of material substance and can be used potently against the spiritual Forces....The Members of the Hierarchy are hard put to it to turn the tide in favour of that true and more spiritual civilisation which is on the way.[8]

> The World Crisis was, as you know, inevitable, but physical warfare could have been avoided if right psychological methods had been employed,...and if the spirit of sacrifice had also been demonstrated by the world aspirants. The need for group sacrifice has not met with adequate response, except in those cases where it has been imposed by governments upon their nationals. Such is the sorry history of what is taking place today.[9]

On June 30, 1940 DK gave the second stanza of the Great Invocation. In this message DK did not bandy words but called for all spiritually minded people, aspirants, and disciples to stand up for freedom and fight the forces of evil. This was a wake-up call alerting humanity that the use of prayers alone for peace was futile, and could no longer be effective without definite action.

> Will you use prayers for peace, and then patiently wait for the forces of good to fight your battle and for God to do the work? I tell you that your prayers and your wishes are unavailing when divorced from right and potent action.[10]

At the end of this message Djwhal Khul commented that the first stanza was not used as potently as it should have been.

> The Great Invocation was rendered relatively powerless, from the angle of dynamic usefulness, because the majority of those who used it turned it into a peace prayer. It was instead a great spiritually militant invocative demand. This must not happen with this Stanza of Invocation. It is a demand; it is also an authoritative affirmation of existent fact; it sets in motion agencies and forces hitherto quiescent,

> and these can change the face of the world battlefield; it invokes the Prince of Peace, but He carries a sword, and the effects of His activity may prove surprising to those who see only the needs of the form aspect of humanity.[11]

The Prince of Peace mentioned in the quotation above is the "the Rider from the Secret Place." Attention is drawn to this remark in order to show how DK is reiterating that certain illusions and glamours in the beliefs of spiritually minded people may be surrounding the ideal of the Christ and the Hierarchy in regard to war and the need to combat evil forces which threaten human liberty. It is also an indication of the possibility that humanity can call forth this Rider if the invocative demand is coupled with positive action. This somewhat mystical reference to the Rider is a prelude to the more direct appeal for the reappearance of the Christ which became possible once the tide of WWII was turned in favor of the Allies.

According to DK, this turning point came between December of 1941 and April 1942. It was during this period that America entered the war after the Japanese attack on Pearl Harbor. Having been forced to drop its neutral position, the USA was able to mobilize its national will and resources to fight the Axis forces. In a message dated December, 1941 DK states:

> The determination and the inner purpose of humanity will be so definite during the period when the Sun will begin to move northward—from December 25th until June 22nd, 1942—that the future of humanity for many hundreds of years will be decided.[12]

DK next urges all his students to use and distribute both stanzas of the Great Invocation for,

> ...one will invoke the Rider from the secret place...the other will invoke the Lords of Liberation.
>
> The blended invocation and the united call from the different levels of the human consciousness will bring a mighty appeal to bear upon the hidden Centres of the "Saving Force." It is this united appeal which must now be organised.[13]

The combined efforts of all those who stood against the Axis powers were apparently succeeding from the viewpoint of DK because in a message dated August, 1942 He stated:

> The critical point is now passed, and the humanitarian grasp of the issues involved, and the unity existing among the Allied Nations, guarantee the inevitable defeat of the Axis Powers.[14]

DK gives some indication of how important the use of the Great Invocation was in the following passages from August 9, 1945 entitled "The Release of Atomic Energy." He discusses the profound effects of splitting the atom and the fact that the race between the Allies and the Axis to develop a bomb caused "enormous tension in hierarchical circles."[15] If they [Axis] had succeeded "it would have led to a major planetary disaster."[17] Djwhal Khul states further that:

> You will now understand the meaning of the words used by so many of you in the second of the Great Invocations: *The hour of service of the saving force has now arrived.* This "saving force" is the energy which science has released into the world for the destruction, first of all, of those who continue (if they do) to defy the Forces of Light working through the United Nations.[17]

Finally, comes a relatively shocking passage:

> The evil forces were closer to success than any of you have ever dreamed. They were so close to success in 1942 that there were four months when the members of the spiritual Hierarchy had made every possible arrangement to withdraw from human contact for an indefinite and unforeseen period of time...
>
> The necessity to withdraw was averted. I may not say in what manner, beyond telling you that the Lords of Liberation took certain unexpected steps. This They were led to do owing to the invocative powers of humanity, used consciously by all those upon the side of the will-to-good and unconsciously by all men of goodwill.[18]

According to this information, the use of the first two stanzas of the Great Invocation along with the enormous efforts of the Allies combined to defeat the Axis powers and the Forces of Darkness. The final passage through this planetary crisis led to the decision of the Rider to now come forth, and this in turn led to the giving out of the third and final stanza of the Great Invocation. This third stanza is the most potent of the three, and according to Djwhal Khul sums up the complete new teachings of the Christ (formerly called the Rider) for the Aquarian Age.

The Great Invocation: Stanza Three

> Each epoch has its own word. This word is as a key to the lock. Ancient Teachings continually spoke about a potent word which was contained in a precise and brief formula. Immutable, like a crystal of known composition, it is impossible to alter in any way the words of these formulas: impossible either to lengthen or to shorten. The guaranty of Cosmos is in the casting of these words.[19]

The third stanza appears next and it is printed in every book written by Alice Bailey. The format as laid out in those books is the one that will be used to explore the deeper aspects of the Great Invocation later in this book. It appears as follows:

From the point of Light within the Mind of God
Let light stream forth into the minds of men.
Let Light descend on Earth.

From the point of Love within the Heart of God
Let love stream forth into the hearts of men.
May Christ return to Earth.

From the centre where the Will of God is known
Let purpose guide the little wills of men—
The purpose which the Masters know and serve.

From the centre which we call the race of men
Let the Plan of Love and Light work out
And may it seal the door where evil dwells.

Let Light and Love and Power restore the Plan on Earth.

From what is written by Djwhal Khul about the Great Invocation, this third stanza is the most powerful and significant prayer ever used on our planet. In *The Reappearance of the Christ* DK says:

> The agony of the war, and the distress of the entire human family led Christ, in the year 1945, to come to a great decision—a decision which found expression in two most important statements. He announced to the assembled spiritual Hierarchy and to all His servants and disciples on Earth that He had decided to emerge again into physical contact with humanity, *if* they would bring about the initial stages of establishing right human relations; secondly, He gave to the world (for the use of the "man in the street") one of the oldest prayers ever known, but one which hitherto had not been permitted to be used except by the most exalted, spiritual Beings. He used it Himself for the first time, we are told, at the time of the Full Moon of June, 1945, which is recognised as the Full Moon of the Christ, just as the Full Moon of May is that of the Buddha. It was not easy to translate these ancient phrases (so ancient that they are without date or background of any kind) into modern words, but it has been done, and the Great Invocation, which may eventually become the world prayer, was pronounced by Him and taken down by His disciples.[20]

Two things are especially interesting about this passage: first, the fact that the "phrases" are of very ancient origin, and second, the fact that the Christ was only permitted to use the Great Invocation in June of 1945, for prior to this date only "the most exalted spiritual Beings" had used it. These two points indicate the great potency and importance of this invocation. These statements make clear we are not dealing with an ordinary prayer created just recently at a time of humanity's need.

> If one may venture to speak in such terms (reverent and symbolical), the reward accorded to the Christ, as He announced His decision [to reappear in the world, JB] as final and irrevocable, was the permission or rather the right to use a certain great Invocation—never before granted....The right to use certain great Words of Power or "Stanzas of Direction" is never lightly accorded. The decision of Christ to appear again among men, bringing His disciples with Him, drew forth this permission from the Lord of the World, the Ancient of Days.[21]

This quotation lays further emphasis on the tremendous magnitude of this invocation by showing that the Lord of the World, Sanat Kumara Himself, granted permission for the Christ to use it. This special permission, along with the facts of the invocation's ancient origin and use only by "exalted spiritual Beings" until 1945, adds a whole new perspective and significance to this sacred "Stanza of Direction." But, before we investigate these deeper and larger issues it is best to examine the words themselves, for much food for thought exists on the outer surface of this invocation that provides nourishment to the soul.

Commentaries On the Great Invocation

Since 1949 some articles about the Great Invocation have been written by various students of the esoteric philosophy taught by Djwhal Khul through AAB; however, the literature available on the Great Invocation is not extensive. No books are written specifically about the Great Invocation alone, although individual chapters and discussions appear in some esoteric and spiritual books as part of a wider topic. World Goodwill[22] produces a 16-page pamphlet entitled *The Great Invocation: The Use and Significance of the Great Invocation*.

One of the earliest commentaries on the Great Invocation is an article written by Foster Bailey which appeared in the June-July 1951 issue of *The Beacon*. In this article Mr. Bailey interprets the invocation by the various stanzas. An extensive extract from this article gives not only a fine analysis of portions of the Great Invocation, but also serves as a typical example of how the Great Invocation is usually interpreted:

> In the first stanza the words "From the point of Light within the Mind of God" are a direct reference to the divine source of light which is the Universal Soul. This Soul includes all souls in all kingdoms, and is the source of light for the animal soul and for the individual human soul and for the soul of humanity as a whole....
>
> In the second stanza the words "From the point of Love within the Heart of God" refer specifically to the occult Hierarchy of the planet, of which the Christ is the Head....
>
> The combined effect of the merging of this light and love in the form of spiritual energy, as invoked by these two stanzas, produces that loving understanding which fecundates the hearts of all men....
>
> The third stanza deals with "The centre where the Will of God is known." This is Shamballa, the centre from Which the Hierarchy draws its life; the centre from which the Christ and those standing closest around him draw the knowledge of the Plan....It is the focal point on this planet for the reception of the direct potency of the will of God....
>
> The fourth stanza specifically directs the invoked energies into that centre of the divine manifestation which is humanity as a whole. The Invocation conforms to the fundamental Plan itself in its recognition that it is only humanity in its own right and by its own evolution

> and spiritual effort, which can bring the Divine plan into manifestation on this planet....
>
> The Invocation closes with a powerful mantric series of words that gathers up its meaning and focuses it on the exact point of the ultimate purpose. This restoring of the Plan on earth by humanity itself with the aid of the Christ and the Hierarchy, is the grand climax of the whole evolutionary process to date.[23]

Foster Bailey's commentary provides a wonderful beginning for an exploration of some basic principles of the ageless wisdom. The Great Invocation is appealing to so many people because it contains the fundamental qualities found in most of the world's religions. In stanza one the Mind of God is stated to be the source of spiritual Light, and the call goes forth for this Light to enter into the human world providing spiritual guidance and wisdom to all humanity. Foster Bailey relates this universal Light to the "Universal Soul" which refers back to the world soul of Plato and Plotinus.

Table 3. Triplicities of the Great Invocation.

Great Invocation	Stanza One	Stanza Two	Stanza Three
Ageless Wisdom	Light	Love	Will
	Mind of God	Heart of God	Will of God
Greek	Nous	Logos	Pneuma
Christian	Holy Spirit	Son	Father
Hindu	Brahma	Vishnu	Shiva
Mahayana Buddhist	Nirmanakaya	Sambhogakaya	Dharmakaya
Egyptian	Isis	Horus	Osiris

Reference is made in the second stanza to the Heart of God, and the broad and sweeping theme of Love. The invocation calls for Christ to return to Earth. Many religions recognize the principle of divine intervention through a savior. Christianity teaches the second coming of Christ; the Jews await the Messiah; the Buddhists expect the future Buddha to appear as Maitreya, and the Islamic faith speaks of the coming Imam Mahdi. This stanza also relates directly to Hierarchy which represents the Heart of God with the Christ as its Leader. Stanza three deals with the Will of God and relates to Shamballa. These aspects of the Great Invocation appear in table 3 along with corresponding representations of deity from various religions and philosophies.

Foster Bailey offers further commentary on the Great Invocation in two of his books. In *Things To Come*, he points out the power and importance of the three aspects in relation to humanity:

> The Great Invocation is unique in that it invokes all three divine aspects in one spoken world-wide prayer. Light invokes the third aspect, love invokes the second aspect and will invokes the first aspect. All three will eventually be lived by in the human family. The potency of all three combined is unimaginably tremendous....
>
> The Great Invocation as a whole acts as a word of power. The words themselves are a divine energy vehicle. When pronounced clearly and intelligently this energy is released. Therefore, The Invocation prevails in its own right if only it is used.[24]

In another book by Foster Bailey entitled *Reflections*, he comments briefly on the need for cooperation between human beings:

> A key word for the Great Invocation is *cooperate*, not merely follow. The Christ uses the Great Invocation to hasten God's Plan and to evoke spiritual potency for his work and when we rightly use the Great Invocation we are cooperating with him.[25]

The themes of the three aspects, the Christ, humanity, and cooperation are all central and vital to the meaning of the Great Invocation. Mary Bailey (who later married Foster after Alice's death), retired president of Lucis Trust, discusses the Great Invocation in her book, *A Learning Experience*. Discussing the importance of the three aspects of light, love, and power, she says:

> We need a much deeper and more inclusive understanding of the three basic energies the Invocation presents, because they, in turn, embody the significance of the Christ's work throughout the Aquarian era.[26]

Without the cooperation of humanity—freely given—the Plan of God cannot succeed. This idea is brought out in stanzas four and five which link the restoration of the Plan to humanity. The human race has come of age and must now accept its responsibility as a co-partner in the evolutionary process of our world. This increasing sense of responsibility is evident in the environmental and world population crises, to name only two areas of global concern. The Christ, representing all humanity, is said to use the Great Invocation daily. If it is accepted that this world prayer is a vital factor in the spiritual evolution of the world, then the effect of people saying the Great Invocation at least once a day becomes a powerful service in cooperation with the Christ and the Hierarchy, as well as with Sanat Kumara and Shamballa.

Invocation as a Tool for Spiritual Emergence

Prayer has always played a part in the life of humanity. The appeal to a Higher Force, to God, is an intrinsic part of all religions. The concept of invocation as explained by Djwhal Khul involves a greater use of the mind and the will than in the past, especially as it has been applied to religious practice. In discussing the possibility of a world religion in the next century, DK states that such a religion will be based on the "science of invocation and evocation."

> The science of invocation and evocation will take the place of what we now call "prayer" and "worship." Be not disturbed by the use of the word "science." It is not the cold and heartless intellectual thing so oft depicted. It is in reality the intelligent organisation of spiritual energy and of the forces of love, and these, when effective, will evoke the response of spiritual Beings Who can again walk openly among men, and thus establish a close relation and a constant communication between humanity and the spiritual Hierarchy.[27]

Djwhal Khul goes on to explain that in the future the practice of invocation will fall into two parts. The first part will involve large numbers of people trained to invoke those spiritual forces of the planet Who, when called, will approach humanity; this involves the Hierarchy of Masters and the Christ. Along with this invocative appeal to Hierarchy is the demand for "light, liberation, and understanding." The idea is to raise the level of approach to God and the spiritual Hierarchy from a purely personal, emotional, devotional level to a point that is mental and less emotional yet filled with compassion and heart energy. This is meant to be an act of invocative service.

Djwhal Khul describes the second part of prayer as an invocative psycho-spiritual tool of greater potency and conscious direction than available today. DK says:

> There will also be the skilled work of invocation as practised by those who have trained their minds through right meditation, who know the potency of formulas, mantrams and invocations and who work consciously. They will increasingly use certain great formulas of words which will later be given to the race, just as the Lord's Prayer was given by the Christ, and as the New Invocation has been given out for use at this time by the Hierarchy.[28]

When the Lord of the World gave the Christ permission to use this ancient invocation, DK referred to this decision by saying, "The right to use great Words of Power or 'Stanzas of Direction' is never lightly accorded." This indicates the magnitude, power, and sacredness of the Great Invocation, and at the same time it demonstrates the tremendous importance of Christ's decision to reappear in the world. It is a mantram of ancient origin and able, if used properly, to effect great spiritual change. The Tibetan defines mantrams in this way:

> A mantram is a combination of sounds, of words and of phrases that, through virtue of certain rhythmic effects, achieve results that would not be possible apart from them....
>
> The potency of a mantram depends upon the point in evolution of the man who employs it. Uttered by an ordinary man it serves to stimulate the good within his bodies, to protect him, and it will also prove of beneficent influence upon his environment. Uttered by an adept or initiate its possibilities for good are infinite and far-reaching.[29]

Referring specifically to the Great Invocation DK goes even further.

> No one can use this Invocation or prayer for illumination and for love without causing powerful changes in his own attitudes; his life intention, character and goals will be changed and his life will be altered and made spiritually useful.[30]

In a video-taped interview,[31] Mary Bailey tells the story of the night Alice Bailey received the Great Invocation from Djwhal Khul. According to the story, Djwhal Khul was so intent on the words of the invocation being exact that He almost materialized in the dictation room in order to accomplish the transmission. This was something that had never been considered in all the years of their work together as far as anyone knows. Apparently, this particular mantram was so important, it had to be recorded as close to the ancient phrases as possible using specific English wording.

Beyond the obvious fact that this invocation is a mantram, a "Word of Power," and a "Stanza of Direction," is the suggestion that its use will not only affect the one who uses it but, perhaps more importantly, it will stimulate and accelerate the spiritual evolution of the entire planet.

> For the reception of this last part or final stanza of the great hierarchical "Invocation for Power and Light," all previous teaching you have received and all your earlier meditation work was simply an elementary prelude. In receiving this Invocation, in its use and distribution, you have been participating in a cosmic event of tremendous importance.[32]

The fact that this Great Invocation was not a mantram suddenly formulated in order to meet the spiritual needs of humanity during recent world crises is another indicator that it has some deeper, more fundamental relationship to the Plan and purpose of our planet. Evidence of this can be found in the following quotation:

> The final stanza of the "Invocation for Power and Light," as it is called in the Archives of the Masters, is apparently simple. It has, in these Archives, an indicatory symbol beside it which indicates the era or period in human history during which it can and should be used. It is interesting to us to note that the evolution of humanity is in line with the indicated timing.[33]

The possible implications and significance of this statement by DK will be explored in chapter 4. For now, it is enough to know that sufficient reason exists to explore the Great Invocation for any clues that may reveal an esoteric meaning lying behind the words of its outer form.

Notes

1. Alice A. Bailey, *Discipleship In the New Age,* vol. II, 157.
2. See Bailey, *The Externalisation of the Hierarchy,* 123.
3. Ibid., 125.
4. Ibid., v.
5. Ibid., 21.
6. Ibid., 26.
7. Ibid., 133.
8. Ibid., 171.
9. Ibid., 171.
10. Ibid., 233.
11. Ibid., 250-51.
12. Ibid., 337.
13. Ibid., 338.
14. Ibid., 367.
15. Ibid., 493.
16. Ibid., 493.
17. Ibid., 497.
18. Ibid., 493-94.
19. *New Era Community*, 42-43.
20. Bailey, *The Reappearance of the Christ*, 30-31.
21. Ibid., 72-73.
22. World Goodwill is a branch of Lucis Trust, the umbrella organization which oversees the publication of the Alice A. Bailey books, the operation of the Arcane School, and various other service activities.
23. Foster Bailey, "The Great Invocation," *The Beacon* Vol. XXX No. 3-4 (June-July 1951): 81, 82, 83.
24. Foster Bailey, *Things To Come*, 127.
25. Foster Bailey, *Reflections*, 115.
26. Mary Bailey, *A Learning Experience*, 114.
27. Bailey, *The Reappearance of the Christ,* 151.
28. Ibid., 152.
29. Alice A. Bailey, *A Treatise on Cosmic Fire*, n. 926.
30. Bailey, *Discipleship in the New Age,* vol. II, 168.
31. Mary Bailey, *Bridge to the Future,* video, 1984.
32. Bailey, *Discipleship in the New Age,* vol. II, 187-88.
33. Ibid., 157.

3

Numerical Symbology

The ancient philosophers considered numbers the basis of everything in the cosmos, both physical and spiritual. Pythagoras and Plato believed the archetypal world of ideas could be expressed through the symbolism of number and proportion. Our modern civilization uses numbers to quantify the physical world. However, the ancients did not use numbers solely to quantify items; they also used numbers to qualify objects. Numbers and their relational proportions were used to express beauty in the physical world, while representing, at the same time, the beauty of the archetypal conceptual dimension of existence. Our examination of the Great Invocation will use numbers qualitatively as well as symbolically. Through the use of correspondence and analogy the symbolic language of numbers can often indicate hidden relationships that do not appear to exist on the surface. From his wonderful book *Jesus Christ, Sun of God: Ancient Cosmology and Early Christian Symbolism*, David Fideler writes:

> From the Greeks, the Jewish kabbalists adopted the practice of gematria, interpreting the meaning of sacred words and phrases by their numerical values. Words or phrases with the same numerical value were taken as having the same meaning, opening the door for a

> unique form of scriptural interpretation. The word *gematria*, however, is based on the Greek word *geômetria* or geometry, and...there exists definitive evidence that gematria constituted a sacred language of Greek theology and was used before the time of Plato.[1]

This passage shows the antiquity of gematria or as the Tibetan Teacher Djwhal Khul calls it "esoteric numerology." Through the symbolic connections revealed by numbers certain clues may be revealed about the Great Invocation that are not immediately noticeable. In addition, the numbers themselves may reveal particular qualities which again will indicate hidden relationships between seemingly disconnected parts. The following hypothetical situation provides a simple example of this idea. If you were reduced to the size of an ant and were only able to exist in two dimensions of length and width (surface plane) and you suddenly saw before you an area of five separate and distinct obstructions you would not understand the true nature of these strange "forms." However, if the third dimension of depth was suddenly added to your sensory equipment you would see that the five separate forms were actually the fingertips of a hand placed on the surface of your world. With the added dimension of depth you now become aware of an entirely new view of your world. Five distinct "objects" are now seen to be one connected unit.

The words of the Great Invocation can be thought of as the "five marks" on our surface world, while the "hand" represents the true hidden (esoteric) nature of the Great Invocation lying just beyond our normal sensory world. Through the symbolism of their numeric meanings and correspondences, the words of the Great Invocation may open a greater world of meaning to our sight. The Great Invocation will be examined in several ways.

- **Numerologically**. The values of the words are determined through the substitution of numbers for letters. The qualities, analogies, and correspondences of the various components of the Great Invocation can then be examined according to numerical symbolism.

- **Structurally**. The Great Invocation can be studied simply by its form or structure. The structure of the Great Invocation can be examined by counting the number of stanzas, sentences, lines, words, and letters forming the entire prayer. The resultant numbers are then examined according to their symbolic meaning and association with ideas and archetypes of the ageless wisdom. Table 4 which follows provides the total number of stanzas, lines, words, letters, and sentences in the Great Invocation.

Table 4. Structure Table.

Stanza	Line #	# of Words	# of Letters	# of Sentences
1	1	10	37	0
	2	9	36	1
	3	5	22	1
Total	3 Lines	24 Words	95 Letters	2 Sentences
2	4	10	37	0
	5	9	36	1
	6	5	22	1
Total	3 Lines	24 Words	95 Letters	2 Sentences
3	7	10	37	0
	8	8	34	0
	9	8	37	1
Total	3 Lines	26 Words	108 Letters	1 Sentence
4	10	10	36	0
	11	9	31	0
	12	9	34	1
Total	3 Lines	28 Words	101 Letters	1 Sentence
5	13	11	44	1
Total	1 Line	11 Words	44 Letters	1 Sentence
5 Stanzas	13 Lines	113 Words	443 Letters	7 Sentences

Table 5 lists all the major components in the Great Invocation which, like table 4, is based purely on the structure of the Great Invocation and not on the numerological values of the words. Of special importance, however is the fact that all the components added together equal 5. As you will soon discover, this is highly symbolic.

Table 5. Structure Synthesis.

Components	Quantity
Great Invocation	1
Stanzas	5
Sentences	7
Lines	13
Words	113
Letters	443
Key Words	21
Key Word Letter Total	95
Structural Total	698
Root Value	6 + 9 + 8 = 23 2 + 3 = 5

- **Key Words**. In addition to these obvious components, various words in the Great Invocation are capitalized. I have termed these "key words" and identified twenty-one of them in the Great Invocation. The total number of key words and letters comprising the key words are included as part of the Great Invocation's structure. Capitalized words excluded from this total are those at the beginning of each line, due to the usual practice of capitalizing the first word of a line in poetic expression. Table 6 contains the twenty-one key words along with the numerological values of each word. A detailed examination of these values appears in chapters 4 and 6.

Table 6. Twenty-one Key Words.

Key Word	# of Letters	AN	RAN	Root
Light	5	56	29	11
Mind	4	40	22	22
God	3	26	17	8
Light	5	56	29	11
Earth	5	52	25	7
Love	4	54	18	9
Heart	5	52	25	7
God	3	26	17	8
Christ	6	77	32	5
Earth	5	52	25	7
Will	4	56	20	2
God	3	26	17	8
Masters	7	95	23	5
Plan	4	43	16	7
Love	4	54	18	9
Light	5	56	29	11
Light	5	56	29	11
Love	4	54	18	9
Power	5	77	32	5
Plan	4	43	16	7
Earth	5	52	25	7
Total 21	95	1103	482	176

Esoteric Numerology

This book employs several methods of number/letter conversion for interpreting the Great Invocation. One method converts the English alphabet according to the numeric order of each letter. For instance, the letter A is equivalent to 1, and the letter Z is equivalent to 26. (We will simply use "equal to.") The numeric value that results from this method is called the alpha number, a term used by William Eisen in his book *The Universal Language of Cabalah*. Whenever a word in this book has been converted to an alpha number it will be abbreviated as AN. The following table illustrates this method.

Table 7. Alpha Numbers—AN.

A	1	N	14
B	2	O	15
C	3	P	16
D	4	Q	17
E	5	R	18
F	6	S	19
G	7	T	20
H	8	U	21
I	9	V	22
J	10	W	23
K	11	X	24
L	12	Y	25
M	13	Z	26

To find the AN value for the word "NUMBER" look up each letter in table 7 and find the total by adding the values of letters together. The letter values are shown here as: 14 (N) + 21 (U) + 13 (M) + 2 (B) + 5 (E) + 18 (R) = 73. So, the word "NUMBER" has an AN value of 73.

Another conversion technique is called the RAN method which means "reduced alpha numbers." This simply means that all the letters of the alphabet are reduced to single digits when employed to find the value of a given word. Table 8 illustrates how the alphabet is converted to single digits.

Table 8. Reduction Process.

A	1	N	14, 1 + 4 = 5
B	2	O	15, 1 + 5 = 6
C	3	P	16, 1 + 6 = 7
D	4	Q	17, 1 + 7 = 8
E	5	R	18, 1 + 8 = 9
F	6	S	19, 1+9=10, 1+0=1
G	7	T	20, 2 + 0 = 2
H	8	U	21, 2 + 1 = 3
I	9	V	22, 2 + 2 = 4
J	10, 1 + 0 = 1	W	23, 2 + 3 = 5
K	11, 1 + 1 = 2	X	24, 2 + 4 = 6
L	12, 1 + 2 = 3	Y	25, 2 + 5 = 7
M	13, 1 + 3 = 4	Z	26, 2 + 6 = 8

This method of conversion is the system used most often by numerologists for interpreting birth dates and names for individuals seeking information about their personal lives. Table 9 is the result of the process shown in table 8 and appears as follows:

Table 9. Reduced Alpha Numbers—RAN.

1	2	3	4	5	6	7	8	9
A	B	C	D	E	F	G	H	I
J	K	L	M	N	O	P	Q	R
S	T	U	V	W	X	Y	Z	

As can be seen in the above table the letter J now equals 1 instead of 10 because the 1 and 0 have been added together thus reducing the value of the letter J to 1. Using this method for the word "NUMBER" yields a different total: 5 (N) + 3 (U) + 4 (M) + 2 (B) + 5 (E) + 9 (R) = 28 (RAN).

In addition to the fact that the two methods result in different totals, 73 AN and 28 RAN respectively, both these totals can ultimately be reduced to their root value, which in this case is 1. This is done as follows: AN value 73, 7 + 3 = 10, 1 + 0 = 1 and RAN value 28, 2 + 8 = 10, 1 + 0 = 1. Even though the word "number" has a root value of 1, it also has a value of 73 and 28 depending on the method used to convert it.

One very important difference between standard numerology and the methods employed in this book is this: standard numerology reduces all words to their root values, but in this book a word or phrase can be expressed in its AN, RAN or root value form. The exception to this rule is when a word results in a total of 11 or 22. Then the number is not reduced any further. Therefore, 11 does not become 2 and 22 is not reduced to 4; they remain 11 and 22 and are called master numbers. A summary of these methods follows using several different words as examples:

Number—AN value 73.
Root value 1—7 + 3 = 10, 1 + 0 = 1.
Number—RAN value 28.
Root value 1—2 + 8 = 10, 1 + 0 = 1.

Christ—AN value 77.
Root value 5—7 + 7 = 14, 1 + 4 = 5.
Christ—RAN value 32.
Root value 5—3 + 2 = 5.

Will—AN value 56.
Root value 11—5 + 6 = 11.
Will—RAN value 20.
Root value 2—2 + 0 = 2.

Another type of number we will sometimes employ is called a "triangular number." These numbers are obtained by totaling all the numbers from 1 up to and including the number in question in order to arrive at a total. This total is directly related to the original number. For instance, the number 10 is a result of the addition of 1, 2, 3, and 4 (1 + 2 + 3 + 4 = 10). Therefore, the numbers 4 and 10 have an inherent relationship. Table 10 lists the first fourteen numbers with their resultant triangular numbers at the right.[2]

Table 10. Triangular Numbers.

1	1	1
2	1+2	3
3	1+2+3	6
4	1+2+3+4	10
5	1+2+3+4+5	15
6	1+2+3+4+5+6	21
7	1+2+3+4+5+6+7	28
8	1+2+3+4+5+6+7+8	36
9	1+2+3+4+5+6+7+8+9	45
10	1+2+3+4+5+6+7+8+9+10	55
11	1+2+3+4+5+6+7+8+9+10+11	66
12	1+2+3+4+5+6+7+8+9+10+11+12	78
13	1+2+3+4+5+6+7+8+9+10+11+12+13	91
14	1+2+3+4+5+6+7+8+9+10+11+12+13+14	105

Figure 1. The Tetraktys.

The graphic representation above in which the first four numbers are added together is actually called the Tetraktys of the Pythagoreans. Since the Greeks had no written symbols for numbers they expressed numbers as dots. The Tetraktys was laid out in a triangle of dots as illustrated above. This diagram shows quite clearly how the first ten numbers form a triangle. Tier one contains one dot; tier two, two dots; tier three, three dots; and tier four, four dots. Therefore, adding tier one and tier two is the same as adding 1 + 2, yielding 3. The Pythagoreans considered the first ten numbers as Perfect and Divine. Since a triangle of four tiers depicted this perfect state (1 + 2 + 3 + 4 = 10), this pattern is often called the Divine Tetraktys.

In the two instances Djwhal Khul performed a numerological analysis of several words, He did not use the alpha numbers (AN) as shown in table 7, but the style of table 9, the reduced alpha numbers (RAN). This is not to say one is more valid than the other or that DK does not believe a particular method to be true, but only that He did not use it in these instances. Experience shows both methods to be of great value, and therefore both methods are employed in this work. The method used to find a word value is indicated by AN or RAN after the number.

Each of these methods provides valuable information concerning the esoteric meaning of various terms and their relationships. Following are the two most extensive examples of numerological analysis given by DK in his work with Alice A. Bailey.

Djwhal Khul and Esoteric Numerology

Numerology has hitherto been studied primarily, and rightly, from the substance aspect, but not so much from the standpoint of conscious energy. The Triad, for instance, is usually looked upon by our students as the triangle formed by the manasic-buddhic and atmic permanent atoms; the cube stands for the lower material man, and the five-pointed star has frequently a very material interpretation. All these angles of vision are necessary, and must precede the study of the subjective aspect, but they lay the emphasis upon the material rather than upon the subjective; the subject nevertheless should be studied psychologically.[3]

The following passage is a practical example of what the Tibetan calls "esoteric numerology":

It is interesting to note that the numerical value of the word "four" is the same in detail as that of the word "force", if you eliminate the number five. For humanity, it is the fifth energy which leads to the battlefield, the energy of the discriminating mind, and when that has been in due time used, controlled and transmuted, "only the four remains and force has gone." Note the detail of the numbering:

F O R C E
6 6 9 3 5 .....29.....11.Number of adept, using energy.
F O U R
6 6 3 9 ....24......6. The creator, unifying the
subjective and the objective.

It is apparent that *force* in the first group ends in separativeness, for five is the number of the mind and of man. Number nine, the number of initiation, is hidden midway in force, but the climaxing figures indicate activity and separation. In the second group of figures, activity precedes the nine of initiation, and that nine is the culmination. But five is left out. Man is no longer really human or separative. He is the perfected four of the lower three and the soul. Putting the truth quite simply, let it be borne in mind that mankind, the fourth kingdom, which is an expression of the fourth creative hierarchy of human monads, is swept by the instinct or impulse towards harmony, and is thus primarily under the influence of the fourth ray. This harmony is achieved through the use of the energy of the fifth ray of knowledge. Then through gained and applied knowledge, the result is beauty and the power to create. Then the ray of the fifth Lord will be withdrawn from the major cycle governing humanity, and wisdom and intuitional buddhic response will characterise humanity. There is a close interplay in this major cycle, as far as mankind is concerned, between the two ray Lords of Harmony and of Knowledge. It is again in this numerical relation of four and five that the number nine emerges, which is the number of initiation. An adept of the fifth initiation is one who has achieved complete harmony through right knowledge. This takes place at the fourth initiation and is demonstrated or proven at the fifth.[4]

This rather lengthy passage has been included in order to illustrate the Tibetan's detailed and inclusive method of analyzing words—in this instance "force" and "four." In the next passage Djwhal Khul analyzes the word "Shamballa." Although this is another lengthy extract, it contains valuable clues to the esoteric meanings of various numbers.

To this centre we give the name Shamballa, the component letters of which are numerically: S.H.A.M.B.A.L.L.A. or 1.8.1.4.2.1.3.3.1. This word equals the number 24 which in its turn equals 6. I would call your attention to the fact that the word has in it nine letters, and—as you know—nine is the number of initiation. The goal of all the initiatory process is to admit mankind into realisation of and identification with the will or purpose of Deity. The number 6 is the number of form or of manifestation which is the agent or medium through which this realisation comes and by which the consciousness is unfolded so that it can become the foundation of the higher process which is instituted at the third initiation. That initiation is closely related to the third major centre, Shamballa; it is the third, from the angle of man's perception and understanding, but the first from the angle of Deity Itself. Again, 6 being the number of the sixth ray, it is therefore the number of idealism and of that driving force which makes mankind move forward upon the path and in response to the vision and press upward towards the light. It is in reality devotion to an unseen goal, ever on ahead, and an unswerving recognition of the objective. Like all other divine qualities, it has its material counterpart, and that is why 666 is regarded as the number of the Beast or of materialism, the number of the dominance of the three worlds prior to the process of reorientation and the expression of developed idealism and purpose. The third aspect expresses itself through pure materialism, and hence the three sixes. In an ancient book on numbers the initiate is defined as "the one who has experienced and expressed 666 and found it naught; who has dropped the 6 and become the 66, and thus has found himself upon the WAY; later, again, he drops the 6 and becomes the perfected 6-form, the instrument and expression of spirit.

The number 24 is of deep interest, expressing as it does the double 12—the greater and the lesser zodiac. Just as the number 6 expresses *space*, so the number 24 expresses *time*, and is the key to the great cycle of manifestation. It is the clue to all cyclic appearance or incarnation. Its two figures define the method of evolution; 2 equals the quality of love-wisdom, working under the Law of Attraction and drawing man from one point of attainment to another; whilst 4 indicates the technique of conflict and the achieving of harmony through conflict; 4 is also the number of the human hierarchy, and 2 is the number of the spiritual hierarchy. Technically speaking, until the third initiation, the initiate is "occupied with the relationship of the 2 and the 4; these, when placed side by side, connote relation; and when placed the one above the other, the initiate passes from the 4 into the 2." Needless to say, there is much more to say anent these figures, but the above will suffice to show the satisfactory nature of esoteric numerology—not numerology as understood today.

I would have you note that the sounds which compose the word "Shamballa" are predominantly along the line of will or power or of first ray energy. Of the nine letters, six are on the first ray line of force, 1.1.1.3.3.1.—spirit and matter, will and intelligence. Two of them are along, the second line of force, 4 and 2. The number 8 inaugurates ever a new cycle, following after the number 7, which is that of a relative perfection. It is the number of the Christ-consciousness; just as 7 is the number of man, 8 is the number of the Hierarchy, and 9 is the number of initiation or of Shamballa. Forget not that, from the angle of the Hierarchy, the third initiation is regarded as the first major initiation.

These preliminary remarks are intended to convey much esoteric information to those who realise that number gives the clue to the form and purpose of the life which the form veils.[5]

The Work of William Eisen

I have found only one instance of numerological analysis of the Great Invocation. In the second volume of *The English Cabalah: The Mysteries of Phi*, the author, William Eisen, devotes three pages to the Great Invocation.

In his brief analysis Eisen reveals a proportional relationship between the words light, love, purpose, and "universal" plan. Using the natural numbers of the alphabet to convert these words, (the AN method) Eisen indicates how light-56 added to love-54 equals purpose-110. Then love-54 added to purpose-110 equals universal plan-164.[6] In other words purpose is comprised of light and love, and the universal plan contains love and purpose. It is not possible to explain Mr. Eisen's theories underlying these number combinations because they are developed over the course of two large and complex volumes (1360 pages) dealing with numbers, the English alphabet, Cabalah, the Tarot, and other mystical and kabalistic topics.

William Eisen's work is fascinating and comprehensive, but his work with the Great Invocation, although provocative, hardly scratches the surface in comparison to the present work. It is very possible, however, that Mr. Eisen, who died in 1989, would have discovered much within the Great Invocation—along the lines of the present work—if he had pursued this area of study because he was surely a gifted explorer and teacher in his application of the ancient Kabalah to the English language.

Notes

1. David Fideler, *Jesus Christ, Sun of God: Ancient Cosmology and Early Christian Symbolism*, 27.
2. To find a triangular number from any number, add 1 to the number you are working with and multiply them by each other. Divide the result by 2. This result is a triangular number.

   For example to find the triangular number for 5 add 1 to 5 yielding 6; multiply 5 x 6 resulting in 30; divide 30 by 2 giving 15. The number 15 is a triangular number resulting from the number 5. This can be verified by referring to table 10. Conversely, to determine whether a number is a triangular number perform the following operation:

   1. Multiply the number by 8.
   2. Add 1 to the result. (Be sure to press the equal key on your calculator before doing step 3.)
   3. Find the square root of the result of step 2. The easiest way to do this is to press the radical sign found on most calculators.
   4. Subtract 1 from the result.
   5. Divide this number by 2.
   6. If the answer is a whole number (no decimals) then your original number is a triangular number.
   7. Use the triangular number from the first example to confirm your result.

3. Bailey, *A Treatise on Cosmic Fire,* 695.
4. Bailey, *Esoteric Psychology,* vol. I, 346-47.
5. Bailey, *The Rays and the Initiations*, 79-81.
6. William Eisen, *The English Cabalah,* vol. II: *The Mysteries of Phi*, 691.

4

Numerology and the Great Invocation

With the historical context, background, and commentaries of the Great Invocation established, it is time to examine the numerological information for clues to the significance of the Great Invocation. Most of the numbers are interrelated. Some numbers are derived directly from the Great Invocation and others are linked with passages appearing in the various books transmitted to Alice Bailey by Djwhal Khul. Commentaries by Helena P. Blavatsky and others in relation to number symbolism will also be used where appropriate. As explained in chapter 3, some number results are AN (table 7) and others RAN (table 9).

The Number 5: The Essence of the Great Invocation

When all the letters in all the words of the Great Invocation are converted to numbers, added together and reduced to a single digit, the final result is the number 5. Five is a highly significant number in respect to the ageless wisdom, especially in relation to humanity, because the human kingdom is working to perfect manas (Sanskrit for "mind"). Manas is the fifth principle out of the seven which humanity is bringing to perfection through the evolutionary process. Briefly, the seven principles are:

1. The etheric energy body
2. Vitality, Prana
3. Desire
4. Concrete mind, lower manas
5. Abstract mind, higher manas
6. Wisdom, Buddhi, Christ force
7. Spiritual Will, Atma

The ageless wisdom distinguishes between the mental activities of desiring an ice cream sundae, balancing a checkbook, and abstract creativity. These are respectively, desire mind, concrete mind, and abstract mind. During the current fourth round the human kingdom is working to perfect the fourth principle of concrete mind. In the next round, the fifth, humanity will be working to perfect abstract mind or higher manas.

Presently, according to the ageless wisdom, we are living in the fourth round. This fourth cycle indicates the fullest expression of dense matter. We might think of it as the slowest vibratory rate expressed by our planetary Logos. In a footnote of *A Treatise on Cosmic Fire* the Tibetan says:

> *The present Round*, which is the fourth, is the one in which desire, or response to contact and sensation is being brought to its fullest expression. In the next round, the fifth, the fifth principle of mind, or manas, will reach fruition.[1]

Every round is broken down into seven cycles of consciousness development. These developmental cycles of consciousness growth are termed root-races. The root-race can be thought of as a seed planted in the consciousness of a small group of dedicated individuals. The seed represents a new quality or principle of consciousness that will gradually be spread throughout humanity. Today humanity finds itself well into the fifth root-race cycle, a cycle that started more than 10,000 years ago according to the ageless wisdom. (Root-race refers to consciousness development, not physical body type.)

This fifth root-race represents a foreshadowing of the development of the fifth principle in the coming fifth round due to an affinity with 5. Therefore, even though the larger cycle of the fourth round is at its densest point of manifestation, wherein it is developing sentiency and desire, the current cycle for humanity involves the development of the mind relative to sensation and desire.

During this cycle, human beings are learning how to use their minds to achieve mastery over the senses and desire nature. The simplest and most fundamental example of this idea is that reason must control the basic animal passions in order to build and maintain civilization and culture. This is exemplified by the teachings of all the world religions as well as many universal principles laid down by philosophers of the East and West.

The twentieth century has seen an enormous acceleration in the use of the mind in every field of human endeavor. Even though we as a race are in a major crisis of planetary proportions, there is also tremendous opportunity for a breakthrough into a new renaissance of human civilization through the use of the mind. We are beginning to realize that too much emphasis on knowledge, science, and technology creates monumental problems—the potency of the mind is great indeed. Although the mind is a wonderful instrument, it alone cannot solve all our social ills. If reason can provide an atmosphere of civilized living in which the baser selfish desires and instincts are controlled for the betterment of society, then we are freed to explore more refined feelings expressed through the arts. This releases humanity at a higher turn of the spiral to work and play within the greater fourth round evolution of desire and sensory experience. Through the mind's ability to discriminate and reason, the selfish desires and cravings for sensory satisfaction which lead to addictions of every kind—physical, emotional, and mental—are replaced with aspirations toward beauty and harmony expressed through the creative mind.

Thus, we find ourselves in the middle of exponential development of the fifth principle of mind, within the fifth human root-race, and on the verge of either chaos or a quantum leap to a new level of global civilization. Through the proper direction of mind toward a spiritual vision of world unity in diversity, the selfish use of fourth round senses and desires that have brought nothing but pain and suffering can be transformed into joy and beauty. In light of this alone, the fact that the Great Invocation vibrates to the keynote of 5 is of great significance.

In addition to this, humanity represents the fourth kingdom in nature, but its goal is the fifth kingdom. According to the wisdom teachings, a human being enters the fifth kingdom through five specific expansions of consciousness called initiations. The kingdoms of nature are:

1. Mineral
2. Vegetable
3. Animal
4. Human
5. Spiritual - Hierarchy
6. Planetary - Shamballa
7. Solar

We have already seen that the Great Invocation is a tool for invoking spiritual forces into the world of human living in order to save us from sinking into chaos and destruction. The Tibetan states that the Great Invocation has the greatest effect in calling forth aid from the spiritual Hierarchy when it is used with a clear and focused mind. Thus, the number 5, and consequently, the fifth principle of mind is the key to effective use of the Great Invocation. However, it is not simply the use of the mind divorced from spiritual principles of love, freedom, and cooperation. These qualities of life can only be accessed through the integration of heart and mind. The Great Invocation speaks to this process when invoking both the Light and the Love of God.

The ability to use the mind as actively and powerfully as humanity is doing at this time and for the past two hundred years is addressed by the Master Djwhal Khul. He says that the energy of mind has been predominantly active on the Earth since 1775.[2] This energy of mind is called the fifth ray. It is the ray of Concrete Knowledge and Science. Djwhal Khul offers the following comments on the fifth ray:

- The energy of what is so peculiarly called "concrete science" is the quality or the conditioning nature of the fifth ray.
- It is pre-eminently the substance of the mental plane...
- This energy...is the thoughtform making energy....
- It is fundamentally the most potent energy at this time in the planet...
- It is the energy which admits humanity (and particularly the trained disciple or initiate) into the mysteries of the Mind of God Himself.
- It is profoundly susceptible to the energy of Love-Wisdom, and its fusion with the love aspect is given the name of "wisdom" by us, because all wisdom is knowledge gained by experience and implemented by love.
- This energy is essentially a light-bearer...
- This energy transforms the divine ideas into human ideals.[3]

The previously listed points reveal an intrinsic and fundamental relation to the Great Invocation due especially to the final point that the fifth ray "transforms divine ideas into human ideals." The Great Invocation is designed to transform the entire world of human living by invoking the energies of light, love, and power. The fifth ray energy is "essentially a light-bearer...It is profoundly susceptible to the energy of Love-Wisdom...It is the energy which admits humanity into the mysteries of the Mind of God Himself." Clearly, the energy of ray five provides the qualitative fuel which empowers this Great Invocation.

The five senses are the means of communicating with the physical world, and through the fifth principle of mind humans apply reasoning intelligence in order to survive, grow, and evolve as a species. The increased use of the mind is a relatively new event in human evolution, and the Great Invocation is most effective when used with mental focus rather than simply as a devotional prayer. This is not to say feelings don't play a role in prayer and invocation; they do, but the mind is the propelling force of the Great Invocation. Clear, focussed, mental concentration activates the Great Invocation, making it an effective prayer for planetary transformation.

The real shift in this regard is that of empowerment for the group rather than for the individual. This invocation is powerful in group terms and incidentally potent for the individual. It is, therefore, significant that this Great Invocation has been released for human use because it suggests that humanity is maturing in its use of the mind as the fifth principle and can now truly benefit from the use of the Great Invocation. Amplifying this thought is the point that the Great Invocation was released for human use during the current cycle of the fifth ray.

H. P. Blavatsky points out that five is the pentagon, the Makara,[4] the five-pointed Star, the symbol of a planetary Logos, the symbol of the microcosm, and of creation.[5] In material not originally published in the books by Alice Bailey, but published later in a book by Mary Bailey, DK says:

> The five-pointed star stands for achievement....
>
> It stands for man's work and shows him what he has to dominate—through the astral, through the lower mind, through the higher mind or intellect, and through the intuition, he has to find his way back to God.[6]

The number 5 is a recurring theme throughout the Great Invocation, and the number 5 will emerge in various ways as we continue our exploration.

The Five Stanzas

Each of the five stanzas of the Great Invocation will now be examined numerologically. Table 11 not only shows the number 5 as the total of the Great Invocation, but graphically indicates that the Great Invocation contains five distinct stanzas.

Table 11. Root Values of the Five Stanzas.

Stanza One	8
Stanza Two	9
Stanza Three	5
Stanza Four	13/4
Stanza Five	6
Total	32
Reduced Total	5

Stanza One

From the point of Light within the Mind of God
Let light stream forth into the minds of men.
Let Light descend on Earth.

This stanza has a numerological value of 8. The number 8 is a number of power. It implies the ability to control and wield energy in order to accomplish a goal. Esoterically, 8 signifies the spiritual Hierarchy and Christ consciousness. Eight suggests that through the power of Light existing in the Mind of God, humanity will be raised in consciousness. From the individualized consciousness of the human kingdom, humanity will be transformed into the consciousness exemplified by the Christ, head of Hierarchy. Through Hierarchy another connection is made to the number 5 in that the Hierarchy[7] is the fifth kingdom in nature and the goal for humanity.

Stanza Two

From the point of Love within the Heart of God
Let love stream forth into the hearts of men.
May Christ return to Earth.

This second stanza has a numerological value of 9. The number 9 reflects endings and consummations. This number is often associated with humanitarianism and philanthropy. It is appropriate, therefore, that it is connected to the theme of love. All true spiritual teachers and teachings underscore the necessity for love to be the basis of all relationships and evolutionary progress. When the second stanza is sounded with mental and loving intent, the point of Love in the Heart of God is called forth in order to transform human consciousness from that of the separated "me" person to that of the group oriented "we" person. True love does not call for the eradication of the self but for the expansion of the self into a group consciousness of cooperative endeavor. The number 9 speaks to this idea through the humanitarian keynote of the self as it is offered to the group in order to serve the whole.

Furthermore, the concept of endings and consummations introduces the profound subject of initiation, for humanity can be initiated into a new awareness of the group mind and heart via the energy present in this stanza. The Great Invocation was offered to humanity because of the rapid growth in human consciousness exemplified by the strong reaction during WWII against the forces of separatism and fear, and in favor of freedom and right human relationships based on goodwill. Humanity's decision to fight the forces of darkness which resulted in the victory of the forces of light signaled the spiritual guides of the planet that humanity was ready for initiation into group consciousness. It was then that the Great Invocation was given to the Christ and subsequently passed on for use by the people of the world.

Stanza Three

From the centre where the Will of God is known
Let purpose guide the little wills of men—
The purpose which the Masters know and serve.

Stanza three has a numerological value of 5. One interpretation is that the fifth mental principle works best when coupled with the use of will. The call is for the "wills of men" to apprehend the "purpose which the Masters know and serve." This purpose has a relation to the Will of God. Stanza three indicates humanity's maturation to a point of cooperation with the Hierarchy of Masters in working with the purpose of God's will.

The central theme of this stanza suggests how humanity can become a partner in the emerging Plan. The importance of the mind in this process is highlighted by the number 5 and its relation to the mental principle. Furthermore, since the number 5 is also symbolically associated with the spiritual Hierarchy as a kingdom of creation, one may infer that the kingdom of God needs the help of humanity to successfully fulfill the purpose and even calls on humanity to step forward at this time to assume an important spiritual role.

Stanza Four

From the centre which we call the race of men
Let the Plan of Love and Light work out
And may it seal the door where evil dwells.

The numerological value of stanza four is 4. The number 4 involves the practical, mundane aspects of living—limitations imposed by the material world. This number is foundational in respect to the world in which humanity evolves. This stanza, being the fourth in order, represents a convergence of four energy. Stanza four mentions humanity, the fourth kingdom in nature, and the fourth ray of Harmony Through Conflict governs the human kingdom.

In stanza four the importance which humanity plays in the Plan of God is amplified, for it is through humanity that the "Plan of Love and Light" is to "work out." Through the restrictions imposed by the number 4, humanity struggles to achieve harmony.

This process of working within form and substance will eventually "seal the door where evil dwells" and "restore the Plan on Earth."

In addition, this stanza is the only stanza in which the numerological result must be reduced in order to achieve a single digit; the reduction being from 13 to 4 (1 + 3 = 4). In this reduction process we separate 13 into 1 and 3. The 1 symbolizes the soul and the 3 represents the threefold incarnating personality constituted of mind, emotions, and physical body. In order to achieve the final reduction to number 4 we must, in effect, integrate the personality with the soul. This is symbolically demonstrated when we add 1 and 3 together to achieve 4.

Stanza Five

Let Light and Love and Power restore the Plan on Earth.

The final stanza has a numerological value of 6. This number is associated with responsibility and love. In a more negative way it is sometimes associated with materialism, but only because it deals with the form world. Esoterically considered, 6 involves the perfection of form.[8] This is because 6 is a perfect number, being the result of the addition of all its factors except itself. These are 1, 2, and 3 (1 x 6 and 2 x 3). In addition, 6 is a triangular number because it is the result of the addition of the first three numbers, 1, 2, and 3. If this last stanza were treated as a mandate, the numerological keynote of six points toward the restoration of the Plan on Earth through the perfecting of form. This process of perfection might also be described as the redemption of matter.

The Twenty-one Key Words

When examining the Great Invocation, take note that twenty-one words in the Great Invocation are capitalized, excluding leading verse line words. (In order to indicate this fact more clearly these words are printed in bold face type.)

From the point of **Light** within the **Mind** of **God**
Let light stream forth into the minds of men.
Let **Light** descend on **Earth**.

From the point of **Love** within the **Heart** of **God**
Let love stream forth into the hearts of men.
May **Christ** return to **Earth**.

From the centre where the **Will** of **God** is known
Let purpose guide the little wills of men—
The purpose which the **Masters** know and serve.

From the centre which we call the race of men
Let the **Plan** of **Love** and **Light** work out
And may it seal the door where evil dwells.

Let **Light** and **Love** and **Power** restore the **Plan** on **Earth**.

An interesting aspect of these capitalized words is an inconsistency involving two words—light and love. Note the differences in their capitalization in the first two stanzas of the Great Invocation.

This distinction may indicate that the Light of God and the Love of God are to be distinguished from the light that streams into the minds of men or the love that enters the hearts of men. Perhaps the entry of divine Light and Love into the human world of form is symbolized by the lower-case spelling of light and love in stanzas one and two. Symbolically speaking, the Light and Love of God lose their pure divinity as they enter the denser parts of the created world and are therefore shown as lower-case. Alternatively, one might argue that since "Light" is diminished to "light" when it enters the minds of men then why is the word Light capitalized in the third line, when it has descended on Earth?

After examining the Great Invocation in detail it is obvious to me these twenty-one capitalized words have a deep symbolic meaning not easily recognized. There is a basis for the location of these key words in specific stanzas, for the number of letters in these key words and for their numerological value. (These points will be examined as we proceed.) The evidence suggests "light" and "love" were purposely written in lower-case to create and maintain specific numerological consistency on a theme woven throughout this mantram. All these "threads of symbolic meaning" are necessary to hold this "fabric of words" together. This Great Invocation appears to be a tapestry of words intentionally woven into an intricate hidden pattern of deep significance.

Counting the key words in each stanza, we find 5 key words in stanza one, 5 in stanza two, 3 in stanza three, 3 in stanza four, and 5 in stanza five. Using numeric symbolism we can interpret the meaning of the number of key words in each stanza.

The first item we notice is the presence of the number 5 in three of the stanzas, namely stanzas one, two, and five. The fact that these stanzas all have the same quantity of key words (5) indicates that only through the balanced use of both mind (stanza one) and heart (stanza two) can the Plan be restored on Earth (stanza five). Because stanzas one and two both have an equal number of key words we interpret this to mean that humanity must use mind and heart with equal strength. This idea is automatically coupled with stanza five because this stanza also contains five key words. Therefore, by using mind and heart in an equal or balanced manner, humanity can restore the Plan on Earth.

Stanzas three and four contain three key words each. As in the previous stanzas, these two are symbolically linked because they both have an equal number of key words (3). This suggests that the purpose of God (stanza three) will be achieved through humanity's use of intelligent love, and that evil will be barred from entry into the world as a consequence (stanza four). In this instance 3 concerns the three aspects of divinity—Father, Son, and Holy Spirit, or esoterically speaking, the spiritual *life* of God, the spiritual *consciousness* of God, and the spiritual *intelligence* of God. The meaning here is that these three aspects are contained in both God and humanity, and only through the applied will of humanity to the purpose of God can the Plan manifest through humankind.

The Numerology of the Key Words

Now that we have interpreted the meaning of the number of key words in each stanza, we will interpret the meaning of the numerological value of the key words in each stanza. We will do this by adding the values of each key word together in stanza one, and then doing the same for each of the other four stanzas. This procedure and its results are shown in table 12.

Table 12. Root Values of the Key Words in Stanzas One Through Five.

Light + Mind + God + Light + Earth	5
Love + Heart + God + Christ + Earth	9
Will + God + Masters	6
Plan + Love + Light	9
Light + Love + Power + Plan + Earth	3
Total	32
Root Value	5

The five key words in stanza one equal a numerological total of 5, which reemphasizes the importance of the mind principle in humanity. The fact that five key words equal 5 further reinforces the strength of this stanza. In addition, the overall numerological value of stanza one is 8, the number of Christ consciousness and the Hierarchy. Therefore, this stanza emphasizes the use of mind (5) to achieve the power of Christ consciousness and enter the fifth kingdom of the Hierarchy.

The five key words in stanza two total 9 numerologically, focusing attention on humanitarian service and initiation. This is reinforced by the fact that the entire stanza equals 9 also. In addition, the key word values of stanzas one and two combined total 5 (5 + 9 = 14/5). (See table 12 above.) In effect they represent a microcosm of the entire invocation which also totals 14/5, reinforcing the need to synthesize head and heart in order to achieve the greater purpose of restoring the Plan on Earth.

The key words in stanza three equal a value of 6 which again places emphasis on perfecting the form through the application of will. The fact that the overall numerological value of stanza three is 5 indicates it is through the mind that humanity must apply its will to the perfection of the material world. This, of course, is a long range goal for the human kingdom.

The key words of stanzas four and two are symbolically linked via the number 9. The service orientation of 9 supports the practice of right human relationships, the heart energy necessary for group cooperation, and the sealing of the door where evil dwells.

This human endeavor can lead to the group initiation of humanity symbolized by the 9.

Finally, the key words in stanza five have a total of 3, again emphasizing the trinity of God—or esoterically as Power (Father), Love (Son), and Light (Holy Spirit). These three key words of Light, Love, and Power thus sum up the trinity of God that can restore the Plan on Earth. The major factor in this restoration is a more giving and heart-centered humanity (stanza two and four via the 9 keynote), empowered by the purpose of God's Will to perfect the form (natural kingdoms) by being responsible to the Earth (stanza three via the 6 keynote) and enlightened by the Mind of God (stanza one via the 5 keynote).

In other words, the Plan can be restored through three fundamental aspects of God's trinity. First, humanity must become more heart-centered. This is shown by the number 9 (humanitarianism and initiation) which connects stanza two (Love) and stanza four (race of men). Second, the Will of God (stanza three) is fulfilled through the perfection of form (6). This is to be accomplished by humanity when purpose guides the "little wills of men." Right now, the Masters in the Hierarchy serve that purpose, but eventually humanity will work in partnership with the kingdom of God, the Hierarchy. Third, the key to restoring the Plan on Earth (the purpose) will come when the mind of humanity is filled with the Light of God (fifth principle of mind or manas).

The sums of the key words from each of these five stanzas yield a total of 5 (5 + 9 + 6 + 9 + 3 = 32/5), revealing that the key words themselves are a reflection of the entire Great Invocation. The stanzas total 32/5, and the key words within the five stanzas also total 32/5.

Table 13. Root Values of Stanzas and Key Words.

Stanza	1	2	3	4	5	Total	Root
Entire G.I.	8	9	5	4	6	32	5
Key Words	5	9	6	9	3	32	5

In the same way, the Great Invocation from beginning to end equals 5 by the sum of 752 being reduced to a single digit (7 + 5 + 2 = 14, 1 + 4 = 5). Along the same premise the number 113 (the total words of the Great Invocation) also reduces to 5 (1 + 1 + 3 = 5). (See Master List of the Great Invocation, appendix A.)

In turn, the numerological total of all twenty-one key words also equals 5 by the sum of 176 being reduced to its root value (1 + 7 + 6 = 14, 1 + 4 = 5). What's more the twenty-one key words are composed of ninety-five letters and reducing the number 95 yields 5 (9 + 5 = 14, 1 + 4 = 5). See table 6 in chapter 3.

Table 14. The Power of 5.

Terms	AN	RAN	Root
Word of Power	158	68	5
Souls	86	14	5
Masters	95	23	5
Hierarchy	95	59	5
Disciple	77	14	5
Christ	77	32	5
The Light Which Ever Shineth in the East	374	176	5
Sirius	95	32	5

The terms in table 14 clearly denote 5 as a predominant number relating Sirius, the Hierarchy, and the Great Invocation. In essence the Great Invocation is a *word of power* resonating to the number 5. It calls us to our future destiny, the fifth kingdom of perfected *souls*. We enter that kingdom at the fifth initiation as *Masters* of the *Hierarchy*. We each become a conscious working *disciple* of the *Christ*, the head of Hierarchy. We then live in the radiance of what DK calls "*the Light which ever shineth in the East*"[9] and become young aspirants in the Great White Lodge on *Sirius*.

Notes

1. Bailey, *A Treatise on Cosmic Fire,* 571.
2. See list in Bailey, *Esoteric Psychology,* vol. I, 26.
3. Bailey, *The Rays and the Initiations,* 590-92.
4. Sanskrit for crocodile; Capricorn, the tenth sign of the zodiac.
5. Bailey, *A Treatise on Cosmic Fire,* n. 396.
6. Mary Bailey, *A Learning Experience,* 55.
7. The word "Hierarchy" has a AN value of 95 which reduces to 14/5.
8. See discussion of Shamballa in chapter 3 in the section "Djwhal Khul and Esoteric Numerology."
9. Bailey, *Esoteric Psychology,* vol. II, 59.

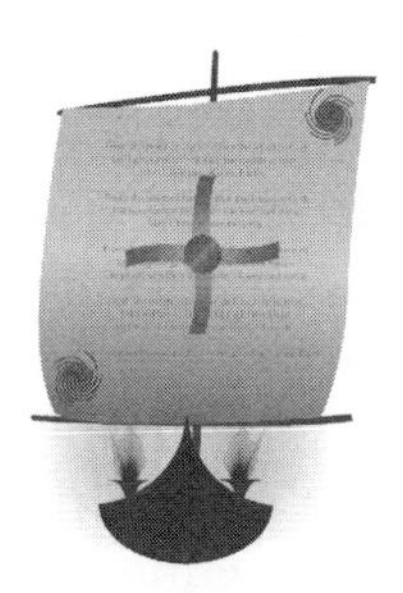

5

Sanat Kumara

In chapter 2 we explored the historical perspective of the Great Invocation from 1935 to 1945. That brief review of the historical context in which the Great Invocation appeared qualified it, in terms of the human struggle, with the forces of darkness and materialism during the twentieth century. The ageless wisdom teaching tells us that the world wars of this century were the culmination of a great conflict between the forces of Light and Darkness which began in old Atlantis long before our ancient history began. In order to understand the full magnitude of humanity's role on Earth at this time, we need to examine the nature of the Being Who created our planet. Since this Being's task is to save through sacrifice, the Law of Redemption is a major factor on our planet. Consequently, the Great Invocation, as a prayer of redemption calling on the Light, Love, and Power of God to restore the Plan on Earth, is closely connected to the Great Work of the One in Whom we live and move and have our being—Sanat Kumara.

Earlier in the section on the "Ageless Wisdom View of God," we pointed out that the ageless wisdom philosophy, as taught by Djwhal Khul, describes various orders of creation brought into manifestation by intelligent cosmic Beings well beyond our level of consciousness. The stars and planets are the physical bodies of these Creators, but these physical forms cannot describe the fullness and grandeur of the Intelligent Lives informing these celestial worlds.

There are a staggering number of creators, deities, gods, demigods, angels, devas, saviors, etc., described by the ageless wisdom teachings. Some of these beings are celestial life forms manifesting as planets, stars, constellations, and entire galaxies. Moreover, there are many other entities in various dimensions who work with these more exalted Celestial Logoi. This complexity is compounded by the fact that many of the same beings have different names depending on the religion, philosophy, mythology, etc. involved. In addition, many of these divine beings take on different names according to how and where they manifest. In effect, they don a different celestial hat according to the particular job they are performing, or role they are playing in the cosmic scheme.

Certain types of these creators are called Kumaras. Sanat Kumara, the Creator of the human kingdom, is of this order. According to Geoffrey Barborka, Sanat Kumara is Sanskrit for "always a youth: regarded as a progenitor of mankind."[1]

Putting a very complex subject in simple terms, the ageless wisdom teaches that the first attempts to create humanity on the Earth failed because the faculty of mind or manas would not function within the animal forms created by the natural evolutionary process. In order to assist in the development of humanity on the Earth, a higher order of intelligence led by Sanat Kumara voluntarily entered into the evolutionary process of the planet in order to instill the principle of mind. According to Barborka in his book *The Divine Plan*:

> Because of having themselves developed the faculty of Mind in previous Manvantaras, [cosmic cycles, JB] as well as the ability to use it with *full* consciousness, they were able to awaken the dormant faculty of Manas [mind, JB] during the Third Race [Lemurian, JB], so that man was able to function intellectually in his turn. These lofty Beings are therefore termed the Lords of the Flame, or Sons of Mind—Manasaputras—or again Solar Gods.[2]

Barborka goes on to list some thirty-four different names given to these solar Gods as they appear throughout *The Secret Doctrine*. He explains that the three categories of names for these beings are the manas aspect, the Agnishvatta aspect, and the Kumara aspect.

> The Manas aspect stresses the phase of the awakening of the Mind principle...The Agnishvatta aspect stresses the evolutionary phase [of the mind, JB]...The Kumara aspect represents the phase of enlightenment by direct assistance, in that the Holy Youths (the literal translation of the word Kumara) actually incarnated in a portion of the human race.[3]

Barborka, citing Blavatsky, points out that the Kumaras

> may indeed mark a "special" or extra *creation*, since it is they who, by incarnating themselves within the senseless human shells of the two first Root-races, and a great portion of the Third Root-race—create, so to speak, a *new race*: that of thinking, self-conscious and *divine* men.[4]

The Kumara theme is important because the Great Invocation is a *mantram of redemption* calling on the Light of God, the Love of God and the Purpose of God to enter the world of human living in order to restore the Plan on Earth. As we have just read, the Kumara role of these advanced spiritual Entities is one of self sacrifice in order to redeem or correct situations which have not gone according to Plan.

The Master DK states that the Being who is evolving through the Earth scheme incarnated on the Earth as Sanat Kumara some eighteen million years ago during the Lemurian root-race:

> The Planetary Logos of our earth scheme, one of the Seven Spirits before the throne, took physical incarnation, and, under the form of Sanat Kumara, the Ancient of Days, and the Lord of the World, came down to this dense physical planet and has remained with us ever since. Owing to the extreme purity of His nature, and the fact that he is (from the human standpoint) relatively sinless, and hence incapable of response to aught upon the dense physical plane, He was unable to take a dense physical body such as ours, and has to function in His etheric body. He is the greatest of all the Avatars, or Coming Ones, for He is a direct reflection of that great Entity who lives, and breathes, and functions through all the evolutions on this planet...He is the Great Sacrifice, Who left the glory of the high places and for the sake of the evolving sons of men took upon Himself a physical form and was made in the likeness of man.[5]

This passage clearly indicates that Sanat Kumara is an Avatar, having sacrificed the freedom of the higher worlds by incarnating in the dense world of human evolution in order to instill the principle of mind in the animal men of the Lemurian epoch. According to HPB the name Sanat

> is the First or "Primeval Ancient," a name which identifies the Kabalistic "Ancient of Days" and the "Holy Aged" (Sephira and Adam Kadmon) with Brahma, the Creator, called also Sanat among his other names and titles.[6]

It is also important to remember that Sanat Kumara represents the incarnated form aspect of the planetary Logos. This idea parallels the nature of the human soul which incarnates in the physical world through a physical form. This is called the personality, and part of the consciousness of the soul is in the physical body. The person has a name, a family, a job etc. Throughout the life of the person in incarnation the soul on its own plane of consciousness exists also. When the person "dies" the portion of the consciousness formerly in the physical body returns to the main consciousness of the overlooking soul. This is a rough analogy of Sanat Kumara in relation to the planetary Logos.

Esoteric Numerology of Sanat Kumara

In chapter 2 we discussed in some detail the history and circumstances leading up to the release of the Great Invocation for use by humanity. One of the more intriguing aspects of this story involves the granting of permission by Sanat Kumara for the Christ to use the Great Invocation and then pass it on for use by humanity. As you may recall, Sanat Kumara, along with certain other exalted Beings of Shamballa, has apparently known of and used the Great Invocation for eons. Does this sacred mantric sound relate directly to Sanat Kumara and His role as planetary savior? If so, what role does the Christ, head of Hierarchy play in the larger story? There is numerological evidence suggesting an intimate connection between Sanat Kumara and this Great Invocation.

We have already examined the twenty-one key words numerologically in the previous section. We now turn our attention to the possibility that there is encoded numerological information contained in the Great Invocation which points to more esoteric underpinnings.

Remembering that Sanat Kumara is the original Savior of the Earth, let us first look at the numerological value of these three words. First we will compare their reduced alpha numbers (RAN).

S A N A T K U M A R A
1 + 1 + 5 + 1 + 2 = 10 2 + 3 + 4 + 1 + 9 + 1 = 20 Total: 30

S A V I O R
1 + 1 + 4 + 9 + 6 + 9 = 30

Interestingly, we see that "Sanat Kumara" and "savior" both equal 30. There is a numerological correspondence between Sanat Kumara and the word "savior," indicating at least some subjective relationship. However, if we examine the number 30 more closely we find a fascinating link between these two terms and the Great Invocation. The factors required to produce 30 are: 2 x 15, 3 x 10, and 5 x 6. Using esoteric numerology, we will combine these factors and products to find their root essence.

Table 15. Factors of 30.

<table>
<tr><td rowspan="3">Factors</td><td>2</td><td>15</td><td>30</td></tr>
<tr><td>3</td><td>10</td><td>30</td></tr>
<tr><td>5</td><td>6</td><td>30</td></tr>
<tr><td>Total</td><td>10</td><td>31</td><td>90</td></tr>
<tr><td>Root</td><td>1</td><td>4</td><td>9</td></tr>
<tr><td>Total</td><td colspan="3">1 + 4 + 9 = 14, 1 + 4 = 5</td></tr>
<tr><td>Root</td><td colspan="3">5</td></tr>
</table>

Referring to table 15, note we have totaled the factors in each column, reduced them numerologically, and then added them together yielding a final number of 5—the value of the Great Invocation. Moreover, we can be even more specific in showing what appears as an esoteric code within the Great Invocation. By adding the unreduced factors and products together we arrive at a total of 131 (10 + 31 + 90). There is one significant phrase in the Great Invocation with an AN value of 131, and that phrase is "God is known."

G O D	I S	K N O W N
7 + 15 + 4 = 26	9 + 19 = 28	11 + 14 + 15 + 23 + 14 = 77

Total: 131

This fact by itself is interesting, but added to it we find that this phrase lies at the exact *middle* of the Great Invocation. There are 113 words in the Great Invocation. By simple arithmetic we see that 113 - 3 = 110 and that 110 ÷ 2 = 55. Thus there are 55 words before and 55 words after the phrase "God is known." Furthermore, these 55 words are a symbolic correspondence to the AN value of Sanat, which is also 55.

S A N A T
19 + 1 + 14 + 1 + 20 = 55

Let's examine the entire name using the AN value along with the word savior.

S A N A T	K U M A R A
19 + 1 + 14 + 1 + 20 = 55	11 + 21 + 13 + 1 + 18 + 1 = 65

Total: 120

S A V I O R
19 + 1 + 22 + 9 + 15 + 18 = 84

In the above comparisons we see no apparent correlation, nevertheless there is another interesting relationship between these two terms not immediately obvious. This involves the word "kumara." Note that kumara has a value of 65, however, as shown in the diagram below the plural form "kumaras" equals 84, the AN value of savior. Thus, there is a correspondence between Sanat Kumara and savior using the RAN method, and a relationship between kumaras and savior using the AN method.

K U M A R A S
11 + 21 + 13 + 1 + 18 + 1 + 19 = 84

Another interesting relationship also appears here in relation to the name "Jesus," the savior of Christianity. Christian theology teaches that God became "man" through "Jesus" in order to save humankind. The AN value of "Jesus" equals 74 and the RAN value of "man" equals 10. Thus, the man (10), plus Jesus (74) equals the savior (84). Put in another way, the perfected Man Jesus (84) is a reflection or example in the human world of the kumaras (84) Whose nature is of the divine world.[7]

As mentioned earlier, Sanat Kumara was fully aware of the Great Invocation before He gave Christ permission to use it in 1945. By going into the numerology of Sanat Kumara we are laying the groundwork for the next step in our investigation. We have applied esoteric numerology to the name of Sanat Kumara in order to demonstrate the depth, range, and possibilities of this technique. We are simply unraveling that which may have been deliberately tied together.

This example of esoteric numerology is a sample of what is coming as we proceed directly into the Great Invocation. By using the same techniques found in this chapter we will show an intimate connection between Sanat Kumara and the Great Invocation. Esoteric numerology is not so much a question of number mysticism as it is knowledge of how to construct symbols based on universal truths by gathering the correct building blocks.

The relationship between words and numbers is powerful. As we are discovering, this relationship works at different levels and even through the transliteration of foreign words, such as the Sanskrit name, Sanat Kumara. Why this number/letter correspondence works is not the subject of this book. However, since Djwhal Khul translated the Great Invocation into English and also gave examples of esoteric numerology (chapter 3), it is possible that He placed numerological symbolism in the Great Invocation and in other parts of his writings as well. Accordingly, we are using esoteric numerology (gematria) as a working hypothesis in order to reveal correspondences between seemingly dissimilar subjects.

In effect, two conditions can exist simultaneously. One, esoteric numerology reveals a relationship between numbers and letters. This is clear from a study of Greek and Hebrew gematria and the examples shown here. This appears to be a natural phenomenon of language. Second, someone with enough knowledge of how this number/letter relationship works could design and construct words, phrases, and sentences in order to convey two or more meanings. In other words, letters, words, phrases, etc., can be deliberately constructed in order to communicate an esoteric message within the outer exoteric message.

In fact, throughout history secret societies have encrypted their doctrines in order to keep the uninitiated from their activities and teachings. This method was also a way to preserve the teachings, so they would be available to future students or disciples of a given mystery school or organization. Probably the best example of this idea is found in Masonry. Other examples are the Kabbalists, the Rosicrucians and the Knights Templar, to name a few.

The question naturally arises as to whether the Tibetan has used this encrypting process through special terminology, word spelling, quotation marks, italicized words, phrases, and numbers. If this is a plausible possibility, then our next question is why? Why would DK code information within his books? Mostly for the reasons given above, but also as a teaching method. The books DK dictated to Alice Bailey are definitely esoteric in varying degrees, but there may be keys to understanding the esoteric ideas cleverly embedded within those words themselves. There are various techniques for delivering information to students at different levels of understanding. There are hints, occult blinds, the scatter technique, and what I believe are numerological clues. I do not believe this is done to mislead or confuse the student (although it is done to discourage superficial curiosity seeking); on the contrary, it is designed to activate our abstract minds. The student who studies esoteric work is being trained to think synthetically rather than linearly. The concrete logical mind is being used to activate and train the higher mind, and eventually the intuitive mind—that of pure reason.

In light of this, if the Tibetan has encoded the Great Invocation in this way, I believe He has done this in order to grab our attention, to make us realize beyond any possibility of doubt that there is much more to the world we inhabit than what our five senses alone tell us.

At the very least we can say that if Djwhal Khul has deliberately embedded coded terminology in his writings in order to communicate more esoteric information, it is not without precedent, as indicated by the information provided by David Fideler who points out:

It is well known that the Christian gnostics, who claimed to possess a form of secret knowledge (*gnôsis*), employed the gematria and mathematical symbolism in their teachings, for such is reported by the early church fathers Irenaeus, Hippolytus, Tertullian, and Jerome. Hippolytus accuses the gnostic teachers Valentinus and Marcus of having taken over their numerical symbolism from the Pythagoreans....Hippolytus also refers to another early Christian teacher, Colarbasus, "who attempts to explain religion by measures and numbers."[8]

Sanat Kumara is the First Kumara, the Lord of the World, the Ancient of Days. Sanat is the Life expression of our entire world at this time, the divine incarnation of the planetary Logos. The name Sanat has a value of 10 RAN and 55 AN. Let's end this section by quoting two Greek philosophers, who are commenting on the numbers 10 and 55. Speaking about the number 10 or the decad, the Greek philosopher Iamblichus states:

It has encompassed seminally within itself all things, both solid and plane, even and odd and even-odd, perfect in all manners of perfection...Hence it was reasonable for God to use it as a measure for things and as a gnomon [carpenter's square, JB] and straight edge when he added things to one another and fitted them together harmoniously....

Hence the Pythagoreans in their theology called it sometimes "universe," sometimes "heaven," sometimes "all," sometimes "Fate" and "eternity," "power" and "trust" and "Necessity," "Atlas" and "unwearying," and simply "God" and "Phanes" [name of the Creator in Orphic cosmogony, JB] and "sun."[9]

In addition to the AN value of Sanat equaling 55, in table 10 on page 47 we find an interesting fact—the addition of the numbers 1 to 10 also equal 55. (In fact both numbers are triangular.) The number 55 is rather extensively described in the chapter "On the Decad" in *The Theology of Arithmetic*. This extract is from Anatolius:

Moreover, the decad generates the number 55, which encompasses wonderful beauties. For in the first place, this is formed by doubling and trebling the systematic sequence of numbers—the doubles are 1, 2, 4, 8 (i.e. 15), the triples are 1, 3, 9, 27 (i.e. 40), and the addition of these makes 55. Plato also mentions these sequences in the passage on the generation of soul which begins, "He removed one portion from the whole," and so on [Timaeus 35b].

> Moreover, the sequence of the first five triangular numbers generates 55 (3, 6, 10, 15, and 21 make 55) [see table 10, JB] and again, the sequence of the first five squares generates 55 (1, 4, 9, 16, and 25 make 55); and according to Plato the universe is generated out of triangle and square.[10]

The diagram below (figure 2) is called a Lambda, for the Greek letter "L." Keith Critchlow wrote in the forward to *The Theology of Arithmetic*:

> When Plato proposed the portioning by number of the Same, Other and Being in their unified mixture (Timaeus 35b-c), he set up what has subsequently been called his Lambda. It is a portioning arranged into two "arms," each with three intervals.[11]

> In *Timaeus*, Plato declared that the primary sequence of numbers by which the universe gains life is 1, 2, 3, 4, 9, 8, 27.[12]

There is much more to the Lambda diagram which is beyond this author's knowledge; nevertheless, it is important to our subject since it describes Plato's philosophy of creation based on number. The previous extract from Anatolius is describing the Lambda numbers in the diagram. By progression 1 x 1 = 1, 1 x 2 = 2, 2 x 2 = 4, 2 x 4 = 8. These even numbers total 15. On the right side of the diagram are the odd numbers. 1 x 1 = 1, 1 x 3 = 3, 3 x 3 = 9, 3 x 9 = 27. These odd numbers total 40. When added together 15 + 40 = 55. Out of the unmanifest comes the one; from the one comes duality. From duality comes triplicity, and out of triplicity come the four. Thus, the final statement of Anatolius "according to Plato the universe is generated out of a triangle [1, 2, 3, JB] and square [4, 8, 9, 27, JB]." These passages clearly indicate the high value the Greek philosophers placed upon the numbers 10 and 55 in relation to God and the nature of the universe. They also reinforce the esoteric numerology of Sanat (10 RAN, 55 AN), the First Kumara, the Ancient of Days.

Figure 2. The Lambda

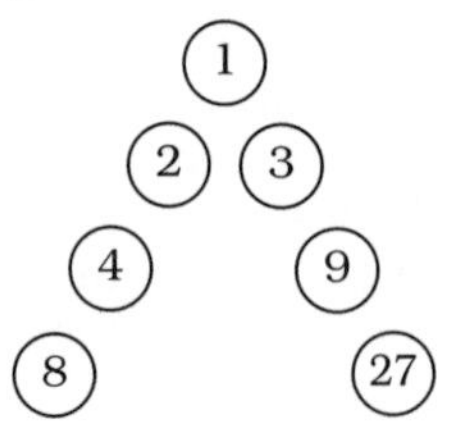

Notes

1. Geoffrey A. Barborka, *The Divine Plan*, 554.
2. Ibid., 133.
3. Ibid., 134.
4. Ibid., 134.
5. Alice A. Bailey, *Initiation, Human and Solar*, 28-29.
6. Blavatsky, *The Secret Doctrine,* vol. 1, Adyar ed., 161.
7. This very point is further strengthened by the fact that both "Jesus" and "messiah" equal 74. Paradoxically, Lucifer also equals 74. In her *Theosophical Glossary*, however, HPB offers the following in regard to Lucifer: "The planet Venus, as the bright 'Morning Star.' Before Milton, Lucifer had never been a name of the Devil. Quite the reverse, since the Christian Saviour is made to say of himself in *Revelations* (xvi.22) [actually 22:14, JB] 'I am ...the bright morning star' or Lucifer." Blavatsky, *The Theosophical Glossary,* s.v. "Lucifer."
8. Fideler, *Jesus Christ, Sun of God*, 27-28.
9. Iamblichus, *The Theology of Arithmetic,* trans. Robin Waterfield, 109-10.
10. Ibid., 115.
11. Ibid., 13.
12. Ibid., 29.

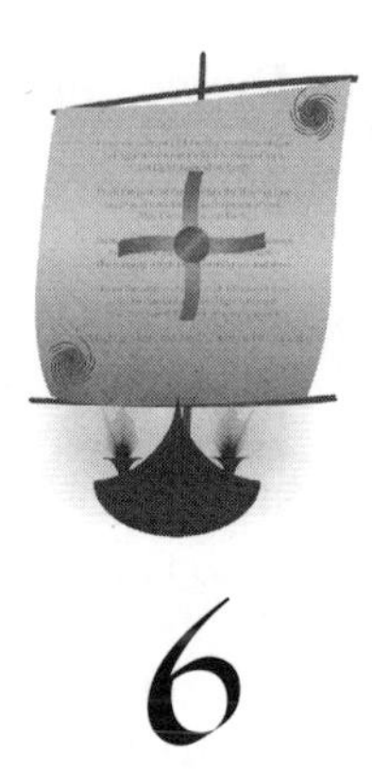

6

The Twenty-one Key Words: A Hidden Pattern

There is a distinct possibility that the twenty-one key words of the Great Invocation are capitalized words because they are especially important. This idea might be stated as a question: If there is hidden esoteric symbolism in the Great Invocation, are the capitalized words a clue to such a possibility?

In chapter 4 we spent some time interpreting the numerological meaning of the key words according to the five stanzas. In the last chapter we examined the name "Sanat Kumara" using a more esoteric numerological approach. Our investigation revealed some very interesting correspondences between the name Sanat Kumara and the word savior. These relationships are numerically real, but more importantly, they are consistent with everything Djwhal Khul says about the nature of Sanat Kumara. Since it was Sanat Kumara Who gave permission for the Christ to use the Great Invocation in 1945, there is the distinct possibility that the Great Invocation contains information specific to Sanat Kumara.

This chapter will lay out the detailed results of investigating the twenty-one key words found in the Great Invocation. We will look at the key words from several angles, but first let's start with the number 21 itself.

The number 21, from an arithmetical perspective, is the result of 3 x 7, or 7 + 7 + 7. This rather mundane information is significant because the numbers 3 and 7 are the two most important numbers used by Djwhal Khul in his presentation of the ageless wisdom. It should be pointed out that although DK stresses the fundamental importance of 3 and 7 in His teaching, He is simply following through and expanding on much of what the ancient philosophers of the mystery schools taught their students. As we have already mentioned, the foundation of all creation is based on the triplicity. Out of this fundamental trinity emanates the fundamental sevenfold nature of all life as we know it. According to DK, we live in a septenary system which is based on three foundational aspects of will, love, and intelligence. This combination produces at least twenty-one possible energy combinations. It should be pointed out, however, that there are many other energy combinations and qualities governing our lives, but we are only concentrating on the energy theme of the number 21.

The Secret Doctrine of Helena P. Blavatsky contains some interesting references to the number 21. Anyone who has read or glanced through this six volume work knows it is not light reading. Published in 1888, *The Secret Doctrine* is a major source of information concerning the relatively modern presentation of the ageless wisdom, with exhaustive cross-references to major religious and philosophical ideas. It describes in great detail the origin of the universe, our solar system, and the creation of mankind on the Earth.

Much of *The Secret Doctrine* is based on the stanzas of Dzyan. According to HPB, these stanzas explain the mysteries of creation. The stanza which concerns our study of the Great Invocation is the fourth one of the seven which deal with cosmic evolution. (Later in *The Secret Doctrine* Blavatsky explores twelve more stanzas from the Book of Dzyan which deal with the evolution of man on the Earth.)

The fourth stanza begins as follows:

> Listen, ye sons of the earth, to your instructors—the sons of the fire. Learn there is neither first nor last; for all is one number, issued from no-number.[1]

HPB then explains the identity of the sons of fire:

> With these verses the mystic sense of the solar and lunar symbols is connected. The Pitris are Lunar Deities and our Ancestors, because they *created the physical man.* The Agnishvatta, the Kumaras (the Seven Mystic Sages), are Solar Deities, though they are Pitris also; and these are the "Fashioners of the *Inner* Man." They are "The Sons of Fire,"...evolved from Primordial Fire.[2]

This passage clearly shows that the Sons of Fire are the Kumaras who created the spiritual aspect of humanity, as opposed to the Lunar Lords who created the form aspect. The Kumaras are the Solar Deities or Solar Pitris Who created humanity as individually evolving self-conscious souls. If we think of our physical bodies as vehicles for the "I" consciousness, then that order of Creators called the Lunar Deities created the forms in which the human consciousness is embodied. The ageless wisdom teaches that there is a vehicle or form body for each of the types of consciousness we express. For example, we have emotions comprised of emotional substance which forms itself into an emotional body or field. Our thoughts are confined to a mental body, and our physical sense of self with its five senses is embodied in a physical body. The Lunar Deities created the various bodies—physical, emotional, and mental. The Solar Deities or Kumaras created the individualized human soul that inhabits the bodies created by the Lunar Deities.

The fourth stanza continues:

> Learn what we, who descend from the primordial seven, we, who are born from the primordial flame, have learnt from our fathers....
>
> From the effulgency of light—the ray of the ever-darkness—sprang in space the re-awakened energies; the one from the egg, the six, and the five.[3]

The specific point of interest in this segment is "the one from the egg, the six, and the five," which HPB says, "give(s) the number 1065, the value of the First-born."[4] Blavatsky goes on to explain that the numbers 10, 6, and 5 are an anagram for the Hebrew letters Yod, Hé, Vau, Hé or Jehovah. In the Hebrew alphabet Yod is equal to 10, Hé equals 5, and Vod equals 6, with the second Hé repeating the 5. These four Hebrew letters are called the Tetragrammaton.

Blavatsky further stresses the importance of this number by inserting a footnote which reads:

> In the Kabalah, the same numbers, viz. 1065, are a value of Jehovah, since the numerical values of the three letters which compose his name—Jod [Yod, JB], Vau, and twice Hé—are respectively 10, 6, and 5; or again thrice seven, 21....By means of Temura, the anagrammatical method of the Kabalah, and the knowledge of 1065 (21), a universal science may be obtained regarding Cosmos and its mysteries (Rabbi Yogel). The Rabbis regard the numbers 10, 6, and 5 as the most sacred of all.[5]

One intriguing aspect of this explanation by Blavatsky is the rearrangement of the three letters. For, in actuality Jehovah is spelled using Yod, Hé, Vau, Hé which gives the numbers 10, 5, 6, and 5 again. These add up to 26, which is the number for God in the Hebrew Kabalah.[6] However, HPB is quick to point out that according to Rabbi Yogel, a universal science regarding the mysteries of the universe can be obtained by means of Temura or the rearrangement of the letters (anagrams), which also rearranges the numbers.

A close examination of the twenty-one key words in the Great Invocation displays a distinct pattern suggesting a relation to Blavatsky's all-important number 1065. The placement of the key words results in the following number pattern: the key words in stanzas one and two are added together equaling 10; the key words in stanzas three and four are added together equaling 6 and stanza five remains with five key words equaling 5. This 10, 6, 5 pattern is the composite 10, 6, 5 number (1065) mentioned by HPB in relation to the Kumaras.

Table 16. Key Word Pattern.

Stanzas	Total Key Words
1 and 2	10
3 and 4	6
5	5
Total	21

HPB further states that, "in the Mahabharata, the Prajapati are twenty-one in number, or ten, six, and five (1065), thrice seven."[7] According to *The Encyclopedia of Eastern Philosophy and*

Religion, the term Prajapati is Sanskrit and means "lord of creatures."[8]

In *A Treatise on Cosmic Fire* DK defines Prajapatis as:

> The Progenitors; the givers of life to all on this earth....Cosmically, they are the seven Rishis of the Great Bear; systemically they are the seven planetary Logoi, and from the standpoint of our planet they are the seven Kumaras.[9]

This definition by the Tibetan delineates three specific levels of expression for the Prajapatis—cosmic, systemic, and planetary, thus giving 3 x 7 or 21 Prajapatis or Kumaras. There is an additional clue to the number 21 in another statement from *A Treatise on Cosmic Fire* which reads:

> It has been stated that a mystery lies hid in the 777 incarnations....Primarily this number applies to the planetary Logos of our scheme and not so much to other schemes. Each Heavenly Man has His number and the number of our Heavenly Man lies hid in the above three figures.[10] [11]

Note that DK refers to the "three figures" rather than the number 777. This could mean that He is hinting at 3 x 7 or 7 x 7 x 7. We will have more to say about 7 to the third power later.

Theoretically, the placement and number of these key words may be designed to point out to us that Sanat Kumara, the Lord of the World is intimately connected with the Great Invocation. This is indicated through the esoteric numerology of the name Sanat Kumara. Referring back to the previous chapter, the RAN value of "Sanat" equals 10 and the AN value of "Kumara" equals 65. Connecting Sanat (10) to Kumara (65) gives the number 1065. Thus we see that the name "Sanat Kumara" is encoded within the pattern of key words when stanzas one and two, and stanzas three and four are combined. Might this be one reason why Djwhal Khul wanted the Great Invocation written exactly as He gave it to Alice Bailey? Incidentally, recalling that the number 21 refers to the Kumaras in general, it is intriguing to see that the word "Kumaras" equals 21 (RAN).

K U M A R A S
2 + 3 + 4 + 1 + 9 + 1 + 1 = 21

Relative to the Earth, the number 10 indicates perfection if it is numerologically associated with the Lord of the World, Sanat Kumara.[12] The first two stanzas represent the number 10 and suggest that perfection is achieved only when both head and heart are synthesized in human expression. This is represented for the spiritual student by the two paths of mysticism and gnosis, the former being the path of the heart and the latter being the path of the head. At some point on the spiritual path Light and Love are integrated, and the transfigured initiate emerges as the soul-infused disciple. This is indicated at the end of stanza two, "May Christ return to Earth." The Christ, Representative of divine Love-Wisdom, incarnated on Earth through the man Jesus, returns again through the achievements of the spiritually enlightened disciples of the modern world.

The number 6 within the 1065 encompasses stanzas three and four. This is noteworthy in light of the fact that the numerological value of the key words present in both stanzas also totals 6. As mentioned earlier, the number 6 involves the process of perfecting the material form, or the redemption of matter. Through the Will of God (Sanat Kumara, the planetary Logos), some divine purpose is being worked out, and humanity is meant to know the purpose and manifest the Plan on Earth (stanzas three and four). The presence of the number 6 here suggests that this is to be done through the refinement and care of the material world by humanity. The environmental movement is an example of humanity's recognition of its responsibility in caring for the Earth.

Finally, the number 5 in the fifth stanza shows once again that Light, Love, and Power can restore the Plan on Earth through the human kingdom's development of manas/mind. The fifth root-race (current humanity) is meant to develop the fifth principle of mind.

A Mission of Planetary Redemption

Even though the Great Invocation was not used by the Hierarchy prior to 1945, there is nothing in DK's writings to suggest that He did not know that such a mantram existed. Following this reasoning, it is possible that DK was laying the groundwork for the possible introduction of such a world prayer that would contain esoteric information about Sanat Kumara, and the role of our planet in relation to the star systems in close proximity to our own solar system.

Ultimately, the star Sirius may hold the key to the origin and nature of the Great Invocation. Recall the Tibetan's words from chapter 2: "In receiving this Invocation, in its use and distribution, you have been participating in a *cosmic event* of tremendous importance" [emphasis, JB]. DK does not use words randomly. In the books by DK cosmic means beyond our solar system. This is illustrated by a previous reference (n. 9) regarding the Prajapatis or Kumaras in which Djwhal Khul says:

> *Cosmically*, they are the seven Rishis of the Great Bear; *systemically* they are the seven planetary Logoi, and from the standpoint of our *planet* they are the seven Kumaras. [emphasis, JB]

This is one example of how DK uses the terms cosmic, systemic, and planetary when referring to various spiritual Beings. The point to note is, by using the term "cosmic" the Tibetan is indicating that the Great Invocation and its use is related to something beyond our tiny planet and solar system. By using the word "cosmic" DK is dropping a hint that we humans on this planet are more intimately connected with the cosmos than we suspect; that the Great Invocation is somehow related to the life activities of cosmic Entities Who transcend our world, and that some great purpose is being worked out on Earth through humanity. Intertwined in all this is the esoteric fact that the Christ, the Hierarchy, and humanity are now able to use the Great Invocation. Since it was Sanat Kumara Who gave the Christ permission to use it in 1945, we now turn to Sanat Kumara for clues to this "cosmic event" in which we are all participating.

In chapter 5, Sanat Kumara is referred to as the "Great Sacrifice." Through Sanat Kumara's direct incarnation on the Earth over eighteen million years ago, the fundamental keynote of redemption through sacrifice has influenced the growth process of planet Earth.

> The basic sacrifice which the planetary Logos made was when He decided to incarnate or enter into the form of this planet. This was from pure choice, motivated by His "fixed determination" to function as the Saviour of the planet, in the same sense as the world Saviours come forth for the salvaging of humanity. Sanat Kumara is the prototype of all world saviours.[13]

In chapter 5 we also demonstrated a numerological comparison between Sanat Kumara and savior. Using the RAN method we found that they both equal 30. (It is interesting to note that the number 30 represents the accepted age at which Jesus was baptized by John and began His role as the savior or messiah in the Gospel story.) We now turn to an even more fascinating aspect of this God/savior theme.

To begin, we must return to the term "Kumaras." Earlier we showed how the RAN value of Kumaras equals 21 and related this number 21 to the Prajapatis (the Progenitors or Kumaras—givers of all life to Earth) and the twenty-one key words of the Great Invocation. Calculating the AN value of "Kumaras" yields a result of 84.

	K	U	M	A	R	A	S	
AN	11 +	21 +	13 +	1 +	18 +	1 +	19	= 84
RAN	2 +	3 +	4 +	1 +	9 +	1 +	1	= 21

Total 84 + 21 = 105

As you can see from the example above the combined total of "Kumaras" using both calculation methods yields 105. The number 105 is significant since it is the AN value of the word "saviour." We have already discovered that the AN values of both "savior" and "Kumaras" equal 84, but what is important here is that the British spelling of savior contains a "u." All the Alice Bailey books use the British style of spelling and by including the "u" in savior, the value of the word is increased by 21 equalling 105.

S	A	V	I	O	**U**	R	
19 +	1 +	22 +	9 +	15 +	**21** +	18	= 105

This fact shows a certain internal consistency to the idea of the Kumaras being associated with saving and redemption according to the Hindu philosophy, and the latest presentations of the ageless wisdom given by HPB and Djwhal Khul. It is also interesting to see that by the addition of the 21st letter of the English alphabet this correlation between the Kumaras and saviors is maintained—especially since the number 21 is so closely linked with the Kumaras and the twenty-one key words of the Great Invocation. This is all very fascinating for what it shows in relation to esoteric numerology and gematria, but it takes on more significant proportions because of the following information given by Djwhal Khul in *A Treatise on Cosmic Fire*:

> It has been stated that one hundred and four Kumaras came from Venus to the Earth; literally the figure is one hundred and five, when the synthesising Unit, the Lord of the World Himself, is counted as one.[14]

It is not clear as of this writing who stated that there were 104 original Kumaras involved in the Earth's early evolution, but for some reason DK wanted it clearly known that the total was really 105. The fact that "saviour" happens to equal 105 may have no further significance beyond that of mere coincidence, except for the following fact—the addition of the numbers 1-105 equals 5,565. (See procedure in n. 2, chapter 3.) This total of 5,565 is very significant because it is made up of 55 and 65 which are the AN values of Sanat (55) Kumara (65). The implications of this fact suggest the Tibetan may have deliberately placed this value of 105 into print in order to show a connection at some future date between Sanat Kumara and His role as *saviour* of the Earth.

In addition, another unexpected encoding emerges here in the form of the ancient Hebrew name for God which is Yod Hé Vau Hé. Blavatsky is not so interested in the god Jehovah, whom she considered a personified tribal deity, but with the esoteric origin of Jehovah which is rooted in the universal symbolism of number. As mentioned earlier, Blavatsky refers to the numbers 10, 6, and 5 as the Hebrew name for Yahweh or Jehovah. This is certainly correct according to the Hebrew use of gematria, except that the numbers are jumbled. The 10 for Yod is in order, but Hé 5 and Vau 6 are reversed. Instead of 10, 5, 6, 5, Blavatsky simply refers to the numbers 10, 6, 5, in which she has either dropped the first 5 (Hé), or dropped the last 5 (Hé) and transposed 5 and 6.

Why did HPB make these changes? The only reason appears to be that this is the order in which they appear in the fourth stanza of Dzyan quoted earlier in this chapter. Since DK claims to have dictated parts of *The Secret Doctrine* to HPB, is it possible that years later, through Alice Bailey, the Tibetan is using the number 105 to make the point that the ancient God Yahweh is related in some way to the 105 Kumaras who came to the Earth to aid the evolutionary process of our planet? Figure 3 illustrates how Yod Hé Vau Hé can be translated into the 105 Kumaras without rearranging or dropping a Hebrew letter.

Figure 3. YHVH Equals 105 Kumaras.

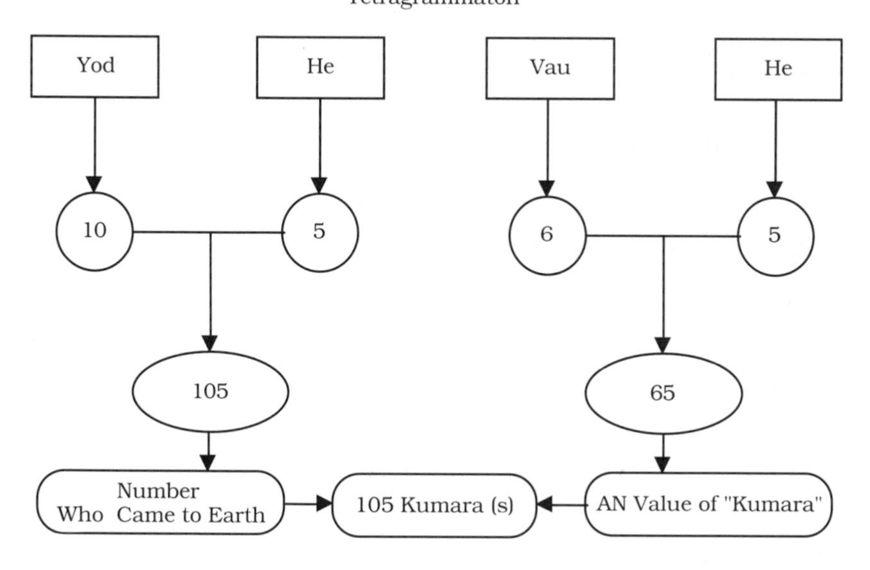

How might this number 105 relate to the Great Invocation? First of all, the 104 Kumaras are led by the first Kumara who we now know is Sanat Kumara. These Beings incarnated on the Earth in order to fulfill some mission of redemption. This entailed a great sacrifice and set in motion a prototypal Plan of spiritual "rescue" involving the restoration of a saving force that would release or save the victims from some kind of evolutionary process that had somehow gone astray. Sanat Kumara is the planetary savior—a prototype or archetype. Liberated, enlightened humans model themselves after Him if they choose to play the role of world Saviors and become spiritual Teachers of humanity. This concept is reflected in the Maitreya Buddha of Buddhism, the avatars of Hinduism, the Imam Mahdi of Islam, the Messiah of Judaism, and the Christ of Christianity. The Great Invocation is a world prayer that can be influential in invoking the return of the World Teacher who will be a model of Sanat Kumara, just as all the past saviors and avatars have been.

According to the ageless wisdom tradition, the Great Invocation calls on God (Sanat Kumara) to set in motion those forces which will allow another one of His representatives to come forth from the higher spiritual worlds in order to carry the Plan forward. The Great Invocation is one other link in the golden thread of our planetary life stretching back to the time when the Kumaras first came to the Earth eighteen million years ago. The Great Invocation is part of an evolving Plan—a blueprint, perhaps—containing some of the information pertaining to the purpose and will of God, manifesting through Sanat Kumara.

The number 105 signals the presence of 5565—Sanat (55) Kumara (65). This number is encoded in the Great Invocation through the symbolic correspondence to the twenty-one key words. For 5565 can be reduced to 21 by 5 + 5 + 6 + 5 = 21. The number 5565 is also reflected, as we have seen, in the pattern of the key word placement within the Great Invocation. Does this number 5565 hold any more clues connecting the symbolic structure of the Great Invocation and Sanat Kumara? Yes it does, and again, the twenty-one key words play a central role.

Sixes and Fives

The name Sanat Kumara contains eleven letters. This is reflected in the twenty-one key words by the fact that there are actually only eleven different key words, the remaining ten being duplicates (table 17 p. 92). In effect, there are two groups of key words in the Great Invocation—one group of eleven originals, and another group of ten duplicates. Examining the numerological value of Sanat Kumara once more we see that Sanat has a value of 55 which reduces to 10 and Kumara has a value of 65 which reduces to 11, indicating a direct correspondence to the key words and their repetition throughout the Great Invocation. Clues to the meaning of the eleven essential key words and the ten duplicates are found by referring back to their original coding as 65 and 55 respectively.

First let's take the number 65, separate it into 6 and 5, and examine the word "Kumara." Turning to number 6 first, remember that the Kumaras are a special kind of spiritual Being responsible for the creation of humanity. These lofty Beings brought manas or mind to animal man, thus creating the human race. Djwhal Khul explains the symbolic function of the number 6 while discussing initiation or the expansion of consciousness:

> The goal of all the initiatory process is to admit mankind into realisation of and identification with the will or purpose of Deity. The number 6 is the number of form or of manifestation which is the agent or medium through which this realisation comes and by which consciousness is unfolded.[15]

Later on in the same extract the Tibetan quotes an "ancient book of numbers" and explains that the material aspect of the world is contained in the number 666. The initiate drops one 6 and enters the Way of initiation, and later drops another 6 and "becomes the perfected 6-form, the instrument and expression of spirit."[16] This indicates that the number 6 is part of a process of consciousness expansion called initiation which brings form to perfection.

Now let's examine the 5 in 65. As we have already discussed in chapter 4, the number 5 plays a major role in the perfection of form and in the evolutionary development of humanity's consciousness through the use of mind, the fifth principle. The number 5 symbolizes the mind. It is through the mental principle and its use that the perfection of form is brought about. The wisdom teachings tell us the Kumaras exemplify this process because these Beings developed the faculty of mind in cycles long past, before the Earth was created. That process is symbolized in the word "Kumara" and its number value—65 or 11.

The number 55 refers to the name "Sanat," and to the number 10. Ten is the redemption of matter—the *achieved goal* of the process represented by 65 (11), which is the use of the mind. Earlier the number 10 was shown to represent perfection and Deity. Not only does 5 + 5 = 10 but the addition of 1-10 equals 55. (Interestingly, the addition of 1 through 11 equals 66—the number of the initiate mentioned above, and according to DK, 11 is the number of the adept using energy. See "Djwhal Khul and Esoteric Numerology" in chapter 3.) In the context of the key words we can postulate that the eleven original key words symbolize the process of perfecting form through the development and use of mind. And alternately, we can say that the ten duplicate key words symbolize the goal of that process—that is, redemption of matter. The goal of planetary redemption is achieved (10) through the adept's use of the energy of mind (11). The entire name "Sanat Kumara" sums up this grand design through the numbers 10 and 11 and their symbolic presence in the Great Invocation as the twenty-one key words.

Table 17. Key Word Duplication.

Original Words	Duplicate Words			Duplicate Total	Combined Total
Light	Light	Light	Light	3	4
Mind				0	1
God	God	God		2	3
Earth	Earth	Earth		2	3
Love	Love	Love		2	3
Heart				0	1
Christ				0	1
Will				0	1
Masters				0	1
Plan	Plan			1	2
Power				0	1
11	5	4	1	10	21

Taking this analysis one step further let's turn our attention to table 18, opposite page. In this table we have divided the key words into two groups. One group composed of the key words which appear only one time in the Great Invocation. These six non-repeating key words are: Mind, Heart, Christ, Will, Masters, and Power. There are five key words that appear more than once in the Great Invocation. They are: Light, God, Earth, Love, and Plan.

As table 18 shows, the theme of six and five is repeated once again within the eleven original key words. The non-repeating key words represent the *process* of using the energy of mind discussed in table 17. Using the actual key words this process can be described as follows: Form is brought to perfection by the work of the **Christ** and the **Masters**. This process depends on the application of the **Will**, the **Mind**, and the **Heart**. This activity of the spiritual Hierarchy generates the needed **Power** to consummate the purpose of Sanat Kumara. Turning to the repeating key words we find that:

The *goal* is to restore **God**'s **Plan** of **Light** and **Love** on **Earth** and thus redeem substance.

Table 18. Non-repeating and Repeating Key Words.

Non-Repeating Key Words	Letter Count	AN	Repeating Key Words	Letter Count	AN
			Light	5	56
Mind	4	40			
			God	3	26
			Earth	5	52
			Love	4	54
Heart	5	52			
Christ	6	77			
Will	4	56			
Masters	7	95			
			Plan	4	13
Power	5	77			
Totals 6	31	397	5	21	231

You will notice that the bottom of table 18 includes the word count, letter count, and AN totals of the eleven original key words divided into two groups of non-repeating and repeating words. These numbers suggest some interesting meaning and symbolism. When working with gematria and esoteric numerology it is easy to progress deeper and deeper into analysis. These deeper levels are often worth exploring and enjoying just for the experience. It is very much like magnifying a fractal image on a computer. There are millions of levels and possibilities that open up for our examination, but they may not all be significant. Gematria and esoteric numerology offer a rich field of exploration. The challenge is to learn the relative value and significance of what we find. In other words, how does a given piece of information fit into the larger picture? What relevance does it have? How important is it in relation to the overall design? The Great Invocation is like a fractal that offers many levels of exploration. The deeper levels are sometimes microcosmic reflections of the greater whole. Simply looking at the bottom line of the repeated key words in table 18 shows they are comprised of twenty-one letters, and they have a numerological value (AN) of 231 which reduces to a 6. More significant perhaps is that 231 is a triangular number derived from the number 21. By now these numbers are familiar ones, but they give an example of information at the microcosmic level of the Great Invocation, which reflects similar information found at its macrocosmic level. It is not new information but simply similar information embedded at deeper levels within the greater whole.

The six/five theme revealed by the eleven original key words and their correspondence to "Kumara" can be expanded to the entire Great Invocation by searching for all the words which contain five letters, repeat five times, and have a numerological value of 5. The same can be done for all the words that contain six letters, repeat six times, and have a numerological value of 6. Tables 19, 20, 21, and 22 show all the possible five/six combinations in the Great Invocation.

Tables 19 and 20 show all the words in the Great Invocation repeated five and six times. The only three words repeated five and six times are "Light," "let," and "and." As shown, their total reduced AN values come to 10, 6, and 5 respectively, and their total RAN values come to 55, 6, and 5. The correlations with all we have seen in connection with the Kumaras and Sanat Kumara are clearly evident.

Table 19. Words Repeated 5 and 6 Times—AN Value.

Words	AN Value	Total Value	Reduced Value
Light 5x	56	280	10
Let 6x	37	222	6
And 5x	19	95	5

Table 20. Words Repeated 5 and 6 Times—Root Value.

Words	Root Value	Total Value	Reduced Value
Light 5x	11	55	10
Let 6x	1	6	6
And 5x	1	5	5

Next let's turn our attention to tables 21 and 22. Table 21 shows the number of words in the Great Invocation with five and six letters. There are twenty-three five letter words in the Great Invocation. This group contains 115 letters (23 x 5 = 115). There are eleven words with six letters. This group contains 66 letters (11 x 6 = 66). The total quantity of letters of all the five and six letter words is 181.

Table 21. Words with 5 and 6 Letters.

Words With—	Quantity	x Letters	Total Letters
Five Letters	23	x5	115
Six Letters	11	x6	66
Total Quantity of Letters Contained in All the Words With Five and Six Letters			181
Reduced Total			10

Table 22 shows all the words in the Great Invocation with a root value of 5 and 6. There are eleven words with a root value of 5; their combined root value total is 55 (11 x 5 = 55). There are twenty-one words with a root value of 6. Their combined root value is 126 (21 x 6 = 126). The combined root totals of these two groups of words *also* equal 181, just like table 21.

Table 22. Words with a Root Value of 5 and 6.

Words With—	Quantity	Total Root Value
Root Value of 5	11	55
Root Value of 6	21	126
Total Combined Root Value of All 32 Words.		181
Reduced Total		10

There is a distinct relationship between all the combinations of five and six within the Great Invocation. This relationship is indicated by the identical total of 181 in tables 21 and 22, and also in the fact that the number 181 reduces to 10, the number of perfection. We see then, that the combination of 6 and 5 (or 11) is transformed into 10 when we are working with the combined words and letters of the entire Great Invocation. The esoteric meaning indicates that through the combined energies represented by 5 and 6 (or 11) the 10 of perfection is achieved.

The Great Invocation reinforces the importance of numbers 5 and 6 in relation to the process of spiritual perfection. Turning to table 23, note that the fifth word (Light) of the Great Invocation has a root value of 11. The same holds true for the sixth word (within)—it also equals 11. If we put 5 and 6 together to form 56, we find that word position fifty-six is "God" with a root value of 8. Since we have put 5 and 6 together in order to locate the fifty-sixth word of the Great Invocation, we must *combine it* with its inverse partner, which is 65 to complete the process. Word position sixty-five (of) has a root value of 3. Combining the root values of words fifty-six and sixty-five yields another 11 (8 + 3). In fact 56 + 65 = 121 which is the square of 11.

Furthermore, if we add 5 and 6 to get 11, the eleventh word position contains "Let" which equals 37 (AN) or 10 (RAN) which is significant in relation to Sanat Kumara as we will soon see. If we multiply 5 and 6 our result is 30 (savior, RAN). The thirtieth word "within" has an AN value of 83 and a RAN value of 38, both of which reduce to the root of 11.

The presence of all these elevens in conjunction with the

combinations of numbers 5 and 6 reveals the inherent energy integrity of the Great Invocation. This underlying pattern of interrelated numeric harmonies expresses a coherent energy pattern running throughout this powerful mantram. The Great Invocation exhibits signs of being an energy template or circuit made up of word/number combinations carrying specific esoteric information.

Table 23. Word Positions Based on 5 and 6.

Word Position	Word	Root Value
5	Light	11
6	within	11
56	God (8)	11 (8 + 3)
65	of (3)	
132	Totals	33

There is a meaningful message contained in the positions occupied by these four words within the Great Invocation. The words combine to form the phrase "God of Light within." As table 23 shows, the combined total of their four positions in the Great Invocation equals 132. This number also equals the phrase "the Heart of God," found in the Great Invocation. These eight words combine to form the phrase "God of Light within the Heart of God." This God of Light was known as Thoth to the ancient Egyptians, Hermes to the Greeks, and Mercury to the Romans. According to DK, Mercury is the revealer of spiritual will (atma), spiritual love (buddhi), and spiritual mind (manas).[17] Perhaps in this sense Hermes becomes the thrice Greatest, known as Hermes Trismegistus.

Djwhal Khul says that it was "...Hermes, Who initiated the process of enlightenment for our race, the Aryan [fifth root-race, JB]."[18] In the book *The Reappearance of the Christ*, in a discussion of ancient world Teachers the Tibetan states that at "some unknown date *Hermes* came and, so the records say, was the first to proclaim Himself as 'the Light of the World.' "[19]

There have been other Gods of Light, Saviors, World Teachers, and Avatars; there was Hercules, Vyasa, Krishna, Buddha, and the Christ. Each of these is a God of Light. They all emerged from the spiritual Hierarchy, the Heart of God—thus, our phrase "God of Light within the Heart of God." All these World Teachers come forth from the Heart of God, the Hierarchy. This is the great Heart chakra of Sanat Kumara, the center of Love. These Saviors (33 RAN, the total root value of the four words in table 23) are all the highest adepts using energy, which is DK's interpretation of the number 11. (See chapter 3, "Djwhal Khul and Esoteric Numerology.")

All these fives and sixes are mirrored through their numerological and structural makeup which again reflects the important numbers 10, 6, and 5. Because we have mentioned so many number combinations it is prudent to mention once more that this 10 and 11 (6 + 5) theme is reflected in the 21 key words and their breakdown into 10 duplicate and 11 original words. (See tables 17 and 18.) Beyond our interpretation of the 10, 6, 5 numeric symbolism contained within the Great Invocation, the Tibetan offers more esoteric puzzles which may well baffle us, yet add to the weight of evidence suggesting a definite plan in the design of the words and overall structure of the Great Invocation.

> The whole mystery of this principle is hidden in two fundamentals: The mystery of the resolution of the six-pointed star, into the five-pointed star.[20]

The Tibetan continues his remarks about the importance of 5 and 6 in a footnote.

> *The Secret Doctrine* says that: "It is on the Hierarchies and the correct number of these Entities that the mystery of the universe is built."
>
> Ten—The line and the circle. The symbol of the heavenly Men...The ten are sumtotal...
>
> Six—The six-pointed star. The subjective life and the objective form overshadowed by Spirit....
>
> Five—This is the pentagon, the Makara, the five-pointed Star.... In the merging of the five and the six you have the totality of manifestation, the male and female blended in the Divine Hermaphrodite.[21]

This extract is particularly interesting because DK not only tells us 5 and 6 must be synthesized in order to bring about the "sumtotal" of 10, but He also makes a point of specifically discussing—10, 6, and 5—in the exact order of their appearance in stanza four of Dzyan, as well as the key word pattern in the Great Invocation. The Great Invocation appears to contain the very number essences upon which "the mystery of the universe is built."

Further evidence of Sanat Kumara's intimate connection with the Great Invocation involves the correlation of the number of letters in His name and those word positions in the Great Invocation with which we just worked. As figure 4 shows, not only do word positions five and six equal 11 when combined (see Word Position Index in appendix B), but the words located in those two positions each reduce to 11, thus equaling the letters forming the name "Sanat Kumara." One instance of this correlation can be granted to chance, but let's look at two more.

Figure 4. Sanat Kumara 5 and 6.

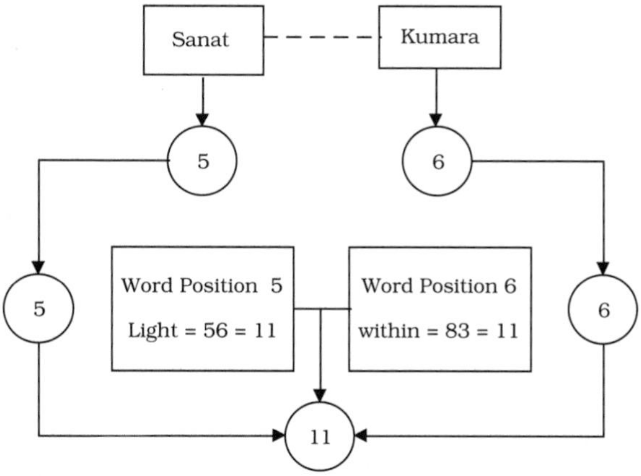

Sanat
Kumara
5
6
5
Word Position 5
Light = 56 = 11
Word Position 6
within = 83 = 11
6
11

Using the numerological value of Sanat Kumara we will now perform the same exercise as before. (See figure 5.) First, we will use the AN values of Sanat Kumara, 55 and 65 respectively. The Word Position Index shows the 55th word of the Great Invocation is "of" and the 65th word is also "of." They both have a value of 21. When we reduce the value of Sanat we get 10, and when we do the same with Kumara we get 11. Adding the two values together yields 21. Again we have a direct correlation between the name Sanat Kumara and the words of the Great Invocation.

Figure 5. Sanat Kumara 55 and 65.

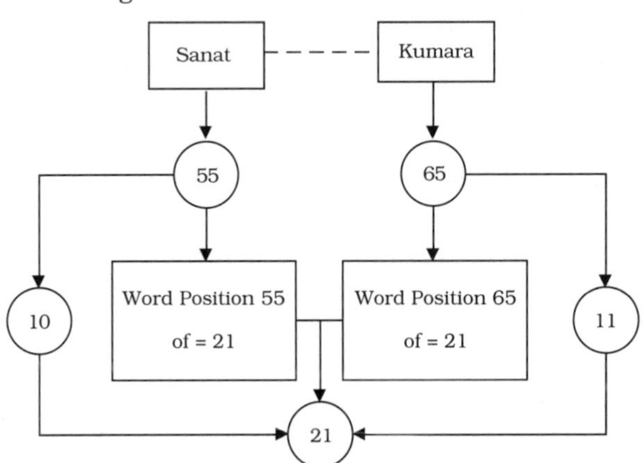

But what if we add 21 (of) and 21 (of) together resulting in 42? We find that the 42nd word of the Great Invocation is also "of" which gives us another value of 21. If we add these three together we obtain a result of 63 (21 + 21 + 21 = 63)—the AN value of avatar. As we already know, Sanat Kumara is the first Avatar of our planet.

Now let's perform the same exercise one more time (figure 6) using the RAN values for Sanat Kumara. These values are 10 and 20 respectively. Looking at the Word Position Index we find word ten is "God" and word twenty is "Let." These two words have values of 26 and 37. Adding these two together results in 63—again we have the value for Avatar! (Also recall that the RAN value of Sanat Kumara equals 30 (10 + 20) which equals "Savior.")

Figure 6. Sanat Kumara Savior/Avatar

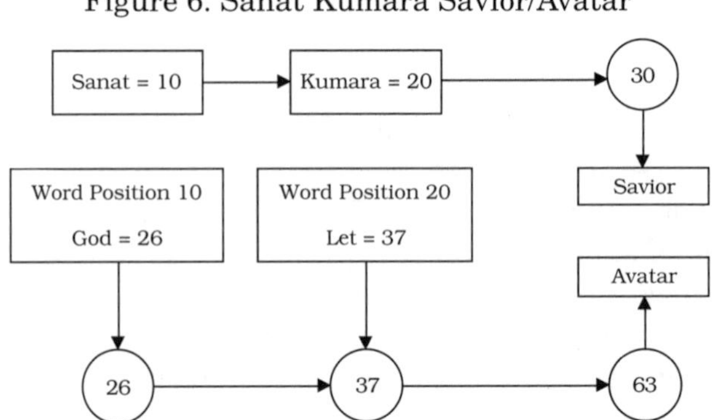

The numerological and symbolic lesson is quite clear—Sanat Kumara is the Lord of the World, the Great Sacrifice. The numeric symbolism of His name is imprinted throughout the Great Invocation. As the prototypal Savior of Earth, Sanat Kumara passes this torch of redemption to the human souls who choose the line of the Savior as their field of planetary service. Through the process of spiritual initiation, the human soul becomes the liberated spiritual soul and enters the Hierarchy of Light and Love. These Masters then work under the Christ, the Leader of Hierarchy. This quintessence of human evolution on our planet is the Spiritual Agent of Sanat Kumara. The Christ is both an office and a Man-God. The Christ is the Intermediary between the Father in heaven, Sanat Kumara, and humanity. This mediating process is beautifully represented through the key words of the Great Invocation.

The Hidden Sevens of Sanat Kumara

We now have an appreciation for the versatility of the name and number combination of Sanat Kumara. The numbers reveal themselves through the words in the Great Invocation (as just demonstrated) and by the distribution of the key words in the five stanzas. In addition, the story of the 105 Kumaras reveals the numerological value of Sanat Kumara by the extension of 105 to 5565.

We are now going to use the number 5565 as a medium for showing the connection between the prototypal planetary savior, Sanat Kumara and His human/divine counterpart, the Christ. As mentioned in the previous section, the Christ is the Agent between the Heavenly Father and humanity. The Christ is the Avataric Bridge linking the Lord of the World, Sanat Kumara, to the world of human living. The Christ and the Hierarchy receive, step down, and distribute the spiritual Will and Purpose of the Lord of the World to humanity in the form of the Plan.

The process of stepping down the energy of Sanat Kumara and Shamballa to the Christ and the Hierarchy is reflected in the relationship between the numbers of Sanat Kumara and the twenty-one key words. Sanat equals 55 (AN), which reduces to 10 (5 + 5). This corresponds to the ten duplicate key words. Kumara equals 65 (AN), which reduces to 11 (6 + 5). This corresponds to the eleven original key words. We now have two sets of key words, one set of ten and one of eleven. The ten duplicate key words contain 43 letters which reduce to 7 (4 + 3). Their numerological value is 475 (AN), which reduces to 7 (4 + 7 + 5 = 16/7). The eleven original key words contain 52 letters which also reduce to 7 (5 + 2), and their numerological value equals 628 or 7 (6 + 2 + 8 = 16/7). Thus, these two sets of key words equal 7 both numerologically and through their total letters.

Figure 7. The Hidden Sevens of Sanat Kumara.

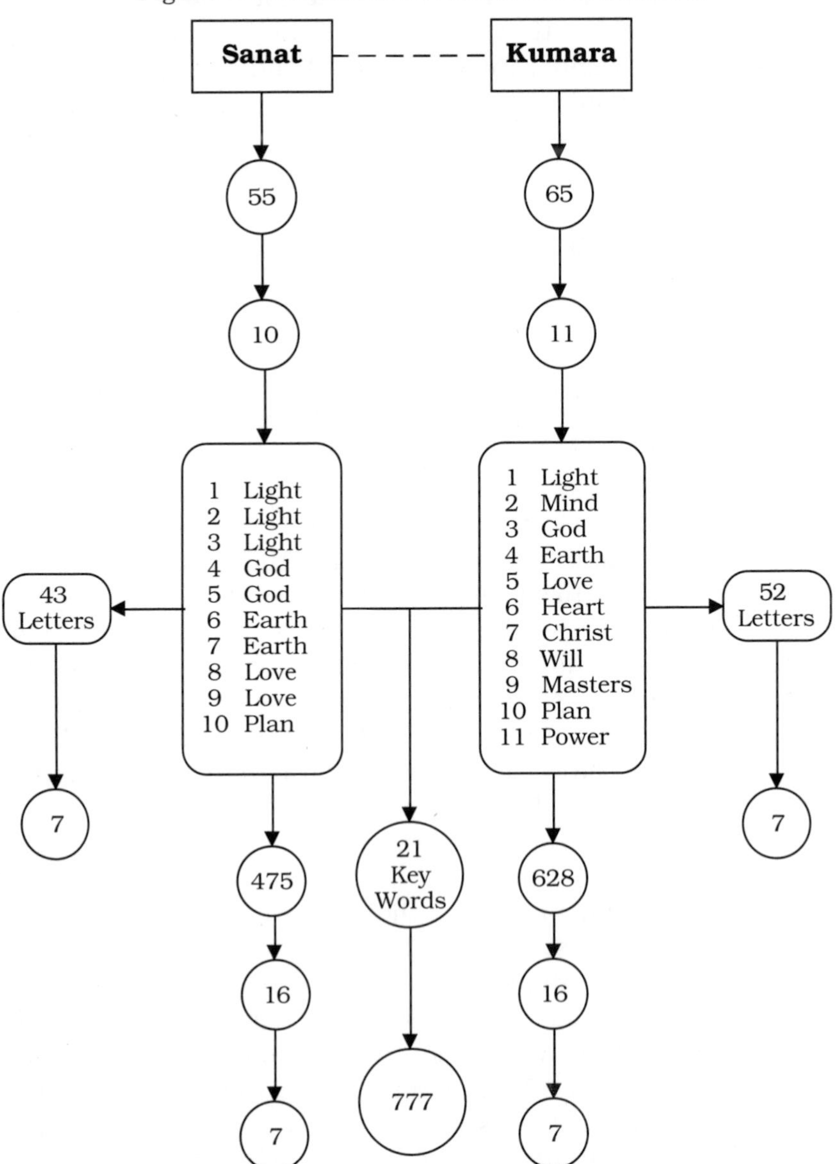

Using the name of Sanat Kumara as a basis for separating the key words into two groups, two sets of 77 (AN value of Christ) emerge. In effect Sanat Kumara symbolically pours the energy of His Will through the key words, forming a series of sevens relating Christ—77 to the 777 of the planetary Logos, Sanat Kumara.

A curious side note to the 10 and 11 key words is found in the book *Letters on Occult Meditation*:

> The total number of petals in the centres, if we eliminate the spleen which has a purpose all its own, and the three lower organs of creation, is one thousand, one hundred and ten, the total number signifying the perfection of the microcosm.[22]

Note that this number is 1110 or 11 and 10, the numbers of the two sets of key words in figure 7.

The Christ, the Six, and the Five

In the last section we saw how the eleven original key words are divided into six non-repeating and five repeating key words. This pattern reflects the word Kumara with its value of 65. We also saw how the eleven key words reflect the process and result of perfecting form through the development and correct use of the fifth principle of mind. In this section we will bring our subject closer to the human dimension through the incarnation of the Christ in human form through Jesus 2,000 years ago.

As we are discovering, the Great Invocation contains information connecting its numerically symbolic word structure with Sanat Kumara. We have learned that Sanat Kumara sacrificed Himself through direct incarnation on the Earth in order to carry out some redemptive purpose. And we have also learned that all world saviors are redemptive agents of Sanat Kumara sent into the world of material form to further the Purpose and Plan of Sanat Kumara for our planet.

Jesus the Christ is the latest of these human/divine messengers to come forth from the higher worlds of spirit. The Christ is specifically named in the Great Invocation and is called on to "return to Earth." Is there information about the Christ, the latest world savior, also hidden within the Great Invocation? Yes there is, but the symbolism points more to the message than to the messenger. Yet, paradoxically, the messenger is the living proof of the message's essential truth and hope.

The Christ represents the perfect human being incarnated through the physical form—the perfected "6-form" of Jesus the man. The reason the number 6 is a perfect number is because it is the sum of all its factors apart from itself. 1 x 6 = 6 and 2 x 3 = 6. The factors apart from 6 are 1, 2, and 3. 1 + 2 + 3 = 6. Thomas Taylor writes:

> The Pythagoreans, as we learn from the extracts from Nicomachus, denominated the hexad, "the form of form, the only number adapted to the soul, the distinct union of the parts of the universe." [23]

This can be interpreted by indicating that the numbers 1, 2, and 3 represent the three aspects or trinity and they are united through the number 6.

The symbolism of the number 6 is also demonstrated by the twenty-one key words in which 21 is the result of adding the first *six* numbers together—1 + 2 + 3 + 4 + 5 + 6 = 21. Just as symbolic, if not more so, in referring back to table 6 (on page 43), note that no key word has a root value of 6 and only one key word contains 6 letters: the word "Christ." This symbolizes the esoteric law that the Christ principle—the saving, redeeming force of life—must be present in order to complete the evolutionary plan of spiritualizing form.

At the same time, it is important to note that the AN and RAN totals of Christ equal 77/14/5 and 32/5 respectively. Jesus Christ symbolizes the synthesis of the six-pointed star—the perfected form, and the five-pointed star—the perfected human soul. He represents the template, the apotheosis of the human soul's evolution in form. This six-five relationship is symbolized in the name "Sanat Kumara" and "Jesus Christ" both of which have five letters in the first name and six letters in the second name. This relationship is also shown in the value of Kumara—65, which is 6 and 5 joined together. (Later we will see how the reverse—5 and 6—join to form 56, which is another important number related to the Great Invocation.)

The connection between the six and the five is beautifully symbolized in the Great Invocation itself by the fact that only ten words other than the word "Christ" have six letters—the symbolism being that the perfection of ten is achieved through the work of Christ in perfecting the form. This is actually illustrated by the arrangement of these eleven words: "Christ" is placed exactly in the sixth position of the eleven words, with five words ahead of it and five words following it. (See table 24. Note that the word positions show the exact order of the words within the Great Invocation.) This middle placement is beautifully symbolic not only because Christ represents the middle principle in the Christian Trinity, but also because the Christ Principle is the essential factor in the entire process of redemption. Christ is the mediator between humanity and the Father. The soul is the mediator between the personality and the spiritual monad. Hierarchy is the mediator between Humanity and Shamballa. Sanat Kumara is the mediator between all the lifeforms of the Earth and the solar Logos. The midpoint is key to all spiritual advancement. This table clearly illustrates this very point.

Although the midpoint placement of Christ is the main theme of table 24, there are also some other interesting values contained within it. The word "Christ" is the only word of the eleven words with a root value of 5, and in relation to the key words, "Christ" is the only word with 6 letters. Therefore, symbolically speaking, the word "Christ" in the context of the Great Invocation illustrates an important concept.

Table 24. Christ, the Middle Principle.

Word Position	Word	AN Value	Root Value
6	within	83	11
13	stream	76	22
30	within	83	11
37	stream	76	22
41	hearts	71	8
45	Christ	77	5
46	return	96	6
51	centre	65	11
63	little	78	6
77	centre	65	11
102	dwells	75	3
Totals 511	66 Letters	845	116
Root 7	3	8	8
7 + 3 + 8 + 8 = 26 = 8—Christ Consciousness			

Viewing the entire Great Invocation, the non-key words symbolize humanity, the individual key words symbolize Hierarchy, and the key words as a group, represent Sanat Kumara and Shamballa. Christ as the only word with six letters among the key words is the perfection of form within the Hierarchy. He stands for achievement—the success of human evolution. This is further demonstrated in table 6 on page 43. Note that the Christ, God and Plan are the only three words that equal 11 when their number of letters is combined with their root values. This indicates even more clearly that the Christ is the first human being to fulfill the Plan (11) of God (11). Therefore the Christ represents the agent or bridge of transfiguration between Shamballa, Hierarchy, and Humanity.

Referring again table 24, the ten non-key words with six letters symbolize the perfection of form in potential. These words represent a future possibility. The Christ comes into their midst from the kingdom of God, the Hierarchy. His presence among the ten non-key words illustrates two things: first, the presence of the Christ principle at the heart of every atom of substance; second, the centrality of the Christ as World Savior and Teacher Who dwells in the midst of the form world (number 6) in order to redeem, transform, and liberate humanity from its imprisonment in matter. All of this is demonstrated by the placement of these words within the Great Invocation.

The totals at the bottom of table 24 indicate another interesting bit of information. All the factors relating to the six-lettered words reduce to 26 (God) and then to 8. Djwhal Khul says number 8 is "the number of the Christ-consciousness."[24] Turning once again to David Fideler's book *Jesus Christ, Sun of God* we find the following:

> The number of the physical world is six, the number of the spiritual world is eight....The number 8, the ogdoad, symbolizes the new order of Christianity, and JESUS, 888 [using Greek gematria, JB], was known as the Ogdoad to the early Christian gnostics.[25]

David Fideler also points out that:

> The early Christians maintained that *Iêsous* was "a name above all names." Origen, the early church father, even went so far as to boast about how the name of Jesus possessed more magical efficacy than those of the pagan divinities.
>
> In the same way that the names of Apollo, Hermes, Abraxas, and Mithras were designed to represent aspects of the Universal Logos, the values of both *Iêsous* (888) and Christos (1480) are obtained from 74,

> the most characteristic number from the magic square of the Sun. It is unlikely that this is a coincidence, for, as Dr. Eisler has pointed out, the name *Iêsous* is "an artificial and irregular Greek transliteration" of the Aramaic name Joshua, designed to bring out the number 888.[26]

Using Greek gematria, Jesus (888) is a result of 12 x 74 and Christos (1480) is a result of 20 x 74 . Fideler sums up by saying

> both Jesus (888) and Christos (1480) are related to the magic square of the sun. Both are multiples of 74, the square's most characteristic number, as is the number 666, which is the sum of all of the numbers which comprise the magic square of the sun.[27]

Let's briefly examine this subject of magic squares before continuing our discussion. There are seven fundamental magic squares traditionally recognized by Hermetic philosophy. These seven magic squares correspond to the seven known planets of the ancient Chaldeans, namely Saturn, Jupiter, Mars, the Sun, Venus, Mercury, and the Moon. These are categorized according to the number of squares needed to symbolize each planet from the smallest to the highest. Thus, Saturn is a 3 x 3 square, Jupiter 4 x 4, Mars 5 x 5, the Sun 6 x 6, Venus 7 x 7, Mercury 8 x 8, and the Moon 9 x 9. Although the subject of magic squares is interesting, our main concern here is the symbolism of the Sun. This magic square represents the energy of 6 in various degrees of refinement from the mundane to the sublime, thus the 6 x 6 grid. These levels of increasing refinement from the physical to the spiritual are measured by the total value of the numbers found in the four corners of any magic square.

The magic square of the Sun is reproduced in figure 8A below. By adding the four corner numbers together we obtain a result of 74. David Fideler is demonstrating the fact that the Greek Gnostics named "Jesus" according to an octave of 74. Thus, 12 x 74 or 888 is the value for Jesus in Greek and the value for Christos is 20 x 74 or 1480.

Figure 8A. Magic Square of the Sun.

6	32	3	34	35	1
7	11	27	28	8	30
19	14	16	15	23	24
18	20	22	21	17	13
25	29	10	9	26	12
36	5	33	4	2	31

Remember the earlier extract by Djwhal Khul in chapter 3 which is partially repeated here: "In an ancient book on numbers the initiate is defined as 'the one who has experienced and expressed 666 and found it naught...'" In *Esoteric Astrology* DK states:

> Six is the number of the great work of the period of manifestation, is the number of "the Beast," which is the lower nature as far as man is concerned, and is all that which seeks to destroy the higher life, but also that which can be controlled and directed finally by the soul.[28]

In other words, this passage is saying the Christ principle serves as the perfecter of form. The form aspect is represented by the number 6 and according to the ancients, 6 represents the physical sun. Through the divine incarnation of the Christos (1480) as Jesus (888), the 666 of form—the physical sun—is redeemed and transfigured into the perfected 6-form of the spiritual sun. Since the ancients recognized the Sun as the giver of all physical life and light on our planet, the Greek words Jesus and Christos were created to symbolize the higher spiritual counterparts of the physical sun. (Note that Djwhal Khul uses the terms physical Sun, Heart of the Sun, and central spiritual Sun quite often, and we will be referring to these three aspects of the Sun in future chapters.)

Jesus Christ is the giver of spiritual life—the Son/Sun of God, thus the association with the magic square of the Sun and the number 74. This ultimate perfection is demonstrated in the Greek name *Iêsous Christos* which equals 2368 (888 + 1480). Interestingly, the number 2368 reduces to the perfect 10 (2 + 3 + 6 + 8 = 19/10). Incidently, the AN value of Jesus Christ (in English) totals 151 which is the equivalent of "The Great Work" (of alchemy).

Let's return to the symbolic structural placement of Christ at the center of the six letter words. This symbolic midpoint placement of Christ is also illustrated by the Cabalistic Tree of Life. The Tree of Life is composed of ten Sephiroth which can be considered as archetypal ideas, creative forces, or angelic intelligences. Kether, the crown, corresponds to the One Manifested Godhead, the originating mover of Creation out of which the other nine Sephiroth emanate, while Chokmah relates to the stars. The other eight Sephiroth are associated with the Sun and the seven known planets of the ancient Chaldeans. For instance, Binah, the third Sephira is equated with Saturn, understanding, and the divine feminine aspect; Chokmah, the second, is equated with the stars, wisdom, and the masculine aspect. Each one of the ten Sephiroth are connected by lines which are called paths. There are twenty-two pathways on the Tree of Life and these correspond to the twenty-two letters of the Hebrew alphabet. These along with the ten Sephiroth make up the thirty-two Paths of Wisdom.

Figure 8B. The Tree of Life.

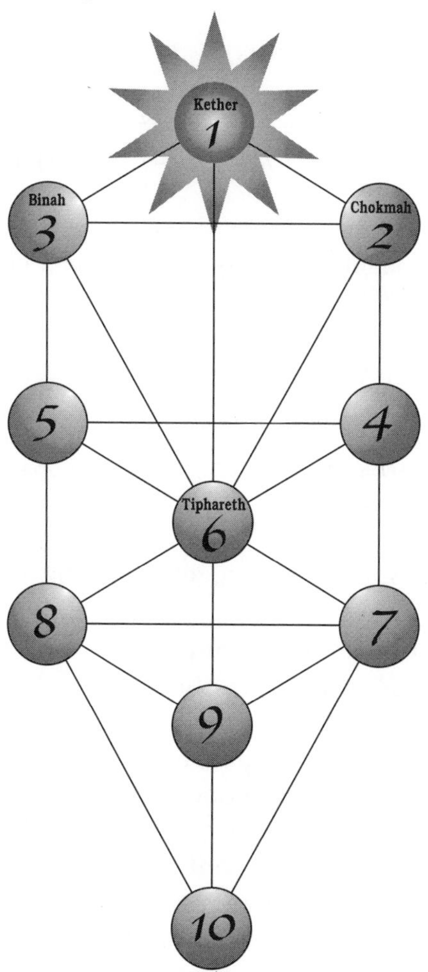

The number 32 is interesting because it relates directly to the magic square of the Sun mentioned earlier—32 x 74 = 2368—the Greek *Iêsous Christos*. Fideler calls this product "the Illuminating Knowledge of the Solar Logos."[29] This number is the highest level of the magic square of the Sun because it expresses the highest level of attainment within our solar system relative to planet Earth. Thus, walking all 32 paths of the Tree of Life leads to the perfected God/Man—Jesus Christ (151) the product of "The Great Work (151). Again, we see how the various systems of ancient thought overlap and show remarkable cross correspondences. Despite the fact that many systems do not correspond in complete detail, they should generally correspond at least to some degree if they truly represent the ageless wisdom teachings.

Referring to *Godwin's Cabalistic Encyclopedia*, we find that the number 21 is related to the "mystic number of the sixth Path (Tiphareth)." In his Introduction, Godwin explains the Hebrew four letter name of God (YHWH—*Yod*, *Heh*, *Vav*, *Heh*—Tetragrammaton):

> The four consonants are often described as a family: *Yod* is the Father...The first *heh* is the Mother...The final *heh* is the daughter.

Concerning the letter Vav, Godwin says

> *Vav* is the Son and includes the Sephiroth 4 through 9, although it is particularly associated with Tiphareth. Tiphareth is therefore associated with Christ.[30]

Bringing the various factors together we have—

- The number 6 is a perfect number.
- David Fideler's work with the magic square of the Sun and its connection to the number 6 and Jesus Christ.
- The sixth Sephira of Tiphareth on the Tree of Life and its association with the Sun and the Christ.
- Tiphareth's location at the center of the Tree of Life just like the Sun's location at the center of the solar system.
- The eleven words of the Great Invocation with six letters, along with the word "Christ" at the center symbolizing the Sun at the center of the solar system and Tiphareth at the center of the Cabalistic Tree of Life.

At this point it is important to remember that the Christ as World Savior is the human counterpart of Sanat Kumara, the prototype of all world saviors. The purpose of our planet is that of sacrificial redemption. This is illustrated in the following table of items which all equal 105 and a root of 6—the number of redemption.

Table 25. The Number 105.

Word or Phrase	AN Value		Dsecription
Tiphareth	105		6th Sephiroth of the Cabalistic Tree of Life
Saviour	105		Western term for Avatar
Earth Scheme	105		Evolutionary Vehicle for our planetary Logos
The World	105		Tarot card 21 of the Major Arcana
Kumaras	AN 84	RAN 21	84 + 21 = 105

We end this chapter with the words of Djwhal Khul:

> This theme of redemption (which underlies all the initiatory processes) is hidden in the karmic responsibilities of Sanat Kumara; stage by stage, initiation by initiation, the disciple arrives at an understanding of redemption. First of all, he learns to bring about the redemption of his threefold personality; then the concept enlarges along paralleling lines as he seeks the redemption of his fellowmen; later, he shares the redemptive work connected with all true hierarchical endeavour and becomes an "active part of a redeeming Ashram." At the later initiations, and after the fifth Initiation of Revelation, he sees with a new clarity some of the karmic liabilities which have led the planetary Logos to create this planet of suffering, sorrow, pain and struggle; he realises then (and with joy) that this little planet is essentially unique in its purpose and its techniques, and that on it and within it (if you could but penetrate below the surface) a great redemptive experiment is going forward; its prime implementing factors and its scientific agents are the "sons of mind who choose to be the sons of men and yet for all eternity remain the Sons of God." These "sons of mind" were chosen, in that far distant time when the fourth kingdom in nature came into being, to carry forward the science of redemption.[31]

Notes

1. Helena P. Blavatsky, *The Secret Doctrine,* vol. 1, 150.
2. Ibid., 151.
3. Ibid., 152.
4. Ibid., 153.
5. Ibid., 154.
6. Incidently, the English word "God" also has a value of 26 by the RAN method.
7. Ibid., 154.
8. *The Encyclopedia of Eastern Philosophy and Religion*, s.v. "Prajapati."
9. Bailey, *A Treatise on Cosmic Fire,* n. 692.
10. Ibid., 306.
11. Curiously the RAN value of "prajapatis" is 111 and 7 x 111 = 777.
12. If the numbers 1 through 10 are added together, the result is 55. The AN value of "Sanat" equals 55—a composite of the five key words in stanzas one (5) and two (5).
13. Bailey, *Discipleship in the New Age,* vol. II, 286.
14. Bailey, *A Treatise on Cosmic Fire,* 387.
15. Bailey, *The Rays and the Initiations,* 79.
16. See earlier extract by DK in chapter 3.
17. See Alice A. Bailey *Esoteric Astrology*, 354.
18. Bailey, *The Externalisation of the Hierarchy,* 39.
19. Bailey, *The Reappearance of the Christ,* 104.
20. Bailey, *A Treatise on Cosmic Fire*, 395.
21. Ibid., n. 396.
22. Alice A. Bailey, *Letters on Occult Meditation*, 80.
23. Thomas Taylor, *The Theoretic Arithmetic of the Pythagoreans,* 192.
24. See earlier section on "Djwhal Khul and Esoteric Numerology" in chapter 3.
25. Fideler, J*esus Christ, Sun of God,* 270.
26. Ibid., 264.
27. Ibid., 266.
28. Bailey, *Esoteric Astrology,* 128.
29. Fideler, J*esus Christ, Sun of God*, 265.
30. David Godwin, *Godwin's Cabalistic Encyclopedia*, xvii.
31. Bailey, *Discipleship in the New Age,* vol. II, 385-86.

7

Isis-Sothis, The Queen of Heaven

Our Celestial Family

We have already seen how the great spiritual centers of Shamballa and Hierarchy are closely connected to the Great Invocation. We have explored to some degree the symbolic presence of the number 1065 in the twenty-one key words and their connection to Sanat Kumara. Now we must step into a more complex area of esoteric teaching involving cosmic relationships, because the numerical correspondences and symbols found within the Great Invocation not only include our planet, but extend beyond it. According to the ageless wisdom, the Earth is part of a solar system which is governed by the star Sirius, known to the ancient Egyptians as Isis-Sothis. Before we explore this deep and mysterious relationship and the role the Great Invocation plays in it, we will briefly describe the star systems comprising the celestial neighborhood in which our planet is located.

In chapter 1, the universe was described as filled with living beings. Intelligent life not only lives on planets and in solar systems, but the planets and stars are intelligent conscious lives in their own right. To grasp the full nature of Djwhal Khul's description of our planet in relation to the universe, it is necessary to think about stars and planets in terms of life and consciousness, rather than as clusters of material elements haphazardly thrown together by blind natural forces.

As pointed out in the beginning of the book, from the ageless wisdom viewpoint everything in the universe is alive, conscious, and intelligent. The degree of conscious development is dependent on any given lifeform's experience in relation to its environment, whether it is an atom, a plant, a human being, or a solar system. Everything is alive and evolving in some way, but not necessarily in the physical universe. The wisdom teaches that most of the living entities of the universe exist in dimensions other than the physical. The Tibetan describes this state of affairs beautifully in *A Treatise on Cosmic Fire*:

> The confines of the heavens Themselves are illimitable and utterly unknown, Naught but the wildest speculation is possible to the tiny finite minds of men and it profits us not to consider the question. Go out on some clear starlit night and seek to realise that in the many thousands of suns and constellations visible to the unaided eye of man, and in the tens of millions which the modern telescope [first published in 1925, JB] reveals there is seen the physical manifestation of as many millions of intelligent existences; this infers that what is visible is simply those existences who are in incarnation. But only one-seventh of the possible appearances are incarnating. Six-sevenths are out of incarnation...
>
> Realise further that the bodies of all these sentient intelligent cosmic, solar and planetary Logoi are constituted of living sentient beings, and the brain reels, and the mind draws back in dismay before such a staggering concept.[1]

The idea that the stars and planets of the universe are living intelligent entities is not new. The ancients believed the celestial bodies were Gods with distinct qualities and influences which affected the Earth and its inhabitants; this was the basis of mythology and astrology. The idea that the Earth is under the influence of stars which are living intelligent Beings, billions of miles from our planet, flies in the face of modern day science and the current worldview of reality. However, in order to think in new ways, to open ourselves to new ideas (actually, according to DK, ancient and ageless), we must suspend our preconceived notions about the nature of things. Science is a long way from bottom line definitions of the nature of life and consciousness in the universe; it has barely scratched the surface of our own planet. Relatively speaking, science knows a great deal about the physical world but almost nothing about anything which lies beyond the five senses of our physical bodies. Science knows far more about physical bodies and forms than it does about the lives working through those forms.

The teachings of the ageless wisdom consider the present cycle of scientific investigation temporary in terms of its materialistic worldview. Djwhal Khul states in various parts of his writings that scientific discoveries will inevitably lead investigators beyond the strictly material realm into dimensions of existence which were once thought of as pure superstition. In the book *Esoteric Astrology,* the Tibetan says:

> The heavens, the constellations, signs and planets mean one thing to the Hierarchy and another thing to the astronomers and still another thing to the astrologers, whilst they are simply bewildering galaxies of light to the average citizen. I feel the need to remind you of this and to point out to you that astronomical facts are only relative as regards the true and factual nature of that about which scientific pronouncement is made; they are declarative of life and potency but not as science and the average man understand them. From the standpoint of esoteric truth, they are simply embodied Lives and the expression of the life, the quality, the purpose and the intent of the Beings Who have brought them into manifestation.[2]

This concept of influence and relationship between planets, solar systems, and stars was touched on earlier in the section "A Mission of Planetary Redemption" in chapter 6 by mentioning that Sanat Kumara came to the Earth from Venus. This is a deep and profound mystery, and even though Djwhal Khul has provided some information about this event, many questions remain and much has been left unsaid. Before we approach the topic of Sanat Kumara and Venus we must explain how the Earth is related to the solar system and how the solar system fits into the local celestial scheme of things. Despite the fact that we are treading on unsure ground and striking out into "unknown territory," we must continue to move forward in the direction indicated by the clues that have been discovered so far.

Beginning at the strictly physical level, our Earth is a planet within our solar system. Specifically speaking, it is the third planet from the Sun. As far as we have been able to ascertain, our Earth appears to be the only planet in the solar system to have life as we know it. It appears very lonely out there.

Our Sun is classified as a G2 star, meaning that it is a relatively average star compared to thousands of others making up our galaxy. Our Sun, along with approximately 100 billion other stars, lies about two-thirds from the center of the Milky Way galaxy in one of its spiral arms. Our galaxy has been estimated to be some 100,000 light years in diameter and is described as a spiral in shape, although new data appears to indicate that our galaxy may have somewhat different characteristics. Since light travels at approximately 186,000 miles per second or about 6.6 billion miles per hour (!) you can see that just one light year is a huge distance by human standards. Therefore, in order to get from one side of our galaxy to the other we would have to travel at the speed of light for 100,000 years. Despite these immense distances, esoteric teaching, particularly astrology, declares that the stars and planets relate to and influence each other as well as all the lifeforms inhabiting the worlds. Quoting Djwhal Khul on this matter:

> In esoteric astrology we are, therefore, dealing with the Life and Lives which inform the "points of light" within the universal Life. Constellations, solar systems, planets, kingdoms in nature and microscopic man are all of them the result of the activity and the manifestation of energy of certain Lives whose cycle of expression and whose infinite purposes lie outside the comprehension of the most advanced and illumined minds on our planet.[3]

In respect to the immensity of the galaxy, esoteric cosmology and astrology are only concerned with the stars and constellations in relatively close proximity to our Earth. As mentioned briefly in chapter 1, Djwhal Khul describes a cosmic Logos, a living Intelligence, called the One About Whom Naught May Be Said, in Whom our solar system and consequently, our Earth exist. DK identifies some of the constellations which make up this vast cosmic Intelligence. There are seven solar systems (all unnamed), of which ours is one, Ursa Major (the Great Bear), the Pleiades, Sirius, and the twelve constellations making up the zodiac. There may quite possibly be other constellations within the stellar body of the One About Whom Naught May Be Said, but the Tibetan is less clear about their identity.

The constellations given above, however, are more than adequate for putting into perspective the esoteric cosmological model taught by Djwhal Khul. We are going to concentrate primarily on Sirius. In order to put these star groups into some perspective, consider the distances of the three most important constellations relative to our solar system: the Pleiades are the farthest from Earth, about 430 light years, while the stars of the Great Bear range from 49 to 190 light years from the Earth, counting from the closest of the group to the most distant. The star Sirius is the closest of the three constellations. Only 8.7 light years from the Earth, Sirius is the fifth closest star to our planet and solar system. Taking all three objects into consideration in relation to the overall size of our galaxy shows that they are actually our regional neighbors, and relative to the Pleiades and the Great Bear, Sirius is our next door neighbor.

Physical distance plays some part here, but the more significant point is the subjective relationship (psychological and spiritual) existing between these cosmic Lives—a relationship transcending the space/time dimension. The primary level of interaction for these celestial Lives takes place at higher energy states compared to the human level of existence. In a universe that contains intelligent life at the level of planets and solar systems, as well as at the level of human life, we need a wider and more inclusive view of reality. If dimensions of being exist beyond the physical world we inhabit, then our entire perspective of human living is expanded beyond measure.

For most people the question of intelligent life existing on other planets in the universe is a fascinating idea. The esoteric teaching of the ageless wisdom takes this basic idea and extends it much further by saying the planets on which life exists and the solar systems containing those planets are *themselves alive, conscious and intelligent Entities*. This higher order of life is the macrocosm and we are the microcosm or lives contained within this larger order of life. St. Paul was stating a fundamental esoteric truth when he described God as "the One in Whom we live, and move, and have our being" (Acts 17:28). Djwhal Khul sometimes refers to humanity as the cells within the body of the planetary Logos. Drawing a rough analogy, in this kind of universe, humanity and the lifeforms existing on the various worlds can be compared to sub-atomic particles existing at the quantum level of reality. In such a universe the human lifespan of 80 years is a mere nanosecond in the conscious life of a planetary or solar Logos.

If the universe appears physically ordered according to size—from atoms to galaxies, with man somewhere in between—the ageless wisdom extends the hierarchical scale to include consciousness. The consciousness of an atom, a man, a planetary logos, and a solar logos are "sized" accordingly. Djwhal Khul describes the consciousness limits of the preceding four units of consciousness as the "ring-pass-not." Naturally, an atom has a minute ring-pass-not and its conscious radius is bound by the form in which it is found. Speaking of the other three basic units of consciousness DK says:

> Space, again, is included in the ideas of consciousness, and its utilisation of matter. Space, for the Logos, is literally the form wherein His conscious activities and purposes are worked out—the solar ring-pass-not. The space wherein a planetary Logos works out His plans is similarly as much of solar space as His consciousness is developed enough to use. Man again repeats the process and his ring-pass-not is included in the radius of his consciousness, and may be very circumscribed as in the case of the little evolved, or may be inclusive of a portion of planetary space of great extent, and even in the case of the very highly evolved may begin to touch the periphery of the sphere of influence of the planetary Logos in Whose body he is a cell.[4]

Summing up so far we have the following:

- Everything in the universe is conscious to some degree.
- Celestial objects such as stars and planets are conscious Lives of immense intelligence.
- The life forms inhabiting these celestial worlds are also conscious.
- Viewed from above downward Humanity is the lowest unit of life that has self-consciousness.
- All other life forms, including atoms, are conscious but not self-aware.
- All the lives, including man, living within the ring-pass-not of a planet and solar system are considered integral parts of the "bodies" of these Cosmic Beings.
- Most importantly, these so-called bodies include more than the physical form. The rings-pass-not of solar and planetary Beings include many dimensions of existence beyond the physical plane.

- Finally, these celestial Entities communicate and exchange energy with one another and, therefore, affect all the conscious entities living within their spheres of influence. This cosmic relationship is the basis of astrology.

Below is a general outline of the various celestial relationships which affect our Earth and all its kingdoms of nature, including humanity.

The One About Whom Naught May Be Said.
- A. The three celestial groups consisting of
  - 1. The Great Bear
    - a. The seven stars of the Big Dipper
  - 2. The Pleiades
    - a. The Seven Sisters
  - 3. Sirius[5]
- B. The twelve constellations of the zodiac.
- C. The seven solar systems
  Our solar system is one of these seven—
  The Grand Man of the Heavens, the solar Logos.
- D. The various planets in our solar system—
  The Heavenly Men, the planetary Logoi.

These are the most important celestial Intelligences mentioned by Djwhal Khul in respect to our solar Logos and our planet. The lives of these Beings are impossible to fathom, but as human beings living within the periphery of their rings-pass-not we are nonetheless affected in varying degrees by their evolutionary development at cosmic levels, most of which we are not yet aware. The effects of these stupendous Lives are indirectly experienced by humanity via Sanat Kumara. Such effects are felt over long periods of time and affect whole races, nations, and civilizations. It is only through the zodiacal constellations that individual lives are affected directly by these Beings. The important point to remember about all these Entities is this: Their influence on our world comes through the *energy* they radiate, and not through direct contact with the physical bodies of these cosmic Beings. Such contact would be comparable to a human being attempting to communicate with a sub-atomic particle. Contacts with higher life expressions are stepped down and mediated from group to group. This idea is the basis of the great chain of being or hierarchy (not to be confused with the "Hierarchy" which specifically refers to the Christ and the Masters of Wisdom who guide the evolution of consciousness on our planet).

For instance, within the ring-pass-not of our planetary life on Earth, the center called Shamballa is comprised of very advanced Beings who communicate their purposes to the less advanced Hierarchy of Masters. The Masters exist in various grades of development, yet only the most advanced members of the Hierarchy can receive the energy coming from Shamballa. This energy is first received by the Christ and other advanced Members of the Hierarchy Who "step it down" before distributing it to the other Masters. These Masters in turn modify the energy further so that their disciples at the physical level can comprehend in human terms the work to be done at the physical plane level for the overall Plan of God to be carried out. In this way the Purpose of God working through Shamballa is stepped down into a Plan by the Hierarchy's advanced Members, and eventually distributed to various Masters who work more closely with humanity. Summing up, we might say an idea in the Mind of God which concerns the world of human living is stepped down by various spiritual Beings until the divine idea appears in the human world as, for example, brotherhood, goodwill, or world peace.

In terms of the great cosmic design, Sanat Kumara is contributing to some greater Plan in service to the solar Logos. In turn, the solar Logos is contributing to some higher Purpose in respect to Entities existing at a cosmic scale of life encompassing greater, more extensive areas of consciousness within our galaxy. So, in our little corner of the galaxy, and within the ring-pass-not of the One About Whom Naught May Be Said, our solar Logos has a particularly close association with the Cosmic Beings ensouling the Pleiades, the Great Bear, and Sirius.

Narrowing down this relationship even further, our solar Logos is especially linked with Sirius, which is the second or Christ aspect at the cosmic level of existence. We are closely connected to Sirius because our solar Logos is bringing that second aspect to perfection at the physical plane level through our current solar system. Thus, our solar system is the medium for bringing the Christ energy of Sirius to the densest level of existence. The middle soul aspect expresses both the Love of the Father or first aspect and the Intelligence of the Mother or the third aspect. The fundamental and primary quality of our solar system is Love. In other words, God is Love.

This solar system is the second of three solar manifestations or "incarnations." In the present solar incarnation, the second aspect of love-wisdom is being brought to perfection. In the first solar system the third aspect of active intelligence was brought to perfection. In the next or third manifestation of the solar Logos, the first aspect of Will or Purpose is the goal.

Table 26. Cosmic and Planetary Triplicities.

First Aspect	Second Aspect	Third Aspect
Great Bear	Sirius	Pleiades
Life	Consciousness	Form
Spirit	Soul	Body
Will	Love	Intelligence
Father	Son	Holy Spirit
Shamballa	Hierarchy	Humanity
Sanat Kumara	The Christ	Leaders

The Great Bear, Sirius, and the Pleiades appear in this table for two reasons. One is in order to illustrate their relationship to the three fundamental aspects. The second reason is to indicate that these three star systems control and govern the evolutionary development of our entire solar system.

The Great Bear is associated with the first aspect, Sirius with the second aspect, and the Pleiades with the third aspect. Because our solar system is developing the second aspect of love, and Sirius is the second aspect influencing our solar system (on a cosmic scale), all the items in the middle column of table 26 are fundamentally connected no matter how distant they may be from one another, no matter whether we think in terms of physical, psychological, or spiritual evolution.

As we shall see, there is a fundamental connection between the sun Sirius and the Christ which inevitably includes the Great Invocation. A case can be made for this cosmic link by piecing together the various but scattered bits of information given by

Djwhal Khul in his various books. Beyond that investigative process however, the Great Invocation itself offers hints and clues to a possible link with Sirius through esoteric numerology.

The Christ, Sirius, and the Great Invocation

In 1945, as WWII was drawing to a close, the Tibetan began releasing information about the Great Invocation and the reappearance of the Christ as the World Teacher for the Aquarian Age. Scattered within these writings were a few statements by DK that implied a connection between the Great Invocation, the Christ, and Sirius.

As a result of the defeat of the Axis powers during WWII, the Christ announced to the Hierarchy that He would incarnate in physical form once again. As a result of His decision, DK indicates the Lord of the World, Sanat Kumara, gave the Christ permission to use a very ancient mantram known as the third stanza of the Invocation for Power and Light, or what is now popularly known as the Great Invocation. In the book *Discipleship in the New Age,* vol. II, DK writes "This mantram is peculiarly and essentially Christ's Own Mantram."[6] This is an interesting remark by the Tibetan when juxtaposed with the following statement about the Christ's use of the Great Invocation: "He used it Himself for the first time, we are told, at the time of the Full Moon of June, 1945."[7] Remember, it is "so ancient" that the phrases are "without date or background of any kind," and only the most exalted spiritual Beings—including Sanat Kumara—had been sounding this ancient mantram for countless eons; yet "this mantram is peculiarly and essentially Christ's Own Mantram."

The next hint dropped by the Master DK is when He is discussing the use of the Great Invocation by Alice Bailey and others in the discipleship group working with Djwhal Khul in the 1930's and 1940's. He tells them, "In receiving this Invocation, in its use and distribution, you have been participating in a cosmic event of tremendous importance."[8] A *cosmic event*—not planetary, not systemic (of our solar system), but cosmic. Is the Tibetan hinting at a relationship between the Christ, the Great Invocation, and Sirius?

In the book *The Rays and the Initiations* DK notes that:

> This Sirian influence was not recognised, and little of it was definitely focussed in the Hierarchy, until Christ came and revealed the love of God to humanity. He is the expression, par excellence, of a Sirian initiation, and it is to that high place He will eventually go.[9]

Did the Christ—the first Sirian Initiate—receive permission to use His own mantram held in trust by Sanat Kumara and used by these Exalted Beings for ages because the Great Invocation is a Sirian Word of Power? And might it be possible that since the Christ finally earned the right to use it and then passed it on to the Hierarchy of Masters to use, and it was finally given in word form for humanity to use that we have all been participating in a *cosmic event of tremendous importance*? The question naturally arises as to what importance the star Sirius has in relation to our Earth and solar system.

DK states that Sirius is closely related to Sanat Kumara and consequently to our Earth:

> There is a relationship of very ancient date between our Lord of the World, Sanat Kumara, and the Lord of Sirius, and this exists in spite of the fact that our planet is not a sacred planet.[10]

Perhaps this relationship is relevant to the evolution of the human kingdom on our planet. We already know from our previous investigations into the nature of Sanat Kumara that He made a "great sacrifice" by lowering His vibratory nature enough to allow Him to take etheric form on Earth, even though He is not registered by our physical senses. The effect of Sanat Kumara incarnating onto the etheric level of our world was the creation of the human kingdom. The wisdom teachings tell us that the individualized human soul was created and embodied in the animal men wandering the Earth approximately eighteen million years ago. At that moment in time the human consciousness, which had a sense of individual selfhood, was born.

While discussing the principle of freedom in a section on the subject of Sirius, the Tibetan mentions that "This divine principle represents an aspect of the influence which Sirius exerts on our solar system and particularly on our planet."[11] He then adds that:

> It is the principle of freedom which enables Sanat Kumara to dwell on the Earth...It is responsible for His being known as the "Great

> Sacrifice," for (under the control of this law) He created our planetary life and all that is within and upon it, in order to learn to wield this law with full understanding, in full consciousness, and yet at the same time to bring release to the myriad forms of His creation.[12]

According to the information provided by Djwhal Khul, Sirius is of paramount importance to our solar system as well as to our tiny planet. In the words of DK:

> This great Sun which is to our solar Logos what the Monad [the divine life in each human being, JB] is to the spiritual man, has a peculiar part to play where our Earth is concerned. It might be considered by those with a sound sense of occult proportion that our tiny planet with its planetary Logos (one of the "imperfect Gods" of *The Secret Doctrine*) would be too small to enter in the slightest way into the consciousness of that Supreme Illumined Entity Who is greater even than our Solar Logos. Such, however, is the case.[13]

We are only able to construct a crude outline of a profound mystery lying beyond our capacity to comprehend in its true reality as we attempt to summarize the relationship between Sirius, the solar Logos, Sanat Kumara, the Christ, and the Great Invocation. Although DK "explains" this mysterious relationship with Sirius using the scatter technique of esoteric writing, we are still left with huge gaps in the story. According to Djwhal Khul, these gaps are deliberately left in various parts of His books (and other teachings of the Hierarchy) because certain information is considered too potent for public distribution.

Thus, we are dealing with several layers of information in DK's esoteric writing:

1. There is the teaching itself which provides the needed information on any given topic of esoteric practice, philosophy or history of events, e.g., the life of Christ.
2. Hints are placed in the teaching for students who are able to go deeper into a given topic if the student is willing and able to do so.
3. Sometimes one bit of information cannot be given without revealing something else which must remain hidden. In such instances occult blinds are placed in the work. An example of an occult blind is in the assigning of colors to the seven rays. Students generally visualize color during meditation. This activity attracts energy into the psychological field of

the meditator. If the true color (ray energy) was invoked before a student was ready to receive it, various negative reactions would likely occur in the student's life. The important point is, this does not mean students should not meditate; it doesn't mean colors should not be used. It does mean, however, that a particular color may in fact be directly connected to a more esoteric color, which the student will *gradually* assimilate into his or her psychological system via the exoteric or outer color. A blind has been drawn over the reality as a temporary protection of the student while they still proceed with meditation and the use of color.

4. The last aspect in the layering of esoteric writing involves the deliberate withholding of information on a given topic without any hope of uncovering the true nature of that topic. Although some details can be given to the public, much is left unsaid and must be accepted on faith until more information is made available. In effect, the keys are withheld. These instances, and there are many of them in DK's writing, are usually associated with the mysteries of initiation, which surface gradually in a series of revelations.

The challenge for us is the probability that we are dealing with all four of these layers as we investigate the Great Invocation and its possible relationship to Sirius. Despite these limitations we must move forward as best we can, because the clues for pursuing this mystery have been given to us. We must assume that the Tibetan placed this material about Sirius and related topics in our hands because there is a message in it that can be deciphered. Our main uncertainty is knowing how much of the story we are meant to uncover.

The esoteric clues assembled to this point reveal the following: Our solar system is the physical embodiment of a solar Being on a scale of existence far beyond our human stage of evolution. This solar Logos shares Its Conscious Life, in some mysterious way, with the Logos of the star Sirius. In fact, DK describes this region of space as "a great force centre which we generalise by calling it by the name of the sun Sirius." DK says both systems are separate in time and space, but our solar system is subjectively influenced and operates under the governance of the Sirian system. In addition to this, Sanat Kumara, our incarnated planetary Logos, has a special relationship with the Sirian Logos. Through the help of the Sirian

Logos, Sanat Kumara was able to make a "great sacrifice and take etheric form" on Earth. This sacrificial act generated those conditions which brought the human kingdom with its free-willed mental nature into existence.

As a result of the evolutionary process of consciousness expansion, animal man developed into civilized man; some even developed beyond the human kingdom and entered into the fifth kingdom called the spiritual Hierarchy. One of those animal men evolved into the One we call the Christ. He became the first human (working through the form of Jesus 2,000 years ago) to achieve a level of conscious evolution which equaled the first degree of the Sirian level of consciousness expansion. The esoteric teachings call such expansions initiations.

Finally, in 1945, the Christ made a decision to return to Earth in physical form rather than just "overlighting" humanity with His spiritual Presence. As a result, Sanat Kumara granted the Christ permission to use an ancient mantram which no human or Member of the Hierarchy had ever used before—it is, according to the Tibetan, "a formula which has been in possession of the Hierarchy ever since it was founded on Earth." Only Sanat Kumara and His Assistants in the sixth kingdom had used this mantram. Despite this, however, DK states that this "Word of Power" is essentially Christ's own mantram. This seems to suggest that Sanat Kumara has held it in trust for the use of the first Initiate of the Sirian degree.

Did Sanat Kumara sacrifice Himself for these millions of years in order to carry out a special mission for the Great Lives Who inhabit the region of Sirius? By finally using the Great Invocation are we human beings, after millions of years, now engaged in some greater evolutionary Plan of cosmic importance? Might we be the subject of some special experiment in consciousness evolution being directed and supervised by advanced Lives from the region of Sirius? Are we, in fact, now using a Sirian mantram especially prepared for us over 18 million years ago—before we even existed on this planet as human beings ensouled in animal bodies? The words used by DK earlier in this book are brought into sharper focus in this context:

> It [the Great Invocation, JB] has in these Archives, an indicatory symbol beside it which indicates the era or period in human history during which it can and should be used. It is interesting to us to note that the evolution of humanity is in line with the indicated timing.

Who prepared those projections of the evolutionary timing of humanity? Did this "Word of Power"—this Great Invocation—originate in the Sirian solar system? The Master Djwhal Khul has more hints to offer, but first let's gather information about Sirius from other sources.

Sirius: Isis-Sothis

The star Sirius was identified with Isis by the ancient Egyptians. The following two passages clearly depict this. In H.P. Blavatsky's *Theosophical Glossary* we read:

> Sirius (Gr.) In Egyptian, *Sothis*. The dog-star: the star worshipped in Egypt and reverenced by the Occultists; by the former because its heliacal rising with the Sun was a sign of the beneficent inundation of the Nile, and by the latter because it is mysteriously associated with Thoth-Hermes, god of wisdom, and Mercury, in another form. Thus Sothis-Sirius had, and still has, a mystic and direct influence over the whole *living* heaven, and is connected with almost every god and goddess. It was "Isis in the heaven" and called *Isis-Sothis*, for Isis was "in the constellation of the dog", as is declared on her monuments....Being connected with the Pyramid, Sirius was, therefore, connected with the initiations which took place in it. A temple to Sirius-Sothis once existed within the great temple of Denderah. To sum up, all religions are not, as Dufeu, the French Egyptologist, sought to prove, derived from Sirius, the dog-star, but Sirius-Sothis is certainly found in connection with every religion of antiquity.[14]

Turning to *Burnham's Celestial Handbook* we find further confirmation of the Isis-Sothis-Sirius connection:

> Sirius was the revered "Nile Star" or "Star of Isis" to the ancient Egyptians; its annual appearance just before dawn at the summer solstice heralded the coming rise of the Nile, upon which Egyptian agriculture- and in fact all life in Egypt- depended. In about 3000 BC this "heliacal rising" occurred about June 25, and is referred to in many temple inscriptions where the star is called the "Divine Septe" (or Sopet or Sothis) and is identified with the soul of Isis. In the temple of Isis-Hathor at Denderah appears the inscription: "*Her Majesty Isis shines into the temple on New Year's Day, and she mingles her light with that of her father Ra* [the Sun, JB] *on the horizon.*"[15]

Isis was the wife and sister of Osiris. Together they were the chief Goddess and God of ancient Egypt. According to the myth, Osiris was sealed in a coffin by his jealous brother Set. The coffin was placed in the Nile where it eventually floated out to sea. Isis searched for the coffin in many lands before she discovered it. She took Osiris back to Egypt, but Set found the body once again and cut it into fourteen parts. Isis found all the parts except the phallus, which was lost in the Nile and swallowed by a fish. Isis, however, fashioned a new phallus out of gold, managed to reassemble Osiris, and bring him back to life. Thereupon, she was able to conceive a son by him who was called Horus. Isis raised Horus secretly in the Nile delta, and when he was mature enough, through Osiris' guidance from the underworld, Horus eventually avenged his father's death by defeating Set in battle and regaining control of his father's empire.

Although there is much more detail to this myth, it is not too difficult to see a distinct similarity to the nativity story of Christianity, especially the mysterious conception of Horus from the gold phallus of Osiris. David Fideler points out that:

> Harpocrates, a form of the Egyptian solar divinity Horus, represents the new-born sun as an infant. His mother was the goddess Isis, and he is often represented seated upon her lap. This iconography of the goddess with her divine, solar child is thought by many scholars to have prepared the way for the Christian iconography of the "Madonna and child."[16]

The point of this brief description of the Osiris-Isis story is to clarify the central role Isis played in the religious lives of the ancient Egyptians, but it should be mentioned that Osiris also held an equal if not more important place in the Egyptian religion. Osiris represents life everlasting. His life symbolizes renewal due to his death and resurrection. Without Isis' intervention, however, this rebirth would not have happened, and Horus would not have been born to avenge his father's death.

We are dealing with the three primary aspects of God in this Egyptian myth. We need to realize that even though Osiris, Isis, and Horus are three distinct deities in the myth, they are actually three expressions or aspects of One Life lying beyond our ability to comprehend except through Its aspects. All three aspects of the divine trinity are simply different expressions of God; they appear separate in the objective world of time and space. In simple terms, they work as a team, but they cycle in and out of power according to the circumstances of life. This basic triplicity operates at every level of the universe, from the atom to a solar system. Thus, Osiris, Isis, and Horus are three aspects of One Source of Life. If we use the information about Sirius provided by Djwhal Khul, we can say that Sirius is a candidate for the Source of the life of our solar system and by default our Earth. Therefore, we will theorize that Isis represents one of three aspects of the Sirian system, namely the feminine or third aspect—the Great Mother. We must be careful, however, not to confuse sexual forms in the physical world with the archetypal polarities which are the causes responsible for the effects we call male and female.

Isis had a wide influence on Egyptian and Greek religion. The cult of Isis absorbed the goddesses of other religions wherever it spread in the ancient world. The name Isis is actually the Hellenicized version of her original Egyptian name, Ast, which means throne.[17] She is usually depicted with a headdress of a solar disk and carrying the Egyptian ankh, the symbol of immortality. In the words of the famed Egyptologist Sir Wallis Budge:

> An examination of the texts of all periods proves that Isis always held in the minds of the Egyptians a position which was entirely different from that of every other goddess...it is correct to say that from the earliest to the latest dynasties Isis was the greatest goddess of Egypt...[18]

Manly P. Hall offers many insights about the Goddess Isis in his monumental book *The Secret Teachings of All Ages*. Referring to the magical powers associated with Isis, Manly Hall writes:

> The mysteries of Hermeticism, the great spiritual truths hidden from the world by the ignorance of the world and the keys of the secret doctrines of the ancient philosophers, are all symbolized by the Virgin Isis. Veiled from head to foot, she reveals her wisdom only to the tried and initiated few who have earned the right to enter her sacred presence, tear from the veiled figure of Nature its shroud of obscurity, and stand face to face with the Divine Reality....
>
> The priests of Isis became adepts in the use of the unseen forces of Nature. They understood hypnotism, mesmerism, and similar practices long before the modern world dreamed of their existence....
>
> Plutarch describes the requisites of a follower of Isis in this manner... he alone is a true servant or follower of this Goddess, who after has heard, and been made acquainted in a proper manner with the history of the actions of these Gods, searches into the hidden truths which lie concealed under them, and examines the whole by the dictates of reason and philosophy.[19]

Quoting Budge once more:

> It is said that Isis was well skilled in the use of words of power, and it was by means of these that she restored her husband to life, and obtained from him an heir. It is not known what the words were which she uttered on this occasion, but she appears to have obtained them from Thoth, the "lord of divine words," and it was to him that she appealed for help to restore Horus to life after he had been stung to death by a scorpion.[20]

These various descriptions provide some perspective on the enormous breadth of influence which Isis had in the ancient world. Isis is a veiled mystery, all powerful, and able to perform magic. She is the Great Mother of all, the wife and sister of Osiris, and the mother of Horus, and is even transformed much later into Mary, the mother of Jesus. Isis is the Queen of Heaven, Isis-Sothis, Sirius.

Isis is the personification of the power of the word to "bend reality" and override the law of physics. Is this not the magical power of the Great Invocation as described by DK? In so many words, the Tibetan tells us that when this Great Invocation is used with mental focus and with fixed intent it has the power to effect great change in the lives of all who use it. Djwhal Khul states that the Great Invocation is the most effective tool we have for invoking the reappearance of the Christ, the World Teacher for the Aquarian Age.

Isis Unveiled

It is only natural to question any possible connection between a world prayer for peace and an ancient Egyptian goddess. But remember, Isis represents Sirius and it is through the help of the Lord of Sirius, according to Djwhal Khul, that the human kingdom along with its civilization and culture on our Earth was brought into manifestation by Sanat Kumara.

Hints of such a possibility are found in the book *Hermetica*, which is a collection of the teachings ascribed to Hermes Trismegistus, who will be discussed in detail in chapter 10. This extract entitled "Kore Kosmu" is in the form of a dialogue between Isis and her son Horus.

> Tell me then, mother, How did Earth attain to the happy lot of receiving the efflux of God? And Isis answered: Mighty Horus, do not ask me

> to describe to you the origin of the stock whence you are sprung; for it is not permitted to inquire into the birth of gods. This only I may tell you, that God who rules alone, the fabricator of the universe, bestowed on the earth for a little time your great father Osiris and the great goddess Isis, that they might give the world the help it so much needed.[21]

In a very real sense, Isis personifies the constellation Virgo, the Virgin. Speaking about Virgo, Djwhal Khul states that "its symbology concerns the whole goal of the evolutionary process which is to shield, nurture and finally reveal the hidden reality."[22] This sums up the above quotation in which Isis tells Horus that their role is to help the world. Later in the same text Isis describes the gifts and knowledge she and her husband Osiris have given to humanity. We will detail these gifts in the next chapter, but we must not get ahead of our investigation.

Let's just say at this point that Isis represents a spiritual energy of great wisdom and power. She is that force which fosters the growth of the Christ in every human heart. She is a symbol and personification of the cosmic virgin mother who can perform magic, who knows words of power taught to her by Thoth. Note that Thoth is also Mercury, and it is Mercury which rules Virgo.

The Great Invocation symbolizes Virgo and Isis in that it is a word of power which the Tibetan says is the most effective tool we have for invoking the reappearance of the Christ. As we will soon see, the goddess Isis, an aspect of the Sirian system and personification of Virgo the virgin, nurturer of the Christ, is intimately connected with the Great Invocation. Is it possible that the Great Invocation is an ancient Word of Power from the Lord of Sirius, given to our Earth for use by humanity when we were finally evolved enough to use it?

We have already examined the key words and their relation to Sanat Kumara. In chapter 5, we briefly mentioned the significance of Sanat Kumara in relation to the middle phrase of the Great Invocation, "God is known." This showed that there were 55 words ahead of this phrase and 55 words following it. We then evaluated the symbolism of the number 55 in its correspondence to the numerological value of "Sanat." Now let's continue our journey by delving deeper into the heart of the Great Invocation—its middle word.

The word found at the very middle of the Great Invocation is "IS." The AN value of "is" equals 28. There is more to this word beyond its obvious meaning which Webster's defines as the third person singular tense of the verb to be. Philosophically it is certainly true that reality is, the universe is, and God is. But beyond this there does not appear to be anything more to find here. There is one interesting aspect about the word "is," however—it is half of the word Isis. We now know that Isis was associated with the star Sirius by the ancient Egyptians, so this fragmented form of Isis (is) could be a clue to further insights.

Simply put, if "is" has a value of 28, than Isis naturally has a value of 56 because Isis is "is" repeated two times. It then follows that because there are 113 words in the Great Invocation, there are fifty-six words ahead of "is" and fifty-six words following "is," and these fifty-six words correspond to the numerological value of Isis. In effect we can say that the middle word of the Great Invocation is half of Isis or that Isis is found *half veiled* at the heart of the Great Invocation. This is definitely an occult blind left for discovery in the sense that the word "veiled" equals 57, and the fifty-seventh word of the Great Invocation is the middle word "IS." Therefore, the fifty-seventh word is *veiling* or *hiding something*. In addition, the phrase "Isis veiled" equals 113 which corresponds to the 113 words comprising the Great Invocation. In other words, the Great Invocation symbolizes the veiled Isis.

In addition to all the above, it must be added that 56 is also the RAN value of *"the sun Sirius*." Therefore, Sirius is not only identified with Isis in the religion of ancient Egypt, but Sirius is also present in the esoteric numerology and structure of the Great Invocation itself.

Figure 9. Isis is Sirius.

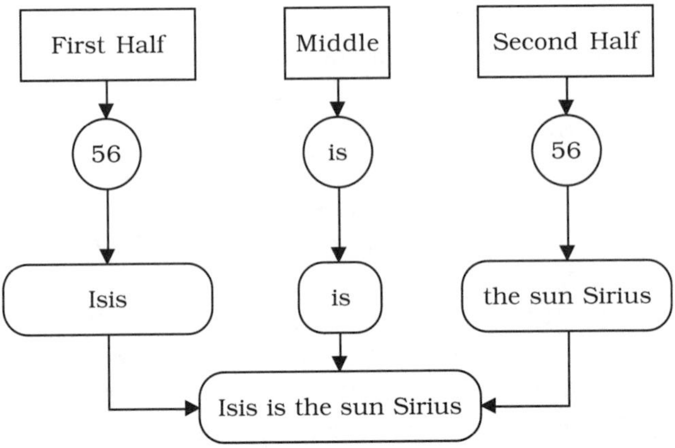

First Half
56
Isis
Middle
is
is
Second Half
56
the sun Sirius
Isis is the sun Sirius

The theme of Isis and her veiled nature is symbolically represented on the mysterious set of cards called the Tarot. Because their symbolism is so universal and they are often traced back to ancient Egypt, they may contain further information about Isis-Sothis and her identification with Sirius.

The Tarot and Ancient Egypt

The Tarot is a deck of seventy-eight cards of symbolic pictures used for divination. The deck consists of twenty-two major trump cards, or major arcana, and fifty-six minor arcana. The minor arcana containsfour suits of fourteen cards each. Modern day playing cards have their origin in the Tarot.

Opinions differ as to the age of the Tarot. Some researchers believe the cards originated in fourteenth century Europe, while others think they originated in ancient Egypt. Arthur Edward Waite did not believe the Tarot originated in Egypt, but he felt the cards contained universal symbology that could have been expressed in any culture that taught the Mysteries of Initiation. Thus Egypt, India, China, Chaldea, and Greece, among other countries qualified.

The reason for bringing the Tarot cards into this investigation has more to do with the symbols contained on the cards than with their origin. If these cards represent the ageless wisdom in their depiction of symbols, then they are probably quite old and universal in their essential meanings. We have chosen the Rider-Waite deck for the simple reason that it is the original (perhaps classic) and probably best known of the Tarot decks published this century.

The High Priestess—Arcanum II—is of specific interest to our study because she is the veiled Isis. In his classic work *The Pictorial Key to the Tarot,* A. E. Waite has this to say about The High Priestess:

> It is sometimes held to represent the Divine Law and the Gnosis, in which case the Priestess corresponds to the idea of the Shekinah.[23] She is the Secret Tradition and the higher sense of the instituted Mysteries.[24]

Waite's reference to the Mysteries concerns spiritual initiation and revelations about the nature and origin of human existence, the nature of God, and the world. According to DK, initiation is of the greatest importance in relation to Sirius, thus revealing a connection between The High Priestess (the veiled Isis), Sirius, and initiation.

Figure 10. The High Priestess.

The term *Shekinah* is also significant, meaning a Hebrew goddess or feminine archetype relating to the Holy Spirit. This is the third, or Mother aspect which is one of the three aspects expressed by Sirius. The Tibetan says the *Shekinah* is "the light which 'ever shineth in the East.'"[25] Waite continues:

> She has been called Occult Science on the threshold of the Sanctuary of Isis but she is really the Secret Church, the House which is of God and man....she is the spiritual Bride and Mother, the daughter of the stars and the Higher Garden of Eden. She is, in fine, the Queen of the borrowed light, but this is the light of all. She is the Moon nourished by the milk of the Supernal Mother.
>
> In a manner, she is also the Supernal Mother herself—that is to say, she is the bright reflection. It is in this sense of reflection that her truest and highest name in [sym]bolism[sic.] is *Shekinah*—the

> co-habiting glory....There are some respects in which this card is the highest and holiest of the Greater Arcana.[26]

When Waite describes The High Priestess, Isis, as the "Secret Church," he is describing the spiritual Hierarchy, agent of the second aspect of the divine trinity on our planet. When he calls The High Priestess the "House which is of God" we may interpret this to mean Shamballa, the first aspect of the trinity. When Waite tells us The High Priestess is Shekinah, she then represents the Great Mother, the third aspect of the trinity, divine Intelligence, Sophia-Wisdom.

Sirius represents each one of these aspects in relation to our planet. Sirius is the origin of our planetary Hierarchy and of the process of initiation. The sun Sirius administers the Law of Karma throughout our solar system and therefore governs the activities of Shamballa. Sanat Kumara was only able to incarnate on Earth through the aid of the Sirian Law of Freedom. And finally, Sirius is the origin of the divine Intelligence of manas that flows into our solar system. Jason C. Lotterhand, in his book *The Thursday Night Tarot*, describes The High Priestess in this way:

> On the scroll, the word "Tora" reveals that Tarot speaks the Law of Nature, or Isis. The High Priestess is Isis Veiled in this picture, and Isis Unveiled in The Star card (Key 17). Isis is very much like Alma Mater, as we call our universities. Alma mater, the all-embracing Mother, integrates all of life's different departments and brings them into unity.[27]

Lotterhand goes on to explain that The Star (Arcanum XVII) represents Isis unveiled and that this symbolizes the revelation of nature's secrets as the woman in Arcanum XVII is naked or unveiled as opposed to the mysterious veiled High Priestess. Lotterhand states that "Isis has an occult connection with the star Sirius, which is said to have an overseeing helping function for Earth. Sirius is like the main star in Key 17."[28] Turning back to Waite, we find him describing The Star card as "Dog-star, or Sirius." Later Waite describes the woman on the card: "...the figure will appear as the type of Truth unveiled, glorious in undying beauty, pouring on the waters of the soul some part and measure of her priceless possession."[29]

Following Waite's comments on the "waters of the soul," note that five rivulets of water flow from the pitcher in the left hand of the figure. Four rivulets appear to remain on dry land while the fifth mixes with the water in the pool. The number 5 is prominent once more, but divided into 4 and 1. The four streams are the four elements of nature, while the fifth is the etheric energy underlying physical matter, returning to its universal source in the pool.

The water flowing from the pitcher in the right hand fills the pool, creating seven concentric rings. This could be interpreted as a symbolic reference to our own solar system, with its sun and seven sacred planets. The overall meaning in the context of our subject suggests the supervision and mentoring of life in our solar system by Sirius. Again the presence of the numbers 5 and 7 correlate with the number theme of the Great Invocation.

Figure 11. The Star.

The presence of the central star with seven identical (but smaller) stars suggests once more the idea of a parent and its seven offspring. (This is mirrored in the pool with its central source of water flowing from the pitcher, along with the seven emanating ripples.) Each star possesses eight rays of light. Esoterically, the number 8 symbolizes the Christ consciousness. This suggests a central star or emanating source of Christ energy—a Cosmic Christ—spawning or developing new sources of Christ energy representing the second aspect of Love-Wisdom.

The stars, therefore, are grouped as 1 and 7. These two digits comprise the number of The Star card itself (17). Since there are seven stars with eight rays each, there are fifty-six rays of energy. As we have just seen, the number of these rays is the value of Isis and "the sun Sirius."

Overlooking this entire scene is the ibis, perched on a tree at the right. The ibis is the Egyptian symbol for Thoth-Hermes, who, as we learned earlier in this chapter, is the god associated with numbers, alphabets, words of power, and most importantly, Isis and Sirius.

The symbolism of The Star card provides a rich source of interpretation, nevertheless, the presence of the numbers 5, 14, 17, 7, 8, and 56 correlate quite well with our investigation.

The third Tarot card related to the Great Invocation is The Sun, Arcanum XIX. This card is important to our study because of the relationship between our sun or solar Logos and the sun Sirius. Before we explain the connection of The Sun card to the Great Invocation, it is important to establish a clearer connection between our sun and the sun Sirius. Several examples of this connection were given earlier, but I will offer a few more now.

In the book *A Treatise on Cosmic Fire* DK is describing the Laws of Thought. First He tabulates three cosmic laws. The first law is entitled the Law of Synthesis:

> It is the law governing the thought form of that One of the cosmic Logoi in Whose consciousness both our system, and our greater centre [Sirius? JB], have a part.[30]

> The system of the Sirian Logos is on the cosmic mental plane, and in a subtle way, incomprehensible to us, our Logos, with His system, forms a part of a still greater Logos.[31]

> The second law is the *Law of Attraction and Repulsion.* Fundamentally, the law describes the compelling force of attraction that holds our solar system to the Sirian.[32]

Before describing the seven laws of our own solar system, DK tells us an intermediate law exists:

> Which is the synthetic law of the system of Sirius. This law is called by the generic term, the Law of Karma, and really predicates the effect the Sirian system has on our solar system. Each of the two systems, as regards its internal economy, is independent in time and space, or (in other words), in manifestation. We have practically no effect on our parent system, the reflex action is so slight as to be negligible, but very definite effects are felt in our system through causes arising in Sirius. These causes, when experienced as effect, are called by us the Law of Karma...
>
> The Lipika Lords of our system, the systemic Lords of Karma, are under the rule of a greater corresponding Lord on Sirius.[33]

As explained earlier, this scale of being is roughly analogous to atoms forming molecules, and molecules forming cells, and cells forming organs, and organs forming part of an organism. DK illustrates this idea with this final example of cosmic relationships:

> Each one of us, in due process of evolution, forms part of one of the Heavenly Men [planets in our solar system, JB], Who Themselves form the seven centres in that greater Heavenly Man, the Logos [our solar system, JB]. Yet, though we are merged with the whole, we do not lose our identity, but forever remain separated units of consciousness, though one with all that lives or is. In like manner our Logos loses not His identity, even though He forms part of the Consciousness of the Logos of Sirius. In His turn, the Sirian Logos forms one of the seven Grand Heavenly Men, who are the centres in the body of ONE OF WHOM NOUGHT MAY BE SAID.[34]

These extracts (and there are others) clearly indicate that our solar system has a definite connection to the sun Sirius and its system. In fact, the Tibetan is saying that we are subordinate to this greater system of Sirius—it is our parent system and administers cause and effect in our system, namely the Law of Karma. In light of this and the correspondences to Isis in the Tarot, it is not too much of a stretch to include The Sun card, Arcanum XIX, in this analysis.

Using a bit of simple arithmetic with the numbers of these three cards we discover The Sun (19) minus The High Priestess (2) equals The Star (17). In other words, when the veil of Isis is removed from the Sun it reveals the unveiled Isis—The Star; or 19 - 2 = 17. This is symbolically represented on the Sun Tarot card depicted in the

Figure 12. The Sun.

Waite deck, if not in other designs. Looking at the card, note there are 10 sets of straight and wavy alternating rays of light streaming from the Sun. These rays spell "is" ten times and ISIS five times—the straight rays being the letter "I" and the wavy rays being the letter "S." But, there is one straight ray left over—a letter "I." This is very significant because ISIS has a numerological value of 56 and 5 x 56 = 280. When we add the additional "I" valued at 9 we get a final total of 289. The number 289 is the square of 17, and 17 is the number of "The Star" or Sirius! The Sun is the cosmic veil covering the star Sirius. In addition, the presence of the ten wavy lines and the eleven straight lines also corresponds to the ten and eleven key words found in the Great Invocation. The twenty-one key words contain 95 letters and Sirius equals 95 AN.

An additional set of fascinating clues emerges in an intriguing book entitled *The Sirius Mystery*, by Robert K.G. Temple. In his book Temple tells about the Dogon, an African tribe living in the former French Sudan of Mali that possesses detailed knowledge about the star Sirius and its invisible (except through a telescope) companion star Sirius B. The entire religion of the Dogon is based on Sirius and its invisible companion (and possibly a third star, Sirius C):

> The Dogon were in possession of information concerning the system of the star Sirius which was so incredible that I felt impelled to research the material. The results, in 1974, seven years later, are that I have been able to show that the information which the Dogon possess is really more than five thousand years old and was possessed by the ancient Egyptians in the pre-dynastic times before 3200 B.C., from which people I show that the Dogon are partially descended culturally, and probably physically as well.[35]

Speaking about the sacred Dogon traditions Temple goes on to say:

> I have now been able to trace these back to ancient Egypt, and they seem to reveal a contact in the distant past between our planet Earth and an advanced race of intelligent beings from another planetary system several light years away in space.[36]

The research conducted by Temple adds much to what we have already uncovered about the ancient Egyptians. Part of Temple's investigation involves the Egyptian god Anubis, the son of Isis' sister Nephthys and Osiris. (Some sources say the father was Set, the brother and killer of Osiris.) Anubis assisted Isis and her sister Nephthys during the funeral of Osiris by embalming and wrapping Osiris' body in linen. Anubis also presides over the weighing of the heart of the deceased, ensuring the scale is properly balanced beforehand. Temple tells us:

> Anubis is variously represented as jackal-headed and dog-headed in Egyptian art. Wallis Budge adds: "Thus much, however, is certain, that in ancient times the Egyptians paid the greatest reverence and honour to the Dog."[37]

Beyond the obvious connection to the Dog Star Sirius exists a very curious link between Isis, Anubis, and The High Priestess Tarot card. Citing Plutarch Temple continues:

> And when the child (Anubis, child of Nephthys by Osiris) had been found, after great toil and trouble, with the help of dogs which led Isis to it, it was brought up and became her guardian and attendant, receiving the name Anubis, and it is said to protect the gods just as dogs protect men.[38]

Temple is trying to make the point that Anubis may symbolize an orbit around Sirius A (Isis) because Anubis (Sirius B or C?) is always with Isis protecting her.

This intimate connection is further illustrated in the Tarot card of Isis as The High Priestess (figure 10). There are six letters depicted on this card—B, J, T, O, R, A. The letters B and J stand for the Hebrew words Boaz and Jachin, the pillars in the temple of Solomon, or the universal pairs of opposites e.g. Yin and Yang. The TORA is the scroll of the Hebrew Law and also an anagram for ROTA or Latin for wheel from which TAROT is derived. The really fascinating aspect of these letters, however, is that they equal 66 (AN) when added together, and 66 is also the value of Anubis. Is this a coincidence or another clue hidden within the Tarot (among other places) pointing to some connection between Sirius and our Earth?

Having said all this, let's follow this Egyptian thread further with Temple:

> A name similar to Anubis...and which is also associated with Isis-Sothis (Sirius) is Anukis, a fellow-goddess of Sothis who, along with the goddess Satis, sails in the same celestial boat with Sothis in the Egyptian paintings. There are thus the three goddesses together, possibly a description of Sirius A, Sirius B, and Sirius C, and emphasizing that the Sirius system is really thought to be a three-star system.[39]

The idea that the ancient Egyptians believed three Goddesses (stars) sailed together in the same "celestial boat" coincides with DK's remarks when He refers to Sirius as a system. Temple goes on to describe Anukis:

> The goddess Anukis holds two jars from which she pours water, possibly indicating two watery planets around her star? All the references to the Sothis heavens are to a watery, reed-growing paradise. Many archaeologists have surmised that this refers to some specifically Egyptian locale. But no one is sure. What is known is that the

> heaven is almost invariably associated with the Sirius system and is described as being prolific of vegetation and watery.[39]

The following quotation is again from Waite's *The Pictorial Key to the Tarot* in which he is describing the 17th Arcanum, The Star:

> The female figure in the foreground is entirely naked. Her left knee is on the land and her right foot upon the water. She pours Water of Life from two great ewers, irrigating sea and land.[40]

Perhaps there is something to be said about the correlation of Waite's imagery on the Tarot with ancient Egyptian religion. This is especially true when we convert the names of these three goddesses to numbers; we arrive once more, at the value 289 or the square of 17, the number of The Star. Also note the 10, 6, 5 number pattern of the word lengths which corresponds to the pattern of the twenty-one key words.

Table 27. Three Goddesses of Egypt.

Name	AN Value	Word Length
Isis-Sothis	146	10
Anukis	75	6
Satis	68	5
Total	289	21

The threefold theme is an important part of our investigation. After all, we have discovered much about the Great Invocation by dividing it into three parts—a beginning, middle, and end. The three Egyptian goddesses equal the square of 17 or 289. The number 289 correlates quite well with the Tarot, and remarkably it also correlates to three phrases within the Great Invocation. Moreover, the three phrases are not just a set of unrelated words, but are in fact the three aspects of the fundamental triplicity of the ageless wisdom. These three phrases are the "Mind of God," "Heart of God," and "Will of God." Together they add up to 289 the square of 17 (17 x 17) and are found in the first three stanzas of the Great Invocation.

Therefore, these phrases are esoterically linked with The Star card Sirius. Note that these three phrases are composed of 28 letters, the perfect number found at the center of the Great Invocation.[41]

Table 28. The Three Aspects.

Phrase	AN Value	Length
Mind of God	87	9
Heart of God	99	10
Will of God	103	9
Total	289	28

We are not attempting to correlate the three goddesses with these three aspects or with the possible three stars in the Sirian system. It is remarkable enough to see the relationship between the three phrases of the Great Invocation, the three goddesses of ancient Egypt, the alternating rays on The Sun card, 289, the square of 17, and the 17th Star card, Sirius. These three goddesses and the three aspects of God from the Great Invocation also correlate with Sirius in an unexpected way described by DK:

> The influences of Sirius, [are] three in number.[42]
>
> [The three degrees of Masonry, JB] are related to the three major groups of Lives on Sirius, for there are there no kingdoms of nature, such as we possess.[43]

Several intriguing questions can be asked as we end this section: When the Great Invocation is divided into three parts, does it yield clues associated with Sirius because it is modeled according to the three major groups of Lives Who dwell there? Is the Great Invocation structured according to Sirian energy patterns, such as the three Sirian influences, due to its origin on Sirius? If so, is this inherent, like DNA, or has the Great Invocation been deliberately worded in order to indicate its place of origin?

Let's finish this section by examining this veiled/unveiled theme using esoteric numerology. Referring to the table following, we might say that the Great Invocation is "Isis veiled" or The High

Priestess prior to studying it with esoteric numerology. When we discover The Star veiled by The Sun (card) at the center of the Great Invocation, we see "Isis Unveiled." We then realize that The Star is the sun Sirius. The numerological value of "the sun Sirius" (182) equals The Star (91) doubled (2 x 91 = 182). In addition, we can also state that 182 equals 91 + 91 or 9191, which translates into ISIS (using RAN values 9 for I and 1 for S). The numerological values of the three crucial elements in table 29 equal 443, which is the *number of letters* contained in the Great Invocation. This means that the true nature of the Great Invocation (Isis Veiled as The High Priestess) is revealed as a Word of Power related to the sun Sirius when the veil of Isis is removed (Isis Unveiled, The Star).

Table 29. Sirius Unveiled.

Isis Veiled	113
Isis Unveiled	148
The sun Sirius	182
Total	443

God is Known

Further proof of this veiled connection is found at the middle of the Great Invocation once again, only this time via the middle phrase "God is known." These three words have an AN value of 131 and a RAN value of 50.[44] In many ways Sanat Kumara is the "God (Who) is known" because the 55 words ahead of "God is known" and the 55 words following it equal the value of "Sanat" which is also 55 (AN). But, as we have seen, the ageless wisdom acknowledges hierarchies of deities, many creators at different levels of the universe and in different dimensions beyond the physical level. Therefore, the phrase "God is known" may have different levels of meaning as does the entire Great Invocation.

For now, however we will focus on the RAN value of "God is known," which equals 50.[45] There are at least two significant factors which are of interest in relation to the number 50. First, Temple devotes an entire chapter of his book to the number 50. The chapter is entitled "The Sacred Fifty." The number 50 is especially sacred to the Dogon tribe because, according to their religion, Sirius B has an orbital period of 50 years in its movement around Sirius A. (Indeed this is proven astronomically as discussed earlier in *Burnham's Celestial Handbook.*) In this particular chapter, Temple mentions the "fifty great gods" called the Anunnaki. Temple says:

> They were literally restricted to the level of being a numerological cipher. They are continually invoked and are of importance—but they never did anything but sit on their thrones and "be fifty."[46]

Temple then proceeds to examine the fifty heroes of the Sumerian tale of Gilgamesh, and the fifty Argonauts of Jason. Temple offers much more information on this subject, but suffice it to say, some symbolic connection exists between the value of 50 at the center of the Great Invocation and the importance ascribed to the number 50 by the Dogon and the various mythologies of the ancients.

Divine Intervention

Temple relates the Dogon belief that the visitors from Sirius came to the Earth and set up a civilization here:

> Nommo is the collective name for the great culture-hero and founder of civilization who came from the Sirius system to set up society on the Earth. Nommo - or, to be more precise, the Nommos - were amphibious creatures...
> The system of Sirius, which is known as "land of the fish", and is the placenta of Nommo, is specifically called the "double placenta in the sky", referring to the fact that it is a binary star system. The "earth" which is in the Sirius system is "pure earth", whereas the "earth" which is in our solar system is "impure earth".
> The landing of Nommo on our Earth is called the "day of the fish."[47 48]

In *A Treatise on Cosmic Fire,* DK describes cosmic avatars from Sirius which appear similar to the Dogon reference to Nommo. Djwhal Khul writes:

> Their appearance in a solar system is very unusual...
> Such entities from Sirius appear at the occasion of the initiation of the solar Logos...The effect of such a visit as that of the Avatar from Sirius is seen as the sumtotal of civilisation and culture, viewing these from the standpoint of the entire system and in one flash of time.[49]

Did this visit of an Avatar from Sirius eventually set in motion the needed forces which led to the physical/etheric embodiment of Sanat Kumara on Earth?

Temple's detailed study of the Dogon tribe and their intimate knowledge of Sirius suggests some form of intervention by more advanced beings from that system. Apparently when these beings intervened in Earth affairs they taught those early humans the laws and principles of civilization, culture, science, and religion. Although this describes the Dogon view of pre-history, it also describes, in so many words, the arrival of Sanat Kumara and the 104 other Lords of the Flame on Earth some eighteen million years ago.

According to Temple, the Dogon people and their religion can be traced back to the Egyptians. Many stories of Atlantis and other lost civilizations can be found which describe an advanced civilization created by Gods or visitors from other worlds. Generally speaking, Atlantis was eventually destroyed by cataclysms resulting from a war between the forces of light and darkness. (This topic was discussed briefly in chapter 1.)

Researchers such as R. A. Schwaller de Lubicz, John Anthony West, and recently Graham Hancock believe there is evidence of a lost civilization prior to the Egyptians which was highly advanced. In his book *Serpent in the Sky,* West offers the following thought:

> How does a complex civilization spring full-blown into being? Look at a 1905 automobile and compare it to a modern one. There is no mistaking the process of "development." But in Egypt there are no parallels. Everything is there right at the start.
>
> The answer to the mystery is of course obvious, but because it is repellent to the prevailing cast of modern thinking, it is seldom seriously considered. *Egyptian civilization was not a "development", it was a legacy.*[50]

The Tibetan describes this lost civilization to some extent in the following passages:

> In those far-off times, the only people who had any true measure of intelligence were the disciples and initiates; they guided and guarded infant humanity...The Hierarchy was, in those days, present upon the earth as the priest-kings.[51]

DK goes on to explain that humanity was almost entirely emotional and aspirational at that time and had little mental development as is the case today. The people had a desire for beauty and "emotional completion."

> This was fostered in the people by the Hierarchy through the gift of various inventions and by the use of the instinctual masses of men in building great and beautiful cities and stupendous structures, the remnants of which persist until today. This was done under the expert guidance of the initiates and adepts who employed their knowledge of the nature of matter and energy to produce much that today man is gropingly endeavoring to discover and make possible. All that the modern processes of civilization have made possible, and much more than that which today comes under the name of scientific discovery were known in old Atlantis, but they were not developed by men themselves but given to them as a free gift, much as people today give to a child beautiful and wonderful things which the child uses and enjoys but which he does not understand in any way....Sanitation, hygiene, means of transportation and air machines were developed and of a very high order; these were not the result however of man's achievement but gifts from the Hierarchy, developed or constructed under wise guidance. There was command of air and water because the guides of the race knew how to control and master the forces of nature and of the elements, but none of it was the result of human understanding, knowledge or effort. The minds of men were undeveloped and not adequate to such a task, any more than is the mind of a little child.[52]

This rather lengthy extract on Atlantis clearly indicates a connection between the information provided by DK and the investigations of other researchers into the ancient past, especially Temple's work in regard to the Dogons' religious teaching about the god Nommo who brought civilization to mankind. Robert Eisler expands on this theme of divine gifts bestowed on early humanity in a discussion of the Babylonian God Oannes. In a chapter interestingly entitled "The Fishergod as A Culture-Hero," Eisler is describing the writings of a Babylonian priest named Berossos:

> This Neobabylonian Bël-priest relates, that in the first year after the creation of the world a "rational being" emerged from the Persian Gulf and landed on the shore of Babylonia. It had the body of a fish; under its fish-head, however, there was a human face and under its fish-tail a pair of human legs....This being, called Oannes, passed the day among men without partaking of any food, and taught them the art of writing as well as all sciences and crafts, the building of cities, the surveying of land, the observation of the stars, and finally the sowing and harvesting of all kinds of grain and plants.[53]

These activities sound very much like the work of Nommo and the priest-kings of the Hierarchy described by the Tibetan Djwhal Khul.

The real thrust of Eisler's book traces the origin and development of the "Fisher God" Orpheus from the ancient Greeks up to the time of Christianity and the early church with its adoption of the fish motif with Jesus as the Fisher of men. Before leaving Robert Eisler we offer one more comment by him:

> There is no doubt that this Neobabylonian Oannes story represents the most explicit extant version of the myth describing the Fish or Fishergod as lord and teacher of all wisdom. Yet traces of the same combination of ideas are not only found in the Greek, but also in other branches of Aryan tradition.[54]

All these commentaries indicate intelligent beings—be they Gods, demi-Gods, or extraterrestrials—visiting the Earth in prehistoric times and conferring high technology, science, civilization, and culture on early infant humanity. H.P. Blavatsky gives the following information:

> As to Enoch, Thoth or Hermes, Orpheus and Cadmus, these are all generic names, branches and offshoots of the seven primordial Sages—incarnated Dhyan Chohans or Devas, in Illusive, not mortal bodies—who taught Humanity all it knew, and whose earliest disciples assumed their Master's names.[55]

Along the same theme, HPB discusses a similar order of Intelligence called the Kabiri. This word is of Phoenician origin according to HPB (*Theosophical Glossary*), and means deity or god:

> They were also, in the beginning of times, the Rulers of Mankind, when, incarnated as Kings of the "Divine Dynasties," they gave the first impulse to civilization, and directed the mind with which they had endued men to the invention and perfection of all arts and sciences. Thus the Kabiri are said to have appeared as the benefactors of men, and as such they lived for ages in the memory of nations. To these Kabiri or Titans is ascribed the invention of letters...of laws and legislature, of architecture, as also of the various modes of magic, so called, and of the medical use of plants. Hermes, Orpheus, Cadmus, Asclepios, all those Demigods and Heroes...all are generic names.
>
> It is the Kabiri who are credited with having revealed the great boon of agriculture, by *producing* corn or wheat. What Isis-Osiris, the once living Kabirim, did in Egypt, that Ceres is said to have done in Sicily; they all belong to one class.[56]

We see that there is ample evidence from various sources that some form of higher intelligent life may very well have once visited the Earth either from another world and/or another dimension in order to guide and nurture the young human race to adulthood.

Temple's reference to amphibians is intriguing when we recall that the unclothed woman on The Star card has one foot on top of the water and the other on dry land. This might be symbolic of an amphibian life form, or perhaps it indicates control over the forces of nature. The references by the Dogon to Sirius as the "land of the fish" and the coming of Nommo to Earth as the "day of the fish" are quite significant in connection with the phrase "God is known" (RAN 50) due to the symbol of the fish used by early Christians. Christianity was born in the age of Pisces the fish; and did not Jesus tell his disciples to be fishers of men? Another curious link with fish is found in the Hebrew letter associated with The Star card of the Tarot. The Hebrew letter is *Tzaddi*—the fishhook!

The belief by the Dogon that our Earth is an "impure earth" compared to the "pure earth" of Sirius is somewhat descriptive of one of seven Earths that is inhabited by "demons and spirits." (See note 48.) (Recall DK's statement that we have a peculiar relationship to Sirius despite the fact that our Earth is a non-sacred planet.)

So far we have shown how the middle phrase "God is known" corresponds to various clues concerning Sirius. It has already been shown how the middle word relates to Isis, especially in relation to The High Priestess who partially veils the Tora on the Waite depiction of her, just as the word "is" half veils the word "Isis."

The great goddess Isis is identified by many names in ancient history; she is nature, wisdom, the Divine Mother, Sophia, and the Queen of Heaven. Blavatsky calls the Egyptian goddess Neith the Queen of Heaven in her *Theosophical Glossary*. In reference to Neith, Temple quotes E. A. Wallis Budge:

> One of the oldest goddesses of Egypt. She was the goddess of hunting and weaving, but was identified with many other goddesses such as Isis.[57]

(An interesting aspect of the goddess Neith is the fact that her name equals 56 using the RAN method, which is, of course the same value as Isis.) In G. A. Gaskell's *Dictionary of All Scriptures and Myths*, "Queen of Heaven" is "A symbol of the principle of buddhi, or the Wisdom-nature." Cross references include, Buddhi, Goddess, Isis, Lady, and Wisdom.[58] The phrase "The Queen of Heaven" has an AN value equal to 171, which is quite significant because this number relates directly to the three middle words of the Great Invocation—"God is known." These three words are the fifty-sixth, fifty-seventh, and fifty-eighth words in the Great Invocation. When these three word positions are added together they equal 171, the same value as "the Queen of Heaven"!

In effect, the very center of the Great Invocation is telling us that "God is known" through some relationship with "the Queen of Heaven" who is Isis or Sirius. Might this not be another way by which the Master DK is indicating the mysterious relationship existing between Sanat Kumara and Sirius, depicted in the Great Invocation through the fifty-five (Sanat) words preceeding and following the phrase "God is known"?

If this were not enough, we find that Nephthys, the sister of Isis, when combined numerologically with Isis totals 171 (56 [Isis] + 115 [Nephthys] = 171). In his book *The Gods of the Egyptians*, E.A Wallis Budge offers the following comments about Nephthys:

> She always appears as the faithful sister and friend of Isis, and helps the widowed goddess to collect the scattered limbs of Osiris and to reconstitute his body...and her commonest titles are, "dweller within Senu," "lady of heaven"...Like Isis, Nephthys, was believed to possess magical power. [Another one of her titles was] "mighty one of words of power."[59]

Budge goes on to add these interesting points gathered from comments made by Plutarch in his *Isis and Osiris*:

> From the above paragraphs it is clear that Nephthys is the personification of darkness and of all that belongs to it, and that her attributes were rather of a passive than active character. She is the opposite of Isis in every respect; Isis symbolized birth, growth, development and vigour, but Nephthys was the type of death, decay, diminution and immobility. Isis and Nephthys were, however, associated inseparably with each other, even as were Horus and Set...Isis, according to Plutarch represented the part of the world which is visible, whilst Nephthys represents that which is invisible, and we may even regard Isis as the day and Nephthys as the night.[60]

At this point in our investigation let us take a breath and assess the situation. We have a world prayer, the Great Invocation, which is supposed to be the most powerful and ancient mantram or "word of power" ever used by humanity. We have been steadily led to the heart of the Great Invocation where we have discovered a pattern of words both in structure and numerological correspondence that reveals a specific relation to Isis, who the ancient Egyptians identified with the star Sirius.

The three words at the middle of the Great Invocation—"God is known"—are the fifty-sixth, fifty-seventh, and fifty-eighth words of this word of power. These three word positions total 171. Not only does this value equal "the Queen of Heaven" or Isis but it also equals Isis/Nephthys (the inseparable polar opposite sisters of the ancient Egyptians). Quoting once more from *The Sirius Mystery* by Temple we find the following thoughts by the author:

> I had begun to suspect that the sister-goddess of Isis, who is called Nephthys, represented a possible description of Sirius B, the dark companion star that described a circle around Sirius...But I must confess that I was not prepared to discover this following passage [from *The Gods of the Egyptians* by Budge, JB]: On the subject of Anubis Plutarch reports (944;61) some interesting beliefs. After referring to the view that Anubis was born of Nephthys, although Isis was his reputed mother, he goes on to say, "By Anubis they understand the horizontal circle, which divides the invisible part of the world, which they call Nephthys, from the visible, to which they give the name of Isis; and as this circle equally touches upon the confines of both light and darkness, it may be looked upon as common to them both - and from this circumstance arose that resemblance, which they imagine between Anubis and the Dog, it being observed of this animal, that he is equally watchful as well by day as night."

Temple continues:

> This description could be taken to be one of the Sirius system. It clearly describes Isis (whom we know to have been identified with Sirius) as "the confines of light" and "the visible", and her sister Nephthys is described as being "the confines of darkness" and "the invisible", and common to both is the horizontal circle which divides them - the horizontal circle described, perhaps, by the orbit of the dark companion about the bright star? And here, too, is an explanation of the symbolism of the dog which has always been associated with Sirius, which has borne throughout the ages the name of the "Dog Star."[61]

At first glance it may appear that we are straying too far afield, but we need to look more deeply into what this all means. First of all we are receiving the "message" that "God is known" as

Isis/Nephthys, the Queen of Heaven, or Sirius. We have discovered that this "God(dess)" is dual in the sense that Sirius is a binary star system (and perhaps a triple). Surprisingly, we are suddenly talking about *orbits of stars*. Symbolically speaking, what does an orbit represent? It indicates perfect balance between two opposing forces, or in this case, two celestial bodies. There is the mutual attraction and repulsion held together in balance by a third factor of balanced relationship.

This beautifully describes the structure of the Great Invocation as we have already seen. The word "is" valued at 28 represents one half of the fifty-six words placed before and after it. In fact, this mirroring becomes even more clear when the two sets of fifty-six words are each divided in half again yielding four sets of twenty-eight words each, with the word "is" resonating its value of 28 in the center. (Note that Osiris was slain either in the 28th year of his reign as king or in his 28th year of life.[62]) Beyond this structural pattern of resonating balance between the two parts of the Great Invocation is a rather amazing fact. When we divide the Great Invocation in half as described above—excluding the middle word "is"—there is an identical numerological balance between the first half and the second half—*they are equal in value!* Each half of the Great Invocation equals 2648.

Figure 13. Numeric Poise.

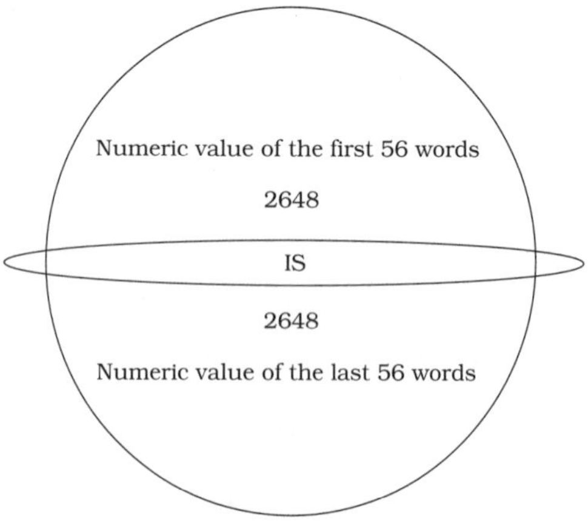

Numeric value of the first 56 words

2648

IS

2648

Numeric value of the last 56 words

This perfect balance between the first and second halves of the Great Invocation symbolically suggests a balanced relationship between two parts which is mediated by a third factor, namely the middle word "is." Thus, we have Isis symbolically representing the active, light side of existence—Yang Spirit, perhaps, and Nephthys representing the passive, dark side, Yin Substance (not evil) with "is" at the midpoint symbolic of the mediating soul linking spirit and substance. Through this revealed pattern we can clearly see another level of meaning to the Great Invocation which describes the universal principle of the trinity found in most religions and philosophies.

Let's extend this idea a bit further using esoteric numerology. If we reduce the value of the first half of the Great Invocation, we arrive at a value of 2. This is accomplished by reducing 2648 as follows: 2 + 6 + 4 + 8 = 20 and 2 + 0 = 2. Obviously, we arrive at the same result with the second half of the Great Invocation. We then reduce the middle word "is" (28) as follows: 2 + 8 = 10 and 1 + 0 = 1. Placing these three numbers together according to their order within the Great Invocation yields 2, 1, 2, or 212. The number 212 equals "the Dog Star Sirius." And if that is not enough to clue us in on the inner meaning of the Great Invocation, the number 212 also equals "the lifting of the Veil."

Figure 14. The Unveiled Dog Star

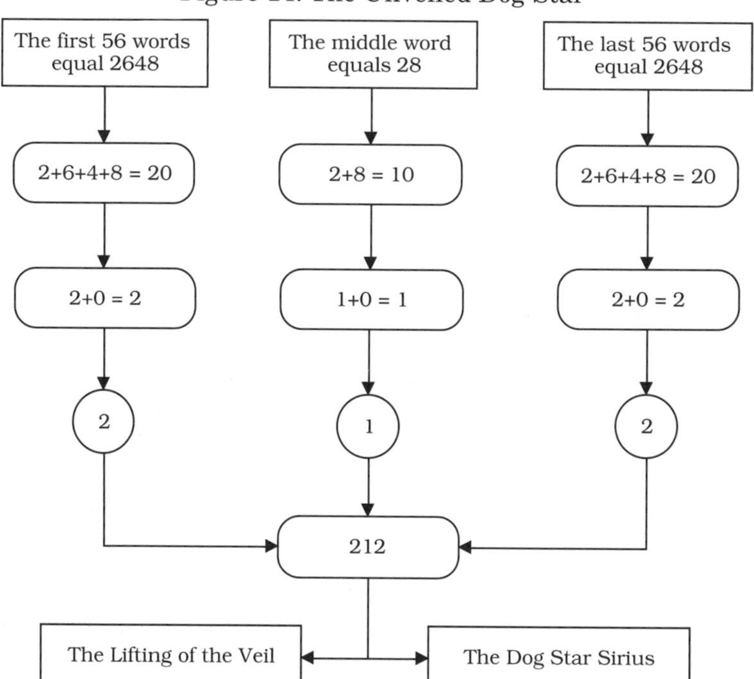

All of this discloses that finding the midpoint of the Great Invocation leads to the discovery of a vital message pointing to the Dog Star Sirius with all the implications suggested by this connection given to us by the ancient Egyptians (and others), and especially by the Master Djwhal Khul Himself. We are not finished with this theme, however, for there is one more intriguing aspect to this part of our investigation.

The Celestial Ship

In the book *A Treatise on Cosmic Fire* Djwhal Khul describes what He calls the "seven cosmic Paths." These seven Paths are called:

Path I	The Path of Earth Service
Path II	The Path of Magnetic Work
Path III	The Path of the Planetary Logos
Path IV	The Path to Sirius
Path V	The Ray Path
Path VI	The Path of the Solar Logos
Path VII	The Path of Absolute Sonship[63]

According to DK:

> These terms are the generic names given in the mystic parlance of the Lodge of Masters to the seven methods of work, of endeavor and of aspiration whereby the perfected sons of Earth's humanity pass on to specific cosmic Paths or streams of energy... [64]

It is not our purpose to go into all these paths in detail but to focus specifically on the Path to Sirius and its symbol. The Tibetan gives the symbol for five out of the seven paths. Quoting from *A Treatise on Cosmic Fire*, DK offers the following description of the symbol for the Path to Sirius: "two wheels of electric fire, revolving around an orange Cross, with an emerald at the centre."[65] The words used in this description come to an AN value of 862. Two items are fascinating about this description. The first is that the "two wheels of electric fire" suggest two stars orbiting around a central body described as an "orange Cross with an emerald at the centre." Interestingly, the terms "orange Cross" and "emerald" combined have a numerical value of 192 (AN). This equals the term "the Great White Lodge" which relates directly to our Hierarchy, and as we shall soon see, the Great White Lodge *on Sirius*.

The second point of interest pertaining to this symbol is perhaps even more intriguing; it involves the numerical value of the entire description—862 (AN). The number 862 is the arithmetical extension of 41.024089. The triangular number resulting from the addition of the first forty-one numbers (1-41) is 861. This number 41 is significant because it equals the name "Argo," the ship of Jason and his *fifty* argonauts. Therefore, the numerological value (862) of the words DK uses to describe this symbol of the Path to Sirius is the closest number possible to 41 and its triangular result 861.

According to the myth, at the end of the voyage of the Argonauts, the Greek goddess Athena placed the Argo in the sky where it is known as Argo Navis or Carina. Thus, the Argo is the celestial ship. Remember the numerical value of the three middle words "God is known" equals 50 (RAN) which corresponds to the fifty argonauts. Also, recall that these three middle words are the fifty-sixth, fifty-seventh, and fifty-eighth words of the Great Invocation which together total 171. This number 171 equals the phrase "the celestial ship." If this were not enough, the phrase "Argo, the celestial ship" equals 212, or "the Dog Star Sirius"

Table 30. The Celestial Ship.

The Celestial Ship	171
Argo, the Celestial Ship	212
The Dog Star Sirius	212

The Greek word Argo, however, which refers to the ship used by Jason and the Argonauts, goes much deeper than the Greek epic. In his allegorical story *The Golden Ass* (also entitled *Metamorphoses*), Lucius Apuleius (c. CE 120-180) describes his adventures of being accidentally transformed into an ass for a year before finally returning to human form. After suffering many indignities and humiliations, Lucius finds himself by the sea, where under the inspiration of the full moon, he asks the goddess Isis to help him. (Incidentally, prior to his prayer Lucius immerses his head in the water seven times, stating that the divine Pythagoras relates the number 7 to ritual.) Significantly, Lucius opens his prayer to Isis by addressing her as *the Queen of Heaven*.

As Lucius lays down to sleep, Isis suddenly appears out of the sea in the light of the moon. Lucius offers a detailed description of Isis, but of significance to our study, Lucius states that she held a golden vessel or boat in her left hand. During her brief visit with Lucius, Isis tells him she will transform him back to human form if he attends a ceremonial procession of her priests as they dedicate a new ship to her. Lucius agrees, and the next day he follows Isis' instructions, is returned to human form and goes on to become an initiate of the Mysteries of Isis. More on this in chapter 8. The important point here is the connection between Isis and the ship. This is all the more remarkable due to the numerological correspondence between "the Queen of Heaven" and "the celestial ship" and their connection to the exact middle of the Great Invocation. I believe we are dealing more with the symbolism of the ship than with an actual ship, such as the Argo.

In his monumental book *Anacalypsis*, Godfrey Higgins traces the word *Argo* back to the Sanskrit term *Argha*. Here is what Higgins has to say regarding this topic:

> The Argha is represented by a vessel of copper by the Brahmins in their sacred rites. It is intended to be a symbol or hieroglyphic of the universal mother. It is very often in the form of an elliptic boat or canoe, having both ends similarly pointed....In the centre of it is an oval rising, embossed, which represents the Linga. But it is to be seen in the shape described in the plate [in Higgins' book, JB] repeated in every variety of the way, in every temple of India. By the union of the Linga and Yoni, or Ioni, it is intended mystically to represent the two principles of generation—to represent them as one. This boat as I have already intimated, was the Argo of Greece, the name of the mystic ship in which the Ionians, who lived in Argos, sailed to seek the golden fleece of the Ram.[66]

Blavatsky says the following about the word Argos:

> It comes from *arg or arka*—the female generative power symbolized in the Moon—the navi-formed Argha of the Mysteries, meaning *the Queen of Heaven*.[67] [Emphasis mine, JB]

Higgins offers much more information about Argha, but we will confine ourselves to the theme of Isis and the Goddess' relation to

Sirius. Higgins again:

> In the mysteries of Egypt and Greece a ship was commonly used—this was the Argha. But it has been remarked by Mr. Bryant that this ship was not a common ship, but was of a peculiar construction; was, in fact, a mystic ship. It had both ends alike, was a correct, very much elongated, ellipse, and was called...Amphiprumnaus. Hesychius says..."*Amphiprumna are used in voyages of salvation.*" This alludes to the processions in which these ships were carried about, in the middle of which was placed the phallus.[68]

Higgins later points out that the word Argha does not mean ship in Sanskrit but is rather the name *of* a ship. Argha, he maintains, is simply a vessel or container.

> The Argha was not only the Yoni, but the surrounding ether in which the Yoni and Linga floated. It was also the boat in which the male and female generative principles, when reduced to their simplest form, floated during the sleep of Brahma. It was the ark of Noe, or of Mind...in which the germ of the animated nature or principles of generation were preserved. But it was in one sense as the Arga, the Preserver or Saviour, viz. as the Ark. It was the vessel in which the covenant of God was carried. But the most important point is, that, as the ship of Noe, it was the Saviour.
>
> Every one has heard of the celebrated boat of Isis among the Egyptians, Greeks, and Romans. But the Northern nations also worshiped her in the form of a ship. This ship was placed in the constellations and called the Argo. In Egypt this was called Sothis or the Star of Isis. This very well connects the Arga and Isis and Saviour—the ship in which the seed of nature was preserved. The Egyptians, Greeks, and Romans, all had festivals in the spring season to the ship of Isis.[69]

Blavatsky adds further weight to the significance of the Argha, Ark, ship, boat or vessel to the ancients in a discussion of the death and resurrection initiations of the Mysteries of Egypt. Speaking of the initiate, HPB says:

> While the postulant represented the Sun...the Sarcophagus was symbolic of the female principle. This, in Egypt; its form and shape changed with every country, provided it remained a vessel, a symbolic "navis" or boat-shaped vehicle, and a *container*, symbolically, of germs or the germ of life....The Navis, or ship-like form of the crescent, which blends in itself all those common symbols of the Ship of Life, such as Noah's Ark, the Yoni of the Hindus, and the Ark of the

> Covenant, is the female symbol of the Universal "Mother of the Gods,"and is now found under its Christian symbol in every church, as the *nave* (from *navis*).[70]

These extracts reveal a much deeper and intricate history of the Argo or Argha. It is one that includes a vessel which operates at various levels with various meanings. It would appear that the Greek myth of Jason and the Argonauts is an inherited story, with various versions and outcomes, which despite these alterations, retains the primary idea of a magical ship or vessel that carries its heroes through the many dangers and adventures of life in order to fulfill a mission. If anything, this is the esoteric root of our investigation into the Great Invocation, and its meaning for humanity. For in a very real sense the Great Invocation is a vehicle that carries—and at the same time—is the word of power which can invoke the Christ and restore the Plan on Earth. As Hesychius said in the above quotation, "amphiprumna are used in voyages of salvation." Was not the coming of Sanat Kumara a "voyage of salvation?" And might not "the Queen of Heaven," the Argha or Argo—the celestial ship—at the exact center of the Great Invocation represent the divine vessel that carries the mantram of salvation to humanity? The symbol of Sirius described by DK appears to reveal the Argo as part of a clue to the source of the Great Invocation.

This particular clue is related to the third or feminine aspect of Sirius in that it is described as a vessel or container. This container is sacred because it carries the seeds of Life. Perhaps it carries the human monads or solar angels on their mission of redemption to the Earth as part of the saving force of Sanat Kumara. This third aspect is often referred to by the Tibetan as the Brahma aspect.

In the book *Initiation, Human and Solar* DK is discussing the secrets revealed to the initiate during the third, fourth, and fifth initiations. The secrets revealed at the third initiation concern the Brahma aspect. One of the mystic phrases revealed is: "The Boat of Mystery which Ploughs the Ocean." In light of all we have discussed about Isis and the Argo and their connection to Sirius, this phrase is certainly intriguing.[71]

The AN value of "The Boat of Mystery which Ploughs the Ocean" equals 437. This number is significant because it is the product of 19 x 23. The number 19 represents the value of the letter found at the exact center of the Great Invocation, the letter "s."

(More about the number 19 in chapter 9.) The number 23 is significant because it represents the intermediate reduction of all the elements constituting the Great Invocation. (See table 5.) What's more, if 23 is reduced to the root value 5 and also multiplied by 19 the result is 95—the value of Sirius.

Earlier in this chapter we related The High Priestess to the divine Feminine, Sophia-wisdom aspect of God. This is sometimes termed *Shekinah* which DK relates to "the Light which ever shineth in the East." This phrase is an esoteric and Masonic reference to Sirius and the Mysteries of initiation.

We have already established that the ninety-five letters of the key words correspond to Sirius (95). The twenty-one key words have a total root value of 176. (See table 6.) This number is the very same RAN value of *"the Light which ever shineth in the East."* Furthermore, the RAN value of "The Boat of Mystery which Ploughs the Ocean" *also* equals 176.

"The Boat of Mystery which Ploughs the Ocean" could be a number of things. It might be our Earth, or it could be our solar system. Maybe the boat represents Sirius as it ploughs the ocean of space with its companion and offspring, our solar system. This is one more mystery which appears connected (at some level) with the Great Invocation, Sanat Kumara, our solar Logos, and Sirius. From the standpoint of esoteric numerology one thing is certain:

- "The Boat of Mystery which Ploughs the Ocean" is related to the Great Invocation via the numbers 19 and 23 and the root total of the key words 176. It is conceptually linked with the Argo, the celestial ship.
- The key words are related to Sirius by the number 95.
- "The Light which ever shineth in the East" refers to Sirius and is related to the key words by the number 176.
- Both phrases are linked to each other, as well as to the key words of the Great Invocation by 176. (See table 6.)

Notes

1. Bailey, *A Treatise on Cosmic Fire,* 1059.
2. Bailey, *Esoteric Astrology*, 257.
3. Ibid., 9.
4. Bailey, *A Treatise on Cosmic Fire,* 281.
5. DK refers to this star as "...a great force centre which we generalise by calling it by the name of the sun Sirius." Ibid., 624.
6. Bailey, *Discipleship in the New Age,* vol. II, 173.
7. Bailey, *The Reappearance of the Christ,* 31.
8. Bailey, *Discipleship in the New Age,* vol. II, 188.
9. Bailey, *The Rays and the Initiations,* 415.
10. Ibid., 414.
11. Ibid., 416.
12. Ibid., 416-17.
13. Ibid., 413-14.
14. Blavatsky, *The Theosophical Glossary,* s.v. "Sirius."
15. Burnham, *Burnham's Celestial Handbook,* vol. 1, 391.
16. Fideler, *Jesus Christ, Sun of God,* 262.
17. The Egyptian word "ast" is also applied to Osiris. This suggests that Osiris and Isis may be two aspects of one universal principle. Egyptologists are not certain about the origin of the name Ast.
18. E. A. Wallis Budge, *The Gods of the Egyptians,* vol. 2, 203.
19. Manly P. Hall, *The Secret Teachings of All Ages,* 46, 48.
20. Budge, *The Gods of the Egyptians,* vol. 2, 214-15.
21. Walter Scott, ed and trans., *Hermetica*, 491-93.
22. Bailey, *Esoteric Astrology*, 251-52.
23. Blavatsky considers Shekinah to be "the veil of Ain-Soph the Endless and the Absolute." Blavatsky, *Theosophical Glossary,* s.v. "Shekinah."
24. Arthur Edward Waite, *The Pictorial Key to the Tarot,* 13.
25. Bailey, *Esoteric Psychology,* vol. II, 59.
26. Waite, *The Pictorial Key to the Tarot,* 76-79.
27. Jason C. Lotterhand, *The Thursday Night Tarot*, 38.
28. Ibid., 291.
29. Waite, *The Pictorial Key to the Tarot*, 139.
30. Bailey, *A Treatise on Cosmic Fire,* 567-68.
31. Ibid., 571.
32. Ibid., 568.
33. Ibid., 569-70.

34. Ibid., 571-72.
35. Robert K.G. Temple, *The Sirius Mystery,* 1.
36. Ibid., 5.
37. Ibid., 64.
38. Ibid., 71.
39. Ibid., 64.
40. Waite, *The Pictorial Key to the Tarot,* 136.
41. Note also that when read in a line the three word lengths are 9, 10, 9. If the 10 is reduced numerologically to 1 the result can be read as 9, 1, 9. These three digits can be written as 9 19 where 9 = i and 19 = s or IS, the middle word of the Great Invocation.
42. Bailey, *Esoteric Astrology,* 300.
43. Bailey, *The Rays and the Initiations,* 418.
44. It should be noted that when "God" 17, "is" 10, and "known" 23 are reduced to their root values they equal 8, 1, and 5 respectively which total 14/5. The Great Invocation also has an intermediate value of 14 before reaching the final root value of 5.
45. Once again we see the number five emerge, this time at the center of the Great Invocation through the reduction of 50 to 5—5 + 0 = 5.
46. Temple, *The Sirius Mystery,* 99.
47. Ibid., 31-32.
48. A fascinating cross reference exists between Temple's research and the cabalistic meaning of the number 50. According to *Godwin's Cabalistic Encyclopedia* one of the Hebrew meanings of the number 50 is *Dagh Gadhol*—Great Fish, another is *Yam*—Sea and a third is *Adamah*—Earth; one of the seven Earths. The commentary on *Adamah* is "Receives light from the stars and planets, but is inhabited by demons and spirits." Could this apply to the coming of the Great Fish God in order to redeem or save the inhabitants of one of the seven Earths from the demons and spirits of materialism?
49. Bailey, *A Treatise on Cosmic Fire,* 723-24.
50. John Anthony West, *Serpent in the Sky*, 1.
51. Bailey, *Externalisation of the Hierarchy,* 121.
52. Ibid., 121-22.
53. Robert Eisler, Ph.D., *Orpheus—The Fisher: Comparative Studies in Orphic and Early Christian Symbolism*, 43-44.
54. Ibid., 45.
55. Blavatsky, *The Secret Doctrine,* vol. 3, n. 270.
56. Ibid, 363.
57. Temple, *The Sirius Mystery,* 97.

58. G. A. Gaskell, *Dictionary of All Scriptures and Myths*, s.v. "Queen of Heaven.
59. Budge, *The Gods of the Egyptians,* vol. 2, 255-56.
60. Ibid., 258.
61. Temple, *The Sirius Mystery,* 63-64.
62. Budge, *The Gods of the Egyptians,* vol. 2., 188.
63. Bailey, *A Treatise on Cosmic Fire,* 1242.
64 Ibid., 1243.
65. Ibid., 1261.
66. Godfrey Higgins, Esq., *Anacalypsis,* vol. 1, 336.
67. Blavatsky, *The Secret Doctrine,* vol. 3, n 414.
68. Godfrey Higgins, Esq., *Anacalypsis,* vol. 1, 344.
69. Ibid., 798.
70. Blavatsky, *The Secret Doctrine,* vol. 4, 30-31.
71. An interesting twist on this bit of information is that this phrase is found on page 171 of *Initiation, Human and Solar,* which is the number value of "the celestial ship" and "Isis-Nephthys."

8

The Mysteries of Initiation

As we have already seen Sirius holds a special place in the ageless wisdom. In no other area however, is this more so than in that of initiation. We spent some time explaining initiation in chapter 1 because the subject is so closely linked with Sirius. According to Djwhal Khul, the entire process of initiation is a method of mind and consciousness expansion. These expansions and revelations of a greater reality beyond the normal awareness of human beings are also known as the Mysteries.

According to HPB, the Mysteries were not always so. During an earlier epoch in human history, at the time of the Atlantean civilization, mankind was taught openly about the nature, origin, and purpose of life and man's place in the scheme of things, but this knowledge was eventually misused and abused. Quoting Blavatsky:

> Selfishness was born out of desires and passions hitherto unknown, and but too often knowledge and power were abused, until finally it became necessary to limit the number of those *who knew*. Thus arose Initiation....The need of veiling truth to protect it from desecration becoming more apparent with every generation, a thin veil was used at first, which had to be gradually thickened according to the spread of personality and selfishness, and this led to the Mysteries. They came to be established in every country and among every people,

> while to avoid strife and misunderstanding exoteric beliefs were allowed to grow up in the minds of the profane masses.[1]

In his comprehensive book *Morals and Dogma: Ancient and Accepted Scottish Rite of Freemasonry*, Albert Pike describes the mystery religions of the ancient world as follows:

> Among most of the ancient Nations there was, in addition to their public worship, a private one styled the Mysteries; to which those only were admitted who had been prepared by certain ceremonies called initiations. The most widely disseminated of the ancient worships were those of Isis, Orpheus, Ceres and Mithras....Plato said that the object of the Mysteries was to re-establish the soul in its primitive purity, and in that state of perfection which it lost....Proclus held that initiation elevated the soul, from a material, sensual, and purely human life, to a communion and celestial intercourse with the Gods.[2]

Manly P. Hall offers some additional information on this subject:

> The best evidence of the significance of the Mysteries is to be found in the lives and writings of those who received the initiations. Among the most famous were Pythagoras, Plato, and Aristotle; yet these same men acknowledged that, in comparison to the wisdom contained in the adytum of the Mysteries, they knew and taught only as small children. Incredible as this may seem, it bears out the thoughts of Porphyry who wrote that the initiates during their trials participated in a divine splendor and the gods themselves attended the initiators.[3]
>
> Of course not everyone who took part in the Mysteries reached the same level of initiation. In fact the Eleusinian Mysteries were divided into the Lesser and Greater. The Lesser Mysteries of Eleusis involved many candidates, and these were concerned with purification of the body, mind, and emotions. This stage of the Eleusinian rites was designed to aid the practitioner in self-improvement and character building through purity of thought and body. Those who successfully passed the lesser rites were called the *mystae*, or those who saw through a veil or mist. When we remember that as many as twenty-five thousand persons attended a single performance of the rituals in the temple at Eleusis, it becomes obvious that such a number could not be regarded as sharing in a common illumination. The initiates of the lower grades were therefore spectators—not participators—in the body of mystical doctrine.[4]

Manly Hall goes on to explain that the majority of *mystae* never progressed past the Lesser Mysteries, but those who did had gone through five stages or degrees of initiation. Entering the fifth degree and the Greater Mysteries really meant the initiate had entered a life of philosophy and spiritual inquiry involving a major life commitment. According to Hall's various sources, the initiation rites into the Greater Mysteries lasted eight or nine days. The climax of the ceremony is described in this manner:

> In his introduction to Taylor's *Eleusinian and Bacchic Mysteries*, Dr. Alexander Wilder summarizes the climax of the initiation rite as follows: "...Demeter seals, by her own peculiar utterance and signals, by vivid coruscations of light, and cloud piled upon cloud, all that we have seen and heard from her sacred priest; and then, finally, the light of a serene wonder fills the temple, and we see the pure fields of Elysium, and hear the chorus of the Blessed;—then, not merely by external seeming or philosophic interpretation, but in real fact, does the Hierophant become the Creator and revealer of all things; the Sun is but his torch-bearer, the Moon his attendant at the altar, and Hermes his mystic herald." This summation is partly derived from Porphyry.[5]

The goddess Isis also played a role in the Mysteries of initiation. A concise account of an initiation experience related to Isis comes from Lucius Apuleius, in his book *The Golden Ass* which we discussed at the end of chapter 7. Lucius was so overwhelmed by the redeeming power and compassion of Isis, he became an initiate of her Mysteries. Lucius explains to his readers that he, as an initiate, cannot give the details of his initiation. He then offers only the following information:

> I approached the confines of death. I trod the threshold of Prosperine; and borne through the elements I returned. At midnight I saw the Sun shining in all his glory. I approached the gods below and the gods above, and I stood beside them, and I worshiped them.[6]

The initiations of the various Mystery Religions of antiquity were meant to give hope and upliftment to the human spirit. Although most of what was communicated to the candidates of the Greater Mysteries remains untold, enough is known to say that, generally, they concerned the immortality of the human soul and the revelation of a divine world beyond that of the mundane life of human living. The initiate was granted a brief glimpse of, and true experience, in the "regions" beyond this world. Through the secret methods of the high priests of the mysteries, the soul of the initiate was set free to travel into the heavenly worlds beyond the veil of

Isis. Plato beautifully describes the effects of the initiation experience in the Phadreus:

> Beauty it was ours to see in all its brightness in those days when, amidst that happy company, we beheld with our eyes that blessed vision, ourselves in the train of Zeus, others following some other god; then were we all initiated into that mystery which is rightly accounted blessed beyond all others; whole and unblemished were we that did celebrate it, untouched by the evils that awaited us in days to come; whole and unblemished likewise, free from all alloy, steadfast and blissful were the spectacles on which we gazed in the moment of final revelation; pure was the light that shone around us, and pure were we, without taint of that prison house which now we are encompassed withal, and call a body, fast bound therein as an oyster in its shell.[7]

According to Djwhal Khul, the requirements for initiation are constantly being adjusted to the evolving psychological and spiritual growth of humanity. The initiates of today receive more advanced training and must meet higher standards than the initiates of 2,500 years ago. This is as it should be because as humankind evolves, so must the training given to those who are ready to advance beyond the veil of the outer world. The revelation of divinity is expanded to meet the needs of a rapidly advancing humanity.

Although the secrets of initiation have been kept from the general public due to concerns about the possible misuse of this knowledge by the masses, the latter part of the nineteenth century witnessed a reversal of this practice, at least in part. Since then much esoteric information has been released to the public through the work of H.P. Blavatsky, Helena Roerich, Rudolf Steiner, Alice Bailey, George Gurdjieff, Lucille Cedarcrans, and other messengers and teachers of the spiritual Hierarchy. All of this effort is part of a Plan of preparation for the reappearance of the World Teacher and the emergence of other Members of the Hierarchy into the outer world of human activity. A major part of that Plan involves the restoration of the ancient mysteries to their place of respected influence in the spiritual, cultural, and scientific spheres of civilization. This restoration can come only after humanity settles many of its wars and selfish habits of prejudice and separatism.

Until the Tibetan began dictating his books to Alice Bailey in 1919, Blavatsky and other teachers of the ageless wisdom either would not tell or simply did not know how or where the Mystery Religions originated. Most said they originated on Atlantis and spread to India, Chaldea, Egypt, and the Americas during the destruction of the Atlantean civilization, which according to most accounts actually took thousands of years. The final destruction occurred around 10,450 BCE.

In the book *A Treatise on White Magic*, the Tibetan gives an account of the establishing of the "Temple of Ibez" in the center of South America about seventeen million years ago as the first physical outpost of the "Shamballa Fraternity." Although Sanat Kumara and His Assistants remained on etheric levels in the center known as Shamballa, They decided that the Mysteries needed to be taught from a central physical location in order to meet the needs of a "rapidly awakening humanity."

In the beginning of this process, during the Lemurian period, infant humanity needed conscious development in the physical domain. This early stage of physical development and coordination is equated with Hatha yoga. Techniques to bring about physical plane focusing and integration were taught. As time progressed the feeling aspect of mankind was developed and integrated with the physical. Djwhal Khul relates that this stage was entered upon during the Atlantean period, and the teachers concentrated on developing love as a positive emotion. This stimulated the devotional, aspirational, mystical path to God. In Indian yoga this can be equated with Bhakti yoga.

As the ages passed, the psychological evolution of humanity reached a point where mental development and integration were possible, as demonstrated by the great schools of philosophy and science which began to appear about 2500 years ago in Asia and the Mediterranean rim. (Not as much is known about the mystery schools of the Americas, but recent findings indicate a sophisticated civilization and culture developed along different lines than that of Asia and the Mediterranean regions.) DK comments:

> Gradually the teaching was re-organized, and the curriculum increased; little by little the mysteries were developed as the people became ready for them until we have the marvelous Schools of the Mysteries of Chaldea, Egypt, Greece and many others.[8]

Before considering the relationship between the Mysteries and Sirius, we should remember that the Mysteries of initiation are meant to be revealed to humanity. That which was esoteric thousands of years ago is exoteric now, and that which is esoteric and hidden from modern humanity today will become exoteric in the future. When humanity demonstrates its ability to use power with love and wisdom, then power and knowledge will be made known to us. Maybe we are learning the needed lessons and passing the tests of wisdom as we begin to dismantle our nuclear weapons, for the hidden power of the atom was certainly revealed to us in all its terrible might. We are meant to gain knowledge, but knowledge is relative truth, always revealing a greater truth of which the former is but a part. The Mysteries of initiation have always been and are still concerned with the gradually unfolding revelation of truths contained within truths that are eternal. According to H.P. Blavatsky:

> Initiation, though it contained neither rules and principles, nor any special teaching of science—as now understood [more than 100 years ago, JB]—was nevertheless science, and the Science of sciences. And though devoid of dogma, of physical discipline, and of exclusive ritual, it was yet the one true religion—that of eternal truth. Outwardly it was a school, a college, wherein were taught sciences, arts, ethics, legislation, philanthropy, the cult of the true and real nature of cosmic phenomena; secretly, during the Mysteries, practical proofs of the latter were given. Those who could learn truth on all things—*i.e.*, those who could look the great Isis in her unveiled face and bear the awful majesty of the Goddess—became Initiates.[9]

Sirius and the Process of Initiation

> These ancient Mysteries were originally given to Humanity by the Hierarchy, and were—in their turn—received by the Hierarchy from the Great White Lodge on Sirius. They contain the clue to the evolutionary process, hidden in numbers and in words; they veil the secret of man's origin and destiny, picturing for him in rite and ritual the long, long path which he must tread.[10]

The evolutionary process to which Djwhal Khul refers is that of consciousness expansion. Humanity is the lowest self-conscious kingdom of nature. We are that form of conscious life that interfaces directly with the natural world of animals, plants, and minerals found on our planet. The Mysteries are said to tell the story of how and why the human kingdom exists. The Mysteries explain with ever increasing clarity, degree by degree, revelation by revelation, the nature, role, and purpose of the human kingdom in relation to the world and the Cosmos.

According to the philosophy of the ageless wisdom, the human kingdom is only now arriving at its destined point of usefulness to the higher spiritual kingdoms of the Hierarchy and Shamballa. Humanity, Hierarchy, and Shamballa are meant to work together in conscious cooperation as part of the greater Purpose of Sanat Kumara, the planetary Logos. Consciousness development has evolved from self-awareness to a rapidly forming group-awareness. It has literally taken millions of years of evolution for humanity to reach the initial stages of group consciousness. By group consciousness we mean such qualities as brotherhood, the sharing of resources, cooperation, and goodwill.

DK offers few details about this greater Purpose, but within the context of our investigation to this point, the evidence suggests that our tiny planet has a definite role to play in the Purpose of the greater Lives of our solar system and Sirius. As we have already shown, the rapid development of the Christ as a member of the human kingdom signals a major success of human and spiritual evolution on our planet. Recall DK's earlier description of Christ and His accomplishment: "He is the expression, par excellence, of a Sirian initiation, and it is to that high place He will eventually go."

This effort to spur the evolution of human consciousness has required the sacrifice of Sanat Kumara along with His other spiritual Assistants. The effect of this "descent" to physical plane levels created a tremendous stimulation of animal men that led to the creation of individualized consciousness, and thus the human kingdom. Spirit had become anchored in the primitive brain of primate animal man as individual self-conscious mind. Our Progenitors then nurtured infant humanity until we learned to take care of ourselves to some degree. In addition to the establishment of natural evolutionary processes within the human kingdom, opportunity for more rapid development was offered through specialized teaching and training. The Teachers and Instructors of early man taught a more rapid method of consciousness evolution known as initiation. An example of the tremendous opportunity for rapid spiritual evolution through the process of initiation can be illustrated by referring to the most advanced member of the Hierarchy, the Christ. DK says:

> So rapid was the development of the Christ that in Atlantean days He found Himself upon the Path of Probation as did also the Buddha[11]....From the angle of evolution the rapid unfoldment of the

> evolution of Christ was, and has been, *totally unparalleled.* It has never been duplicated....He, therefore, stands uniquely alone.[12]

This unparalleled evolution of the Christ which led Him to become the first human to achieve the Sirian level of initiation was gained through the initiatory method of evolution instituted by the Lives of the Sirian system. This method of evolution is experimental and more rapid than the normal evolutionary process peculiar to the Earth. We, therefore, have two methods of growth available to us on our planet—one natural to our world, and another introduced into our planetary system from Sirius. The book *Initiation, Human and Solar* contains this important information:

> One great fact to be borne in mind is, that the initiations of the planet or of the solar system are but the preparatory initiations of admission into the greater Lodge on Sirius.[13]
>
> The three planetary schemes wherein the great experiment of initiation is being tried are the Earth, Venus, and one other. Venus was the first sphere of experiment, and the success of the endeavour and the force generated was the cause of a similar effort being made on our planet.[14]

This passage clearly indicates the experimental nature of initiation in our solar system and the extraordinary stimulation being experienced by all life on our planet due to the "training" of Sanat Kumara. Here we must remember the Hermetic law "as above, so below." We are the microcosm in the macrocosm. Although we have free will as individual souls, we still come under the laws of "the One in Whom we live and move and have our being." Free will, however, governs the *speed* of our evolution as human beings, and we are all free to choose the normal, slower method or the more rapid Way of Initiation.

> Initiation is in the nature of a great experiment which our planetary Logos is making during this round. In earlier and perhaps in later rounds the whole process will follow natural law. In this round and on this chain, our planetary Logos on His high level is what is esoterically called "sitting for yoga," and is definitely undergoing certain processes of training in order to stimulate His centres.[15]

It is difficult to comprehend the true nature of this concept since our experience of life is limited to the human dimension.

Nevertheless, if we are indeed created in the image of God and if we are the microcosmic reflection of a greater macrocosmic Life, then our own development as human beings will mirror, to some degree at least, that greater Life in which we live. For example, let us take the life of a young woman who gains an entry level position in any given career field. This new employee can work efficiently and successfully in her field, gradually gaining experience and skills which lead to advancement. But, as we know, this same person can commit herself to further study and education in order to learn as much as possible about her field of work. This involves much sacrifice of time, labor, and money but leads to greater capacity to work and serve. Furthermore, this intensified study may lead to groundbreaking discoveries and innovative ideas which introduce revolutionary transformations into the entire field of work and study. This extra effort and dedication on the part of this particular person will affect many areas of her own field of work and may very well spill over into other areas of society affecting whole groups of people.

Although analogies are not perfect across all lines, we can extend this concept to that order of Life of which the Tibetan speaks—our planetary Logos is voluntarily submitting to intensified training in this particular cycle of His Life expression. We as conscious beings contained within this greater Life are intrinsically involved in that greater process. That process involves an intensified training program administered by Great Cosmic Lives connected with the solar system of Sirius, but not necessarily on the physical plane. Another analogy might be that the life expression, plans, desires, and thoughts of an individual are not directly perceivable by examining the cells of that person's physical body, but the effects of that person's life expression—their thoughts and feelings may be detectable in their cells as health or disease.

The breakdown in this particular analogy comes at the cellular level. Cells are not self-conscious free-willed intelligent entities in the same way as are human beings. Humanity is meant to play a conscious role in the life expression and training program of Sanat Kumara on our planet. According to DK, the mysterious symbol attached to the Great Invocation indicates the date when humanity should be ready to use this special word of power. This implies a very long range Plan which began with the implanting of mind in animal man and continued with the Christ reaching the Sirian level of initiation 2,000 years ago. This successful anchoring of

Sirian influence within the Hierarchy by the Christ culminated with Sanat Kumara granting the Christ permission to use the *ancient Word of Power* now known as the Great Invocation.

The long range Plan mentioned in the above paragraph also includes the planet Venus because the Sirian process of initiation was first tried on that planet. Apparently, the advanced Lives Who guide our solar system targeted the Earth as the next planet in this cosmic experiment of rapid evolution. This process of accelerated growth was scheduled to begin with Earth's human kingdom, but for unknown reasons, the instinctual presence of mind (manas) in animal man needed additional stimulus to come into full activity. This additional stimulus was supplied by Sanat Kumara and the Lords of the Flame who sacrificed Themselves and incarnated directly into the substance of planet Earth. The enormous energy impact of this descent into material substance created the human kingdom on Earth and the individualized human soul was born.

DK tells us that the planet Venus was involved in this special effort by Sanat Kumara, and there is a definite relationship between our two planets.

> Each Heavenly Man is linked with one of His Brothers under the Law of Mutual Attraction...Such a link is found between the planetary Logos of the scheme we call Venus, and the Logos of our scheme. This psychic interaction has its cyclic ebb and flow, as ebbs and flows all life force. In Lemurian days came a period of close interaction which brought about an incarnation on the physical planet of the Logos of our scheme, the Head of the Hierarchy, and the One Initiator. This could not have been effected had not the planetary Logos of the Venus scheme been in a position to link up closely with ours.[16]

In another passage from *A Treatise on Cosmic Fire* we find:

> It is not permissible to say much about this mystery, that "Venus is the Earth's alter ego," nor is it advisable, but certain ideas may be suggested which—if brooded on—may result in a wider grasp of the beauty of nature's synthesis, and of the wonderful correlation of all that is in process of evolution. Perhaps some idea may be gained if we remember that, in an occult sense, Venus is to the Earth what the higher Self is to man. The coming of the Lords of the Flame to the Earth was all under law and not just an accidental and fortunate happening.[17]

This naturally sets up a connection between the Earth, Venus, and Sirius since these are the two planets in our solar system which have undergone the experiment of initiation instituted by the Lord of Sirius. But does the Great Invocation fit into this relationship? It would appear to, simply from the logical flow of the entire story of evolutionary development described by the Tibetan—from Sirius to Sanat Kumara; to Christ as the first human Sirian Initiate and the first human to use the Great Invocation; to the theme of initiation itself, and the relationship between Venus and our Earth. Holding these connections in mind, let's look at the numbers involved to see if they reinforce the possibility of such a link. (See figure 15 below.)

Figure 15. The Cosmic Bridge.

	777	
Incarnated As Sanat Kumara The Great Sacrifice	Number Of The Planetary Logos	Custodian Of The Will Of The Lord Of Sirius
Origin Of The Process Of Initiation	"Sirius" = 95	Origin Of All The Planetary Hierarchies In Our Solar System
The First Planet In Our Solar System To Undergo The Experiment Of Initiation	"Venus Scheme" = 134	Aided Sanat Kumara In Establishing Mind On Earth In Human Form
The Second Planet In Our Solar System To Undergo The Experiment Of Initiation	"Earth Scheme" =105	The Total Life Expression Of The Planetary Logos Of Which The Physical Earth Is One Part
A Power Mantram Of Ancient Date Used Only By The Most Advanced Beings On Earth	Total Letters Of The Great Invocation = 443	First Used By Christ In 1945 As Head Of The Hierarchy
Formula For The Great Work Of Cosmic Alchemy	95 + 134 + 105 + 443 = 777	Implemented Through The Process Of Initiation By The Great White Lodge On Sirius

As figure 15 depicts, when the numerological values of Sirius, Venus Scheme, Earth Scheme, and the 443 letters of the Great Invocation are combined they equal 777 (95 + 134 + 105 + 443 = 777). This is really quite remarkable when we consider that each of these factors are connected by the common thread of initiation. For as we have just seen, the process of initiation first involved Venus, and then Earth, and is of Sirian origin. The Great Invocation is conceptually involved because it is linked with redemption through the invocation of Light, Love, and Power—the qualities which will restore the Plan on Earth. Consequently, when the 443 letters comprising this mantram are combined with Sirius, Venus, and Earth, 777—the number of the planetary Logos, incarnated as Sanat Kumara, emerges before our eyes. We close this section with the following passage from *A Treatise on Cosmic Fire*:

> It has been stated that a mystery lies hid in the 777 incarnations. This figure provides room for much speculation. It should be pointed out that it does not hold the number of a stated cycle of incarnations through which a man must pass, but holds the key to the three major cycles previously mentioned [cycles pertaining to a planetary Logos, JB]. Primarily this number applies to the planetary Logos of our scheme and not so much to other schemes.[18]

Sirius and the Great Invocation

Does the Great Invocation contain any additional numeric or symbolic evidence of its connection to the great sun Sirius? We have already indicated a symbolic connection of the middle word "is" to the goddess Isis and, therefore, by association to the star Sirius. In addition, we have linked Sirius to initiation; Sirius to the Christ; and Christ to the Great Invocation. All these factors suggest at least an inferential connection between Sirius and the theme of the Great Invocation—namely, the invocation of spiritual Light, Love, and Power for restoring the Plan on Earth. The fact that the Plan is to be restored tells us there has been an interruption of that Plan. We now know through our brief examination of the Mysteries of antiquity that there was indeed an interruption of a Plan which involved the education and guidance of humanity by a group of advanced Lives who sacrificed themselves in order to instill mind or manas in animal man. Clearly this suggests some greater Plan or agenda which extends beyond our tiny planet. If the Great

Invocation is so ancient, does this antiquity suggest some link with Sirius through its Agents? Djwhal Khul describes such an Agent as:

> That great Entity Who is the presiding Lord of the Lords of Karma. He is the repository of the law during manifestation, and He it is Who is the representative in the solar system of that greater Brotherhood on Sirius Whose Lodges are found functioning as the occult Hierarchies in the different planets.[19]

This passage shows that a representative from Sirius heads the Lords of Karma in our solar system. More interesting perhaps is the statement that the Brotherhood on Sirius has "Lodges...functioning as the occult Hierarchies in the different planets."

These various planetary hierarchies are described here as outposts or Agents of a greater "parent" Hierarchy on Sirius. When referring to the Hierarchy of our planet, DK states: "The entire work of the Great White Lodge is controlled from Sirius..."[20] Djwhal Khul becomes even more specific about the relationship between the Earth (via Sanat Kumara) and Sirius. He says:

> The relationship as it expresses itself is between the Hierarchy and Sirius, and not between Shamballa and that stupendous Sun. The energy evoked in response to this relationship enters the Hierarchy via the Heart of the Sun, creating as a consequence a triangle of spiritual energy of enormous potency....
>
> [There is] A stream of energy coming from the sun, Sirius; this enters directly into the Hierarchy and carries with it the principle of buddhi, or cosmic love. This, in a mysterious way, is the principle found at the heart of every atom.[21]

These short passages are quite important in establishing a deep and profound connection between the source of cosmic love—Sirius, and our Hierarchy headed by the Christ, the first Sirian Initiate on our planet. It is worth repeating a passage quoted earlier:

> This Sirian influence was not recognised, and little of it was definitely focussed in the Hierarchy, until Christ came and revealed the love of God to humanity. He is the expression, par excellence, of a Sirian initiation.[22]

Continuing our exploration of number correspondences, we first return to the word "is" at the center of the Great Invocation.

We know the word "is" has a value of 28, and so far we have used this number as a pointer to the goddess Isis ("is" being half of Isis). The number 28, however, has some interesting meanings which relate to our discussion in a number of ways. First, an Egyptian cubit is comprised of 28 digits, thus linking this central number to an Egyptian theme such as Isis. (This theme will expand as our study continues.) The Egyptians based the digit on the width of one finger and a cubit on the distance from the elbow to the fingertips. Thus, a cubit was the distance between the elbow and the fingertips, or 28 digits.

Second, the number 28 is the height in cubits of the curtains of the Hebrew Tabernacle of the Old Testament. Here we see that the most sacred religious object of the ancient Hebrews had curtains or "veils" of 28 cubits in height. Third, and most symbolic of all, the number 28 is a perfect number. A perfect number is one in which all its factors (apart from itself) added together equal itself. Thus, the factors 1 + 2 + 4 + 7 + 14 = 28.

Returning once again to the Tarot, the name of the 17th Tarot card, The Star, has a RAN value of 28. So, the star can be found at the center of the Great Invocation in the numerical form of "is." We can also show that the AN value of The Star (91) is composed of a 9 and a 1, which corresponds to the RAN values of "I" (9) and "S" (1) or "IS."

In addition, the words "goddess" and "heaven" have RAN values of 28. We have already identified the goddess Isis as both Sirius and "the Queen of Heaven" (171). Therefore, Sirius as "the Queen of Heaven" is at the physical center of the Great Invocation through the corresponding value of the three middle words "God is known" (171). Added to all this, however, we discover the presence of "The Star," the "goddess," and "heaven" at the center of the Great Invocation. These terms are now revealed, but they and the others we have mentioned have been veiled to this point. Therefore, the placement of the word "is" at the middle position is more than appropriate in light of the symbolism of the 28 cubit long curtains of the Hebrew Tabernacle which covered or veiled the Holy of Holies where the Ark of the Covenant was concealed. Strange as it may seem, the word "curtained" equals 95 (AN), the same as Sirius, and "the Holy of Holies" equals 182 (AN), the same as "the sun Sirius."

This fifty-seventh word position of the Great Invocation is one of the most esoteric parts of this word of power because Isis-Sothis, the Queen of Heaven, or the star Sirius, is veiled in this central location and appropriately, the word "veiled" equals 57 (AN).

The word "heaven," however, has an unexpected import beyond "the Queen of Heaven," or the obvious reference to the sky or heavens where the stars are located. Significant, perhaps, is that *Godwin's Cabalistic Encyclopedia* gives the Hebrew word for heaven, *Shamaim*, a value of 390; and curiously, while describing the initiations of Sirius, DK uses the phrase "within the sunshine of the major Sun"[23] which also has an AN value of 390.[24]

This phrase and its relationship to Shamaim (heaven) is esoterically powerful because Godwin indicates that of the seven heavens of cabalism the fourth heaven of *Zebhul* (dwelling) relates directly to Tiphareth. We have already seen how Tiphareth and the Christ are related in the section "The Christ Six and Five" in chapter 6. We next saw how the Christ is related to Sirius and the Great Invocation. Now we find that Tiphareth/Christ is the fourth heaven which corresponds with the fourth "Path to Sirius." (See the section "The Celestial Ship" in chapter 7.) Further, we find that *Zebhul* or *dwelling has a value of 41 in both Hebrew and English* (RAN). Recall that the Argo, the celestial ship, with a value of 41 is the vehicle for the Egyptian goddesses of Isis-Sothis, Anukis, and Satis whose total value comes to 289 or the square of 17—the number DK mentions in relation to the *fourth path to Sirius*. What might this all mean?

This clearly indicates a direct esoteric connection between the fourth heaven of Zebhul and the fourth Path to Sirius connected by the Hebrew word *Shamaim* and the intriguing phrase "in the sunshine of the major Sun" given by the Tibetan—both equalling 390. All of this emerges from the center or heart of the Great Invocation. The Queen of Heaven (171) is the goddess Isis-Sothis or Isis-Sirius. Therefore, *the Goddess of Heaven is the sun Sirius*. This is not only true according to the ancient Egyptians and according to the ageless wisdom, but it is also true numerologically because "the Goddess of Heaven" and "the sun Sirius" both equal 182. And, in fact there is a double layer of esoteric numerology to this correspondence, for if we take the three words "Goddess of Heaven" and replace them with their numeric RAN equivalents we get 28, 12, 28. Reducing these three numbers gives 10, 3, 10 and finally 1, 3, 1 or 131. The number 131 is the AN value of "God is known"! "The Queen of Heaven," "The Celestial Ship," "The Goddess of Heaven," "the sun Sirius," and "God is known" are all interconnected via the middle word and the middle phrase, as well as by the numerical positions of the three middle words in the Great Invocation. At the very least this indicates a distinct connection between the Great Invocation and Sirius. In addition a link exists between Tiphareth and Zebhul—the fourth heaven, the dwelling. Might this dwelling be the vehicle or vessel of containment for the Great Lives of the Sirian system symbolized by a celestial ship called the Argo, Ark, or Argha and which DK describes as that region of space called Sirius?

The Tibetan also mentions the number 14 in relation to this fourth path. The two numbers 14 and 17 are written in a tabulation for the Path to Sirius as: "Hierarchy—veiled by the numbers 14 and 17."[25] The Hierarchy referred to here relates to the Creative Hierarchies of which there are twelve—five esoteric and beyond our current evolutionary cycle and seven exoteric or active within the evolutionary cycle of our Earth. This is a complex subject which goes beyond the scope of this book, but we will discuss the Creative Hierarchies to some degree in the next chapter. Because DK uses number coding in reference to the Path to Sirius, we will first investigate these numbers strictly from a numerological angle. In the next chapter we will go a little further and try to identify the Creative Hierarchy or Hierarchies involved with the Path to Sirius and their connection, if any, to the Great Invocation.

Just as the number 17 has led us to The Star card, the number 14 leads us to the major Arcanum Temperance. This card shows the Archangel Michael standing *on land and in water* pouring what seems to be water from one cup to another. The imagery on this card is very similar to the unveiled Isis in The Star card. (In fact these are the only two trump cards in which the characters are interacting with water in a deliberate way.) Whereas the woman on the Star card is distributing water, the Archangel Michael appears to be keeping the water fresh and alive by pouring it from cup to cup as if recycling it. Blavatsky reports that "In the Talmud, Mikael (Michael) is 'Prince of Water.' " According to HPB " 'Waters' is another name of the 'Great Deep,' the primordial Water of Space, or Chaos, and also means Mother...the Celestial Virgin-Mother of the visible Universe."[26] Perhaps this alludes to a great divinity or higher Intelligence that is the source of the "waters of life" for our particular world and solar system.

Figure 16. Temperance.

I mention solar system here in order to refresh your memory of the relationship earlier described by DK between the sun Sirius and our solar system, which is analogous to the relationship existing between the soul and the incarnating personality. (We must be careful, however, not to stretch this analogy too far when trying to comprehend such lofty celestial Lives.) We can also extend the same idea to the special relationship which exists between Sanat Kumara and Sirius. This leads us to a rather enigmatic object found on the Temperance card. According to both Waite (who designed the cards) and Paul Foster Case, there is a "crown" in the distance on the lower left side of the card. Waite's interpretation is rather vague and esoteric. He states:

> A direct path goes up to certain heights on the verge of the horizon, and above there is a great light, through which a crown is seen vaguely. Hereof is some part of the Secret of Eternal Life, as it is possible to man in his incarnation.

Waite goes on to say that "conventional emblems" and "meanings" must be "renounced" or rejected when pondering this card.

> It is called Temperance fantastically, because, when the rule of it obtains in our consciousness, it tempers, combines and harmonises the psychic and material natures. Under that rule we know in our rational part something of whence we came and whither we are going.

Waite seems to be telling us that this card symbolizes both our origins and destiny after the Great Work of spiritual alchemy has been achieved in this world. He goes on to say:

> It is, moreover, untrue to say that the figure symbolizes the genius of the sun, though it is the analogy of solar light, realized in the third part of our human triplicity.[27]

In other words, we are destined to become spiritualized with the solar light just as the Christ became the sun God indicating the Way of Light ("I am the Light of the world") which all humans are destined to travel. (Recall our earlier discussion about the Sun from the work of David Fideler in his book *Jesus Christ, Sun of God.*)

In his book *The Tarot*, Paul Foster Case offers the following:

> The angel is Michael, archangel of fire, angel of the sun, and ruler of the South (Key 19, The Sun). Michael is also specifically connected with Tiphareth on the Tree of Life.

Of specific interest for us here is the reference to Michael being the ruler of the Sun. Is this an allusion to DK's statement that Sirius rules our solar system? Continuing with Case:

> At the upper end of the path is a crown. It signifies attainment, mastery, and like ideas. It has also a reference to the esoteric meanings of the number 1, which Qabalists call "The Crown." The end of the path of attainment is the realization of the crown of perfect union with the Primal Will.[28]

The primary clue for us in this extract is the crown, which Waite also mentions. The word "crown" has a numerical value of 73 AN and 28 RAN. Both these values are significant. The number 73 equates with Egypt, goddess, redeemer, sacrifice, and interestingly, amphibian. (Note both figures on cards XIV and XVII touch land and water in amphibian style.) Each of these words ties in closely with all the themes we have explored so far (especially the *goddess* of *Egypt*, Isis) which relate the Great Invocation to Sirius.

As for the number 28, we have already shown its significant relevance in relation to the Great Invocation as the central point around which the rest of this amazing mantram revolves. The words "heaven," "goddess," "Egypt," and "The Star" all relate in some way to Sirius. The crown floating in the distant heavens of the Temperance card certainly seems to have some connection with the star Sirius; perhaps it is Sirius itself.

The Hebrew heaven, Zebhul is also connected to the Temperance card. Godwin offers the following information about the fourth heaven of Zebhul: "The fourth Heaven, corresponding to Tiphareth. The heavenly Jerusalem is here, complete with its Temple, upon the altar of which Michael offers sacrifices."[29] Not only does this information reinforce that of the Tarot card Temperance, but it also ties Michael to the fourth path numerically. Interestingly the term "heavenly Jerusalem" equals 196 (AN) which is the square of 14—Temperance and of course, the number veiling the Hierarchy related to the Path to Sirius.

As further food for thought, the following excerpt from *A Treatise on Cosmic Fire* may tie the fourth heaven corresponding to Tiphareth to the fourth Path to Sirius:

> The reason also why the majority of the sons of men follow this Path lies in the fact of its numerical position. These units of the fourth kingdom, the bulk of the fourth Creative Hierarchy on this fourth globe of the fourth scheme in a solar system of the fourth order are innately compelled to seek this fourth Way in order to perfect themselves.[30]

Finally, at the beginning of this section we mentioned how the word heaven related to the Hebrew Shamaim which has a value of 390. We then related this number directly to the phrase "in the sunshine of the major Sun" given by the Tibetan. After this we discussed two numbers which the Tibetan specifically mentions in relation to the fourth path to Sirius, namely the numbers 14 and 17, which we associated with the Tarot cards Temperance (14) and The Star (17). We found that by squaring the number 17 we arrived at the total 289 which equals the names of the three Egyptian goddesses who rode in the celestial ship and the three phrases from the Great Invocation—"Mind of God," "Heart of God," and "Will of God." We also discovered that the square of 14 (196) equals the phrase "heavenly Jerusalem" which directly corresponds with Michael who is on the Temperance card and who is also associated with the fourth heaven of Zebhul.

All of this summarization leads to the final point for this section. When we square 14 (196) and square 17 (289) and add the results together we arrive at 485. The number 485 equals the phrase given by DK, "within the sunshine of the major Sun" (390) and Sirius (95), resulting in "within the sunshine of the major Sun' Sirius" (390 + 95 = 485).

Numerical and Astrological Correspondences and Initiation

We are now at a stage in our study which overlaps number symbolism and certain signs of the zodiac. Djwhal Khul has much to say about the signs and constellations in his writings; in fact He devoted an entire book to the subject, entitled *Esoteric Astrology* (Volume III of *A Treatise on the Seven Rays)*. We will confine ourselves, however, to the astrological signs which relate directly to the numeric and symbolic aspects of the Great Invocation.

In her book *The Labours of Hercules*, Alice Bailey explains the esoteric significance of the astrological signs. Each of the signs represents one of the twelve labors of Hercules from Greek mythology. In her essay on Leo, the fifth sign of the zodiac, and fifth labor of Hercules—the slaying of the Nemean Lion, Bailey states that the constellation Leo contains 95 stars.

> The ninety-five stars in this constellation also have numerical significance for we have there 9 x 10 + 5. Nine is the number of initiation, ten is the number of human perfection, five is the number of man, of the personality, the initiate and his ultimate spiritual achievement.[31]

This brief interpretation of the number 95 is significant in light of all we have stated about Sirius and its tremendous influence on our planet, especially in regard to the process of initiation. Of special significance, however, is the fact that Sirius equals 95. Other significant words and terms of the ageless wisdom that relate to the number value of Sirius are "Hierarchy," "Masters" and "the queen." The last phrase is especially interesting in relation to our discussion about Isis, the queen. The words "Hierarchy" and "Masters," are meaningful because of the close relationship between the Hierarchy (of "Masters") and Sirius.

The fact that Leo contains ninety-five stars (according to Bailey) and that Sirius has an AN value of 95 is a tenuous link at best, but this linkage is further reinforced by DK in the book *Esoteric Astrology*:

> August, which is ruled by Leo, is the month of the Dog-star, or of Sirius, which thus brings Sirius into close relation to Leo. Leo, in the cosmic sense (and apart from our solar system altogether) is ruled by Sirius. Sirius is the home of that greater Lodge to which our fifth initiation admits a man and to which it brings him, as a humble disciple. Later, when the new world religion is founded and is working, we shall find that the major, monthly festival in August, held at the time of the full moon, will be dedicated to the task of making contact, via the Hierarchy, with Sirian force.[32]

In this passage the Tibetan is clearly linking Leo and Sirius, along with the themes of initiation and the Hierarchy. It is also worth noting that Leo has a AN value of 32 which matches the RAN values of Sirius and Christ—32 each.

We might even speculate somewhat on why Alice Bailey even mentioned the ninety-five stars of Leo at all. She doesn't offer star counts in the other chapters on the labors (except in the case of Capricorn), yet in the one labor related to Leo *which is governed by Sirius* she makes it a point to discuss the very number that equals Sirius numerologically. More than that, she even has a section in the Leo chapter of *The Labours of Hercules* devoted to the number 5. Alice Bailey writes:

> This is one of the most interesting labours numerically...From the standpoint of the esotericist, five is the number of man, because man is a divine son of God, plus the quaternary which consists of the lower fourfold nature, the mental body, emotional body, vital body and physical sheath.[33]

Bailey continues:

> But it is in Leo that man becomes what is occultly called the five-pointed star, for that star stands as the symbol of individualisation.[34]

Remember that Sanat Kumara could not have created the human kingdom and individual souls without access to the Law of Freedom which originates on Sirius. Again, notice the reference to the star as a symbol of individualization. (Interestingly, the word "individualisation" with the "s" instead of the "z" equals 192 [AN] which is the same value as "the Great White Lodge.") Bailey goes on to state:

> The Ageless Wisdom of the east tells us that the number five is the most occult and the most deeply significant of the numbers. It claims that the group of celestial and spiritual beings, who took incarnation on earth, manifested through the quaternary, and thus brought into existence the human family, were the fifth group of divine lives and that they combine within themselves, therefore, the dual attributes of the universe, the spiritual and physical...Thus we have the number ten, which is regarded as the number of human perfection and of completion, the number of a perfectly developed and unfolded human being, and the balance achieved between spirit and matter.[35]

The commentary by Bailey reinforces the importance of the number 5 and refers to the number 10 as the goal of man, stressing once more the RAN value of Sanat—10. Since the AN value of Sanat is 55, consider what Alice Bailey says in reference to humanity:

> In order to raise matter into heaven, we have come into manifested existence. In essence and in reality, man is not what he appears to be. He is essentially what he will demonstrate in Aquarius, the opposite sign to Leo. He will then be the man with a universal consciousness, in contradistinction to the self-assertive individuality of the Leo type. The individual in Leo becomes the initiate in Capricorn, and demonstrates as the complete man in Aquarius.[36]

Aquarius is the sign of the world server, but the ageless wisdom teaches that service to the world leads to initiation. And each initiation increases our capacity to serve so that our service eventually grows to world service. This evolution of consciousness only comes through our efforts to improve ourselves and the world around us.

We spiral to perfection at an ever higher turn in the cycle. Therefore, we progress through the signs or labors of Hercules as servers who continuously improve our abilities, skills, and capacities to serve the greater good. Esoteric astrology teaches that we cyclically progress through the zodiacal signs, but that we symbolically progress from Leo the individual to Aquarius the world server as the evolving, expanding initiate of Capricorn, for Capricorn is the sign of initiation. Interestingly, there is an extract from *The Secret Doctrine* which is found in the appendix of *Esoteric Astrology*, "Capricorn is the 10th sign of the zodiac...and has in it *28 stars* [emphasis mine, JB]."[37] It is important to note this because the numeric symbolism of these signs relates directly to portions of the Great Invocation.

Numerologically speaking, Aquarius is the eleventh sign of the zodiac, and Leo is the fifth sign. In the Great Invocation, we find exactly eleven words with a root value of 5, as shown table 31 below.

Table 31. Eleven Words with a Root Value of 5.

Word Position	Word	Qty of Letters	AN	RAN	Root
17	Minds	5	59	23	5
19	men	3	32	14	5
43	men	3	32	14	5
45	Christ	6	77	32	5
52	where	5	59	32	5
58	known	5	77	32	5
66	men	3	32	14	5
71	Masters	7	95	23	5
84	men	3	32	14	5
100	where	5	59	32	5
108	Power	5	77	32	5
663	11	50	631	262	55
6	11	5	10	10	10

(DK states that 11 is the number of the adept using energy.) We can say that the eleven words represent Aquarius, the eleventh sign, and their root value of 5 represents Leo, the fifth sign. Multiplying 11 by 5 equals 55—the AN value of "Sanat." Thus, as Alice Bailey stated the Leo/Aquarius (5 and 11) polarity works to "raise matter into heaven," modeling the redemptive work of Sanat—55. (Adding each together equals 10—the RAN value of "Sanat.") This is indicated in even greater detail by the fact that these eleven words have a combined value of 631/10 (AN), 262/10 (RAN) and 55/10 root value. This value of 10 relates directly to the tenth sign of the zodiac which is *Capricorn*. What's more, these eleven words contain 50 letters (RAN value of "God is known") which reduce to 5 (5 + 0 = 5), returning us to the value of the Great Invocation itself. And finally, the RAN value for these eleven words equaling 262 is equivalent to the combined AN totals of the words "aspirant" (98), "disciple" (77), and "initiate" (87). These three words describe that point in the evolution of the human soul when the *aspirant* enters the spiritual path, becomes a *disciple* and eventually reaches the stage of liberated *Initiate*. (See table 32.)

Table 32. Summary of Numbers 5, 10, and 11.

Item	Corresponds to...
11 Words	Aquarius the 11th sign
5 Letters	Leo the 5th sign
AN, RAN, and Root Values of 10	Capricorn the 10th sign
RAN value of all 11 words = 262	AN Value of "Aspirant, Disciple, Initiate"
Total Root Value 55	AN Value of "Sanat"
11 Words + Values of 10	11 and 10 Key Words (21)
Values of 10 Final Word Position Total = 6 Root Value of 50 Letters = 5	The Sacred Numbers 10, 6, 5

Summing up, Leo and Aquarius are opposite each other in the zodiac and therefore represent two poles of one energy. This Leo/Aquarius polarity indicates the emergence of the individual who achieves material success as a personality. It is the mark of individual, often selfish, human achievement. Once this duality is reversed, the Aquarius/Leo individual expresses the spiritual achievement of the soul or transpersonal self who becomes a powerful leader serving the world. The following points summarize the correspondences between Leo, Capricorn, Aquarius, Sirius, and the Great Invocation:

1. These three signs are related through the numbers 5, 10, and 11. Leo (5) relates to its opposite Aquarius (11) indicating the progress of the individual personality from self server to world server. Numerically considered, 5 x 11 = 55 which is a triangular number—the total of the first 10 numbers added together. Ten is the number of perfection. Leo (5) relates to Capricorn (10) because 5 is the number of man reaching human perfection through initiation by the doubling of 5 to 10.
2. These three numbers are primary themes of the Great Invocation and the ageless wisdom.
3. The three signs of Leo, Capricorn, and Aquarius relate specifically to man's spiritual journey from individualisation to initiation and world service.
4. This journey of the human soul has been fostered through the aid of the great Lives on Sirius.
5. The numbers 10 and 11, or Capricorn and Aquarius, relate numerically to the 10 and 11 (21) key words of the Great Invocation which are composed of 95 letters—the value of Sirius.
6. The number 5 relates Leo, the fifth sign, to the many "5" themes of the Great Invocation and also to Sirius itself because 95 (Sirius) finally reduces to 5.
7. Sirius, according to the Tibetan, governs Leo and these two are related numerically through the number 32. Sirius RAN = 32, Leo AN = 32.
8. There are eleven words with a value of 5 in the Great Invocation.
9. The word "light" (five letters) is repeated five times and has an AN value of 56 (Isis) and reduces further to 11.

10. The word “and” is repeated five times and has an AN value of 19 (19 x 5 = 95, Sirius).

As our study continues, we see a clear strand of numeric correspondences running through the Great Invocation, linking it with distinct and well defined (although sometimes abstruse) themes of the ageless wisdom found in the ancient world as well as in the modern writings of Blavatsky, Bailey, and Djwhal Khul. We are not quite finished with esoteric astrology, but before we go further we must approach the Great Invocation from a new angle. As we move on to the next chapter we will see additional examples, both numeric and symbolic, connecting the meaning and significance of certain zodiacal signs with the Great Invocation.

Notes

1. Blavatsky, *The Secret Doctrine,* vol. 5, 260.
2. Albert Pike, *Morals and Dogma of the Ancient and Accepted Scottish Rite of Freemasonry*, 352-53.
3. Manly P. Hall, *The Initiates of Greece and Rome*, 59.
4. Ibid., 21.
5. Ibid., 28.
6. Marvin W. Meyer, ed. *The Ancient Mysteries, A Sourcebook*, 189.
7. Plato, Phaedrus, *Plato: Collected Dialogues,* trans. R. Hackforth, et. al., 496-7.
8. Alice A. Bailey, *A Treatise on White Magic*, 381.
9. Blavatsky, *The Secret Doctrine,* vol. 5, 265.
10. Bailey, *The Rays and the Initiations,* 330-31.
11. According to the Tibetan, the Buddha had attained a high degree of evolution in a previous cycle of our planetary evolution and held the position of the "Christed" Leader of the Hierarchy prior to the current head of Hierarchy Who attained this position during His incarnation through Jesus 2,000 years ago.
12. Bailey, *Esoteric Psychology,* vol. II, 210.
13. Bailey, *Initiation, Human and Solar*, 17.
14. Ibid., 96.
15. Bailey, *A Treatise on Cosmic Fire,* 829.
16. Ibid., 367.
17. Ibid., 298.
18. Ibid., 306.
19. Bailey, *Initiation, Human and Solar,* 126-27.
20. Bailey, *The Rays and the Initiations,* 414-15.
21. Ibid., 414, 415.
22. Ibid., 415.
23. Ibid., 416.
24. These indirect clues that branch off from our main points are of some importance in the overall treatment of our subject, but they are not as essential in revealing the more pertinent data. I am, however, bringing these other factors into the investigation when they seem at least to be of some interest.
25. Bailey, *A Treatise on Cosmic Fire,* 1260.
26. Blavatsky, *The Secret Doctrine,* vol. 2, 179.
27. Waite, *The Pictorial Key to the Tarot,* 124, 126.
28. Paul Foster Case, *The Tarot*, 156, 155.
29. Godwin, *Godwin's Cabalistic Encyclopedia,* s.v. "Zebhul."
30. Bailey, *A Treatise on Cosmic Fire,* 1259.
31. Alice A. Bailey, *The Labours of Hercules,* 51.
32. Bailey, *Esoteric Astrology*, 299.

33. Bailey, *The Labours of Hercules*, 48.
34. Ibid., 49.
35. Ibid., 49.
36. Ibid., 49.
37. Bailey, *Esoteric Astrology*, 676.

9

The Revealing Cross of Sirius

Part One

Up to this point we have presented many examples of numerological coding within the Great Invocation, suggesting a possible link between this word of power and the system of Sirius. Some of this evidence is inferred from the ageless wisdom presentation of the Tibetan Master Djwhal Khul. Scattered throughout the books DK wrote with Alice Bailey are bits and pieces (some large and some small) of information connecting the sun Sirius with the evolution of our planet.

The Tibetan tells us Sanat Kumara has a close relationship with the great Lord of Sirius, and that without the help of Sirius, Sanat Kumara could not have intervened so directly in the evolution of life on the physical Earth. Without the aid of Sirius, the human kingdom could not have been created; that is, the individualized human soul would not have come into being as dramatically as it did some eighteen million years ago. This required a tremendous sacrifice on the part of the incarnating planetary Logos we call Sanat Kumara; in fact DK tells us this planetary Being is called the "Great Sacrifice."

Through a rather detailed examination of the numbers connected with Sanat Kumara we have found symbolic evidence of His "imprint" within the Great Invocation, especially through the key words. These key words are numerologically and symbolically linked with the "savior" theme of Christianity (Christ), Hinduism (Vishnu), Buddhism (Boddhisatva), Islam (Imam Mahdi), and Judaism (Messiah). We have linked the savior Christ to Sanat Kumara and Sirius through the information supplied by DK as well as through the numeric symbolism contained in the Great Invocation. This connection runs from the sublime "blessing" of Sirius conferred on Sanat Kumara as planetary Savior directly through to the One we know as the Christ, Whose spiritual life expression the Tibetan describes as an excellent example of the true Sirian initiation process. The Christ represents the first human being of the individualization process on Earth to achieve the Sirian level of initiation. He is also the first being of the Hierarchy and Humanity to use the Great Invocation.

Therefore, we are suggesting the Great Invocation is actually a mantric prayer formula—a word of power which is Sirian in origin. It was entrusted to Sanat Kumara some eighteen million years ago when He and 104 other Kumaras came to the Earth and established Themselves here in order to bring manas or mind to animal man. But, is there any evidence within the Great Invocation itself which actually indicates Sirian origin and influence? Is it more than just 113 beautiful words strung together by the Master Djwhal Khul when He gave them to Alice Bailey? Of course we are not suggesting the Great Invocation was written on Sirius in the English language, but we are saying the current version of the Great Invocation as translated by DK into English may contain hidden clues to its source.

Beyond the Sanat Kumara/savior theme we have also found some fascinating parallels in the work of Robert K.G. Temple and the Tarot cards, all of which led us into ancient Egypt and the story of Osiris and Isis. Although at first glance these topics appear wide afield from the Great Invocation, we have shown that the goddess Isis and her resurrection of Osiris through the help of Thoth, (God of alphabets, numbers, words, and magic) does fit in with the theme of redemption, saviors, words of power, initiation, and Sirius. All of these themes are interwoven within the Great Invocation. Not only are the themes and teachings connected, but there are numerological and symbolic interweavings between these themes and the Great Invocation. Now we want to demonstrate an even more direct connection between Sirius and the Great Invocation through the symbolism of the cross. Djwhal Khul writes:

> The sign of the Cross—associated in the Western world with this initiation [the Crucifixion, JB] and with the Christian faith—is in reality a cosmic symbol, long ante-dating the Christian era. It is one of the major signs to be found in the consciousness of Those advanced Beings Who, from the distant sun, Sirius, the seat of the true Great White Lodge, watch over the destinies of our solar system, but Who pay particular attention (why They do so is not yet revealed) to our relatively little and apparently unimportant planet, the Earth.[1]

As you shall see this fascinating piece of information provides us with an opening into deeper aspects of the Great Invocation not readily obvious to investigation unless we proceed with the theory that the Great Invocation may originate with "Those advanced Beings...Who pay particular attention to our relatively little and apparently unimportant planet."

In chapter 7, "Divine Intervention," the Great Invocation was divided into three parts; fifty-six words, the middle word "is," and fifty-six words. Now we will go one step further and divide each group of fifty-six words in half, leaving four groups of twenty-eight words each with the word "is" remaining separate. In effect, we are creating four distinct quadrants from the Great Invocation resulting in a cross with the word "is" placed at the center. Because DK describes the cross relating to the Path to Sirius as equal-armed (see *A Treatise on Cosmic Fire*, page 1260), we are placing four *equal* numbers of words in each quadrant lying between these arms. (In the major Tarot Arcanum, The High Priestess [Isis-Sirius] is wearing an equal-armed cross as she sits on her throne.)

As demonstrated earlier, the 2648 AN value of the first and second halves of the Great Invocation can each be reduced to 2 (2 + 6 + 4 + 8 = 20, 2 + 0 = 2). The middle word "is" can be reduced to 1 (2 + 8 = 10, 1 + 0 = 1). The first half, middle, and second half of the Great Invocation can then be represented as 212, which equals the phrase "the Dog Star Sirius." A very similar result can be obtained using the equal-armed cross representation of the Great Invocation.

As figure 17 shows, there is a resonating number frequency set up between the middle word "is" with a value of 28 and the twenty-eight words in each quadrant of the cross.[2] The middle word forms a triangle of energy with the first half and the second half of the Great Invocation, giving the value of 84 for each triangle (3 x 28). Remarkably, the number 84 is the AN value for "Dog Star." Again, we find the theme of Sirius woven into the structure of the Great Invocation.

Figure 17. The 28 Triangulation.

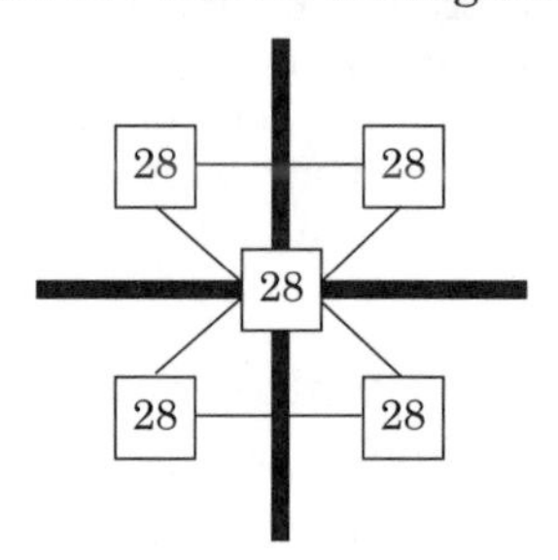

This finding is intriguing in and of itself, but what if we were to investigate the numerological values of the twenty-eight words found in each quadrant of the even-armed cross? Figure 18 below shows the AN values for each group of twenty-eight words.

Figure 18. The Sirian Cross, Level One.

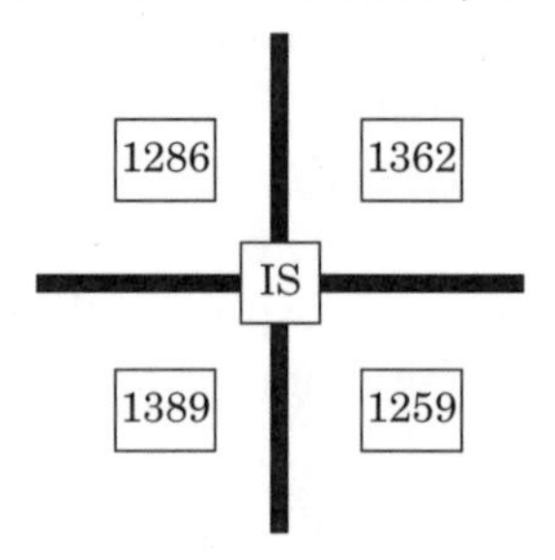

Table 33 divides the Great Invocation into five sections—four sections of twenty-eight words each and one section of one word (the middle word "is"). Starting with the left hand column we see the Great Invocation itself, followed by the number of words in each section, followed by the AN value of each section. These values are then reduced numerologically. Thus, 1286 becomes 17 in the intermediate column (1 + 2 + 8 + 6 = 17) and finally 17 becomes 8 (1 + 7 = 8) in the last column on the right. The question is, of course, do these numbers have any significance in relation to the fundamental theme of the Great Invocation and its possible connection to Sirius?

Table 33. Four Quadrants of the Great Invocation.

Column 1	2	3	4	5
The Great Invocation	Words	AN	Inter-mediate Reduction	Root
From the point of Light within the Mind of God Let light stream forth into the minds of men. Let Light descend on Earth. From the point of	28	1286	17	8
Love within the Heart of God Let love stream forth into the hearts of men. May Christ return to Earth. From the centre where the Will of God	28	1362	12	3
is	1	28	10	1
known Let purpose guide the little wills of men— The purpose which the Masters know and serve. From the centre which we call the race of men Let	28	1389	21	3
the Plan of Love and Light work out And may it seal the door where evil dwells. Let Light and Love and Power restore the Plan on Earth.	28	1259	17	8

Since we divided the Great Invocation into four twenty-eight word sections, what do we find when we look up the numerological value of the 28th word of each of the four sections? Reading table 34 we find that the AN and RAN totals are 136 and 64 respectively.

The phrase “the Will of God” appears in the third stanza of the Great Invocation and is equal to 136 and 64—the same totals found in table 34. We might interpret this to mean that the will of God is related to Sirius in some way. This idea is not without foundation because, according to the Tibetan, Sanat Kumara is “...the Custodian of the will of the Great White Lodge on Sirius....”[3]

Table 34. The 28th Word of Each Quadrant.

28th Word	AN	RAN
Of	21	12
God	26	17
Let	37	10
Earth	52	25
Totals	136	64

More important perhaps, is the numerological fact that the phrase “the Great White Lodge on Sirius” equals 136 (RAN). We discover then, when we divide the Great Invocation into four equal parts which represent the cross motif of Sirius, the final word in each quadrant—namely the 28th—when added together yields a numerological value of 136, reflecting back to us the very theme we are investigating!

Throughout this text we have been using the numeric values of words as cross reference tools to locate corresponding words which might reveal hidden connections between two seemingly unrelated ideas. For instance, the number 56 relates to the goddess Isis (56) and to the fifty-six words of the first and second halves of the Great Invocation; in Egyptian religion, the goddess Isis was identified with the star Sirius. The middle word “is” has a value of 28, which is the same value as the phrase “the star” (RAN). What star? We conclude Sirius because “is” (28) is literally half of “Isis” (is + is or 2 x 28 = 56), and Isis relates to Sirius. We conclude this example by pointing out the phrase “the sun Sirius” equals 56 (RAN), thus completing this cycle of esoteric correspondences.

We are going to expand this concept further by suggesting the possibility that the Great Invocation is a self-referencing word of power. For instance, if Isis and "the sun Sirius" equal 56, does the 56th word in the Great Invocation provide any further insight into the connection between Isis and Sirius? The 56th word of the Great Invocation is "God." This certainly provides some pause for thought.

Another example is the phrase "the star." This phrase equals both 28 (RAN) and 91 (AN). The 28th word of the Great Invocation is the word "of." This is not very revealing, but the 91st word of the Great Invocation is the word "Light." This certainly has meaning in relation to "the star." Let's take this one step further by pointing out that the word "light" equals 56 (AN)! Remember Isis and "the sun Sirius" both equal 56 (and so does "the eastern star").

Before going further I want to add another point of relevance. Just because we can "number hop" through the Great Invocation does not mean every word we try this with will reveal meaningful information. That would be taking matters too far. I am suggesting, however, that some meaningful and significant information might be uncovered through such a process.

We are going to use the number values from table 33 to cross reference the Great Invocation. For example, if the number value is 17, we will find the word in the 17th position in the Great Invocation and note its numerological value. Then we will move to the next value and repeat this process until we have exhausted our number list. We will then combine these values to determine their significance in relation to the themes we have discovered so far. Keep in mind that these values have been derived by configuring the words of the Great Invocation around the equal-armed cross which Djwhal Khul associates with the star Sirius.

In table 33, note that we will not be working with the middle word "is" because it serves as the central axis for the remainder of the cross. This may appear strange in the literal sense, but it bears significance in the symbolic sense because only by removing the middle word "is" from the rest of the invocation does the esoteric meaning reveal itself through the remaining 112 words. Reading down column three, the first set of numbers are 1286, 1362, 1389, and 1259. These numbers present a problem because they are obviously much larger than the number of words in the Great Invocation which, as we know is only 113 words in length. Therefore, how can these numbers serve as an index to the invocation? Only by dividing them into pairs. Thus, instead of 1286 we have 12 and 86. The number 1362 becomes 13 and 62, 1389 becomes 13 and 89, and 1259 becomes 12 and 59. Now we have the following numbers—12, 86, 13, 62, 13, 89, 12, and 59. Since these numbers represent word positions in the Great Invocation, any numbers appearing more than once are superfluous. Therefore, the extra numbers 12 and 13 are eliminated leaving only six distinct word position numbers which are 12, 13, 59, 62, 86, and 89.

The word positions in the Great Invocation corresponding to these six values are in table 35.

Table 35. Values of Level One.

Word Position	Word	AN
12	light	56
13	stream	76
59	Let	37
62	the	33
86	the	33
89	Love	54
321	Totals	289

Our primary interest in this process of analyzing the values of the four quadrants is found in the total value of all the word positions referenced by the numerological information. Therefore, in table 35 we are concerned with the total value of the word positions and the AN values at the bottom of the table. The six items involved have a total value of 321. This number is significant in relation to the Egyptian theme running through the Great Invocation as the number 321 is the numerological equivalent of Osiris (89), Isis (56), Horus (81), and Sirius (95) added together. This of course is the primary Egyptian religious trinity already discussed in some detail earlier, along with the star Sirius, which plays a central role in ancient Egyptian religion and culture.

The number 289 is 17 squared and is directly related to the 17th major Tarot card "The Star." In addition, the number 289 is the numerological equivalent of Isis-Sothis (146), Anukis (75), and Satis (68) who are the three Egyptian goddesses mentioned by Temple as sailing in a celestial boat or ship in an ancient Egyptian scene. Also, the three phrases of real importance in the philosophy of the ageless wisdom and present within the Great Invocation itself—"Mind of God" (87), "Heart of God" (99), and "Will of God" (103)—equal 289.

The results of the next stage of the numerological reduction of these four sections of the Great Invocation appear in figure 19 below. See column four of table 33 and note that the four sections have been reduced to 17, 12, 21 and 17. Since 17 appears twice we will be working with only three numbers and therefore three words, namely those in word positions 12, 17, and 21.

Figure 19. The Sirian Cross, Level Two.

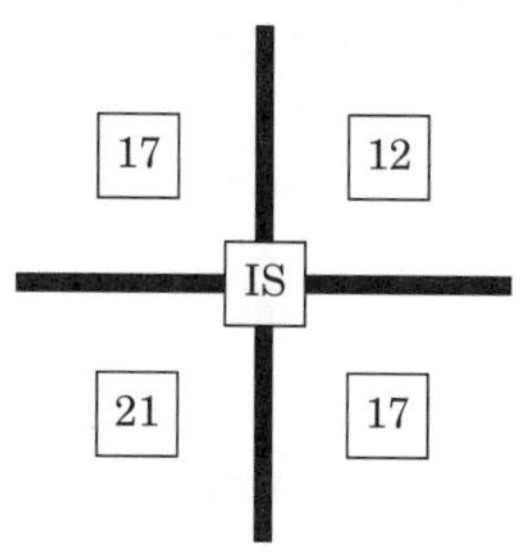

The totals in table 36 are 50 and 171. The number 50 is interesting for two reasons. First, it takes Sirius B 50 years to complete one orbit around Sirius A, thus relating these invocation words to Sirius once more. Second, the number 50 is the value of the middle phrase of the Great Invocation—"God is known." The three words comprising this phrase are the 56th, 57th, and 58th words of the invocation and therefore have a total value of 171, which is the numerological value of the three words referenced in table 36! Thus, there is a natural link between numbers 50 and 171 within the context of the Great Invocation. In addition, the number 171 is of real significance in relation to the Egyptian theme, through such phrases as "the celestial ship" (and its fifty rowers), "the Queen of Heaven" (Isis), "Isis Nephthys," and especially meaningful, "Hermes-Mercury" the "...inventor and god of all arts and sciences...the lord of books, and the scribe of the gods, and mighty in speech."[4]

Table 36. Values of Level Two.

Word Position	Word	AN
12	light	56
17	minds	59
21	Light	56
50	Totals	171

The final or third level of reduction of the four sections of the Great Invocation is shown in column five of table 33; this level of reduction results in numbers 8, 3, 3, and 8. Eliminating the duplicate numbers leaves the numbers 8 and 3. Table 37 displays the totals for the final numerological reduction.

Figure 20. The Sirian Cross, Level Three.

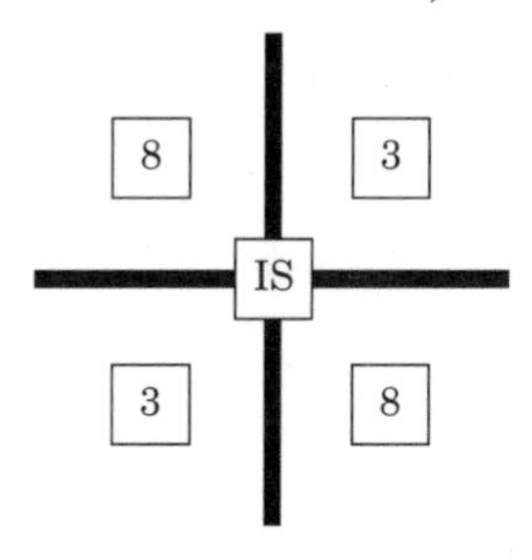

Table 37. Values of Level Three.

Word Position	Word	AN
3	point	74
8	Mind	40
11	Totals	114

As we reach the deepest level of numeric reduction, it appears that many factors are showing themselves to be intimately interwoven and connected at a foundational level. Thus, as shown in table 37, when we add the third and eighth words of the Great

Invocation together we have the number 11. This number corresponds to the eleven original key words constituting the twenty-one key words discussed earlier. DK tells us the number 11 signifies the "adept using energy."

Much of what the Great Invocation is all about relates to the use of energy—a specific kind of energy. Through the use of the Great Invocation we are using the mind to invoke the energies of Light, Love, and Power. We have found this Invocation for Power and Light to be a specifically designed word of power for restoring the Plan on Earth. Blavatsky defines adept in the following way: "In Occultism one who has reached the stage of Initiation, and become a Master in the science of Esoteric philosophy."[5] Interestingly, the terms "initiation" and "energy adept" both equal 120 (AN) and 57 (RAN). In a mysterious way, many of the people of the world today are being initiated into a new way of using energy when they are asked to use the Great Invocation as a form of planetary service. Thus, humanity is learning to be the "energy adept" and achieve planetary initiation under the watchful eyes of the Spiritual Guides of humanity.

The best known and revered Initiate/Adept of the West is Jesus, and His name equals 11 (RAN). The four gospel stories of the New Testament are portrayals of the adept Jesus using energy. The esoteric story teaches that the adept Jesus eventually became the Master Jesus after the crucifixion. Using RAN values, this is indicated numerologically as Jesus (11) the adept (19) using energy prior to the crucifixion (11 + 19 = 30). It was at the symbolic age of 30 that Jesus began His ministry. After the crucifixion, Jesus (11) the adept becomes Jesus the Master. Since the word "Master" has a RAN value of 22, "Master Jesus" now equals 33—the symbolic age of Jesus' crucifixion and resurrection. When combined, 30 and 33 equal 63, the AN value of avatar. This shows the presence of the overshadowing Christ Who was the Avatar of the Piscean Age. Completing the numerological symbolism is the fact that the RAN value of "savior" is 30, and the RAN value of "saviour" is 33, and when combined they *also* equal 63. Thus, one of the key numbers at the core of the Great Invocation is the number 11, indicating the adept using energy.

The other total found in table 37 is the AN value 114. The number 114 equals "Sons of God" (AN)—a term associated by the ageless wisdom with the semi-divine instructors of early humanity and referred to by H. P. Blavatsky in *The Secret Doctrine*:

> It is under the direct, silent guidance of this Maha-Guru [Sanat Kumara, JB] that all the other less divine Teachers and Instructors of Mankind became, from the first awakening of human consciousness, the guides of early Humanity. It is through these "Sons of God" that infant Humanity learned its first notions of all the arts and sciences, as well as of spiritual knowledge; and it is They who laid the first foundation-stone of those ancient civilizations that so sorely puzzle our modern generations of students and scholars.[6]

So then, 114 refers directly to the "Sons of God" who Blavatsky refers to as the Initiates of every mystery school and religion since the great sacrifice of Sanat Kumara created the human kingdom. These very Sons of God are adepts using energy! The numbers 11 and 114 at the heart of the Great Invocation point directly to the Hierarchy of Masters and Teachers who have undergone the process of initiation originating from Sirius. Blavatsky goes on to say:

> The "Being" just referred to, who has to remain nameless, is the *Tree* from which, in subsequent ages, all the great *historically* known Sages and Hierophants, such as Rishi Kapila, Hermes, Enoch, Orpheus, etc., have branched off...He is *the* "Initiator," called the Great Sacrifice.[7]

Here HPB is making the point that although Sanat Kumara is the One Initiator, He brought other great Beings (the 104 Kumaras, Sons of God) with Him along with a host of less advanced light beings, called the Solar Angels, who actually entered into the bodies of many (but not all) of the animal men of eighteen million years ago. Thus was humanity created according to the ageless wisdom. Some of the more advanced Assistants of Sanat Kumara also took form and became the priest-kings who taught humanity art, science, and religion. It was from this line of Teachers that the "Sons of God" emerged. According to the teachings of Djwhal Khul via Blavatsky and Bailey, ancient myths of gods who dwelt amongst early mankind are facts to be taken literally in most cases although many distortions have entered into these stories through the centuries. We are left with legend and myth, bits and pieces of what was once a "golden age," destroyed except for fragments of legendary stories of floods, miraculous deeds of gods and heroes, prophets and saviors, and shattered monuments.

We return again and again to the ancient Egyptians in our investigation of the Great Invocation, a seemingly unlikely "marriage." Yet Egypt played a central role in everything we have previously discussed about the Sons of God, the Mysteries of initiation, and a sophisticated civilization of science, art, and religion created by Sons of God Who once worked openly with humanity. When we look once more at the number 114, we find that a combination of specifically related Sons of God are revealed in terms of two sets of three Egyptian deities. These are "Isis-Sothis, Anukis, and Satis" (82 RAN), and "Osiris, Isis, and Horus" (82 RAN). These two Egyptian triplicities become true Sons of God when Sirius (32 RAN) is included with each group (82 + 32 = 114). Are these not the Egyptian version of Blavatsky's "Sons (and Daughters) of God?" Supporting this idea to some degree we again quote Budge:

> It has already been said that the primitive Egyptians, though believing that their gods possessed powers superior to their own, regarded them as beings who were liable to grow old and die, and who were moved to love and to hate, and to take pleasure in meat and drink like man; they were even supposed to intermarry with human beings and to have the power of begetting offspring like the "sons of God," as recorded in the book of Genesis (vi. 2,4). These ideas were common in all periods of Egyptian history, and it is clear that the Egyptians never wholly freed themselves from them; there is, in fact, abundant proof that even in the times when monotheism had developed in a remarkable degree they clung to them with a tenacity which is surprising. The religious texts contain numerous references to them, and beliefs which were conceived by the Egyptians in their lowest states of civilization are mingled with those which reveal the existence of high spiritual conception.[8]

We see then that the number 114 equates with the Sons of God of the Egyptians, some of whom were Osiris, Isis, Horus, Anukis, Satis, and of course Sothis-Sirius. There is a definite and consistent theme present within the Great Invocation in general, but with the cross arrangement a distinct message involving Sirius, Egypt, and the three principle Gods of the Egyptian resurrection story emerge in the form of numeric symbolism and correspondence.

Let's take this one step further by returning to the phrase "adept using energy."[9]. The fascinating aspect of this phrase is that it corresponds exactly to the "Osiris, Isis, Horus" trinity of the ancient Egyptians. Both these sets of words equal 82 (RAN). Osiris,

Isis, and Horus were not only sons of God (114) related to Sirius, but they were also adepts using energy (82)!

Although the numbers 8 and 3 in the cross diagram reveal a great deal about the underlying energy of the Great Invocation, there is another layer of meaning which reveals the fundamental nature and possible origin of this Word of Power. We have given Djwhal Khul's interpretation of the number 11; now table 38 shows terms important in varying degrees to the overall theme of the Great Invocation.

Table 38. Terms with Root Values of 11.

Terms	AN	RAN	Root
Blue Lodge	83	38	11
Dragons of Wisdom	182	74	11
Great Invocation	173	74	11
Isis-Sothis	146	47	11
Messiah	74	29	11
Neith (Egyptian Goddess)	56	29	11
Redemption	119	56	11
The Hierarchy	128	74	11
The Holy of Holies	182	83	11
The Sirian Lodge	146	74	11
The Sun Sirius	182	56	11
Wisdom	83	29	11

The words in table 38 are special because they must reduce to 11 through *both* methods of numerological reduction, i.e., AN and RAN, in order to appear in it. For instance, you will note the word Isis is not present in table 38, yet we know its value is 56 which reduces to 11 (5 + 6 = 11). This value is the AN total for Isis. When we calculate Isis via the RAN method, however, its value is 20 which reduces to 2. Therefore, Isis does not qualify as a true 11 because we cannot arrive at an 11 value using both methods.

We can go through all the words and phrases in table 38 and fit the majority of them into the thematic context of the Great Invocation. In fact the words "Great Invocation" are in table 38. Such entries as "Isis-Sothis" and "the Sun Sirius" are very powerful symbolic terms which are definitely *central* to the theory that Sirius and the Great Invocation are connected. Actually, it is remarkable (yet consistent) that such words are present at the numerological heart of this most powerful and esoteric world prayer. But, table 38 contains one entry that reflects the 8-3 3-8 pattern of numbers in the final diagram of the cross. That entry is "Blue Lodge." Note its AN value is 83 and its RAN value is 38. No other word with a root value of 11 has this characteristic in the database of esoteric words and phrases. (See appendix E, Esoteric Numerology Lists.)

It should be noted that this database of esoteric and religious terms is a result of research into the nature and origin of the Great Invocation. This database represents terms and concepts specifically born out of the Great Invocation itself and the ageless wisdom teaching from which it has emerged. Thus, within the specialized context and language of esotericism we find very specific messages being broadcast to us along a distinct wavelength. In other words, the symbolism, structure, content, and numerology of the Great Invocation have led to the generation of a database containing specialized esoteric terminology providing clues, which in turn feed back into the Great Invocation. Thus, an information loop is created which spins out the inner meaning of the Great Invocation coded within its words.

Now let's look more closely at the term "Blue Lodge." The Blue Lodge is a Masonic term for the secret work performed in the first three degrees of Masonry. The work of the Blue Lodge is fundamental and foundational to all Masonic work. According to Djwhal Khul:

> Masonry depicts the steady progress of a human being from darkness to light, from ignorance to knowledge and from death to immortality. In the three degrees of the Blue Lodge we have an accurate picture of the progress of the human soul, from the time that that soul appears in human form until the time when the great work

> is accomplished and the candidate for illumination and the worker in the Temple of the Lord ends his career as a risen Master....From the start we will take the position that the Blue Lodge with its three great ceremonies (culminating in the sublime degree of Master Mason) constitute the major Masonic unit, and the E.A [Entered Apprentice, JB] degree, the F.C [Fellow Craft, JB] degree and the third degree contain all the needed elements whereby man can arrive at an understanding of himself and of the universe in which he has to play his little part. We will regard the so-called higher degrees as extensions and elucidations of the three degrees of the Blue Lodge.[10]

The significance of Masonry and the Blue Lodge in relation to the Great Invocation is of major importance because the Tibetan maintains that Masonry is of Sirian origin and influence! Djwhal Khul writes:

> Masonry, as originally instituted far back in the very night of time and long ante-dating the Jewish dispensation, was organised under the direct Sirian influence and modelled as far as possible on certain Sirian institutions and bearing a slight resemblance also to our hierarchical life—as seen in the light of the Eternal Now. Its "Blue Lodge" with its three degrees is related to the three major groups of Lives on Sirius, for there are there no kingdoms of nature, such as we possess; these groups receive all Those Who choose the fourth Path, and train Them in the mode of existence and the type of livingness which is found on Sirius. This will make it plain to you that the least developed of the Sirian Lives are—from our standpoint—all of Them initiates of very high degree.[11]

> This [the Sirian Lodge, JB] is the true "Blue Lodge," and to become a candidate in that Lodge, the initiate of the third degree has to become a lowly aspirant, with all the true and full initiations awaiting him "within the sunshine of the major Sun."[12]

In this last passage DK is indirectly stating once again that our Hierarchy is a "charter member" modeled after the Great White Brotherhood on Sirius. The Tibetan alludes to this idea when He explains that the Lodge (Hierarchy) has two divisions for the Masters Who are its Members:

> a. The — Lodge, comprised of initiates above the fifth initiation, and a group of devas or angels.
> b. The Blue Lodge, comprised of all initiates of the third, fourth, and fifth initiations.[13]

Therefore, when DK says an "initiate of the third degree has to become a lowly aspirant" in the "true Blue Lodge," this means that a human being on Earth who enters our Hierarchy as a third degree initiate is, from the Sirian perspective, equivalent to a person who just enters the spiritual path on Earth and is experiencing the first initiation or birth into the Christ life of spirit. Such a person has entered the Blue Lodge of the Earth's Hierarchy, but is simply a *"lowly aspirant" in the "true Blue Lodge" on Sirius.*

Figure 21. Sirian Initiations.

Initiations Into the Greater Lodge On Sirius

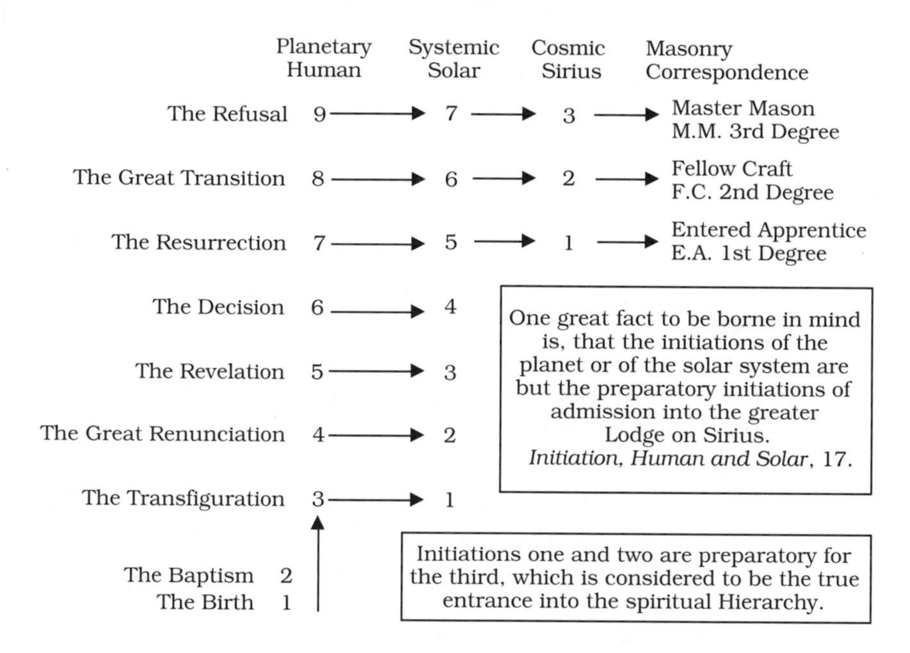

With everything we have discovered about the Great Invocation to this point, with its symbolic and numerological relationship to Sirius, it is truly startling to find the 8-3 3-8 numeric symbol of the Blue Lodge at the core of the Sirian Cross. But, we are not quite finished with these eights and threes, for there are a few more clues waiting to be unveiled.

First, the word "is" has an AN value of 28 which corresponds to "The Star" card in the Tarot using the RAN method. Through its AN value of 91, "The Star" *still* corresponds to the word "is" since it can also be depicted as 91 by substituting 9 for "i" and 1 for "s" using the RAN method. Thus, "is" equals "The Star." using both numerological methods. Thus, "The Star"—91, is hidden at the center of the Great Invocation in the word "is"; it is "veiled" (57) in the 57th position of the Great Invocation.

We say, however, that the numbers found at the core of the Sirian/Great Invocation cross unveil the mystery by revealing the Blue Lodge of Sirius. The numbers surrounding the cross are not only 8 and 3 or 83 and 38 or 33 and 88, but also 8,338. The number 8338 equals "The Star^2 Veiled." In other words, when The Star is multiplied by itself or squared it equals 8,281. When a symbolic veil or occult blind is placed over it, The Star is then veiled (57). Therefore, "The Star^2 Veiled" is $91^2 + 57$ or 8,338 ($8{,}281 + 57 = 8{,}338$). The Veiled Star is *unveiled* by separating 8338 into 83 and 38 revealing the Blue Lodge which we now know (through DK) is found on Sirius.

The Lions Emerge

We must go one step further with these 3's and 8's, although we will now move into more mysterious territory than we have previously explored. I say this because of a cryptic phrase given by the Tibetan in the book *Esoteric Astrology*, which caught my eye as I was reading about the zodiacal sign of Leo. The phrase is "Lions, the divine and tawny orange Flames." Through continuing research into the Great Invocation and esoteric numerology, I have learned to take special notice of peculiar phrases which Djwhal Khul often "drops" into the middle of sentences. Some of these phrases are in quotes and some are not. The above phrase appears exactly as follows:

> Several triangles of force were active when individualisation took place and the "Lions, the divine and tawny orange Flames" came into being and thus humanity arrived upon the planet.[14]

Three things caught my attention when I came across this particular sentence. First, DK is speaking about individualization—when humanity was created. Second, He refers to the color orange, which He has already associated with Sirius via its symbol as an orange cross with a green emerald at the center. (See "The Celestial Ship" in chapter 7.) And third, part of the sentence is placed in quotation marks, although there is no explanation as to the origin of this unusual phrase. Assuming that the phrase was deliberately created and placed in quotation marks, I calculated its numerological value. Interestingly enough its value is 383. I suddenly realized this phrase contained the exact same numbers found in the final numerological reduction of the Great Invocation arranged around the Sirian Cross. Admittedly, one 3 is missing but, 383 can be read as 38 and/or 83 if the 8 is shared between the two 3's. Because the sentence in question has a direct relationship to Sirius, the Blue Lodge (83 38), and individualization, it is just too much of a coincidence to ignore.

All of this information pertains to Leo and according to Djwhal Khul, Sirius governs Leo. It is here the mystery deepens, for on the page directly before the sentence in question we find the following:

> The influences of Sirius, three in number[15], are focussed in Regulus, which is, as you know, a star of the first magnitude and which is frequently called "the heart of the Lion."

DK is referring to the constellation Leo in which Regulus is located. He then adds the following intriguing statement:

> There is more real occultism hidden in the names given to the various stars by astronomers down the ages than has yet been realised, and here you have a case in point.[16]

What is the Tibetan talking about? The clue is hidden in the numeric value of the phrase "the heart of the Lion" which equals 189 (AN). What is the heart of the Lion? It is the star Regulus, which equals 194 (AN). Therefore, if we put the two phrases together, the new phrase that equals 383 is "The star Regulus, the heart of the Lion" (189 + 194 = 383). By providing clues such as these two examples, which both equal 383, is Djwhal Khul telling us that Leo and Regulus are somehow related to Sirius and the effort to create humanity on the planet Earth? If this theory is true it certainly fits very well with the hermetic method of working with numbers, letters, and the giving of hints.

Are there any other connections that fit the Sirian themes associated with 383? While discussing the fourth Path to Sirius the Tibetan lists the effects or consequences on Earth of the Lord of the World's (Sanat Kumara) relationship with the Lord of Sirius.

> The energy evoked in response to this relationship enters the Hierarchy via the Heart of the Sun, creating a triangle of spiritual energy of enormous potency. You have, therefore: Sirius, The Hierarchy, Heart of the Sun.[17]

When we calculate the AN values of "Sirius, The Hierarchy, Heart of the Sun" and add them together they also equal 383. Is the Heart of the Sun related to Regulus? Remember the earlier statement by DK that the influences of Sirius are focused in Regulus, "the heart of the Lion." This may not be literally true as we understand the physical universe, but at the spiritual and psychological levels described by the Tibetan, "reality" as we understand it through our five senses is most likely much different, to say the least. The point is, however, that a definite numerological link via the number 383 exists between these various examples.

There is another instance where the number 383 emerges. It is probably the most cryptic and esoteric example from the standpoint of an occult blind (deliberate or natural).

Following a logical process of investigation concerning lions and the color orange, I found various references to orange in the book *Letters on Occult Meditation* by Alice Bailey. The most pertinent of these references contained what appeared to be possible clues to further information about the connection between orange, Leo the Lion, and Sirius. Here is the passage:

> The synthesis of all the colours, as aforesaid, is the synthetic ray of indigo. This underlies all and absorbs all. But in the three worlds of human evolution the orange of flame irradiates all. This orange emanates from the fifth plane, underlies the fifth principle, and is the effect produced by the esoteric sounding of the occult words "Our God is a consuming Fire." These words apply to the manasic principle, that fire of intelligence or reason which the Lords of the Flame imparted, and which stimulates and guides the life of the active personality. It is that light of reason which guides a man through the Hall of Learning on into the Hall of Wisdom. In the latter hall its limitations are discovered, and that structure which knowledge has built (the causal body or the Temple of Solomon) is itself destroyed by the consuming fire. This fire consumes the gorgeous prison house which man has erected through many incarnations, and lets loose the inner light divine. Then the two fires merge, mount upwards and are lost in the *Triadal Light.*[18]

We will examine the above passage shortly, but first I want to explain the process that led to this discovery of another value of 383. After finding other passages containing references to orange, I turned to the end of the book (*Letters on Occult Meditation*) where I normally record special page references for future use. When I did this I saw that I had recorded one special reference at some earlier time. The reference said "Sirius 262." Turning to page 262, I read that "A Master of the Wisdom is He Who has taken the first initiation that links Him up with the greater Brotherhood on Sirius."[19] Having read this I returned to the reference which is quoted above. Naturally, I was pulled immediately to the phrase in quotation marks, "Our God is a consuming Fire." Calculating its AN value I was shocked to find it to be 262, the corresponding page number that referred to the Master of Wisdom linked with Sirius! Of course it is not beyond reason to view this as a simple coincidence, except for the fact that once again, the Tibetan is talking about orange, the Lords of the Flame, individualisation, the fifth plane, and the fifth principle of manas, all of which are directly associated with Sirius.

Now let's complete the exercise by examining this passage more closely. DK is saying that although the color indigo synthesizes or absorbs all the other colors (vibrations) in the entire evolutionary process, "in the three worlds of human evolution the orange of flame irradiates all." Keep in mind that the symbol of Sirius is an orange cross and that Sirius is found on the cosmic mental plane, the fifth plane, and is the source of manas for our system. DK also tells us that by the esoteric sounding of the words "Our God is a consuming Fire," the color orange is produced. This orange stimulates and guides the life of the active personality and represents the manasic principle of mind and reason brought to Earth through the aid of Sirius, the sacrifice of Sanat Kumara, and the Lords of the Flame. Eventually the consuming Fire will burn the "prison house which man has erected" (the fourth initiation) and the human soul will soon become a Master of the Wisdom (fifth initiation) as the "two fires [the fire of intelligence in man and the consuming Fire of God, JB] merge, mount upwards and are lost in the *Triadal Light*."

The clue which completes the numerological aspect here is the italicized phrase "*Triadal Light*." The AN value of this phrase is 121. "Our God is a consuming Fire" and "Triadal Light" added together equal 383. What then happens to the human being who has taken the fifth initiation and is released into the Triadal Light? "...He is an Initiate of the First Degree in the greater Lodge," meaning the Great

White Lodge on Sirius, or to use Masonic symbolism, the Blue Lodge—83 38.

As an added footnote to all this, the value of "Our God is a consuming Fire" (262 AN) is two times the value of "God is known" (131 AN). In addition, the value of "Triadal Light" (121 AN) is 11 x 11, or the adept using energy x Blue Lodge (11 root value).

I want to conclude this discussion by saying this material has the effect of drawing us deeper and deeper into a mystery which we may never see solved in our lifetimes, assuming we are not creating glamour and illusion from a series of coincidences. I do not believe it is *all* coincidence, however, because too many correspondences are appearing in such a concentrated area of investigation.

To make this point, I have left one more example of 383 for the end of this discussion. To illustrate it properly, we are displaying the level two diagram of the four quadrants prior to reducing them to 8's and 3's (figure 22). By eliminating the duplicate 17, as we did in table 36, we are left with 12, 17, and 21, three numbers that contain the digits necessary to form two other numeric values of primary importance to our subject.

Figure 22. The Sirian Cross, Level Two.

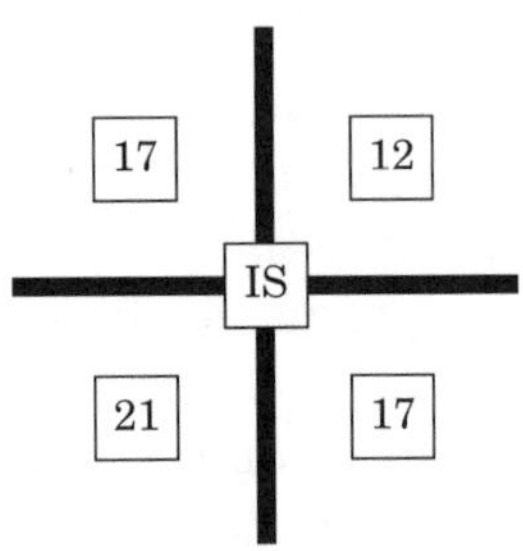

As indicated in figure 23, these six digits contain within themselves the numbers 171 and 212—"the Queen of Heaven, the Dog Star Sirius," which when added together total 383. This is one more example of how numbers carry hidden within themselves distinct patterns relating to archetypal ideas that appear separate from the vantage point of the time/space dimension of the five senses.

Figure 23. Sirius Hidden in Number.

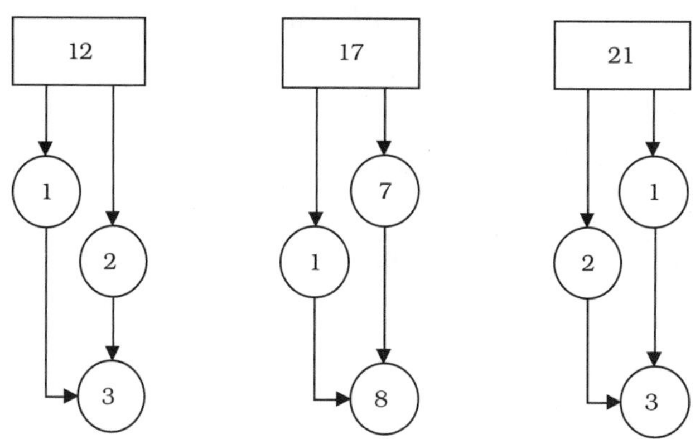

In summary, these three crosses (detailed in tables 35, 36, and 37) have yielded numerical values corresponding to specific esoteric themes involving Sirius, Egypt, and the Mysteries of initiation.

The original four sets of four digit numbers have been reduced to a series of 8's and 3's (root numbers) by dividing the Great Invocation into four sections of 28 words each. Table 39 indicates five rather cryptic, but clearly defined terms and phrases directly related to Sirius in some respect, all with a value of 383.

Table 39. The Number 383.

Phrase	AN	Comments
"Lions, the divine and tawny oranges Flames"	383	Leo, Manas/Mind Individualization.
"The Star Regulus, the heart of the Lion"	383	Three influences of Sirius focused here.
"Sirius, Heart of the Sun, The Hierarchy"	383	Sirius distributes potent spiritual energy
"Our God is a consuming Fire, Triadal Light"	383	The Master of Wisdom becomes an Initiate of Sirius
"The Queen of Heaven, the Dog Star Sirius"	383	Combination of numbers 12, 17, 21

We must seriously consider the esoteric implications of this fact when coupled with the knowledge that the very same numbers—3 and 8—are the "numeric bedrock" of the Great Invocation when it is depicted as the equal-armed cross of Sirius.

The Lion-Man

The Egyptian theme continues to surface throughout this material with the addition of a distinct "lion" theme via the numbers 3 and 8. Naturally, most of us think of the Sphinx when lions and Egypt are mentioned in the same sentence. The lion, however, played an important part in the religion of the ancient Egyptians beyond that of the Sphinx. The most important god of the Egyptians, Osiris, is called the lion-god throughout much of *The Egyptian Book of the Dead.*

The oldest known lion-god of the Egyptians is Aker. This ancient Egyptian god guarded the passage of Ra's solar boat across the sky. The passage is descriptive of the tunnel entrance and exit of the sun as it rose and set each day. The sun god Ra was thought to be entering a tunnel of darkness at dusk from which he would emerge the next day. This idea later evolved to the point where twin lions were said to guard the entrance and exit. These twin lion-gods were named Sef (yesterday) and Tuau (today).

There are also two lion-goddesses named Tefnut and Sekhmet. Tefnut was originally the twin sister of the god Shu. Together they separated heaven and earth, allowing the sun to rise. The other goddess, Sekhmet, was the female counterpart of Ptah of Memphis, the builder and architect who followed the instructions of Thoth/Hermes. This lion-headed goddess was associated with fires and plagues. We must remember that many of the gods and goddesses of the Egyptians actually represent archetypal energies responsible for the creative and natural forces of existence. Sekhmet is one example and she thus represents fiery destruction. Her most prominent title was Lady of Flame.

For purposes of our study, Sekhmet is of particular interest because of her depiction as a human figure with the head of a lion. This immediately brings the Sphinx to mind. The great majority of Egyptologists believe the Sphinx was built by the Pharaoh Khephren sometime during his reign between 2520 and 2494 BCE. Some independent Egyptologists and investigators believe however, that the

Sphinx is far older. John Anthony West is probably the most controversial and prominent critic of the official conclusions of mainstream Egyptologists concerning the age of the Sphinx.

West makes a case for a much older Sphinx by indicating the presence of erosion around the walls of the pit surrounding the statue. His theory was eventually supported by Professor Robert Schoch, a geologist from Boston University. After investigating the site, the professor eventually concluded the age of the Sphinx to be 7000 to 5000 BCE. Although West felt this estimate to be too conservative, it still represented a major break in the official estimate of Egyptologists who scoffed at the idea that the Sphinx could be so old.

Actually, West was following through on the theories of R. A. Schwaller de Lubicz. West writes in the introduction of his book *Serpent in the Sky*:

> *Serpent in the Sky* presents a revolutionary, exhaustively documented re-interpretation of the civilization of ancient Egypt; it is a study of the life work of the philosopher, Orientalist and mathematician, the late R. A. Schwaller de Lubicz.
>
> After two decades of study, mainly on site at the Temple of Luxor, Schwaller de Lubicz was able to prove that all that is accepted as dogma concerning Egypt (and ancient civilization in general) is wrong, or hopelessly inadequate; his work overthrows or undermines virtually every currently-cherished belief regarding man's history, and the "evolution" of civilization.[20]

In a recent work by Graham Hancock and Robert Bauval entitled *The Message of the Sphinx*, the authors penetrate even more deeply into the mysteries of the Sphinx. Through excellent research and investigation, Hancock and Bauval argue a strong case for dating the Sphinx at 10,500 BCE, thus further reinforcing the theories of Schwaller de Lubicz and John Anthony West. Through the use of computer software capable of depicting the sky for any date in history, Bauval and Hancock show that over 12,000 years ago the Sphinx faced the constellation of Leo the Lion at the exact time of the spring and autumn equinoxes. Apparently, the constellation of the Lion was of great interest to the Egyptians for them to have built such a grand monument perfectly aligned to its counterpart in the sky. We may never know why the Egyptians were so interested in Leo, but the ageless wisdom may provide some light on this mysterious subject.

Here are extracts of statements made by the Tibetan concerning the Sphinx.

> In this world period we have the division of the sign of the Sphinx into two signs (the Lion and the Virgin, soul and form) because the state of human evolution and conscious realisation is that of a recognised duality.[21]

> Leo is a part of the Sphinx, and upon this I need not enlarge as we have touched upon this elsewhere. This is a great mystery. Virgo and Leo together stand for the whole man, for the God-man as well as for spirit-matter.[22]

If we couple these statements by the Tibetan with the information provided by Schwaller de Lubicz, West, Hancock, and Bauval we find the Egyptian civilization inherited wisdom and knowledge of the cosmos from advanced initiates of the Mysteries and built this knowledge into the stone monuments found in the deserts of modern day Egypt. The ancients obviously believed Sirius and Leo held the secret of man's nature as both god and animal.

The Egyptians however, were not the only ancient civilization to depict a lion-man. In Hindu mythology, Vishnu incarnated on Earth in various guises in order to save humanity in times of danger; in other words Vishnu was an avatar. In his fourth incarnation (related to the fourth Path to Sirius, perhaps), the god Vishnu took the form of a lion-man named *Narasimha*. According to the *Dictionary of Sanskrit Names,* another name given to Vishnu in his fourth incarnation is *Narahari* (*Nara* = man, and *hari* = tawny, lion).[23] Just as in the Egyptian religion, the Hindu system has many different names for the same god depending on the role the particular deity is playing. Thus, *Hari* is another name for Vishnu and is also associated with *Soma*, the nectar of the gods, because of its brown color.[24] (Interestingly, HPB ascribes golden-green to *Hari* in the glossary of *The Secret Doctrine*.) This hints at the orange and green connection with Sirius and the symbol of its fourth path.

It appears as though we are circling back to the lions, the "tawny orange Flames" mentioned by Djwhal Khul. Returning to the *Dictionary of Sanskrit Names,* we find a cross-reference for the word tawny to be *Kapila*. Thus, *Kapila* is another name for Vishnu! In the glossary of *The Secret Doctrine* we read:

> Kapila (of tawny colour). Name of an ancient sage, identified with Vishnu, considered by some to be the founder of the Sankhya system of philosophy. Name of one of the seven and three Kumaras.[25]

HPB points out that Kapila was not just a sage who founded an Indian system of philosophy:

> Kapila, besides being the name of a personage, of the once living Sage and the author of the Sankhya philosophy, is also the generic name of the Kumaras, the celestial Ascetics and Virgins.... this relates to that primordial period when the "Sons of God" taught to the newly created men those arts and sciences, which have been cultivated and preserved in the sanctuaries by the Initiates.[26]

As the above quotation explains, Kapila has taken various forms throughout the ages, but of special significance to our study is Kapila's identification with the Kumaras, and as Vishnu in the form of Kapila imparting Wisdom and knowledge of art and science to humanity. This is the identical role played by Nommo of the Dogon tribe, Oannes of the Sumerians, and Osiris, with the aid of Isis and Thoth/Hermes of the Egyptians.

We have come full circle in our exploration of the tawny lions described by DK. Lion-gods and lion-men apparently played some mysterious role at least for the ancient Egyptians and Hindus. The esoteric message in all this is that humanity is both animal and divine. We return, once again, to the event held in such high regard by the teaching of the ageless wisdom—individualization—the moment when humanity, the fourth kingdom, was created. The Tibetan explains that the Earth was in the age of Sagittarius when individualization took place,

> but the brain of the then human being failed to register what had happened....Cycles passed and when at a later date the sun was in Leo (approximately eighteen million years ago) the first instances of coordination between brain and mind took place and the human being was definitely self-conscious. He registered his individuality.[27]

The symbolism is certainly obvious—the energy of Leo individuality was embedded in humanity. The new kingdom became a composite of animal bodies implanted with the divine spark of mind. The human soul was created during the time when Leo was in its ascendancy. The Lion-man emerged on the planet. Is this why the great Sphinx sits on the desert facing East? If the priests of the Mysteries of Initiation knew these secrets of man's creation, is it possible they left a marker in the sand at the end of the old Atlantean civilization? As Hancock and Bauval show in their book *The Message of the Sphinx*, the great lion-man of the desert faced the rising constellation of Leo the Lion at the spring and autumn equinoxes in 10,500 BCE. Was this in recognition of the esoteric teaching concerning the time and astrological influences surrounding humanity's creation? All we can do is examine the information available and continue to unravel as best we can the hints and clues provided by the monuments of the past and the ageless wisdom teachings available today.

Part Two

The Creative Hierarchies

The ageless wisdom of the recent past provided by the Tibetan Teacher Djwhal Khul contains many clues about humanity's origin. Some of these clues might be found in DK's teaching about the Creative Hierarchies. These Hierarchies are groups of lives that come into activity within the solar system in order to contribute to its development. The various planetary schemes within the solar system are the vehicles through which these various Hierarchies accomplish their work. At this particular time of the solar system's development, the planet Earth is receiving special focus. This focus has been especially intense during the fourth cycle of our current Earth period when the human kingdom came into being some eighteen million years ago. Although there are twelve Creative Hierarchies, only seven are active in our solar system at this time because five of these groups have completed their work in a previous solar cycle. As for the seven Hierarchies currently active in the solar system Djwhal Khul explains:

> Each of these seven hierarchies of Beings Who are the Builders or the *Attractive* Agents are (in their degree) intermediaries; all embody one of the types of force emanating from the seven constellations [zodiacal signs, JB]. Their intermediary work, therefore, is dual:
> 1. They are the mediators between Spirit and matter.
> 2. They are the transmitters of force from sources extraneous to the solar system to forms within the solar system.[28]

Apparently each of the Creative Hierarchies is associated with one of the paths to the Higher Evolution, because the Tibetan identifies the Hierarchies relating to all except the sixth and seventh paths. Because the subject of the Creative Hierarchies is a mysterious and complex topic, we will confine ourselves to an investigation of the Hierarchy or Hierarchies that may relate to the Path to Sirius.

When DK gave the Hierarchies connected with the Path to Sirius, He simply wrote that they were veiled by the numbers 14 and 17. We have already linked these numbers with the 14th Tarot card, Temperance and the 17th card, The Star. When these two numbers are squared and added together they equal 485, the value of the phrase "in the sunshine of the major sun, Sirius."

Now we want to determine if we can link these two numbers (14 and 17) to the correct Creative Hierarchies through esoteric numerology. The Tibetan writes: "Much light can come to the earnest student through a study of the numbers connected with these Hierarchies."[29] The following table is a reproduction of the number scheme given by DK.

Table 40. The Creative Hierarchies.

Hierarchy	A	B	C	D	E	Sign
One	6	1	7	14	5	Leo
Two	7	2	6	15	6	Virgo
Three	8	3	5	16	7	Libra
Four	9	4	4	17	8	Scorpio
Five	10	5	3	18	9	Capricorn
Six	11	6	2	19	1	Sagittarius
Seven	12	7	1	20	2	Aquarius
Total	63	28	28	119	38	

Note that Sagittarius and Capricorn are reversed in relation to one another. The Tibetan notes that: "This is a temporary emphasis and will change in another world cycle. This is one of the mysteries revealed at initiation." *Esoteric Astrology*, 35.

The first thing to remember is that the first five Hierarchies are not shown because they are no longer in manifestation. Table 40 indicates only the seven groups of Hierarchies now active in our solar system. They are numbered in several ways, however. Column A lists these Hierarchies in their natural order without the five that reached completion in the past solar system. Column B gives their order as one through seven just as they are named. Column C lists them from below upwards (from the human perspective), the opposite of column B. Column D is my own addition which simply displays the total for each Hierarchy based on the numbers DK gives in columns A, B, and C. Finally, column E is the numerological reduction of each Hierarchy based on its individual total. The totals for all the Hierarchies combined are shown in the last row of the table.

Notice the number 38 appears at the bottom of column E. This number represents the reduced numerological total of all the Hierarchies manifesting in our Solar System. Interestingly, as you will recall, the numbers 3 and 8 are found in the final reduced form in the four quadrants of the Great Invocation.

Hierarchy One and Leo

Perhaps even more interesting are the numbers found in column D. Notice the presence of 14 and 17—the two numbers given by DK which veil the Hierarchies concerned with the path to Sirius. Number 14 is associated with Hierarchy One. When we reduce the value of Hierarchy One from 14 to 5 (1 + 4 = 5) we obtain the fifth sign of the zodiac which is Leo, and this is the sign Djwhal Khul gives as associated with the first Hierarchy. Therefore, Hierarchy One is transmitting the energy of Leo into our solar system. Numerologically, Sirius and Leo both equal 32 (Sirius RAN, and Leo AN). Recall DK's words, "Leo, in the cosmic sense (and apart from our solar system altogether) is ruled by Sirius."[30]

Let's examine Hierarchy One in detail. Its names are the "Divine Flames" and "Divine Lives." The sign is Leo, the ruling astrological planet is the Sun, and the color is orange. Remember DK's earlier description of the lives involved in the process of creating the human kingdom: "Lions, the divine and tawny orange Flames." Perhaps DK is describing Hierarchy One in this extract. Blavatsky describes these mysterious Lives in the following passage:

> The highest Group is composed of the Divine Flames, so called, also spoken of as the "Fiery Lions" and the "Lions of Life," whose esotericism is securely hidden in the zodiacal sign of Leo.[31]

These Lives are beyond our ability to comprehend in any detail, but Hierarchy One is the "Son of God Himself, the First Born in a cosmic sense,"[32] to quote DK. This terminology refers to the concept of the Cosmic Christ, the Son, born out of the marriage between Father-Spirit and Mother-Matter at cosmic levels of life beyond the physical dimension of human evolution. The Son that is born, in this particular instance, is a cosmic Entity, who eventually manifests through the form of an entire solar system.

In his description of this first Creative Hierarchy, the Tibetan also uses the term "the burning Sons of Desire."[33] He explains elsewhere:

> By the bringing together of spirit and matter (Father-Mother) in the macrocosm, and their union through the action of the will, the objective solar system, or the Son, was produced—that Son of desire, Whose characteristic is love, and Whose nature is buddhi or spiritual wisdom.[34]

These passages clearly indicate that Hierarchy One is an essential expression of the Life of the Solar System itself. This Hierarchy exists at the highest spiritual level of our solar system from the human standpoint. This plane is called the divine plane of existence; it is the plane of the Logos Itself, and whatever may be the nature of Hierarchy One, it is perhaps, an expression of the Essential Life of our entire solar system, or Son in manifestation.

Before proceeding further we should review the systems aspect of the ageless wisdom philosophy, which we discussed in chapter 7. We must keep in mind the Hermetic maxim "As above, so below." This is our primary anchor in this complex sea of abstractions. We human beings are a tiny sub-system inside a larger life system, which in turn is a sub-system inside a greater Life, and so on to incomprehensible levels of the cosmos. Our solar system is the physical manifestation of a Great Life, a Solar Entity described as a "Son" by the ageless wisdom. Our planet is a Self Conscious Living Being, but at the same time it is a sub-system within the greater solar system or solar Logos. And, we humans are self-conscious beings who are sub-systems within our planet.

Now let's take this one step higher. Our solar Logos is part of a larger cosmic Entity DK calls the ONE ABOUT WHOM NAUGHT MAY BE SAID. This incomprehensible Life is a cosmic Logos.

According to DK, our solar system is the heart chakra of this cosmic Being. Chakra is simply a Sanskrit term meaning wheel of energy. These chakras, or centers, are symbolically depicted as lotuses with varying numbers of petals. Remember the law of correspondence, "as above so below." The ONE ABOUT WHOM NAUGHT MAY BE SAID has seven chakras, and this is reflected in the sub-systems within this cosmic Logos. Thus our solar system contains seven chakras which are the seven sacred planets within the "body" of the solar Logos.[35] Our planet possesses seven chakras or centers of energy, and a human being has seven chakras. This is an oversimplification of a complex topic, but it is essentially accurate and follows the Hermetic axiom, "as above, so below."

These wheels are receivers and transmitters of distinct energy qualities. The heart center is the focus of our attention because our solar system is a heart chakra for the expression of Love energy. All heart chakras at every level receive and transmit the energy of Love. The heart chakra is said to contain twelve petals and our solar system is described by DK as a twelve petalled lotus. The Tibetan describes the symbol of Hierarchy One as, "the Golden Lotus with its twelve petals folded."[36] This indicates, perhaps, the future potential of Hierarchy One when the lotus of Love will open and be in full bloom at the consummation of the systemic evolutionary process.

This chakra also corresponds to the second aspect of the trinity—the Son, the Christ, Vishnu, the Love-Wisdom quality of God—the mediator between spirit and matter. Our solar Logos is an expression of the Cosmic Christ, the Son of God incarnate on the cosmic physical plane. Following through on this theme of the Son aspect, Djwhal Khul says:

> The evolution of the Son, or the cosmic incarnation of the Christ, is of immense importance in the plans of the Being greater than the solar Logos, HE ABOUT WHOM NAUGHT MAY BE SAID. The animating principles of allied constellations and systems watch the progress of the evolution of the Son with keenest attention.[37]

What are these allied constellations and systems?

> *The cosmic Logos* of our system works similarly through three major systems (of which ours is not one), utilising seven solar systems (of which ours is one), for the distribution of His force and having myriads of sevenfold groups as the cells of His body.[38]
>
> 1. The seven stars, composing the Great Bear.
> 2. The seven stars, composing the Pleiades...
> 3. The sun, Sirius.
>
> These compose major triangles of force and all are held within the radius of the Life of that Great Being Whose expressed, manifested

> intention is brought into being through the medium of these three related groups and our solar system.[39]

In other words, the ONE ABOUT WHOM NAUGHT MAY BE SAID contains within Its vast cosmic field of expression at least ten constellations of stars—the Great Bear, the Pleiades, Sirius, our solar system, and six other solar systems. The Great Bear, the Pleiades, and Sirius are controlling constellations which distribute energy to the other seven solar systems, of which ours is one.

Keep in mind that Leo is governed by Sirius, and Sirius is our parent system; "Our Logos [solar Logos, JB], with His system, forms a part of a still greater Logos."[40]

Hierarchy One embodies the energy coming from the constellation of Leo the Lion. Here we find a suggestive numerological correspondence. We noted earlier that the phrase "the heart of the Lion" equals 189. This phrase refers directly to Leo, and perhaps indirectly, to the star Regulus. In an interesting passage, the Tibetan is describing the spiritual goals of a human being, a planetary Logos, and a solar Logos. The goal for a solar logos is, "the development of the principle of cosmic Will which will make Him what has been called a 'Lion of Cosmic Will.' "[41] This is a rather striking phrase that certainly relates to the star Regulus, the heart of the lion. The esoteric clue involves the numerological value of "Lion of Cosmic Will," *for it is also equal to 189*. Is this merely a coincidence, or is this a deliberate phrase designed to link the solar Lives of the first Hierarchy with Regulus in Leo? We cannot know for certain at our present stage of knowledge, but at least we are in a position to raise the question because of all the other numerological correspondences in the Tibetan's writing.

Sirius (along with the Great Bear and the Pleiades) governs and controls our solar system, and apparently the other six solar systems which constitute the cosmic expression of the ONE ABOUT WHOM NAUGHT MAY BE SAID. The sun Sirius is the parent system of our solar system. Sirius is the soul aspect, the Cosmic Christ, and our solar system is the incarnated personality aspect, the Son in manifestation.

Sirius is situated on the cosmic mental plane and is the source of manas (mind) for our system. Our solar system is polarised on the cosmic astral plane, and the goal of our system is full consciousness on the cosmic mental plane. (See appendix D1.) Another clue to the nature of the first Hierarchy might be in the statement by DK that, "The first (sixth) Hierarchy might be viewed as endeavoring to express the *mental* vibration of the solar Logos."[42] Since Sirius is the source of manas or mind, and the cosmic mental plane is the goal for the solar Logos, this first Hierarchy may be working quite closely with the manasic energies associated with Sirius.

Sirius is the cosmic center concerned with the creation of individualized soul consciousness in our solar system through the process of initiation. In order to accomplish this task, Sirius filters its energy through the constellation of Leo, where it appropriates the Leonine energy that bestows sensitivity to the environment. DK says, "The whole story and function of Leo and its influences can be summed up in the word '*sensitivity*...' "[43] This sensitivity evolves from the most basic sensitivity of the human being to the outer world, to that of the ego-personality with its individual selfishness, to an increasing sensitivity to the spiritual soul, and culminating in the "spiritual sensitivity of the God-Man...to the environment."[44]

The purpose of our solar system is the development of consciousness, which is the middle or second aspect. (See table 1.) This follows a plan in which the first solar system developed the third aspect of substance/intelligence, the present (second) solar system is developing the second aspect of consciousness/love-wisdom, and the third solar system will develop the first aspect of spirit/will.

During this second incarnation of the solar Logos, Sirius controls and governs the development of the second aspect in all parts of the solar system. Hierarchy One—the Divine Flames, the Fiery Lions—plays the role, perhaps, of gathering in and synthesizing the essence of experience garnered by the other six Hierarchies of the solar system during their time in manifestation. Speaking about Leo (along with Aries and Capricorn) DK says:

> They are Themselves expressions of the will-to-good and, therefore, constitute the line of least resistance for the dissemination of first ray energy throughout our solar system.[45]

Therefore, Hierarchy One represents the first ray of Will, Purpose, and Power.

The Tibetan states this group of Lives "...emanated from the Heart of the central Spiritual Sun."[46] This implies the dispatch of these "Lions of Life" from that aspect of the Godhead—the central spiritual Sun—which is associated with Will and Purpose. However, since these Lives emerged from the heart of the central spiritual Sun this gives Them a distinct second aspect or Love orientation.

We have already ventured into esoteric areas far beyond our abilities to comprehend, but at the least we have found specific themes that hold together in a definite although diffuse pattern. We know that:

- Sirius governs our solar system.
- Sirius governs Leo and consequently Regulus.
- Regulus is known as the heart of the lion.
- Hierarchy One is associated with Leo, lions, and emanated from the *heart* of the central spiritual Sun. Therefore, we may conclude that Hierarchy One is associated with Sirius via Leo.
- The energies of Sirius are related to the soul or second aspect of our solar Logos—the heart of the sun.
- Sirius relates to the Hierarchy of our planet and to the Christ specifically as the head of Hierarchy via the heart of the sun—all second aspect factors.
- Hierarchy One is "the Son of God Himself...even as the *Christ* was the 'Eldest in a vast family of brothers.' "[47]

Thus, the Christ as the first fruit of human spiritual evolution via the process of initiation instituted by Sirius is a human reflection of Hierarchy One which is influenced by Leo, and which in turn is governed by Sirius.

Hierarchy Four and Scorpio

The other number veiling a Hierarchy associated with the path to Sirius is 17. Note in table 40 that the number 17 is associated with Hierarchy Four, the human Monads and consequently with Scorpio. It is rather curious that seventeen should end up being associated with a Hierarchy related to Scorpio because seventeen returns us to the Egyptians.

In Plutarch's story of Isis and Osiris, he describes the slaying of Osiris by his brother Set or Typhon. As described earlier, Set took a beautiful chest to a royal banquet and offered it as a gift to whomever the chest fit the best. Everyone eagerly took turns getting into the chest without success. Osiris, not knowing that Set had already constructed the chest to perfectly fit him, finally took his turn. As soon as he lay down in it, Set and his accomplices swiftly placed the cover on the chest and nailed it shut, trapping Osiris inside. The chest was then cast into the Nile where it was carried to the sea and lost. The intriguing part of this story lies in the following sentence:

> These things, say they, were thus executed upon the 17th day of the month Athyr, when the Sun was in Scorpio, in the 28th year of Osiris's reign; though there are others who tell us that he was no more than 28 years old at this time.[48]

We have already seen the importance of the number 28 through the middle word and the twenty-eight words in each quadrant of the Great Invocation. Now we see that the number 17 is linked with Scorpio in the Osirian myth. Moreover, table 40 shows Hierarchy Four with a total value of 17. Might this not be another clue to the Hierarchy veiled by the number 17 in the Path to Sirius? Further, when 17 is reduced (1 + 7 = 8) we have Scorpio, the eighth sign of the zodiac.

These number clues link the fourth Creative Hierarchy and Scorpio to 17, and 17 is linked with the Path to Sirius. Furthermore, Scorpio is linked with Sirius numerologically in that they both equal 95 (AN). Therefore, Sirius, Scorpio, and Leo (discussed previously) are all connected through the number 5 (Sirius and Scorpio 95, (9 + 5 = 14, 1 + 4 = 5; Leo 32, 3 + 2 = 5).

DK makes three statements regarding Scorpio which are highly significant in relation to Sirius and its close connection with our planet. They are:

- Scorpio is under the influence or inflowing energy of Sirius....
- We come now to the consideration of a sign [Scorpio, JB] which is of paramount importance in the life of evolving man....
- Scorpio, at this particular stage of human evolution, governs the Path of Discipleship.[49]

These three statements present a clear line of relationship between Sirius, Scorpio, human evolution, spiritual discipleship, and initiation.

We have already established a connection between Sirius and

the Path of Initiation. Now we see that Sirius transmits energy to Scorpio where that energy is absorbed. Through what might be described as a process of cosmic alchemy, the energies of Sirius are filtered through Scorpio. This specially combined energy of Sirius and Scorpio is then transmitted to our solar system and eventually to Earth. The energy coming from Scorpio produces the tests and trials of all disciples who struggle for liberation from the material world. Scorpio is the sign of death and transformation. Scorpio thus works with the redemptive process of initiation at the individual level, mirroring the group or planetary process of initiation in the macrocosm. Sanat Kumara, Who represents the planetary macrocosm, underwent a major initiation which led to the individualization of animal man, and consequently, the creation of the human kingdom. Now we as individualized souls repeat the same process under the influence of Sirius/Scorpio.

Thus, the fourth Creative Hierarchy of human monads is known as the "Lords of Sacrifice" and "Lords of Love."[50] They reflect the essential sacrifice and love of Sanat Kumara Who sacrificed Himself by incarnating during the time when Leo was most influential on our planet. The Tibetan links Leo to Scorpio numerically by showing how the signs of the zodiac can be counted two ways, either from Aries to Pisces or from Pisces to Aries. According to Djwhal Khul, in the earlier stages of the soul's development, the human being incarnates through the signs from Pisces to Aries via Aquarius. When a person's life becomes spiritually oriented the process is reversed and the soul incarnates through the signs in the natural order, from Aries to Pisces via Taurus. This is illustrated in table 41.

As table 41 shows, Leo is the fifth sign and the eighth sign depending on the direction in which the signs are read. Scorpio is the eighth sign when Leo is the fifth, and Scorpio is the fifth sign when Leo is the eighth.

By linking Leo and Scorpio in this manner, the Tibetan is making the point that Leo and Scorpio are crisis points in the development of human consciousness. He describes this as a triangle of energies involving Leo, Scorpio, and Capricorn.[51] Leo brings about self-consciousness at individualization. Scorpio brings about the struggling dual consciousness of the disciple who fights for liberation from the material world. These experiences in Leo and Scorpio eventually lead to Capricorn, which brings initiation and group consciousness. Sirius overlights these three signs because Sirius governs initiation (related to Capricorn) and the development of consciousness (related to Leo and Scorpio). Sirius, thus governs Leo, Scorpio (in relation to discipleship), and our solar system—a system developing the second consciousness aspect related to Love-Wisdom.

Table 41. Zodiacal Signs.

1	Aries	12
2	Taurus	11
3	Gemini	10
4	Cancer	9
5	Leo	8
6	Virgo	7
7	Libra	6
8	Scorpio	5
9	Sagittarius	4
10	Capricorn	3
11	Aquarius	2
12	Pisces	1

In his discussion of Scorpio, Djwhal Khul injects considerable information about Sirius. He says:

> This is the great star of initiation because our Hierarchy (an expression of the second aspect of divinity) is under the supervision or spiritual magnetic control of the Hierarchy of Sirius. These are [along with Scorpio, JB] the major controlling influences whereby the cosmic Christ works upon the Christ principle in the solar system, in the planet, in man and in the lower forms of life expression. It is esoterically called the "brilliant star of sensitivity."
>
> Scorpio is the great constellation which influences the turning point both in the life of humanity and the life of the individual human being. For the first time in the history of both mankind and disciples the energy of Sirius, pouring into the seven groups which form our planetary Hierarchy evokes a response.[52]

These two passages tell us a great deal about the effects Sirius has on the spiritual evolution of humanity. In the first paragraph DK calls Sirius the "star of sensitivity" which links it with the energy of Leo. This sensitizing energy relates Sirius to Leo because it plays a major role in developing the sensitivity of the human being from individualization to the sensitive God-man exemplified by the Christ. This stimulating process of increasing the sensitivity of humanity is obviously becoming effective around the world. This is indicated by an increasing awareness of the dangers of pollution, over-population, and the abuse and misuse of human and natural resources. We are more sensitive to and aware of abuse in every area of society. The same holds true for prejudice whether it is gender, religious, or ethnic. Humanity appears to be going through a phase of super-sensitivity at every level of human activity including the five senses. There is too much light, noise and air pollution, such as auto and factory emissions, cigarette smoke, and even intrusive scents from perfumes. This all indicates an increasing human sensitivity to the environment—both physically and psychologically.

At the same time, this intensified sensitivity is strongly impacting the physical and psychological areas of society. Sirius/Leo is also impacting the spiritual sensitivity of humanity and the Hierarchy. This intensifying stimulation of humanity's sensitivity is combining with and apparently augmenting the Sirius/Scorpio connection, which is designed to turn humanity away from materiality toward spirituality. Thus the earlier statement by the Tibetan: "Scorpio, at this particular stage of human evolution, governs the Path of Discipleship." DK says that for the first time in planetary history, disciples and members of the Hierarchy are responding to Sirius. This means the heart center of our planet—the Hierarchy—is responding to the cosmic heart center Sirius, the source of cosmic Love and Mind flowing into our solar system. In relation to humanity, Sirius transmits Love-Wisdom, the soul energy of the Cosmic Christ, into our solar system and especially into the planetary spiritual Hierarchy of Masters. This heart energy of divine Love penetrates the heart center of every human being and kingdom of nature on our planet, as well as the rest of the solar system. We are permeated with pure Love from Sirius, but it is like a seed in latency waiting to be brought to life and fruition. All of this indicates that the work of Sirius is to develop the Son or Christ aspect within our entire solar system, especially on (and by way of) the planet Earth at this time.

The fourth Hierarchy is called the human Hierarchy, "the Initiates," and its energy is "The WORD made flesh."[53] We humans are this Hierarchy. We as a group represent the Logos in form. We are the mediating soul principle between the higher spiritual kingdoms and the lower kingdoms in nature. At a lower turn of the spiral, we, the fourth Hierarchy, are the planetary medium of redemption, the prototype of which is Sanat Kumara.

The cosmic soul represented by Sirius is working through the personality of our solar Logos—the solar system—in order to infuse cosmic Love into the lower cosmic planes, of which our physical world is the lowest. Our solar system or solar Logos is working to develop the second aspect of Love. Sirius is the Soul on its own plane and our solar system is the Son in manifestation or incarnation as the personality aspect. As above, so below; the planetary Logos incarnated as Sanat Kumara, Vishnu incarnated as Krishna (in one instance), the Christ incarnated through Jesus. In each and every instance, we the microcosm cannot help but reflect the macrocosm—the WORD becomes flesh.

The first Hierarchy of divine Lives governed by Leo carries the impulse from the soul (Sirius) into the solar Logos to develop the fiery Will to love. Humanity, the fourth or middle Hierarchy, plays a key role as the lower reflected mediator of this desire of the solar Logos to manifest Divine Love throughout the solar system. This is in accordance with the great Lord of Sirius Who represents the soul aspect of our solar Logos. It is through the human Hierarchy that cosmic Love can be carried to the deepest and densest levels of the solar body. Without the human Hierarchy, the divine Purpose cannot be fulfilled. The Scorpio connection indicates that the fourth Hierarchy—the "Lords of Sacrifice, The Initiates"—has reached a critical turning point in the evolution of the solar system through planet Earth, for we are finally responding to the cosmic soul aspect of Sirius, the star of sensitivity and initiation.

Number Anagrams

We have discussed the first and fourth Creative Hierarchies in some detail and related them to the Path to Sirius to some extent but have not linked them with the Great Invocation as yet. We have illustrated in a previous chapter how the squares of numbers 14 and 17 when added together equal the phrase "within the sunshine of the major sun, Sirius" (485 AN). Although we did not mention it then, we performed this arithmetic operation based on DK's description of the Path to Sirius when He described the method of training for this path in the following phrase: "rhythmic dancing upon the square." This method actually comprises two phrases, and now we want to complete our analysis by working with the first phrase of the method, which is "duplex rotary motion."[54]

By rotating the numbers 14 and 17 in two directions we can create various numbers from the digits which make up 14 and 17. Figure 24 shows all the numbers which can be generated from 14 and 17.

Figure 24. Duplex Rotary Motion.

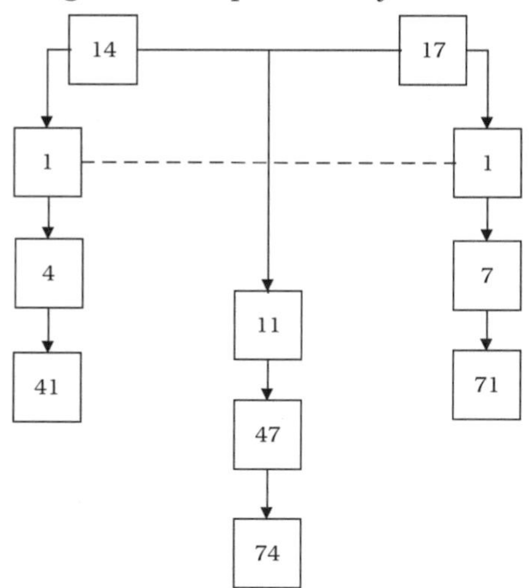

As you can see, we can create nine numbers from 14 and 17. Using the same procedure as with the four quadrants of the Great Invocation, we will locate the words in the Great Invocation which correspond with the two original numbers and the nine additional numbers produced from them. The number one appears two times, therefore as was done in the previous examples, we eliminate the duplicate, bringing the total numbers to ten. We then record their numerological values (AN) and add them together. The procedure and result is shown in table 42.

The number 287 at the bottom of table 42 is the total value of all the word positions combined, and the number 539 is the total of all the AN values of the words themselves. These two numbers link the Path to Sirius, Hierarchies 1 and 4, and the Great Invocation together quite satisfactorily. The number 287 equals "Sirius, the Great White Lodge." The number 539 equals two other phrases—

- Sanat Kumara, The Planetary Logos + The Great Invocation
- The Plan of Love and Light + Invocation for Power and Light

Table 42. Results of Duplex Rotary Motion.

Word Position	Word	AN
1	From	52
4	of	21
7	the	33
11	Let	37
14	forth	67
17	minds	59
41	hearts	71
47	to	35
71	Masters	95
74	serve	69
287	Totals	539

Simply put, these numbers clearly confirm and reinforce what has already been shown—the Great White Lodge on Sirius is connected to the Great Invocation through Sanat Kumara, the planetary Logos. Because 287 and 539 are derived from the original "veiled" numbers, they also indicate that Sirius and the first and fourth Hierarchies may also be involved in the Plan of Love and Light, which includes the Invocation for Power and Light, also called the Great Invocation.

In effect, we have taken two numbers given by the Tibetan (why these two is not clear), rearranged them, found their correspondences in the Great Invocation, and added them all together resulting in the feedback of specific information concerning Sirius, the Great White Brotherhood, the Great Invocation, Sanat Kumara, and the Plan.

This is quite remarkable in itself, but even more so is the fact that all these factors are logically connected according to the ageless wisdom teaching about the special relationship existing between Sirius and Sanat Kumara, and the Plan of Love and Light being resolved on our planet as part of some larger Purpose.

The Fourth and Fifth are the Ninth and Tenth

The heading for this section comes from the book *Esoteric Astrology*. The Tibetan is describing the combined work of the fourth and fifth Creative Hierarchies. If you refer back to table 40, note that Hierarchy Four is ninth and fourth, and Hierarchy Five is tenth and fifth. Just as in table 41 (the astrological signs), DK is counting the Hierarchies from top to bottom and from bottom to top. Therefore, the fourth and fifth are the ninth and tenth.

We have already discussed the quadrants of the Great Invocation at great length in this chapter, but let's complete the exercise and look once more at the middle word "is." Numerologically, it equals 28 (AN) and its two letters equal 9 and 19 respectively. In 919 we find the number symbolism we seek. Again, whether by coincidence or design, the middle word of the Great Invocation corresponds numerically to the combined values of the fourth and fifth, and ninth and tenth Hierarchies (4 + 5 = 9–the letter I, and 9 + 10 = 19–the letter S). The middle word of the Great Invocation thus corresponds to the joining of the fourth and fifth (ninth and tenth) Hierarchies.

Commenting on these two Hierarchies Djwhal Khul states:

> The fourth and the fifth Hierarchies are the ninth and tenth, or the "Initiates" and the "Perfect Ones." All human beings, or "Imperishable Jivas" [Skt. living beings, JB] are those who evolve through a graded series of initiations either self-induced or brought about on our planet with extraneous aid. This they achieve through a "marriage" with the order next to them, the fifth. They are then completed or perfected, and it is owing to this occult fact that the fourth Hierarchy is regarded as masculine and the fifth as feminine.[55]

In this instance, the middle word of the Great Invocation takes on the role of the soul itself which is the middle redeeming principle joining spirit and matter. Through this middle word we are given a graphic image and numerical correspondence to the process of redemption through union and mutual attraction. The graphic image is clearly visible in the Word Position Index (appendix B) in which the upper and lower grids are joined by the 57th middle word "is."

The numerical significance is heightened by the fact that when 9 and 19 are multiplied, they equal 171! This is the value of "the Queen of Heaven," which we now know is Isis-Sothis or Sirius. Yet, there is something even more profound about the number 171 and its relation to the word at the midpoint of the Great Invocation. The Lemurian root-race in which the fourth and fifth Creative Hierarchies joined to form the human kingdom was the 171st major life cycle of the planetary Logos, when He incarnated as Sanat Kumara! It was during this third root-race of the fourth cycle that He came to the planet as the Avatar.

In order to appreciate the significance of this number along with its symbolic and literal placement at the middle of the Great Invocation, we need to understand how a planetary Logos, or Heavenly Man manifests. Again, this is a complex topic, but we will confine ourselves to a general overview in order to stay close to our main subject.

According to the ageless wisdom, a planetary Logos takes form through a planetary scheme. Our solar system is comprised of ten planetary schemes. For instance, the planets Venus, Jupiter, and Earth are separate planetary schemes within our solar system. Each planetary scheme consists of seven chains of worlds. These worlds are called chains because each chain consists of seven globes; thus, the term a "chain" of globes. These globes interpenetrate one another and are found at different levels or planes of consciousness. This is quite similar to the constitution of a human being who has a physical body, an etheric body, an astral body, and a mental body. We only see the physical body; the other bodies are just as real but exist beyond our ability to detect them through the physical senses.[56] Although they are invisible to our physical senses, they still penetrate and surround the outer physical form. The same holds true for the globes of a planetary Logos.

This means the scheme of our planetary Logos comprises forty-nine distinct globes (including our Earth) at different planes of existence. Each one of these globes experiences the attention or concentrated focus of the planetary Logos in turn. From our human standpoint the process works something like this: When a great cosmic Being like a Heavenly Man or planetary Logos comes into manifestation from higher planes beyond anything of which we can conceive, He creates worlds where He can place His consciousness and work out some greater Plan or Purpose. This creative activity is cyclic and proceeds, according to the ageless wisdom, in seven distinct phases called rounds. Therefore, at the beginning of this tremendous evolutionary process, the Logos turns His attention to chain one, globe one, chain one, globe two, globe three, four, five, six, and seven. After the Logos sends His life impulse, purpose, and energy through the seven globes of the first chain, a major cycle has been completed. This major cycle is called a round. This same procedure is repeated six more times in chain one. After seven rounds, the chain one activity or life span is completed and the Logos (after a breather, called pralaya) turns His attention to chain two and the same procedure continues but at a higher, more sophisticated and refined level of activity.

Now we must take this one step further to complete the overview. Seven root-races exist during each round on each globe. These are distinct life waves through which the Logos accomplishes His Purpose. The term root-race is a meager attempt to label the goal and work of the planetary Logos in any given round or on any of the forty-nine globes, but we are handicapped by words and the narrow range of our senses. What kinds of life and activity occur on these other globes is not known, but we do know what is occurring on at least one of them, our Earth.

According to this evolutionary design, our Earth is the fourth globe, in the fourth chain. We are currently in the fourth round, and the consciousness level presently influencing and dominating global civilization is called the fifth root-race. We say consciousness level because as mentioned earlier, the word "race" has more to do with quality of consciousness than skin color or ethnic background. The ageless wisdom views body types as simply vehicles and instruments for developing consciousness.

In order to comprehend the underlying significance of the number 171 in terms of the life cycle of the Heavenly Man, we need to determine the appropriate scale of measurement within the scheme of our planetary Logos. We have four levels of measurement at our disposal, namely—chains, globes, rounds, and root-races. For example, one scheme consists of 7 chains. One chain contains 7 globes. One globe experiences seven rounds. One round on one globe (sometimes called a world period) consists of 7 root-races or life expressions of some kind.

Our purpose in all this is to illustrate the significance of the midpoint in the Great Invocation. We know the middle word "is" has two letters, "i" and "s" which equal 9 and 19 respectively. These correspond to the fourth and fifth Hierarchies which came together to form humanity. We also know 9 x 19 = 171. Among other things, this number also equals the total of the numbers 56, 57, and 58. These numbers are significant because they represent the positions of the three middle words in the Great Invocation, "God is known." We see, therefore, that the middle of the Great Invocation seems to contain a hotspot with an underlying message.

If the middle of the Great Invocation is so important, is there something important we need to know about the middle of a cycle? What about the middle of our Earth Scheme?

Figure 25. The Earth Scheme.

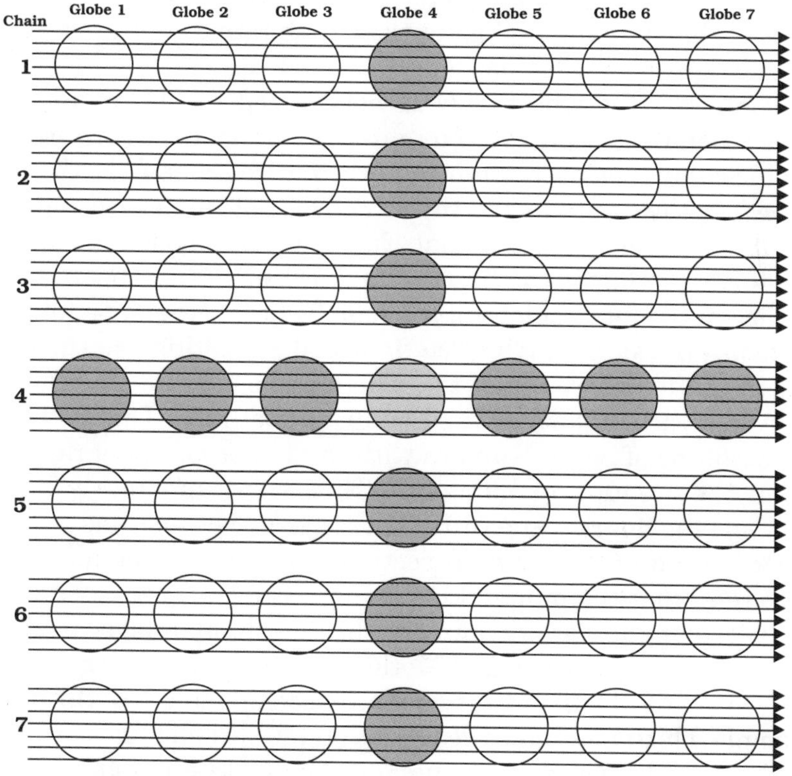

When Sanat Kumara achieved physical/etheric incarnation during the third Lemurian root-race some 18 million years ago He symbolically, figuratively, and perhaps literally mounted the cross of the fourth cosmic initiation. This is graphically depicted here by the exact middle position of the fourth chain, the fourth globe, and the fourth round relative to the entire Earth Scheme.

As we scan figure 25, The Earth Scheme, what chain is found at the middle of the seven? The fourth. Of the seven globes of the Earth Chain, which one is the middle globe? The fourth. If we look at the seven rounds within the fourth globe of the fourth chain, again, which is the middle? The fourth. The exact middle of our entire planetary scheme is found in the fourth chain, the fourth globe, and the fourth round. Translating this 4-4-4 pattern into rounds results in round number 172. The number we are looking for is 171, but the 171st round happened in the fourth chain, on the third globe which is not our dense physical Earth (termed the fourth globe), but the cycle just prior to ours. According to Blavatsky, there was no semblance of human life on the dense Earth globe during this time period since the planet was still in preparation for the higher animal life that would eventually emerge during the coming fourth round. The individualized human souls would eventually use the primate forms of the animal kingdom in the fourth round for the creation of the fourth human kingdom.

Therefore, the clue to 171 is not related to the round, but to some other measurement. The answer lies in the root-races of a specific chain, not in the rounds of the entire scheme. In the words of the Tibetan, "only in the third root-race of the fourth round did conditions permit of His [Sanat Kumara, JB] physical incarnation and of His coming as the first Avatar."[57] Specifically, the mystery of 171 lies in the fourth globe of the fourth chain, otherwise known as the dense physical Earth. (See figure 26.) Locating the third root-race in the fourth round of the fourth globe we find this to be the 171st root-race, known as the Lemurian root-race. This is the time of the coming of Sanat Kumara with the 104 other Kumaras resulting in the creation of humanity. This event apparently brought together the fourth and fifth Hierarchies because, as we have already noted in the previous section, it is through the marriage of these lives that the human kingdom is born.

This planetary event mirrors the cosmic marriage mentioned earlier when the Father and Mother aspects joined in the heavens resulting in the birth of the Son of God. It is the birth of this middle principle which eventually leads to the reuniting of spirit and matter through the Sacrifice of the Son. Might it be possible that our planetary Logos, incarnating as Sanat Kumara, is a product of Hierarchy One, a "Son of God Himself, the First Born in a cosmic sense?" Is Sanat Kumara (the Leader of the Lords of the Flame)

Figure 26. The Earth Chain.

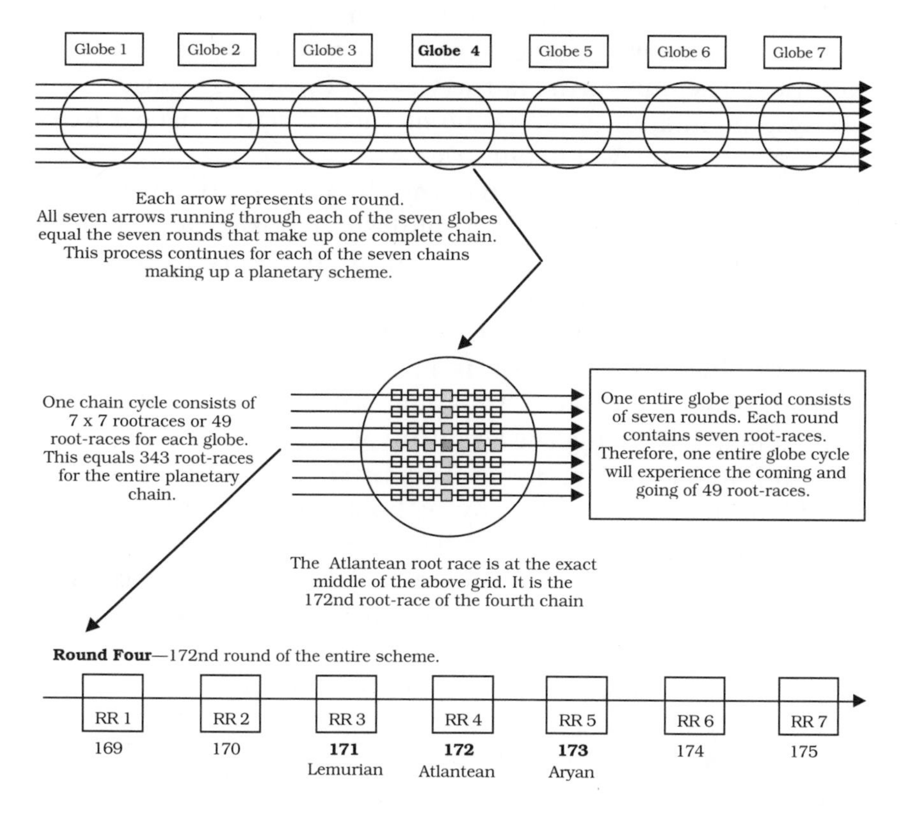

associated with the Fiery Lions of the first Hierarchy which is related to Leo? Did this Heavenly Man emerge from Leo/Regulus, the heart of the Lion in order to serve our solar Logos, thus becoming a Son of the Sun? Since Sirius governs both Leo and our solar system, does this create a special relationship between Sanat Kumara and the great Lord of Sirius? Remember the statement, " 'Lions, the divine and tawny orange Flames' came into being and thus humanity arrived upon the planet." The arrival of Sanat Kumara, the Great Sacrifice, set into motion the marriage of the fourth and fifth Hierarchies, and thus, another Son was born, named Humanity.

The structure of the Great Invocation demonstrates the tremendous significance of the middle aspect in our second solar system (a Son in manifestation) through the placement of the phrase, "God is known" at the center of the mantram.

As you can see from table 43, the sun Sirius, initiation, and the Cosmic Christ equal 171 RAN. Furthermore, they each correspond directly to the word positions at the exact center of the Great Invocation. The sun Sirius is the Cosmic Christ in relation to our solar system, and initiation is the method of consciousness expansion currently employed in our system.

Extending this relationship to the Great Invocation is logical in terms of the ageless wisdom philosophy because the Great Invocation is the word of power used by humanity to restore the Plan on Earth; the Earth, as part of the solar Logos, is therefore, a part of the consciousness of the Lord of Sirius. In addition, this invocative effort by humanity is meant to call forth the Christ's physical presence on Earth, thus mirroring the Great Sacrifice of Sanat Kumara. By using the Great Invocation in this way humanity is fulfilling the work of Sirius. This Great Work is to create a center of Light and Love on the physical plane through the method of initiation. Thus, the Cosmic Christ can fulfill the task of redemption through the agency of humanity. Ultimately, God is known through initiation, revealing the sun Sirius as the Cosmic Christ.

Table 43. God as the Cosmic Christ.

Term	AN	RAN	Word Position	Word in Great Invocation
The sun Sirius	182	56	56	God
Initiation	120	57	57	is
Cosmic Christ	139	58	58	known
Total	441	171	171	

DK says we humans are the cells in the body of the planetary Logos. As we achieve initiation or enlightenment, the cells of the planetary body are filled with the Light and Love of Christ. At the cosmic level it means the Cosmic Christ is irradiating the world of form, suffusing every atom of substance with Love. Such Love is present in each atom already, but it is awaiting release by the human kingdom. Symbolically, the release of atomic energy in this century is a signal that humanity is on the verge of releasing the Love at the heart of the human atom and irradiating the entire planet with divine Light and Love.

The importance of 171 is further reinforced through the middle word of the middle phrase, namely "is," which equals 171 by the multiplication of its two letters "i" and "s" or 9 x 19. We have discussed the various meanings of the word "is," indicating its profound numerical and symbolic connection to Egyptian religion, the Dog star, the "veil" of Isis personifying Sirius—the true Spiritual Sun, and The Sun and The Star Tarot cards. We have also discussed it as numerically symbolizing the connection between the fourth and fifth (ninth and tenth) Hierarchies which combine to create the human kingdom.

Having explored the middle phrase and the middle word in detail, we continue now to the exact midpoint of the Great Invocation where the middle letter "s" is located. This central core of the Great Invocation contains amazing esoteric information about the nature and purpose of our life on Earth.

From the Centre Where the Will of God is Known

The phrase "everything is connected" is a warm fuzzy cliche that is often bandied about in spiritual and religious groups nowadays; but now we are going to see how connected everything *really* is as we study the symbolic and numeric core of the Great Invocation. Once again we will be focusing on the middle of the mantram. We have already spent much time examining the middle phrase and middle word, but now we are going to focus on the middle letter.

The letter "s" is the middle letter of the Great Invocation. Of the 443 letters composing it, the letter "s" is the 222nd. Therefore, the letter "s" occupies the 222nd position of the Great Invocation or the exact middle position relative to the 221 letters preceeding and following it. In fact, this middle letter is the "s" in the middle word "is" and therefore, the "s" in the middle phrase "God is known."

We are discovering that the Great Invocation is plethora of symbolic and literal information regarding the nature of our planetary life and its place in the cosmos. Going back once more to the time of individualization, Djwhal Khul states that when Sanat Kumara incarnated on the Earth globe, He came from another chain within our own Earth scheme. This means Sanat Kumara simply moved from the second chain to the fourth chain within the Earth Scheme. In other words, He did not come to our Earth from some other planet in our solar system. Where these great Entities, these planetary Logoi, originate outside our solar system is another matter entirely, and beyond the scope of our comprehension. We are speaking only in terms of the present life cycle of our Earth Scheme within the present solar system.

Djwhal Khul describes Sanat Kumara's coming to the Earth in the following passage:

> The statement that the great Kumara or the One Initiator came to this planet from Venus is true in so far as it embodies the fact that He came to this dense planet (the fourth) in the fourth chain *from that chain in our scheme which is called the "Venus" chain, and which is the second chain.* He came via the second globe in our chain; His scarcely felt vibration was sensed (occultly) in the second round, but only in the third root-race of the fourth round did conditions permit of His physical incarnation and of His coming as the Avatar.[58]

As figure 27 illustrates, Sanat Kumara came to the Earth along a path from Chain 2, to Globe 2 (within our Chain 4), during Round 2, or 2-2-2. This series of numbers can be read as 222, or as the 222nd letter at the center of the Great Invocation.

However, this is only half the story, since the Tibetan says Sanat Kumara did not actually complete His entire descent to Globe 4 (the dense Earth) until the fourth round of the third root-race. In the last section we explained how this root-race was the 171st of our fourth chain, thus linking it to the middle phrase of the Great Invocation, but the place and timing of the divine Incarnation can be read another way. We can read it as 4-4-3, or as the fourth round of the fourth globe during the third root-race. This series of numbers—4-4-3—corresponds to the 443 letters of the entire Great Invocation.

The total number of letters in the Great Invocation thus tell us Sanat Kumara came to our planet, the fourth globe, in the fourth round, during the third root-race. He began his sojourn and mission of redemption by leaving the second chain and arriving on the second globe of our Earth chain in the second round. This was a major planetary event. The Tibetan explains:

Figure 27. The Descent of Sanat Kumara.

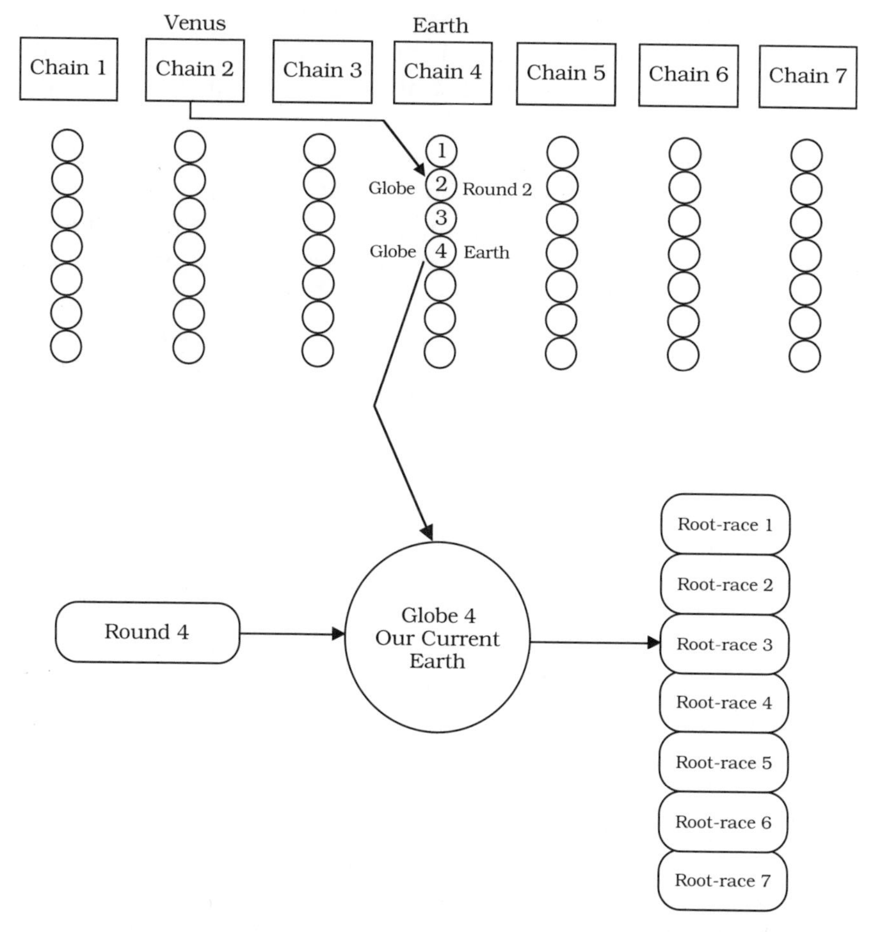

A major incarnation is one in which a planetary Logos takes some initiation. He may, and does, pass through many incarnations without taking initiation. When He does take initiation, it is interesting to note that *He does so during some incarnation in which He takes a vehicle of etheric matter as is the case at this time.*

The Logos of our scheme is preparing for initiation and hence the terrific tests and trials, incident to life on our planet during this cycle, are easily accounted for.

The Logos of our scheme, Sanat Kumara, will take a major initiation in the middle of the fifth round, but is preparing for a minor one at this time.

The Logos of our scheme has been in physical incarnation (having a body of etheric matter) since the middle of the Lemurian root-race, and will remain with us until what is called "the judgement day" in the next round.[59]

The previous extract is very important for understanding the profound significance of the present period of the Earth Scheme. The planetary Logos has entered into physical/etheric incarnation in order to prepare for a major initiation in the near future (relative to the time scale of Sanat Kumara). This preparatory period will require approximately one round. Because Sanat Kumara is preparing for this major expansion of consciousness while incarnated on the planet, this means all the lives of the planet are undergoing accelerated growth. All the kingdoms of nature, including the Hierarchy of Masters, are under intensified pressure due to the focused attention of Sanat Kumara on this aspect of His life expression—our dense globe, the Earth. We are like a chakra in a particular part of His body. His concentrated attention is directed on this center in order to prepare it for more expanded activity at a higher working level.

A major planetary initiative was inaugurated when Sanat Kumara departed chain two and entered our chain via globe two, during round two. Obviously, by placing the letter "s" in the 222nd position of the Great Invocation, DK wanted to communicate something to us about this event. Therefore, if the letter "s" is present in that position, let's investigate its meaning in light of the coming of Sanat Kumara, The Great Sacrifice, The One Initiator, the Lord of the World.

The Letter "S"

"S" is the 19th letter of the alphabet. In order to extract information from the letter "s" we will perform several simple arithmetic operations on the number 19. At this point these operations should be familiar to you.

First, we reduce the number 19:

$1 + 9 = 10$

$1 + 0 = 1.$

Second, we calculate the triangular number derived from 19:

1 through 19 = 190.

Third, we view 19 as the numbers 1 through 9.

Therefore, we calculate the triangular number derived from 9.

1 through 9 = 45.

Next, we will find the word positions in the Great Invocation which correspond with the arithmetic results we have obtained. Those results are the numbers 1, 10, 190, and 45. We have one problem, however. We have a number—190—which is greater than the 113 words found in the Great Invocation. In order to locate this corresponding number we will subtract 113 from 190. Appropriately, the result is 77, for the 77th word of the Great Invocation is "centre," and that is exactly what we are investigating!

The results of our exercise appear in table 44A, which contains all the elements of the number 19, including the number 19 itself. As you can see, the words referenced in the Great Invocation appear to tell a story. They say "From God men, Christ centre." These words describe a spiritual evolutionary process. They describe the descent of Sanat Kumara onto the physical-etheric plane resulting in the creation of the human kingdom. The creation of the human kingdom is meant to fulfill the Great Work of planetary redemption by the Son of God, or Christ-potential of humanity. Individually and collectively, Humanity is the planetary savior. The completion of this process results in the return or ascent back to the centre. Thus, the Great Work of planetary redemption set in motion by Sanat Kumara is completed by the Son, Humanity. The Great Invocation is a key element for bringing the Great Work into fuller operation at the planetary level because it calls on the Christ and spiritual Hierarchy to come forth and work openly in the world; but only humanity can prepare the way by sincerely working for the good of people everywhere.

Table 44A. The Great Work.

Word Position	Word	AN
1	From	52
10	God	26
19	Men	32
45	Christ	77
190 - 113 = 77	centre	65
152	Totals	252

Before examining this process in more detail, note the number 252 at the bottom of table 44A. This number is the total value of the five words we extracted from the Great Invocation by working with the letter "s." The number 252 equals the term "central spiritual Sun." This is significant because the central spiritual Sun always pertains to the will aspect of Divinity. Does Sanat Kumara's mission to this dense material world have something to do with the greater Will of the solar Logos and our parent system, Sirius? "He [Sanat Kumara, JB] is the custodian of the will of the Great White Lodge on Sirius." Is that why all this information is *centrally* located?

The number 152 at the bottom of table 44A is the sum of the five word positions derived from the letter "s." Number 152 dramatically demonstrates the esoteric connection with the number 252, because 152 equals "tawny lions" (AN). Referring back to the end of the section, "Hierarchy One and Leo," (in this chapter) we discovered that the first Creative Hierarchy emanated from the heart of the central spiritual Sun. Now we find that as a result of examining the *central* letter of the Great Invocation, the tawny lions associated with individualization emerge *along with* the central spiritual Sun, which is the source of Blavatsky's "Lions of Life."

The following diagram (figure 28) illustrates the coming of Sanat Kumara in the fourth round, fourth globe, and third root-race through the actual words of the Great Invocation. This great cycle was (and still is) the 172nd round or exact halfway point in the entire cycle of the Earth Scheme, which ideally consists of 343 total rounds. The middle letter "s," as we will learn, symbolizes various things, one of which is the middle round of the Earth Scheme.

By performing numerological operations on the middle letter "s," the Great Invocation yields the words needed to tell the story of Sanat Kumara's mission to our dense globe. That mission is to create self-conscious, intelligent beings who can bridge spirit to the lower kingdoms of nature. The human kingdom performs this act of atonement through initiation into the life of the Christ. Through this bridging process, the energies of the higher planes of spiritual will, pure love-wisdom, and spiritual mind are channeled through humanity and released into the lower planes of matter. The will of God is fulfilled through the human kingdom. The arrival of Sanat Kumara, the prototypal Avatar for our planet, during the middle or 172nd round is demonstrated through the esoteric numerology of the middle letter "s."

Figure 28. The Great Work of Redemption.

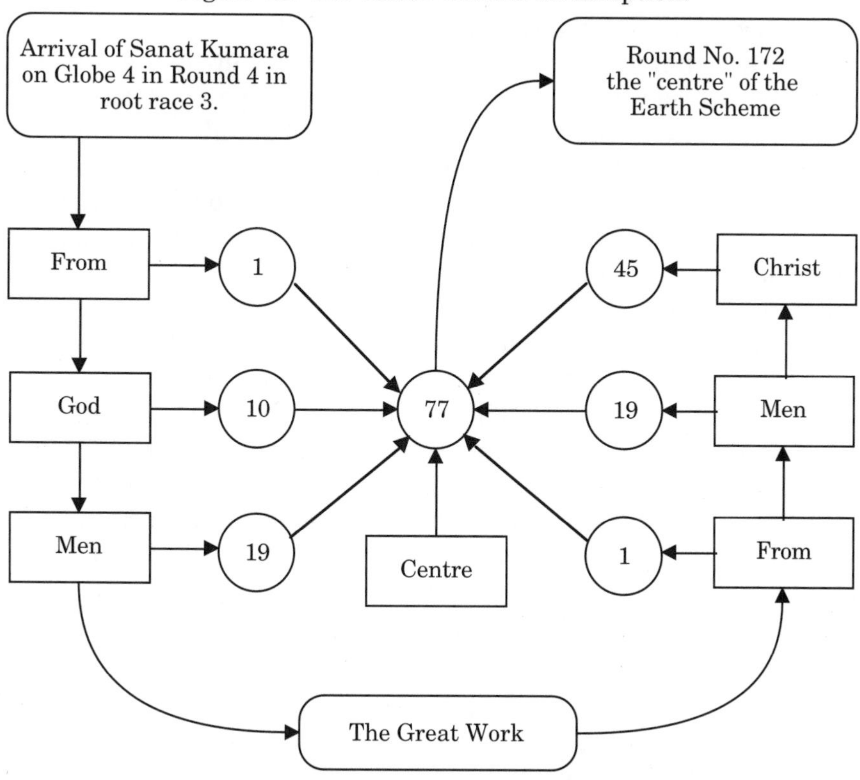

Each word in this diagram is derived from the middle letter of the Great Invocation, the letter "S."
This letter is the 19th letter of the alphabet.
The numerological operations applied to the number 19 are:
19—Word 19 = Men.
1 + 9 = 10—Word 10 = God.
1 + 9 = 10, 1 + 0 = 1—Word 1 = From.
Adding 1 through 9 = 45—Word 45 = Christ
Adding 1 through 19 = 190, 190 - 113 = 77—Word 77 = centre
Adding all the elements together yields 172—
the exact midpoint of the Earth Scheme
(1 + 10 + 19 + 1 + 19 + 45 + 77 = 172).

Therefore, as shown in figure 28, we might say God, or the Cosmic Christ aspect represented by Sirius, willed that humanity be created in order to foster the development of Christ-like Beings on Earth. The Christ is the first human to achieve the goal of the Great Work. As above, so below—the macrocosmic Christ replicates

Itself at the microcosmic level in order to carry Love Divine to the human level and redeem the elemental worlds.

The fact that the letter "s" is the 19th letter of the alphabet allows us to search for numbers which correspond to words and phrases relating to the Great Invocation and corollary themes. For instance, the number 95 is particularly important in our investigation of the Great Invocation because 95 is the value for Sirius. The number 95 is the product of 5 x 19. Since 5 is the value of the Great Invocation, there is a numerological relationship between the Great Invocation and Sirius.

As just demonstrated, the central letter "s" with its value of 19, along with the various numbers derived from it, tells the story of planetary redemption, or "The Great Work." Our premise is that Sirius dominates this redemptive theme which is implemented on Earth through the Sirian technique of initiation. The Great Invocation is a prayer or mantram of redemption associated with Sirius. This theme is dramatically demonstrated once again by the actual words of the Great Invocation—the words located at *multiples of 19*. Table 44B clearly reveals the presence of Sirian influence within the Great Invocation.

Table 44B. Source of the Great Work.

Multiples of 19	Word Position	Word	AN	RAN
1 x 19	19	men	32	14
2 x 19	38	forth	67	31
3 x 19	57	is	28	10
4 x 19	76	the	33	15
5 x 19	95	may	39	12
	285	Totals	199	82

The number 285 equals the AN value of "the central spiritual Sun." The AN sum of all five words equals 199. This number corresponds to "star of initiation." The RAN sum of all five words equals 82, and this number *also* corresponds to "star of initiation." In fact, "star of initiation" is the only term in the "Esoteric Numerology Lists" with the values of 199 and 82. (See appendix E.)

We already know that Djwhal Khul identifies Sirius as the star of initiation by our investigation of Scorpio and Hierarchy Four. The esoteric numerology reinforces this through the RAN total shown in table 44B. When the RAN value of Sirius (32) is added to 82, the result (114) can be translated as "Sirius, star of initiation." This number is consistent with the theme of table 44B since the factors of 114 are 6 x 19.

The middle letter "s" is truly a symbol of the centrality of the Will of the cosmic Lord of Sirius. The themes associated with the central spiritual Sun, the star of initiation, Sirius and the tawny lions all emerge in tables 44A, 44B and figure 28. The placement of letter "s" at the central core of the Great Invocation is like a beacon in the night shedding light on the path of humanity's purpose and destiny. The Great Invocation is not only a gift of Love from God and a Word of Power for fulfilling our destiny as a species, but it tells the story of who and why we are here through the symbolism of numbers.

It is significant that a considerable number of esoteric terms are based on the number 19, since this is the value of the middle letter in the Great Invocation. The symbolic message is that these terms are central to the Great Invocation and the ageless wisdom from which it is derived.

The esoteric terms based on 19 and its significant multiples are listed as follows and appear in condensed form in table 45 at the end of this section. (Note: All numerological values in table 45 are AN unless otherwise noted.)

✠ *19* ✠

represents the letter "s," the middle letter of the Great Invocation.

✠ *38* ✠

relates to the *Blue Lodge* of Sirius. The numbers 3 and 8 are present in the four quadrants of the Sirian Cross.

✠ *57* ✠

is the position number of the middle word of the Great Invocation. The words *human*, *rose*, and *veiled* have a value of 57 (AN). Words with this RAN value include, *initiation*, *energy adept*, and *spiritual soul*.

Humanity was created through the sacrifice of Sanat Kumara, along with the aid of the Lord of Venus and the overarching support and blessing of Sirius. The rosy Cross is the symbol for The Law of Sacrifice governed by ray four.[60] The rose at the center of the cross signifies a life of sacrifice so others may live. The divine prototype for this law is the Cosmic Christ crucified on the Fixed Cross of the heavens. This is the basic and fundamental law governing all manifestation at this time. This, as we have just seen, ties in with Scorpio and Sirius.

The word veiled symbolizes the hidden information contained in the Great Invocation. Human beings can also be seen as veiled from true Life until the spiritual soul is liberated from the wheel of rebirth, and becomes the energy adept through initiation.

✠ 76 ✠

equals *master* (AN). Terms with this RAN value are *Lord of the World* and *Serpents of Wisdom*. A Master is a human being Who is liberated from the world of matter. A Master is a Member of the spiritual Hierarchy. Sirius is the originating Great White Lodge, of which our planetary Hierarchy (along with those in the other planetary schemes of our solar system) is an outpost.

✠ 95 ✠

equals *Sirius*, *Scorpio*, *Neptune*, *Hierarchy*, *Masters*, *I am That I am*, *kundalini*, *the queen,* and *Empress* (all AN); it equals *Argo, the celestial ship* (RAN). (This last item will be discussed in chapter 11.)

Other than the numerological connection between Sirius and Neptune, there is no outstanding relationship which is obvious between these two except the following remark by DK. "Sirius, ...influences our entire solar system psychically via the three synthesising schemes—Uranus, Neptune, and Saturn."[61]

The phrase "I am That I am" refers to the initiate state of being beyond the fifth initiation. This level of initiation definitely relates the Master to Sirius because, as mentioned earlier, the lesser initiations of our planet are preparatory to the initiations of Sirius.

The term kundalini immediately involves several words and phrases from our list. Djwhal Khul injects the subject of kundalini into a discussion of the fifth Creative Hierarchy. As discussed earlier in this chapter, this Hierarchy is a mysterious one that works closely with the fourth Human Hierarchy of Solar Angels. The following extract from *A Treatise on Cosmic Fire* brings several elements of table 45 together.

> The relation of the fifth Hierarchy to a certain constellation has also a bearing upon this mystery. This is hidden in the karma of the solar Logos, and concerns His relationship to another solar Logos, and the interplay of force between them in a greater mahakalpa [previous solar system, JB]. This is the true "secret of the Dragon," and it was the dragon influence or the "serpent energy" which caused the influx of manasic or mind energy into the solar system. Entangled closely with the karma of these two cosmic Entities [two solar Logoi, JB], was that of the lesser cosmic Entity Who is the Life of our planet, the planetary Logos. It was this triple karma which brought in the "serpent religion" and the "Serpents or Dragons of Wisdom" in Lemurian days. It had to do with solar and planetary Kundalini, or serpent fire.[62]

This intriguing passage involves kundalini (95), serpent energy (171), Serpents of Wisdom (76 RAN), the solar Logos (133) and the Lord of the World (76 RAN). Although there is a deep mystery here involving the identity of the other solar Logos connected with ours, the gist of this extract shows a kundalini energy exchange between two solar Entities resulted in a massive influx of manas (mind) into the planet Earth and the coming of the Dragons or Serpents of Wisdom (Initiate Instructors of early humanity). It is not unreasonable to suggest that the other solar system involved was Sirius, since Sanat Kumara, the Lord of the World, has a special relationship with the Lord of Sirius.

"The queen" refers to the Queen of Heaven—Isis or Sirius. The word "empress" refers to The Empress Tarot card. This card is related to Venus, and as we know, Venus aided Sanat Kumara's incarnation as the Avatar of Earth. Venus and the Earth are deeply connected.

Although not in table 45, Hathor is also associated with The Empress card. According to Case:

> *Venus* is the planetary attribution to Daleth [fourth letter of the Hebrew alphabet, JB]. She corresponds to the cow-headed Egyptian goddess Hathor....Venus presides over child-birth...
>
> The Empress is a matronly figure, about to become a mother.[63]

Could Venus be associated with child-birth and motherhood because of the esoteric connection between the Lord of Venus, Sanat Kumara, and the birth of the human kingdom? Obviously, there are layers of meaning here. The fact that the Empress is linked with Sirius numerologically (95) indicates the value of numerical correspondence, while simultaneously opening up the possibility of delving to deeper levels of meaning. For instance, according to Budge:

> She [Hathor, JB] was identified astronomically with the star *Sept*, or Sothis [Sirius, JB], which was called the "second sun" in heaven, she was thereby connected with the rise of the Nile preparatory to the Inundation, and she appeared in the form of this star in the heavens in the neighbourhood of the sun in the second half of July.[64]

The layered meanings of Venus and Hathor indicate "motherhood" at two levels. Venus aids in the birthing of the human kingdom on the Earth through the gift of mind, while Hathor/Sirius is our parent system, the source of mind outside our solar system.

> *The sun "Sirius" is the source of logoic manas*...Venus was responsible for the coming in of mind in the Earth chain. Each was primary to the other, or was the agent which produced the first flicker of consciousness in the particular groups involved....

The Logos	Solar System	Sirius...
Heavenly Man	Earth Chain	Venus[65]

✚ 114 ✚

This number equals *Sons of God* (AN). The RAN valued words appear as two related groups. The first group is *Sirius, Isis-Sothis, Satis,* and *Anukis*. The second group is *Sirius, Osiris, Isis,* and *Horus*. We discussed this group earlier.

✚ 133 ✚

Two terms are associated with this number. They are *solar Logos* and *Lords of Karma*. As we have just seen, our solar Logos is intimately related to Sirius; they share the same consciousness, and Sirius is our parent system. All the karma of our solar system is controlled from Sirius. Therefore, the Lords of Karma definitely fit in with this family of numbers.

✠ 152 ✠

Only one phrase has emerged that relates to this value—*tawny lions* (AN). We have discussed this subject earlier.

✠ 171 ✠

This is one of the most important numbers in the Great Invocation. The three middle word positions (fifty-six, fifty-seven and fifty-eight) total 171. Sanat Kumara incarnated on Earth as the Avatar in the 171st life impulse (Lemurian root-race) of the Earth Scheme. The following terms equal 171—*The Queen of Heaven*, *Isis-Nephthys*, *Hermes-Mercury*, *the celestial ship,* and *serpent energy* (all AN). Except for Hermes-Mercury, who was only mentioned briefly, we have covered these terms in earlier sections. It is worth repeating, nonetheless, that Hermes-Mercury is the Helper, Guide, and general Benefactor of Isis. Hermes-Mercury is central to the numbers and symbolism connected with Sirius and the Great Invocation because he presides over measures, numbers, and words of power. Needless to say, the Great Invocation *is a word of power*, and therefore it comes under the direct influence of Hermes-Mercury.

✠ 190 ✠

Three terms equal the number of perfection, 10 times 19; they are *the Silent Watcher*, *the Throne of Isis,* and the "*adept using energy*." The Silent Watcher is Sanat Kumara and we know He has a special and mysterious relationship to the Lord of Sirius. The Throne of Isis is a term which symbolically refers to the region of Sirius called the Sirian system. Isis is most often depicted in Egyptian paintings with the throne hieroglyphic on her head.

It is quite interesting to note that the Throne of Isis is not only 10 x 19, but also 2 x 95. This might symbolize Sirius seated as the ruling Queen of our system or the presence of multiple stars in the Sirian system. The factor 5 (x 19 = 95) indicates the fifth principle of manas, while 10 x 19 symbolizes perfected manas (relative to our solar system) emanating from the cosmic mental plane where the Sirian system originates—thus, its rulership on the Throne.

The adept using energy symbolizes the expansion of the initiate's consciousness into the world of the fifth kingdom of the spiritual Hierarchy. It is from this kingdom that the Initiate will eventually choose the way of the higher evolution which could be the Path to Sirius as one choice out of seven cosmic paths available.

✚ 247 ✚

Hermes Trismegistus. See chapter 10.

✚ 266 ✚

This number is equivalent to *the burning sons of desire* (AN). Recall the numbers 14 and 17 veil the Creative Hierarchies related to the Path to Sirius. The number 266 is the product of 14 x 19. We found the number 14 is linked with Hierarchy One.

The number 266 also equals *the Brother from Sirius*. This is a title which DK gives to the Lord of the fifth ray.[66] This correlation with the burning sons of desire reinforces the possible connection between Sirius and Hierarchy One.

✚ 285 ✚

The term matching this number is *the central spiritual Sun* (AN). This relates to the first or will aspect of our solar Logos or the Sirian Logos.

✚ 323 ✚

This number is also related to the Path to Sirius because it is the product of 17 x 19. (See number 266 above.) Four different terms combine to yield 323; *Sirius, Scorpio* and *solar Logos*, or *Sirius, Scorpio* and *Lords of Karma*. More mysterious perhaps is the term "*the Transmitters of the Word*." Curiously, this term first appears on page 919 of *A Treatise on Cosmic Fire*, thus perfectly matching letters 9 and 19 of the alphabet or "is." Here is what the Tibetan has to say about this group of Beings:

> The "Transmitters of the Word" on the atomic subplane of each plane are the devas of vast power and prerogative who may be stated to be connected with the Father aspect, and embodiments of electric fire.

> They are all fully self-conscious, having passed through the human stage in earlier kalpas....
>
> Each of these great lives...is an emanation from the central spiritual sun in the first instance and from one of the three major constellations in the second instance.[67]

Since both "the central spiritual Sun" and "the Transmitters of the Word" are multiples of 19, could Sirius be one of the three constellations mentioned by DK, since it too is a multiple of 19? After all, we are investigating a Word of Power that may originate on Sirius. Were the Transmitters of the Word responsible for sending the Great Invocation to our planetary scheme?

✙ 342 ✙

Scorpio to Sirius, the Dog Star. This phrase appears in *Esoteric Astrology* on page 194. It describes the influence Sirius has on the constellation Scorpio.

✙ 361 ✙

The square of 19 equals two combined phrases—*The Throne of Isis, the Queen of Heaven* (AN). In light of all that has been said about these two phrases, it is esoterically justified that they represent the exponential power of 19.

✙ 380 ✙

A combined phrase—*Sirius, the Throne of Isis the Queen* (AN).

✙ 399 ✙

This number represents the product of 21 x 19. I am including it because of the central role played by the twenty-one key words in the Great Invocation, and the fact that they contain ninety-five letters (95 is a multiple of 19). Two very powerful phrases are expressed by the multiplication of 21 x 19. The phrases are *tawny lions, the burning sons of desire* (AN) and *the central spiritual Sun and Sirius* (AN). The first phrase concerns Hierarchy One and Leo, while the second phrase describes the source of Hierarchy One.

According to the Tibetan, "The first great Hierarchy is emanated from the Heart of the central spiritual Sun."[68] The central spiritual Sun is the first aspect, and the word "Heart" implies the second aspect. Sirius is a major second aspect center in the One About Whom Naught May Be Said. Therefore, if the Lives of Hierarchy One emanated from the Heart of the central spiritual Sun, they resonate to Sirius because it is a "Heart" (second aspect) oriented star system. We might also theorize that Hierarchy One is connected with the first aspect of the Sirian system.

We have shown earlier that the twenty-one key words are associated with Sanat Kumara. Djwhal Khul states there is a special relationship between Sanat Kumara and the Lord of Sirius. This is why the twenty-one key words are composed of ninety-five letters. "He [Sanat Kumara, JB] is the custodian of the will of the Great White Lodge on Sirius."[69] To demonstrate the importance of Sanat Kumara's descent into the material substance of the Earth, the Great Invocation is constructed in such a way that the 222nd letter position is located at the exact middle of the mantram. This middle point marks the entry of the Lord of the World into our fourth Earth Chain, and the beginning of His Great Work of Redemption. He came from the *second* Venus Chain to the *second* globe, during the *second* round, and perhaps even during the second life impulse on that second globe (the second root-race). Therefore, when we multiply the value of the letter occupying that special position at the midpoint of the Great Invocation by the number in the Great Invocation representing Sanat Kumara, we multiply 21 x 19.

✠ 437 ✠

The Boat of Mystery which Ploughs the Ocean is discussed in chapter 7, but since this mystery boat is, at the very least, connected to the Argo, it is highly significant that the RAN value of Argo is 23. Thus, the relationship between the central letter "s" and the RAN value of the sacred vessel Argo (19 x 23) equals "the Boat of Mystery which Ploughs the Ocean." In the context of all the multiples of 19 related to Sirius and our solar system, this phrase evokes an image of our two related star systems ploughing through space within the grand cosmic sea of the One About Whom Naught May Be Said.

✙ 1045 ✙

Very powerful esoteric information is contained in this number because it is the result of the interaction of the two factors 19 and 55. The symbolic importance of these two numbers has already been demonstrated. Now we see that their product brings together the *secret of the Dragon* (183 AN) and the value of the description of the symbol of the Path to Sirius (862 AN). The secret of the Dragon involves a relationship between our solar Logos and another solar Logos, which we surmise is Sirius. (See number 95 in this section.)

It was the interaction of these two solar Entities which resulted in an influx of manas on our planet. We know Sanat Kumara was very closely involved in this process, so it is quite fascinating to see Sanat's number 55 here. In addition, the term "fourth Hierarchy," the human Hierarchy, also equals 183 (AN), thus relating the human Hierarchy to the Path to Sirius.

Table 45. The Multiples of 19.

1x	19	The middle letter "s"
2x	38	Blue Lodge (RAN)
3x	57	Human, Rose, Veiled (AN) Initiation, Energy Adept, Spiritual Soul (RAN)
4x	76	Master (AN), Lord of the World, Serpents of Wisdom (RAN)
5x	95	Sirius, Scorpio, Neptune, Hierarchy, Masters, Kundalini, I am That I am, The Queen, Empress (AN) Argo the celestial ship (RAN)
6x	114	Sons of God (AN), "Sirius, Isis-Sothis, Satis, Anukis" (RAN) "Sirius, Osiris, Isis, Horus" (RAN)
7x	133	Solar Logos, Lords of Karma
8x	152	Tawny Lions
9x	171	The Queen of Heaven, Isis-Nephthys, Hermes-Mercury, The Celestial Ship, Serpent Energy
10x	190	The Silent Watcher, The Throne of Isis, Adept Using Energy
13x	247	Hermes Trismegistus
14x	266	The Brother From Sirius, The Burning Sons of Desire
15x	285	The Central Spiritual Sun
17x	323	"Sirius, Scorpio, Solar Logos," "Sirius, Scorpio, Lords of Karma," The Transmitters of the Word
18x	342	"Scorpio to Sirius, the Dog Star"
19x	361	"The Throne of Isis, the Queen of Heaven"
20x	380	"Sirius, the Throne of Isis the Queen"
21x	399	"Tawny Lions, the burning sons of Desire," "The Central Spiritual Sun and Sirius"
23x	437	The Boat of Mystery Which Ploughs the Ocean
55x	1045	Secret of the Dragon + (value of the words describing the symbol for the Path to Sirius) 183 + 862 See chapter 7 "The Celestial Ship."

The Words Made Flesh

A truly amazing relationship exists between the 222nd letter, the 443 letters, and the 113 words of the Great Invocation. This relationship strongly suggests the deliberate planning and design of the Great Invocation in order to record a momentous event in the history of our planet.

To begin, let's review the details of Sanat Kumara's arrival on the Earth. In the previous two sections we have determined that the number 222 refers to the coming of Sanat Kumara to the fourth chain from the second chain during the second round, and arriving in our chain on the second globe. All these twos resonate to the second scheme of Venus, which is a completely different planet and planetary Logos than ours. Keep in mind that the second chain, of *our* Earth Scheme is called "Venus" because it responds to the qualities of the planetary Logos of the Venus Scheme. It is this similarity of vibration, this mutual attractiveness which allows the transfer and movement of various Entities between globes and planes of consciousness.

We next found that Sanat Kumara did not actually reach the physical-etheric level of globe four until the third root-race in the fourth round, which was roughly eighteen million years ago, according to Djwhal Khul. This cyclic arrival of the Avatar on our planet contains the digits 4, 4, and 3, or simply 443.

We now know that 222 and 443 represent the middle letter position of the Great Invocation and the total letters comprising the Great Invocation. Since the letters of the Great Invocation are related to the timing of Sanat Kumara's arrival on our world it is quite possible the number of words have a meaning as well. What might the 113 words of the Great Invocation signify in relation to the coming of Sanat Kumara? The answer lies in the time it took Sanat Kumara to reach the dense fourth globe (our current Earth) of our fourth chain after He transferred to globe two of our chain from chain two. If we count the number of intervening root-races or life impulses of the planetary Logos from globe four, round four, root-race three, we find that exactly 113 life impulses take us back to globe two, round two, root-race two, or 222! (See "113 Steps of Sanat Kumara" in appendix C.)

This indicates that each word of the Great Invocation represents one root-race or life expression of the planetary Logos. In this case, however, this time period of 113 life expressions represents the gradual approach of the planetary Avatar, Sanat Kumara, to our dense physical world where He now lives in etheric form. In effect, whenever we use the Great Invocation we are symbolically retracing the 113 steps of the One Initiator from the time He came to our fourth Earth chain until He was able to emerge onto the etheric levels of the fourth globe.

The first and last words of the Great Invocation express this idea perfectly. The first word, "From," tells us Sanat Kumara has come *from* the Venus chain, while the last word of the invocation, *Earth,* tells us where He arrived. The middle letter "s" at the 222nd position emphasizes the importance of the second or middle aspect of the trinity. This is symbolically represented by 3 twos. It is clear now that the 222 not only indicates the second chain, second globe, and second round, but also reveals that Sanat Kumara came during the second round, to the second globe, and more precisely to the *second* root-race.

Putting this all into perspective gives one quite an esoteric jolt, because the chance of this being a pure coincidence flies in the face of reason. There is creative genius at work here. This Great Invocation was translated into English by Djwhal Khul in 1945. A Treatise on Cosmic Fire was first published in 1925. The information on the coming of Sanat Kumara is supplied by DK twenty years prior to the translation of the Great Invocation into the English words we now possess from its symbolic form on the inner planes.

The number and placement of the letters in question are beginning and ending markers of Sanat Kumara's journey into incarnation, and the 113 words tell us the exact length of His journey. The first word is the marker telling us *from* where Sanat Kumara came, namely the second Globe of the second root-race, in the second round. The last word of the Great Invocation is the time marker "Earth." This tells us where Sanat Kumara arrived 113 root-races or life impulses later.

The presence of this ingenious detail, along with so many other strands of interwoven symbolism are meant, I believe, to pique our curiosity, and open our minds to possibilities of existence lying beyond the narrow range of our limited three dimensional world. The codes and symbolic devices placed within the Great Invocation are designed to shock us into a realization that there are forms of creative genius lying beyond our ability to comprehend. The intricacy and beauty of the complex relationships hidden in the Great Invocation do not only tell us who we are and where we come from, but they also provide a rare glimpse into the mind of a Master. It is through the window of such a mind as this that we are afforded a glimpse of the potential genius of our own future development as enlightened human beings.

With the discovery of this information, it is clear why the Tibetan was so insistent that Alice Bailey record "these words these amazing words" so precisely. Is this additional element of numerological and symbolic structure just another coincidence in a growing list of coincidences, or are we uncovering the work of a Mastermind with a message for humanity?

Notes

1. Bailey, *The Rays and the Initiations,* 692.
2. Recall the interesting symbolism that Osiris was slain either in his 28th year or the 28th year of his reign.
3. Bailey, *The Rays and the Initiations,* 130.
4. Budge, *The Gods of the Egyptians,* vol. 1, 401.
5. Blavatsky, *Theosophical Glossary,* s.v. "Adept."
6. Blavatsky, *The Secret Doctrine,* vol. 1, 256.
7. Ibid., 256.
8. Budge, *The Gods of the Egyptians,* vol. 1, 32.
9. See chapter 3, "Djwhal Khul and Esoteric Numerology."
10. Foster Bailey, *The Spirit of Masonry,* 14.
11. Bailey, *The Rays and the Initiations,* 418.
12. Ibid., 415-416.
13. Bailey, *Initiation, Human and Solar,* 50.
14. Bailey, *Esoteric Astrology,* 301.
15. Recall the earlier extract in which DK states that there are "three major groups of Lives on Sirius." See n. 11.
16. Ibid., 300.
17. Bailey, *The Rays and the Initiations,* 414.
18. Bailey, *Letters on Occult Meditation*, 210.
19. Ibid., 262.
20. West, *Serpent in the Sky,* 1.
21. Bailey, *Esoteric Astrology*, 230.
22. Ibid., 288.
23. *Dictionary of Sanskrit Names,* s.v. "Narahari."
24. *The Encyclopedia of Eastern Philosophy and Religion,* s.v. "Hari."
25. Blavatsky, *The Secret Doctrine,* vol. 6, 460.
26. Blavatsky, *The Secret Doctrine,* vol. 4, 142-43.
27. Bailey, *A Treatise on White Magic,* 440-41.
28. Bailey, *A Treatise on Cosmic Fire,* 1196.
29. Bailey, *Esoteric Astrology,* 36.
30. Ibid., 299.
31. Blavatsky, *The Secret Doctrine,* vol. 1, 261.
32. Bailey, *A Treatise on Cosmic Fire,* 1196.
33. Ibid., 1197.
34. Ibid., 179.
35. These sacred planets are Vulcan (between Mercury and the Sun), Mercury, Venus, Jupiter, Saturn, Uranus, and Neptune.
36. Ibid., 1197.
37. Ibid., 242.
38. Ibid., 353.
39. Bailey, *Esoteric Astrology*, 419.

40. Bailey, *A Treatise on Cosmic Fire*, 571.
41. Ibid., 306.
42. Ibid., 1198.
43. Bailey, *Esoteric Astrology,* 294.
44. Ibid., 295.
45. Ibid., 621.
46. Bailey, *A Treatise on Cosmic Fire*, 1196.
47. Ibid., 1196.
48. Budge, *The Gods of the Egyptians,* vol. 2, 188.
49. Bailey, *Esoteric Astrology,* 197, 193, 195.
50. Ibid., 42.
51. This "Science of Triangles" is very complex and beyond the scope of this book. This example is offered because it relates to our topic. The Tibetan gives many examples of energy triangles in the book *Esoteric Astrology*, which is vol. III of *A Treatise on the Seven Rays* published by Lucis Publishing.
52. Ibid., 197, 198.
53. Ibid., 35.
54. Bailey, *A Treatise on Cosmic Fire,* 1260.
55. Ibid., 1200.
56. There are many cases of psychic sensitivity, of course, in which people report on contact with other dimensions, invisible worlds, and their inhabitants.
57. Ibid., 371.
58. Ibid., 371.
59. Ibid., 374.
60. The Law of Sacrifice is one of the "Seven Laws of Soul or Group Life." A discussion of this law can be found in *Esoteric Psychology,* vol. II page 87 of *A Treatise on the Seven Rays,*. See "Works Cited."
61. Ibid., 378.
62. Ibid., 1203-04.
63. Case, *The Tarot,* 58, 60.
64. Budge, *The Gods of the Egyptians,* vol. 1, 435.
65. Bailey, *A Treatise on Cosmic Fire,* 347.
66. Bailey, *Esoteric Psychology,* vol. I, 77.
67. Bailey, *A Treatise on Cosmic Fire*, 920.
68. Bailey, *Esoteric Astrology,* 38.
69. Bailey, *The Rays and the Initiations,* 130.

10

Hermes Trismegistus

This chapter focuses on the Hermetic aspects of the Great Invocation. The Great Invocation is a word of power. This means it is a word formula for effecting change in the life of the person or group using it. This underlying fact places the Great Invocation squarely in the domain of Hermes, the god of numbers and alphabets. Before we explore the Hermetic aspects of the Great Invocation, let's summarize what we have already discovered about this remarkable word of power.

One of the most impressive features of the Great Invocation is its symmetry. It reveals a definite symbolic structure relating to the ageless wisdom philosophy. We have divided it into three distinct parts, namely, a beginning, a middle, and an end. These three parts reflect the basic triplicity of esoteric, religious, and philosophical teaching. We have separated the Great Invocation according to the middle phrase, the middle word, and the middle letter. Using esoteric numerology and the law of correspondences, all these "dissections" reveal clear and consistent symbolic references to the star Sirius and related themes.

The twenty-one key words and their distribution throughout the Great Invocation direct our attention to Sanat Kumara, while the ninety-five letters making up the key words relate to the star Sirius, whose AN value is 95. The key words thus serve as a bridge between Sanat Kumara, known as the One Initiator, and Sirius, the star of initiation.

We found that the Great Invocation is numerologically equal when divided in two; each half is symbolically linked by the middle word "is," the mediating principle—the second aspect of divinity—the soul.

Following the Tibetan's statement that the cross is found in the consciousness of the advanced Beings of Sirius, we divided the Great Invocation into four parts, thus depicting a cross with twenty-eight words in each quadrant separating the arms. The equal-armed cross arrangement immediately revealed the numerological value of the Dog Star Sirius through the relationship set up between the middle word and any two of the other quadrants of the cross. Using the numerological value of the words in each quadrant, we found a self-referencing system within the Great Invocation revealing yet more information that demonstrates consistent themes related either directly or indirectly to Sirius.

Finally, the actual number of words and letters, along with the middle letter, serve as time markers for the arrival and descent of Sanat Kumara within the Earth chain.

Metaphorically speaking, the application of esoteric numerology to the Great Invocation can be compared to an atom smasher in modern physics. These giant circular machines, called particle accelerators, literally smash atoms in order to determine their composition. As more energy is applied to the accelerator, more sub-atomic particles keep emerging from inside the atoms.

The same seems to hold true for the Great Invocation; the more we seek to penetrate below its surface, the more information it yields. This information is not necessarily infinite, but the message continues to resurface. The Great Invocation is a tremendously potent energy source enclosed within a beautiful casing of words. The words are truly esoteric, because they reveal and conceal occult facts simultaneously. This is real magic. This is the power of the Word, and the Master of magic and Words of Power is Thoth-Hermes-Mercury.

Thoth

The Egyptian god, Thoth, is equivalent to the Greek Hermes and the Latin Mercury. For the ancient Egyptians, Thoth represented the god of numbers, alphabets, words of power, and magic. Clearly, the Great Invocation—its nature, function, meaning, construction, and symbolism—essentially expresses the qualities associated with Thoth. E.A. Wallis Budge describes some of Thoth's attributes:

> He spoke the words which resulted in the creation of the heavens and the earth, and he taught Isis the words which enabled her to revivify the dead body of Osiris in such wise that Osiris could beget a child by her, and he gave her formulae which brought back her son Horus to life after he had been stung to death by a scorpion. His knowledge and powers of calculation measured out the heavens, and planned the earth, and everything which is in them....He was the "scribe of the gods," and possessed almost unlimited power in the Underworld....In the Judgement Scene in the *Book of the Dead* it is Thoth who acts the part of the recording angel...for when once Thoth said that the soul of the deceased had been weighed, and that it had been found true by trial in the Great Balance, and that there was no wickedness whatsoever in it, the gods could not fail to answer, "That which cometh forth from thy mouth is true," "and the deceased is holy and righteous."[1]

This description of Thoth is quite impressive. The function of Thoth is similar to a grand architect or engineer. Through the divine science of numbers, the heavens and worlds are created and maintained. Thoth is able to prescribe formulas which restore health, and he is the scribe of the Gods. Using numbers and words, Thoth scientifically establishes order where there is chaos. Thoth's powers extend beyond the physical world, encompassing the Underworld or inner planes of consciousness following death. Not only does Thoth record the judgement of souls, but he determines their fate. In effect Thoth (among other things) is a Lord of Karma. Therefore, in one sense at least, Thoth is associated with Sirius, because, as you may recall, all karma in our solar system is governed by Sirius.

Thoth also rules words and word formulas called words of power by the ancient Egyptians. From his classic work *Thrice Greatest Hermes*, G.R.S. Mead offers the following:

> It was Thoth who taught these words-of-power and how to utter them; he was the Master of what the Hindus would call *mantravidya*, or the science of invocation.[2]

It should be noted that Djwhal Khul uses the exact terms, "word of power" and "science of invocation" in many parts of his teachings.

It is precisely in the area of word formulas that the great god Thoth emerges as the underlying power of the Great Invocation, for the Great Invocation *is* a word formula, it *is* a word of power. As testimony to Thoth's "powers of calculation," the Great Invocation is filled with numbers. These are not just arbitrary numbers, but numbers which relate to each other; numbers which relate to common themes directly aimed at describing the nature and purpose of our planet through symbolism and correspondence. Here is what Budge states about the power of Thoth in relation to words:

> Thoth as the great god of words was rightly regarded as the judge of words, and the testing of the soul in the Balance in the Hall of Osiris is not described as the judging or "weighing of actions," but as the "weighing of words,"...
> Thoth could teach a man not only words of power, but also the manner in which to utter them, and the faculty most coveted by the Egyptian was that which enabled him to pronounce the formulae and Chapters of the *Book of the Dead* in such a way that they could not fail to have the effect which the deceased wished them to have.[3]

This description of Thoth's role in teaching the proper use of words of power is directly connected to DK's comments on words of power. For instance, the Tibetan says the Great Invocation will be the most effective if it is said with mental focus and intent. The Tibetan's comments on the use of speech and sound are remarkably similar to Thoth's teachings:

> As we well know, there is a branch of magical work which consists in the utilisation of this knowledge in the form of Words of Power and of those mantrams and formulae which set in motion the hidden energies of nature and call the devas to their work....
>
> Therefore, those who seek to learn the occult language, those who yearn to become aware of the words which will penetrate to the ears of those who stand on the other side, and those who seek to utilise the formulae and phrases which will give them power over the Builders, have to unlearn their previous use of words and to refrain from ordinary methods of talking. Then the new language will be theirs and the new expressions, words, mantrams and formulas will be entrusted to their care.[4]

This is a very small sample of what Djwhal Khul has to say about the magical use of sound. The point is, the Great Invocation is basically a Hermetic word formula fundamentally rooted in the ancient practices of Egyptian science and religion. Does this mean the Great Invocation is an expression of ancient Egyptian religion? No. What it does mean, however, is that the Egyptian mystery schools were part of what DK calls "The one fundamental School" of occultism—"...no matter what the offshoots, the basic school of occultism is that one which has its root in the sacred centre of the planet, *Shamballa*."[5] This school operates under the direct supervision of the One Initiator, Sanat Kumara.

Thoth-Hermes is the Egyptian/Greek expression of the fundamental mystery teachings taught by the Brotherhood established on Earth by Sanat Kumara. These fundamental mysteries of initiation concern the origin, nature, and purpose of humanity. In order to grasp this more clearly, let's review the extract by DK from chapter 7 describing these mysteries:

> These ancient Mysteries were originally given to Humanity by the Hierarchy, and were—in their turn—received by the Hierarchy from the Great White Lodge on Sirius. They contain the clue to the evolutionary process, hidden in numbers and in words; they veil the secret of man's origin and destiny, picturing for him in rite and ritual the long, long path which he must tread.

The "clue to the evolutionary process hidden in numbers and in words" surely falls within the domain of Thoth-Hermes. This clearly indicates an esoteric relationship between Hermeticism, the Great Invocation, and Sirius.

From Thoth-Hermes to Hermes-Mercury

Eventually Thoth was given the name of Hermes by the Greeks, and it is by this name that he is best known today. The Egyptians first gave Thoth the attribute of "Thrice Great," and it was as Hermes that he later became known as Hermes Trismegistus, the Thrice Greatest. Antoine Faivre traces the historical evolution of Hermes from Thoth, to Thoth-Hermes, to Hermes-Mercury and finally to Hermes Trismegistus in his informative book, *The Eternal Hermes*. According to Faivre, an early alchemist of Alexandria, "read his name [Trismegistus, JB] as indicating that the operation [alchemical, JB] should be done according to a threefold ontological activity." Faivre provides the following additional examples:

> The *Suda*...[=Suidas] recognized it [the title, Trismegistus, JB] as the sign of the Trinity, an idea supposedly brought to mankind by Hermes...In a treatise dated 1736 and published under the pseudonym of Pyrophilus, one reads that this number is an allusion to the three alchemical principles of salt, sulphur, and mercury. It is most often interpreted as meaning "great philosopher, priest, and king".[6]

These examples of the threefoldness of Hermes reinforce the idea that the Great Invocation is truly Hermetic since so much numeric symbolism is unveiled by dividing it into three parts and examining the esoteric information revealed by the middle letter, word, and phrase.

Later, while discussing Hermes as Mercury, Faivre comments on St. Augustine's opinions on Hermes-Mercury:

> In the same *City of God*, Augustine suggests an etymology for the name "Mercurius" which he says means *medius currens* (running in the middle), "because language 'runs' like a sort of mediator between men."[7]

St. Augustine's idea of Mercury "running in the middle" is quite remarkable in relation to the Great Invocation for the following reason. The name "Hermes-Mercury" equals 171 (AN) and this number, as you may recall, is the value of the three word positions at the exact *middle* of the Great Invocation, namely "God is known" (56 + 57 + 58 = 171). This cannot work with Thoth-Hermes because it equals 139 (AN); nor does it work with Hermes Trismegistus, for it equals 247 (AN). Only Hermes-Mercury (171) can be found "running in the middle" of the Great Invocation.

In *The Secret Doctrine*, Blavatsky relates Mercury to Sirius:

> Says the Egyptian Isis: "I am the Queen of these regions; I was the first to reveal to mortals the mysteries of wheat and corn...I am she who rises in the constellation of the Dog...Rejoice, O Egypt! thou who wert my nurse." Sirius was called the Dog-star. It was the star of Mercury or Budha, called the great Instructor of Mankind.[8]

Earlier in the same volume, Blavatsky offers the following about Mercury:

> He is symbolized in Grecian mythology by one of the "dogs" (vigilance), which watch over the celestial flock (Occult Wisdom), or Hermes Anubis....He is the Argus watching over the Earth, mistaken by the latter for the Sun itself.[9]

At this point we must pause and be clear on what HPB means by the "star of Mercury." First, there is the physical planet Mercury. Second, there is the planetary Logos of Mercury, the Being ensouling that world. Third, there is the quality of energy expressed by Mercury. When HPB says Sirius the Dog star is the star of Mercury, she obviously does not mean the planet Mercury is Sirius, but that there is some source beyond Mercury which is transmitting a distinct quality of energy to that planet. The planetary Logos of Mercury, therefore is the distributing agent within our solar system of the quality of energy emanating from the star Sirius.

Even though Sirius is a star visible at the physical level of the universe, Djwhal Khul says the essential Life Expression of Sirius is actually located or polarized on the cosmic mental plane. From that high level of existence, Sirius distributes manasic energy and cosmic love—pure reason or buddhi into our solar system. Therefore, both mind and love are associated with Sirius and find their expression within our solar system through Mercury.

Returning to HPB's description, we find Mercury, as one of the "dogs" that guards the Occult Wisdom, present in our solar system as the agent of Sirius, the source of the Occult Wisdom also known as the Mysteries. Mercury in the form of "Hermes Anubis" is the protector of Isis. This fits well with Temple's observation in *The Sirius Mystery*:

> A further piece of information from Plutarch about Anubis is: "And when the child (Anubis, child of Nephthys by Osiris) had been found, after great toil and trouble, with the help of dogs which led Isis to it, it was brought up and became her guardian and attendant, receiving the name Anubis, and it is said to protect the gods just like dogs protect men."[10]

We are working with a definite Hermetic correspondence operating on at least two levels, namely, Sirius outside our solar system and Mercury within our solar system. Starting with the Sirian level, we have the dog, Anubis who protects and guards Isis. In Temple's theory, Isis represents Sirius A and Anubis is Sirius B, the tiny white dwarf star which orbits the larger Sirius A every 50 years. Thus, the theory states that this esoteric knowledge of Sirius B racing around Sirius A became mythologized and personified by the ancients in the form of a dog running in circles around its master in order to ward off danger.

The next level of this correspondence is reflected in our own solar system through the quality and life expression of the planet Mercury. In this explanation, HPB first says Sirius was called the star of Mercury, "the great Instructor of Mankind." Blavatsky then says the Greeks likened Mercury to one of the dogs (Argus) or Hermes-Anubis who watches over the flocks (Occult Wisdom). At this point we need to understand that the energy of Sirius (Isis, Anubis) is transmitted to and received by the guardian "dog" Argus (Mercury). The energy of Sirius is manas, mind, wisdom, buddhi, pure reason, and cosmic love. These are the qualities of Thoth-Hermes-Mercury. Hermes is the Master of Wisdom, the God of Light, the great Instructor of Man.

As Argus, Hermes-Mercury "watches over the Earth." Argus was the loyal dog of Odysseus who died after greeting his master when Odysseus returned from his twenty year journey. As Blavatsky explains, in terms of our solar system, Mercury represents Argus the Dog star watching over the Earth. In effect, because Mercury's orbit is so close to the sun, it never strays far from it, just like the loyal dogs Anubis and Argus. In this sense, our sun and Mercury are a symbolic model of the Sirian system in which the tiny white dwarf star, Sirius B orbits the larger Sirius A. Therefore, Sirius A is to our sun as Sirius B is to Mercury. In each case, the smaller unit orbits the larger like the loyal dogs Argus and Anubis.

Is this story a distorted fragment of an ancient truth concerning the protection and guidance of the greater Sirian system over our solar system? Let's repeat extract 1 from chapter 9 indicating that Djwhal Khul may have answered this question in the book *The Rays and the Initiations* some sixty years after *The Secret Doctrine* was published. He is discussing

> Those advanced Beings Who, from the distant sun, Sirius, the seat of the true Great White Lodge, *watch over the destinies of our solar system*, but *Who pay particular attention* (why They do so is not yet revealed) *to our relatively little and apparently unimportant planet, the Earth*. [emphasis mine, JB][11]

Just as the word "is" symbolizes the Star Sirius at the center of the Great Invocation, the symbolic presence of Hermes-Mercury (171) representing the three middle word positions signifies its place as the agent of Sirius in our solar system. Just as our moon reflects the light of the sun onto the Earth, Mercury acts as a figurative "moon," reflecting the higher cosmic mind of Sirius into our solar system. This is depicted in the threefold symbol for Mercury showing the crescent moon, the solar orb and the equal-armed cross of Sirius.

The Return of the Argo

Djwhal Khul may have dropped another clue about Sirius and Mercury in *The Secret Doctrine* when it was written that Mercury was "the great Instructor of Mankind." This phrase has an AN value of 328 or 8 x 41. The number 41 equals the "Argo." In the section "The Celestial Ship" from chapter 7, the Argo (41) symbolizes the star Sirius, the vessel of life. This sacred vessel carrying the seeds of life also symbolizes the Sanskrit Argha or universal mother that gives birth to the son universe. In specific relation to Sirius, it represents the origin of human life in our solar system and on our Earth. Sirius, in its mother aspect, Isis, gives birth to the human kingdom through the agency and sacrifice of Sanat Kumara.

Sixty years after *The Secret Doctrine* was published, Djwhal Khul states in the book *Esoteric Astrology*:

> Mercury was active at the time of individualisation when the "eighth gate" was opened and a major initiation of our planetary Logos took place, producing, in the human kingdom, the process of individualisation.[12]

Just before this extract, Djwhal Khul is noting that Leo can be seen as either the fifth sign or the eighth sign of the zodiac depending on the order in which the signs are read. (See table 41 and discussion of Leo and Scorpio in chapter 9.) He notes that Mercury "...is esoterically called 'the Messenger at the eighth gate.' "[13] We can see then that Mercury (in *The Secret Doctrine*) representing Sirius as "the great Instructor of Mankind" is represented sixty years later as "the Messenger at the eighth gate," thus relating it to Leo and Scorpio, and consequently to Sirius. Thus, by multiplying 8 times 41, or Mercury (agent/messenger of Sirius) times Argo (symbolizing Sirius) we obtain 328 or "the great Instructor of Mankind."

In a sense we can say the universal Argo represents the vessel of wisdom, carrying "the messenger," "the great Instructor of

Mankind." The Argo also symbolizes the vehicle for the ageless wisdom. The Hierarchy of Love-Wisdom, headed by the Christ and supervised by Sanat Kumara, is like a sacred vessel holding these Mysteries which have their source on Sirius. At the individual level, the Argo or Argha is the causal body of the soul, the sacred vessel which holds the accumulated experience and wisdom of the incarnating soul through many lifetimes. These powerful ideas are personified in Thoth, Hermes, Mercury, and Hermes Trismegistus. He represents the underlying, hidden energy of this word of power. He is the cosmic power and life of this sacred sound and the science of sound. In a sense this "Master of Wisdom," as Mead calls the Thrice Greatest, is the esoteric ruler of the Great Invocation. The number symbolism taught to us by the Great Invocation has led us to see the powerful energy of Hermes hidden beneath its outer covering of words.

We see this god of wisdom, pure reason, and buddhi manifesting through the physical planetary form of Mercury, and the celestial form of Sirius; but ensouling these two material forms are living planetary and cosmic Intelligences. At the same time, there is enough evidence to suggest this energy of wisdom, of which the "Thrice-Greatest" is the Master, is manifested on Earth through the various goddesses of antiquity associated with Sophia or Wisdom. These Earth based goddesses might be thought of as feminine Initiates of the celestial Sophia-Wisdom of Sirius—the great Instructors of Mankind.

If Sirius is the source of the Wisdom which the feminine goddesses possess, then the zodiacal sign, Virgo the Virgin, represents the guardian of that sacred Wisdom. In terms of the sacred vessel, Virgo is the cosmic Mother symbolically carrying the hidden Christ within her womb. Later, she gives birth to the Christ child, nourishing and protecting Him until He reaches maturity. From the astrological standpoint, Virgo is ruled by the planet Mercury. Symbolically speaking, it is under the watchful eye of the mother that Mercury, representing the illuminated mind, flourishes and grows in safety. Thus, this rulership symbolizes the close association between Virgo as the protectress of the Wisdom and Mercury as the planetary symbol of that Wisdom. This powerful symbol of the soul's evolution is clearly depicted in the myths surrounding both Isis and Athena.

The Goddesses of Wisdom

We have learned how the great goddess Isis, with the help of Thoth, was able to use the magical formulas he gave her to bring Osiris back to life; and we learned how she performed other magic through the use of words of power. (See "Sirius: Isis-Sothis" in chapter 7.) Beyond these powers, Isis was the most notable and beloved of all the goddesses of the ancient Egyptians. Her influence was widespread. Budge describes her enormous popularity:

> In fact, at a comparatively early period in Egyptian history Isis had absorbed the attributes of all the great primitive goddesses, and of all the local goddesses such as Nekhebet, Uatchet, Net, Bast, Hathor, etc., and she was even identified as the female counterpart of the primeval abyss of water from which sprang all life. From what has been said above it is manifestly impossible to limit the attributes of Isis, for we have seen that she possesses the powers of a water goddess, an earth goddess, a corn goddess, a star goddess, a queen of the Underworld, and a woman, and that she united in herself one or more of the attributes of all the goddesses of Egypt known to us.
> From the works of classical writers we know that her worship spread from Egypt into several places in Western Europe, and she was identified with Persephone, Tethys, Athene, etc.[14]

In his essay *The Mysteries of Isis and Osiris*, Plutarch, the Greek biographer, historian, and philosopher, comments that a statue of Athena at Sais[15] was identified with Isis by the Egyptians. Plutarch says an inscription on the statue read: "I am all that has been and is and shall be, and no mortal has ever re-vealed my robe."[16] The confusion between the identity of Isis and Athena is understandable in light of the fact that both goddesses were so similar in the power and influence they wielded.

This confusion is increased by the fact that many of the attributes Isis shared with Athena actually originated with the more ancient Egyptian goddess, Neith or Net. As the last extract by Budge explains, as time progressed the goddess Isis gradually absorbed earlier Egyptian goddesses, one of whom was Neith. All these goddesses expressed various qualities of the divine feminine aspect of deity. As time passed, Isis became a grand synthetic symbol of the divine feminine in the ancient world. Essentially, all three goddesses are expressions of the buddhic principle of Sophia or Wisdom. In a sense, they are the feminine counterparts of

Hermes, and just as the goddess Isis plays a role in the Great Invocation, the goddess Athena plays a role as well.

Pallas Athena Parthenos

The goddess Athena was a goddess of war, but a protectress rather than an aggressor. She was the goddess of weaving, architecture, and wisdom. The famous Parthenon of Athens is constructed in her honor as Parthenos or virgin.[17] She is said to have invented spinning, pottery, the plough, and cooking. In short, she reminds us of HPB's "the great Instructor of Mankind." Athena seems to have been responsible for bringing civilization and culture to ancient Greece, especially Athens, the center of Greek civilization. The Roman Emperor Julian extols her in this way:

> Unto men Athena gives good things—namely wisdom, understanding, and the creative arts; and she dwells in their citadels, I suppose, as being the founder of civil government through the communication of her own wisdom.[18]

Up to this point there is a small hint of some connection between Athena and the Great Invocation. This connection is dependent, however, on the qualities of light and wisdom which Athena shares with Isis. Since Isis is identified with Sirius, and Sirian themes are woven into the Great Invocation, the goddess Athena is indirectly related to the Great Invocation.

In the section "The Celestial Ship" in chapter 7, we discussed some ideas relating the Argo to Sirius on a symbolic and esoteric level. At the end of the Argonauts' voyage, Athena placed the ship in the heavens where it became the constellation Argo Navis. Although it was not explained in chapter 7, Athena had the power to do this because the Argo was guided and protected by her, and constructed under her supervision. According to the myth of Jason and the Argonauts, the Argo was a very special ship:

> At the foot of Mount Pelion, under Athene's direction, the best shipbuilder in Greece constructed a splendid ship of a kind of wood that does not rot in seawater. It had space for fifty oars and was named Argo after its builder Argus, the son of Arestor. It was the first long ship in which the Greeks dared steer out into the open sea. Built into the prow was a piece of wood from the prophetic oak tree of Dodona, a gift from the goddess Athene.[19]

The Argo, therefore, was an instrument of Athena. It was a vessel of magical and oracular powers, partly due to the special oak wood built into its bow which came from Dodona, the place where the Greek version of Noah's ark came to rest after the Flood. Therefore, another link between Athena and the Great Invocation can be symbolically established on the grounds that the three middle word positions total 171, which correspond to "the celestial ship." The point is, the Argo was built under the direction of the goddess Athena, and later it was turned into the celestial ship through Athena's own power. Therefore, the symbolic presence of the celestial ship at the center of the Great Invocation indicates the presence of the energy of Athena. Before explaining the significance of Athena in relation to the Great Invocation, let's review the numbers of the Argo.

- Argo = 41 (AN).
- The Celestial Ship = 171 (AN)
- Argo, The Celestial Ship = 212 (AN)
- The Dog Star Sirius = 212 (AN)
- Argo, The Celestial Ship = 95 (RAN)
- Sirius = 95 (AN)

Numerologically, Argo, the Celestial Ship, and Sirius are all connected. Could Athena be connected to Sirius as a divine Instructor of Mankind?

Athena, Seven, and the Great Invocation

The goddess Athena symbolizes the number 7, and the gematria of her name in Greek equals 77. In fact, her name in English equals 49 or 7 x 7. Athena was not born like any other being. According to Greek mythology she sprang full-grown from the forehead of Zeus. The goddess Metis, who is Divine Wisdom, was pregnant with Athena when Zeus learned of a prophecy which foretold that Metis would bear a son who would overpower him. Therefore, Zeus swallowed Metis. Soon afterward Zeus developed a tremendous headache. To relieve the pain, Hephaistos, god of Blacksmiths, (Vulcan) split open Zeus' head with an axe and out sprang Athena fully grown, armed and suited in her armor.

The story goes on to say that after Hephaistos freed Athena from the head of Zeus, he asked Zeus permission that Athena be made his bride. In the bridal chamber, however, Athena vanished before Hephaistos consummated their union, and his seed fell to the Earth where Gaia received it. From this event the child Erichthonios was born, and even though his parents were Hephaistos and Gaia, he was entrusted to the care of Athena who became his mother.[20]

This story illustrates why the number 7 is applied to Athena. It is because 7 is not born from any other number nor does it give birth to any number in the decad (1-10). For instance, 2 x 3 = 6, 2 x 4 = 8, 2 x 5 = 10 or 3 x 3 = 9. The best 7 can do in producing numeric offspring is 7 times 1 thus reproducing itself. Seven cannot be born from the decad. For this reason, 7 was treated with great respect by the Pythagorean philosophers—they called it *septad,* a term meaning reverence.

Therefore, the properties of seven were expressed through the name and titles given to the goddess Athena. Her description as Pallas is Greek for maiden. The Greek gematria for Pallas is 343 or 7 x 7 x 7. The title of Parthenos is Greek for virgin. This name has a value in Greek of 515. This number, as the decimal 51.5, is extremely close to the number of degrees in the arcs of a circle divided into seven parts (360 ÷ 7 = 51.428571). The Greeks used the word "parthenos" (virgin) because it equaled 515 which was the closest they could get to the decimal number 51.4, the result of dividing a circle into seven parts.

We have already discovered that the value of the middle word of the Great Invocation equals 28 or 4 x 7. This is a perfect number, and it is also the result of adding the first seven numbers together (1 + 2 + 3 + 4 + 5 + 6 + 7 = 28). We have also illustrated the importance of the twenty-eight words in each quadrant of the Sirian Cross as shown in figure 29 below.

Figure 29. The Five Perfect Numbers.

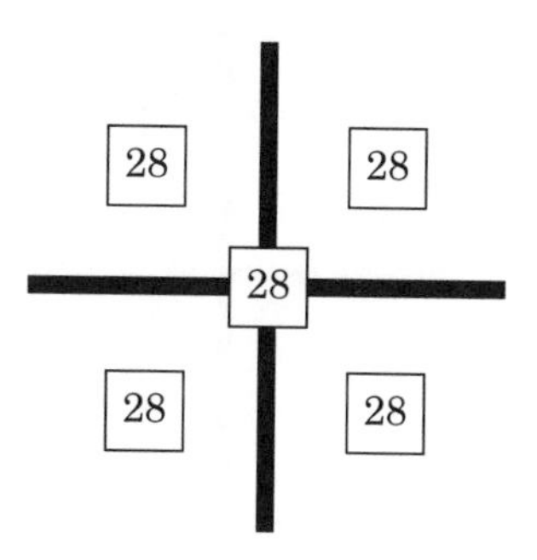

This same symbolism also depicts the presence of Athena, since each quadrant, along with the central number, is a triangular number (28) derived by adding the first seven numbers together.

Since the original diagram shows the value of 28 for the word "is" and 28 mirrored by the twenty-eight words found in each quadrant of the cross, this can also be depicted in the form of 7s as indicated by figure 30. This symbolic representation based on the resonating number 7 of the goddess Athena demonstrates the esoteric structure of the Great Invocation. This underlying septenary pattern is strikingly similar to the emergence of the hidden 7s from the key words as demonstrated in figure 7 in chapter 6.

Seven is, by far, the most appropriate number to have at the foundation and heart of the Great Invocation because it is the most important number found in all the writings of Djwhal Khul. For instance: There are the seven rays, the seven solar systems, the seven planes, the seven sacred planets, the seven ashrams, the seven Spirits before the Throne, the Seven Paths, the seven laws of the solar system, the seven laws of the soul, the seven rounds, the seven root-races, the seven states of consciousness. There are also the forty-nine (7 x 7) planes of consciousness, the forty-nine rays and sub-rays, the forty-nine fires, along with the 343 (7 x 7 x 7) planes of cosmic existence, the 343 rounds in a planetary scheme, and the 343 Life Impulses of a planetary Logos in one chain period of worlds. Finally, there are the 777 incarnations and the number of our planetary Logos—777. These examples indicate to some degree the importance attached to the number 7 in the books by Djwhal Khul. The 7s depicted in figure 30 below are like a signature or seal indicating the primal nature of this word of power rooted in the septenary nature of the cosmos.

Figure 30. The Septenary Cross of Athena.

7	7			7	7
7	7			7	7
		7	7		
		7	7		
7	7			7	7
7	7			7	7

The five 7's found in each quadrant of the cross diagram produce 35. This number is the value of *argha* (AN), which HPB calls "the ark, the womb of Nature; the crescent moon, and a life-saving ship."[21] The Argo (argha) was certainly a ship designed to save the lives of its crew, due to Athena's guidance, just as the Great Invocation (vessel), if used correctly, is designed to save humanity.

The presence of Athena in the sacred vessel of the Great Invocation is evident in another way as well. In chapter 6, the key words were analyzed in various ways, one of which involved dividing them into two groups, the original eleven and the ten duplicates. This same idea holds true for the entire Great Invocation. Even though it is comprised of 113 words, in actuality only fifty-one words are different; the remainder (62) are duplicates of the essential fifty-one. (These appear in tables 46A and 46B, which will be studied momentarily.) One interesting aspect of this core group is the fact that these fifty-one words still have a numerological value of 5, just like the entire Great Invocation. Furthermore, the middle word "where" contains five letters and has a value of 59 (AN) and 32 (RAN), which reduces to 5.

The number 51 is a direct correspondence to the gematria of Parthenos (515) because, as previously explained, a circle divided into seven parts contains seven arcs of fifty-one and a fraction degrees. The essential fifty-one words of the Great Invocation reflect the fundamental presence of the number 7 in its structure. Thus, the fifty-one words constitute the essential soul of the Great Invocation; they represent the infinite unborn nature of the universe manifesting in a sevenfold manner.

Another amazing aspect of these fifty-one words involves the name Pallas Athena Parthenos. The English value of her complete name and title equal 226 (AN), and the fifty-one words are composed of *226 letters*. When reduced to the essential words and letters needed to construct the entire Great Invocation, the goddess Athena is present in the form of the 226 letters constituting the fifty-one words needed to express the sevenfold vibration of this ancient mantram.

Because these 226 letters correspond to the name of the goddess, let's use them to re-enact the birth of Athena. Just as Hephaistos split open the head of Zeus in order to free the full grown goddess Athena from her father's head, we will split these 226 letters in half in order to find the goddess within the Great Invocation. Tables 46A and 46B list the first and second halves of the 226 letters.

Table 46A. The Essential Great Invocation.

Word #	Original Word Position	Word	Quantity of Letters	AN
1	1	From	4	52
2	2	the	3	33
3	3	point	5	74
4	4	of	2	21
5	5	Light	5	56
6	6	within	6	83
7	8	Mind	4	40
8	10	God	3	26
9	11	Let	3	37
10	13	stream	6	76
11	14	forth	5	67
12	15	into	4	58
13	17	minds	5	59
14	19	men	3	32
15	22	descend	54	27
16	23	on	29	11
17	24	Earth	52	25
18	29	Love	54	18
19	32	Heart	52	25
20	41	hearts	71	26
21	44	may	39	12
22	45	Christ	77	32
23	46	return	96	33
24	47	to	35	8
25	51	centre	65	29
First 3 letters of "where"	52	whe	3	36
		Total	113	1374

Interestingly, each half contains 113 letters corresponding to the 113 words in the Great Invocation. Note that the word "where" must be divided in two in order to divide the 226 letters equally. The division of "where" is shown at the bottom of table 46A and at the top of table 46B.

Table 46B. The Essential Great Invocation.

Word #	Original Word Position	Word	Quantity of Letters	AN
Last 2 letters of "where"	52	re	2	23
27	54	Will	4	56
28	57	is	2	28
29	58	known	5	77
30	60	purpose	7	110
31	61	guide	5	46
32	63	little	6	78
33	64	wills	5	75
34	69	which	5	51
35	71	Masters	7	95
36	72	know	4	63
37	73	and	3	19
38	74	serve	5	69
39	79	we	2	28
40	80	call	4	28
41	82	race	4	27
42	87	Plan	4	43
43	92	work	4	67
44	93	out	3	56
45	96	it	2	29
46	97	seal	4	37
47	99	door	4	52
48	101	evil	4	48
49	102	dwells	6	75
50	108	Power	5	77
51	109	restore	7	100
		Total	113	1457

Notice the AN values of the total letters at the bottom of both tables. We will concentrate on these numbers and work with them in the same way as the numbers in the quadrants of the Sirian Cross in the last chapter. Therefore, we will divide 1374 into 13 and 74, and divide 1457 into 14 and 57. These four numbers represent word positions within the Great Invocation. It is significant that even though 62 words, and therefore 62 word positions, have been dropped from the Great Invocation, *these particular word positions* (13, 14, 57 and 74) are part of the 51 words remaining in the version with which we are working. The four words appearing in positions 13, 14, 57 and 74 are shown in table 47 along with their AN values, and totals.

Table 47. Athena, the Virgin Mother.

Word Position	Word	AN
13	stream	76
14	forth	67
57	is	28
74	serve	69
158	Totals	240

Table 47 reveals two totals which are completely descriptive of everything we have discussed to this point. The total value of the word positions equals 158, which corresponds to "Word of Power" (AN). This term speaks for itself at this stage of our investigation. Remarkably, the second number, 240 equals "Athena, the Virgin Mother" (AN). This is truly outstanding in light of what we now know about Athena. Going back to her story, recall that although Athena never gave birth to a child (and thus was considered a virgin), she took on the responsibility of raising Erichthonios, the child of Hephaistos and Gaia. Aside from this aspect of the myth, many of the goddesses of the ancient world were virgin mothers or women who had children through unusual circumstances. The best example of this, of course, is Mary, mother of Jesus.

Let's summarize this information before moving on:

- The Greek name Athena is based on the number 7; thus, the Greek gematria for "Athena" equals 77.
- The English spelling of Athena equals 49 or 7 x 7.
- Pallas is Greek for maiden and equals 343 or 7 x 7 x 7.
- The structure of the entire Great Invocation is an array of 7s.
- Parthenos is the Greek word for virgin; it equals 515 (51.5), referring as closely as possible to the angle formed by divid-

ing a circle into seven parts—51.428571.

- The Great Invocation contains 51 words when all the duplicated words are removed, such as "the," "of," etc.
- These 51 essential words symbolize the sevenfold nature of God.
- There are 226 letters in these essential 51 words.
- The value of "Pallas Athena Parthenos" in English equals 226 (AN).
- When the 226 letters are split in half like the head of Zeus, "Athena, the Virgin Mother" emerges bringing the "Word of Power" with her.

The Adept Using Energy

In chapter 9, we discovered that the Sirian Cross depiction of the Great Invocation, when subjected to a process of numerological reduction, eventually reduced the twenty-eight words in each quadrant to the numbers 3 and 8. The numerological values of the words in the third and eighth positions totaled 114. We found that Osiris, Isis, and Horus along with Sirius equal 114 (RAN), thus corresponding to the numerological "bedrock" at the core of the Great Invocation.

We also discovered that the number 114 equals "Sons of God" (AN). These "Sons of God," according to HPB, were the early Instructors of humanity. Osiris, Isis, and Horus certainly represent such advanced Teachers. And, from what we have discovered about Athena, she must also be considered as one of the "Sons of God." Even though she was obviously female in human form, as was Isis, the term "Sons of God" refers to the middle or second principle of the trinity which represents the Son aspect. This has everything to do with energy relationship, dynamics, and function and little to do with the gender of the animal forms which these divine Instructors ensouled while fulfilling their roles. In other words, the "Sons of God" were primarily Teachers and secondarily male or female. In actuality, Osiris and Isis symbolize two aspects of One Life which has the capacity to both create and give birth, to empower and nurture. The goddess Athena is interesting in this regard because she has no obvious male counterpart, but embodies both feminine and masculine aspects within herself.

The similarities between the Greek goddess and the Egyptian

trinity are quite interesting, but the number values of their names are even more so because they are identical. Pallas Athena Parthenos has the exact same number value as Osiris, Isis, and Horus. Both sets of names equal 82 (RAN). Therefore, Athena is also the "adept using energy" (82 RAN) just like the Osiris, Isis, Horus trinity.

That is only one half of the story, however, because the AN value of these Greek and Egyptian "adepts using energy" equals 226. Therefore, Osiris, Isis, and Horus also correspond to the 226 letters in the fifty-one word version of the Great Invocation. In addition, Osiris, Isis, Horus, and Pallas Athena Parthenos are connected to "the Plan of Love and Light" because this phrase *also equals* 226. And, like Pallas Athena Parthenos, it too contains 21 letters. The fact that "the Plan of Love and Light" equals the number of letters in the fifty-one word version of the Great Invocation is significant because it is the Plan of Love and Light which is being implemented on Earth through the race of men by our divine Instructors. If this is not enough, all three phrases combined contain 57 letters which symbolically relate them to the middle word position of the Great Invocation. Furthermore, since Athena relates to the number 7 and consequently to the underlying septenary structure of the Great Invocation, it is striking to see that by dividing the 443 letters of the Great Invocation by the 57 letters in these three phrases the result is 7.77. There are powerful implications in these esoteric relationships that warrant further examination.

The Work of the Sirian Lodge

We are discussing the Plan of Love and Light. We know almost nothing about this Plan except that humanity, the fourth kingdom in nature, is a primary factor in the Plan's implementation on Earth at this time. The Great Invocation speaks directly to this issue in the fourth stanza:

From the centre which we call the race of men
Let the Plan of Love and Light work out
And may it seal the door where evil dwells.

Recall in the very beginning of the book, we noted that no one in the Hierarchy knows the age of the Great Invocation, but as we have shown in the last chapter, Sanat Kumara may have brought it with Him when He arrived in our fourth chain, and fourth globe some eighteen million years ago. If that is the case, then the Plan of Love and Light is ancient indeed.

Assuming this to be the case, Sanat Kumara and His divine Instructors of Mankind came to this world to implement a Plan of vast proportions that may very well involve the Lives on Sirius. As we have found from our investigation so far, numbers have deep implications in esoteric writing, and DK is a genius in their symbolic and literal use. For example, in relation to the number 4 He tells us the Path to Sirius is the *fourth* of seven. We are told that our solar system is one of the *fourth* order. The Earth is the *fourth* scheme in the solar system. Within our Earth Scheme, our dense physical planet is the *fourth* globe in the *fourth* chain. Humanity is the *fourth* creative Hierarchy, governed by the *fourth* ray of Harmony through Conflict, and is the *fourth* kingdom in nature. The process of initiation, implemented by the Hierarchy, but originating on Sirius, first began in the Atlantean *fourth* root-race. The Egyptian religion, the source of the hermetic teachings in the ancient world was, according to the Tibetan, governed by the *fourth* ray. Last but not least, the *fourth* stanza of the Great Invocation mentions the race of men in relation to the Plan of Love and Light.

The Law of Correspondences plays a powerful role in esoteric writing. Numeric correlations are esoteric bridges connecting subjective archetypal patterns to objective and seemingly separate thoughtforms in the concrete linear mind. Using numbers and subjects which apparently have little or no connection in the usual way of thinking, we will demonstrate a synthetic, subjective, and esoteric relationship existing between "the Plan of Love and Light" as it appears in the fourth stanza of the Great Invocation and the Sirian Lodge.

Here are some numerological facts to consider:

- Fifty-one words of the Great Invocation contain 226 letters.
- Osiris, Isis, and Horus equal 226 (AN).
- Pallas Athena Parthenos equals 226 (AN).
- The Plan of Love and Light equals 226 (AN).
- The phrases "Sirian Lodge" and "the race of men" each equal 113 (AN).
- "The race of Sirian Lodge men" equals 226 (AN).

The Egyptian trinity (226) and Pallas Athena Parthenos (226) are prototypes and archetypes of high initiates associated with the Sirian process of initiation. They are also divine Instructors of mankind Who help implement "the Plan of Love and Light" (226). The number 226 indicates the esoteric connection between these seemingly separate elements. These two ancient examples might also be thought of as "the race of Sirian Lodge men" (226) Who have advanced so far in their evolution that they have entered into the rudimentary levels of consciousness of the greater Lodge of Beings on Sirius.

"The race of men" (113) was created with the help of the "Sirian Lodge" (113); together they equal 226. Therefore, "the Plan of Love and Light" (226) is fulfilled when the work of the Sirian Lodge is symbolically combined with the race of men equaling 226. Since the phrases "the race of men" and "the Plan of Love and Light" are both found in the fourth stanza of the Great Invocation, this indicates another connection between it and Sirius via the fourth Path.

This connection between the Great Invocation and Sirius runs very deep. The profound depth of this relationship is demonstrated by the word positions occupied by the two above mentioned phrases. First let's look at "the Plan of Love and Light."

The phrase "the Plan of Love and Light" occupies positions 86, 87, 88, 89, 90, 91 of the Great Invocation. These word positions (not the values of the words) total 531. The number 531 is also a result of multiplying 3 x 3 x 59. There are three terms specifically related to "the Plan of Love and Light." These are "Sirian Lodge," "Hierarchy," and "the race of men." These three terms each equal 59 (RAN). In addition, each of these elements has three parts.

Sirius has "three major groups of Lives"[22] (symbolically Osiris, Isis, and Horus). Hierarchy has three main divisions—the Manu, the Christ, and the Mahachohan; and human beings (the race of men) are comprised of three parts—monad, soul, and personality. Thus, the three centers—Sirius, Hierarchy, and Humanity each contain three divisions, or 3 x 3. When the RAN value of each one is factored into the formula the result is 531—"the Plan of Love and Light" (3 x 3 x 59 = 531). See figure 31.

These three centers form a triangle which is the basis for the Plan of Love and Light. Symbolically speaking, the Sirian Lodge is the Will aspect (Atma), the Hierarchy is the Love aspect (Buddhi), and the race of men is the Intelligence aspect (Manas). Since these three aspects equal 59, the entire unit equals 177 (3 x 59) which is the same value as "spiritual triad" (177 AN).

Figure 31. The Plan of Love and Light.

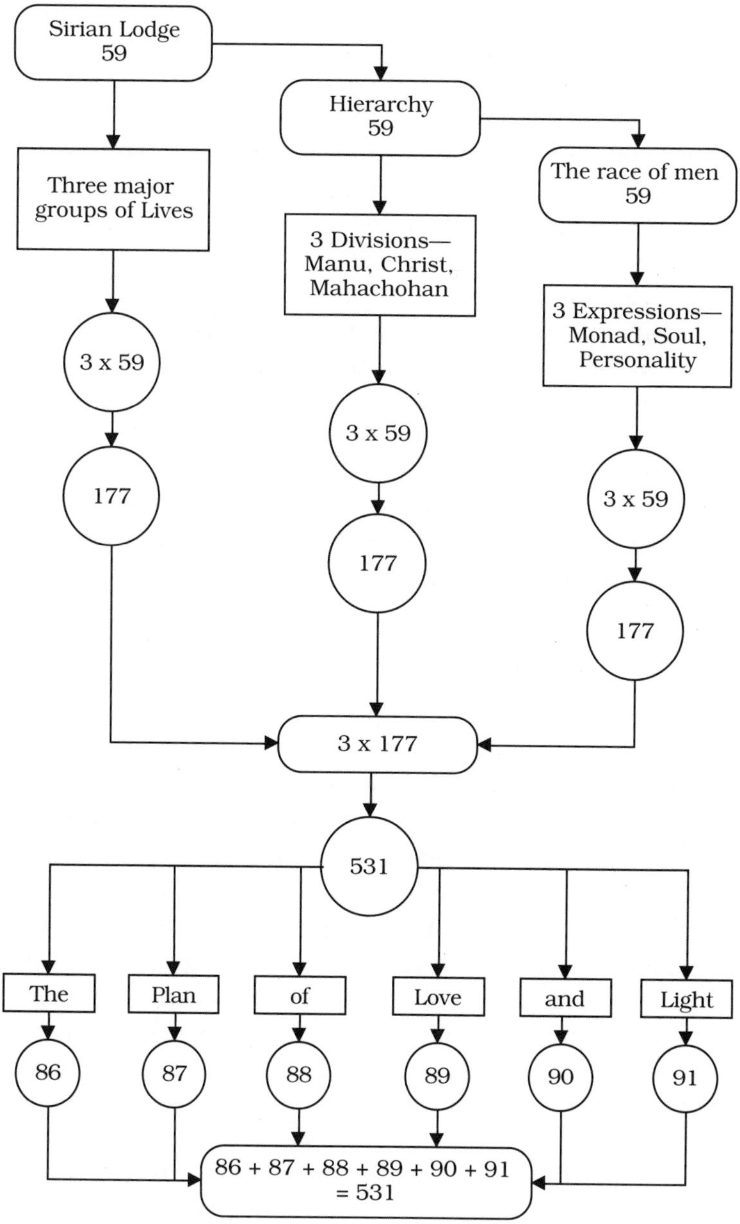

The fact that this phrase is positioned at the exact place in the Great Invocation which yields a number numerically related to Sirius, Hierarchy, and the race of men strongly suggests more than mere coincidence. The entire concept indicates that the Plan of Love and Light involves the Sirian Lodge, our own planetary Hierarchy, and the human race. It might be said that the Great Invocation is a specially designed vessel concealing the mysteries of the ageless wisdom within the confines of its words.

As previously mentioned, the great Lives on Sirius watch over the destiny of our planet for some mysterious reason. Apparently, the race of men is of importance to the Plan of Love and Light originating and administered from Sirius, with its three groups of Lives. The Great White Lodge on Earth is an outpost of the primary lodge on Sirius. "Sirius, the Great White Lodge" equals 287 (AN). Taking into account the three groups of Lives on Sirius and their three influences on the Earth's evolution, we multiply 287 by 3 resulting in 861. This number may seem familiar to you. That is because it is a triangular number resulting from the addition of the first 41 numbers. The number 41 is the AN value of the Argo—Athena's celestial ship. (See chapter 7.) The tie-in with the Great Invocation involves the total value of the word positions for the phrases "the Plan of Love and Light" (531), and "the race of men" (330). The sum of these two phrases is 861 (531 + 330), the same as "Sirius, the Great White Lodge" x 3.

The meaning is direct and simple: The three influences of "Sirius, the Great White Lodge" lead "the race of men" to fulfill "the Plan of Love and Light." Just exactly what those three influences are is unclear, but an obvious choice might be the triple aspects of Will, Love, and Intelligence stepped down to our human level from their source on Sirius. These three influences may also relate to the Tibetan's description of the "three major groups of Lives" found on Sirius. In some mysterious way, these three groups of Lives are related to the Blue Lodge of Masonry. The Tibetan states that those Members of the spiritual Hierarchy Who choose the Path to Sirius are received by these three groups of Sirian Lives Who "train Them in the mode of existence and the type of livingness which is found on Sirius."[23]

The work of the Sirian Lodge is esoterically present in the fourth stanza of the Great Invocation, and specifically indicated by the exact positions of the two phrases "the race of men" and "the

Plan of Love and Light." The emergence of this central idea is a result of both the exact positioning and numerological values of these two phrases within the Great Invocation. The consistency of the Sirian theme of cultivating a human race that can fulfill the Plan of Light and Love on Earth is unmistakable.

The overarching work of the Sirian Lodge might very well be found in the following four statements wherein the Tibetan describes the long range goals of the Plan:

> The first aim and the primary aim is to establish, through the medium of humanity, an outpost of the Consciousness of God in the solar system...
>
> To found upon earth (as has already been indicated) a power-house of such potency and a focal point of such energy that humanity—as a whole—can be a factor in the solar system, bringing about changes and events of a unique nature in the planetary life and lives (and therefore in the system itself) and inducing an *interstellar activity* [emphasis mine, JB].
>
> To develop a station of light, through the medium of the fourth kingdom in nature, which will serve not only the planet, and not only our particular solar system, but the seven systems of which ours is one....
>
> To set up a magnetic centre in the universe, in which the human kingdom and the kingdom of souls [Hierarchy, JB] will, united or at-oned, be the point of most intense power, and which will serve the developed Lives within the radius of the radiance of the *One About Whom Naught May Be Said.*[24]

These four goals of the Plan are implemented through the seven "Rules for Inducing Soul Control." DK explains that these are not rules for the discipleship training of individuals, but that they are

> concerned with those basic trends and those innate tendencies in the divine expression which will ultimately bring about the manifestation of the Oversoul upon our planet.[25]

DK goes on to say that humanity will eventually form an outpost of divine Consciousness on our planet and be

> an expression of the divine Psyche, manifesting eventually those three outstanding psychological characteristics of divinity: Light, Energy, and Magnetism. In the human being, the microcosmic reflection of the Macrocosm, these qualities are expressed by the words: Illumination

> or Wisdom, Intelligent Activity, and Attractiveness or Love.[26]

Djwhal Khul's mentioning of the "three outstanding psychological characteristics of divinity" hints at the three influences of Sirius. In other words, through the Path of Initiation or the work of the Sirian Lodge, humanity will someday be a planet of Initiates expressing the divine Psyche, Oversoul, or Cosmic Christ.

The initiatory process has already produced the Christ as the first fruit of the Sirian Lodge. The achievement of the Christ as the first human being to attain the goal is a guarantee that our planet can become a powerhouse and station of Light in the universe "which will serve the developed Lives within the radius of the radiance of the *One About Whom Naught May Be Said*."

The Light Which Ever Shineth In the East

The work of the Lodge on Sirius is currently focused on our tiny planet Earth. Through a complex series of alignments within our solar system, the Earth now occupies a place of crucial attention in the Plan of Beings far in advance of our Earth humanity. Despite this apparent disproportionate relationship between certain cosmic Lives and our terrestrial humanity, the human kingdom is vitally important in the present solar cycle.

This cycle involves a peculiar window of opportunity occurring at the midway point in the evolutionary Life of the planetary Logos of the Earth Scheme. We are just past the midpoint of that life cycle of our planetary scheme. Since this is a system of cycles based primarily on seven, the fact that we are in the fourth part of the cycle represents a midway point in the overall planetary development.

The planetary Logos of our Earth Scheme is now in physical incarnation. As we now know, He is called Sanat Kumara. According to DK, Sanat Kumara is to take the fourth Initiation in this chain.[27]

> Well may this globe, therefore, be considered the globe of sorrow and of pain, for through it our planetary Logos is undergoing that which the mystic calls "the Crucifixion."[28]

Recall that the planetary Logos incarnated as Sanat Kumara in the fourth round on the fourth globe (our dense Earth) during the third root-race. This act of sacrifice enabled Him to undergo a major initiation. (We must assume the third, since DK says He is now working on the fourth.) As a result of this, the human race was created. We reiterate this point to make it clear that humanity is the *fourth kingdom of nature and the fourth Creative Hierarchy*. In a sense, the human kingdom of monads is the vehicle for the Logos to take the fourth initiation. Therefore, the human race is an intrinsic part of Sanat Kumara's task of attaining the fourth cosmic initiation.

All of this activity is governed by Sirius. Immediately after relating this information about the planetary Logos preparing for the fourth initiation, DK states the following:

> If we link this up with that earlier imparted concerning initiation and the sun Sirius, we will have a clue to the triple cosmic Path.[29]

The Tibetan is referring to the book *Initiation, Human and Solar* in which He describes the various levels of initiation.

> A Master, therefore, is one who has taken the seventh planetary initiation, the fifth solar initiation, and the first Sirian or cosmic initiation.[30]

Although there are many unanswered questions about these cosmic initiations which go beyond the scope of this discussion, the main point here is to understand the supreme importance of Sirius in relation to our development as human beings who will someday take initiation. Beyond the human level, Sirius is also important in relation to the development of our own planetary Logos and to the evolution of the entire solar system, including the solar Logos.

In light of all this, the Great Invocation takes on a truly sacred and profound role in our present planetary circumstances. The situation might be described as follows:

The planetary Logos incarnated as Sanat Kumara during the fourth round of the fourth chain on the fourth globe of the fourth scheme. He underwent a major initiation (perhaps the third), resulting in the creation of the fourth human kingdom. The Great Invocation was entrusted to Him for later use by the newly formed human kingdom. The fourth kingdom was created as a vehicle for Sanat Kumara to take the fourth cosmic initiation.

None of this could have occurred without the intervention of

Sirius. As a result, Sirius is the original source of the Mysteries of man's origin and nature hidden in color, sound, and number. Thus, the Path of Initiation was established on Earth through Sanat Kumara and the divine Instructors of Mankind. In turn, the spiritual Hierarchy came into being on Earth as an outpost of the original Hierarchy of Initiates on Sirius. Sirius as the source of the Mysteries symbolizes "the Light which ever shineth in the East," and Hermes Trismegistus personifies the prototypal Sirian "Light of the World." The Christ was the first human being to attain that Light and so became the Light of the World for humanity.

In the section "Sixes and Fives" in chapter 6, we mentioned briefly that Hermes was the first to proclaim, "I am the Light of the World." Let's look at the esoteric numerology associated with the god of alphabets, numbers, and words of power.

First, if we take the value of all three names of the Thrice Greatest, we have "Thoth Hermes Mercury" equaling 242 (AN). This number is remarkable in the sense that two of its factors are 11 and 22. We already know, according to the Tibetan, the number 11 symbolizes the adept using energy. In *Esoteric Psychology,* vol. I, while discussing the seven rays and the twelve creative Hierarchies DK states:

> The 7 + 12 = 19, and if you add to these 19 expressions of the Life [One About Whom Naught May Be Said, JB] the 3 major aspects of Deity, which we call the life of God, the Father, the love of God the Son, and the active intelligence of God the Holy Ghost, you arrive at the mystic number 22, which is called (in esotericism) the number of the adept.[31]

So we see that 11 is the number of the adept using energy, and the number 22 is the adept himself. Therefore, when we multiply 11 x 22, we get the product 242 or Thoth Hermes Mercury. Therefore, the Thrice Greatest Hermes is the prototypal "adept using energy." Hermes personifies the Thrice Greatest because He is the Universal ADEPT Who is able to work with all three aspects of God, along with the seven rays and twelve Creative Hierarchies. DK is quick to point out that human adepts simply recognize these twenty-two energies but are nowhere near the point of wielding and mastering them.

The next example of esoteric numerology involves the name "Hermes Trismegistus" which equals 247 (AN). The proclamation, "I am the Light of the World" equals 238 (AN). Together these two elements total 485 and equal the phrase "within the sunshine of the major sun Sirius" (485 AN). Hermes Trismegistus is thus related numerologically to Sirius. This might be interpreted to mean that the Light of Hermes is the spiritual Light—the sunshine—of the major sun Sirius.

This idea is borne out by the fact that "Thoth Hermes Mercury" the "God of Light within"[32] (242 + 132 = 374) equals "the Light which ever shineth in the East" (374). This esoteric numerological fact relates Hermes to Sirius at several levels. First, that the Light of the World is God immanent within each individual soul, and this Light is the spiritual radiance of Sirius. Second, this Light of Wisdom is ever present in the East as the true spiritual sun, Sirius hidden behind the disc of the physical sun; the place where the Light is always present, both physically and spiritually. Third, Hermes is the messenger and mediator of the Light of Initiation which has its source on Sirius, and He may be that mysterious Avatar from Sirius Who is now present in our solar system.[33]

The theme of the light in the east continues with the phrase "eastern star" 140 (AN). The combination Hermes Mercury (171), God of Light within (132), and "eastern star" (140) equals 443, which of course is the number of letters in the Great Invocation. These words can be put together as "Hermes-Mercury, God of Light within (the) eastern star" (443). In this instance, the Great Invocation is directly connected to Hermes and Sirius as the eastern star. The Masonic symbolism is clearly evident in this theme, and continues to add esoteric numerological weight to the Tibetan's statements that Masonry has its origin on Sirius.

The Hidden God of Light

A connection between Hermes Trismegistus and the Great Invocation is also found through the phrase "the God of Light." It is generally recognized that Hermes is the God of Light, and we have already quoted DK's statement that Hermes was the first avatar to declare Himself as the Light of the world.

The fascinating thing about the phrase "the God of Light" is the fact that it lies hidden within the Great Invocation. At the end of the section "The Return of the Argo" we discussed the zodiacal sign Virgo. As the guardian of the Wisdom she symbolizes the Great Mother Who carries the Christ Light within her body. In fact, Djwhal Khul relates Virgo to "The Hidden Light of God."[34] Thus, the Great Invocation, like Virgo, is a sacred vessel carrying "the Light of God" or "the God of Light" hidden within its womb. The phrase only becomes visible by using the numeric position of a word in the Great Invocation as an "index" for finding a corresponding word at another location within it.

This technique uses the Word Position Index—a schematic of all 113 words of the Great Invocation (appendix B and figure 32). It is divided into two 7 x 8 grids of fifty-six words each. These two grids are joined by the middle word "is" in the 57th position. Note that the top number of each box indicates the word position and the bottom number indicates the AN value of the word.

Let's use the word "point" as an example of this process of "word hopping." Locate "point" in position 3 and note that its AN value is 74. We now use the numerological value 74 to find the word located in position 74. The 74th position contains the word "serve," with a value of 69. We now use the number 69 to find the 69th word in the Great Invocation. That word is "which," and it has a value of 51. We now proceed to word position 51, which takes us to word position 65. Once word position 65 sends us to word position 21, we find ourselves in an endless loop involving four words, which are "Light," "God," "the," and "of." This loop can be read as "the Light of God" or "the God of Light." This infinity loop is telling us that the Light of God and the God of Light is infinite.

No matter what word we choose in this process we will always be caught in the infinity loop containing the words "the God of Light." Interestingly, the path of this number loop actually traces an infinity sign, despite its disproportionate shape. Try any word within the Word Position Index to prove this for yourself. It is impossible to break out of the Great Invocation because there is no word with a numerological value greater than the number of words (113) within it.

Because the phrase "the God of Light" can only be found by movement through the Great Invocation according to numeric vibration, it is truly Hermetic, hidden and therefore, esoteric. The numeric value of this phrase is 136 (AN) and 73 (RAN). This is really quite remarkable because no matter how we move through the numeric vibrations of the Great Invocation, we always end up in an infinite loop consisting of the numbers 21, 26, 33, and 56, whose combined numerological values equal *"the Great White Lodge on Sirius"*!

Figure 32. Signature of Sirius.

1 From 52	2 the 33	3 point 74	4 of 21	5 Light 56	6 within 83	7 the 33
8 Mind 40	9 of 21	10 God 26	11 Let 37	12 light 56	13 stream 76	14 forth 67
15 into 58	16 the 33	17 minds 59	18 of 21	19 men 32	20 Let 37	21 Light 56
22 descend 54	23 on 29	24 Earth 52	25 From 52	26 the 33	27 point 74	28 of 21
29 Love 54	30 within 83	31 the 33	32 Heart 52	33 of 21	34 God 26	35 Let 37
36 love 54	37 stream 76	38 forth 67	39 into 58	40 the 33	41 hearts 71	42 of 21
43 men 32	44 May 39	45 Christ 77	46 return 96	47 to 35	48 Earth 52	49 From 52
50 the 33	51 centre 65	52 where 59	53 the 33	54 will 56	55 of 21	56 God 26
			57 is 28			
58 known 77	59 Let 37	60 purpose 110	61 guide 46	62 the 33	63 little 78	64 wills 75
65 of 21	66 men 32	67 The 33	68 purpose 110	69 which 51	70 the 33	71 Masters 95
72 know 63	73 and 19	74 serve 69	75 From 52	76 the 33	77 centre 65	78 which 51
79 we 28	80 call 28	81 the 33	82 race 27	83 of 21	84 men 32	85 Let 37
86 the 33	87 Plan 43	88 of 21	89 Love 54	90 and 19	91 Light 56	92 work 67
93 out 56	94 And 19	95 may 39	96 it 29	97 seal 37	98 the 33	99 door 52
100 where 59	101 evil 48	102 dwells 75	103 Let 37	104 Light 56	105 and 19	106 Love 54
107 and 19	108 Power 77	109 restore 100	110 the 33	111 Plan 43	112 on 29	113 Earth 52

As you may recall, the number 136 also appeared in chapter 9 as the value for "the Will of God" and "the Great White Lodge on Sirius" when the four words in the twenty-eighth position in each quadrant of the Sirian Cross were combined. (See table 34.)

We have, therefore, "the Great White Lodge on Sirius," "the God of Light" (or the Light of God), and "the Will of God" each equaling 136. (Recall Djwhal Khul's statement that Sanat Kumara "is the Custodian of the will of the Great White Lodge on Sirius."[35]) This word/number infinity loop can be thought of as a pulsating signal alerting us to the identity, nature, energy, and source of the Great Invocation. It also indicates the steady rhythmic motion associated with the seventh Ray of Ceremonial Order or Magic.

Ray Seven–The Unveiled Magician

In terms of the seven rays and their relationship to our planet at this crucial time in history, ray seven is probably the most important of all. This ray is coming into manifestation as the Aquarian Age is beginning.

Everything we have discussed in this chapter is based on the seventh Ray of Ceremonial Order or Magic. Hermes Trismegistus symbolizes the power of ray seven. He is the "Unveiled Magician,"[36] which is one of the names given to the Lord of the seventh ray. Since the Great Invocation is a word of power, it comes under the influence of ray seven. In the words of DK, "He [seventh ray Lord, JB] guides and directs the production of the form by means of certain occult words."[37] This is exactly what the Great Invocation is designed to do—create those conditions by which the new civilization or form of human living can be constructed. In this sense DK gives the seventh ray Lord the name "The Keeper of the Magical Word."

By using the Great Invocation with clear and focused mental concentration, we are effecting a real transformation of the physical-etheric plane. This is the plane on which the seventh ray is the most powerful. Therefore, another name for this ray Lord is "The Divine Alchemical Worker." Thus, "The Keeper of the Magical Word" is "The Divine Alchemical Worker" who transforms through the use of sounds and mantrams. This is all seventh ray work. While describing the powers of a seventh degree initiate, DK offers the following information about the use of sound:

> On the physical he works primarily with the Words of the seventh Logos, which fall naturally into five groups: Mantrams which deal with etheric matter...Mantrams which deal with dense physical matter...Words specifically connected with the human Hierarchy...Words concerning the deva evolution...Words which affect the life side of manifestation.[38]

The occult science of sound is the most closely guarded knowledge of the Hierarchy because the worlds are created and destroyed through the use of sound. The pacing, rhythm, and proper notes are part of the secret use of mantrams. DK warns that "Until the inner faculty of clairvoyance is somewhat developed, this knowledge of mantrams remains practically useless and may be even a menace."[39]

The Great Invocation is the most powerful mantram of the Hierarchy which humanity can use. Although we use this prayer in the form of words, as we are discovering, these words are intimately "wired" to numeric frequencies resonating on etheric levels. When we activate these words by saying the Great Invocation (or even by mental repetition), it is like throwing the switch to a powerful generator existing on the etheric planes. The effect produced by these word/number frequencies flows from a vast reservoir of spiritual energy directly connected to the seven original word-forms of the sacred Word of Power as it is used by Hierarchy, the Christ, and the Beings in Shamballa.

In other words, humanity is using a form of the original Great Invocation suitable for the evolutionary level of present day mankind, but still containing the inherent and essential vibratory frequency of the original Word of Power as it exists at the highest levels of our planetary Life. It is abundantly clear from the esoteric standpoint that these 113 words which we call the Great Invocation reflect the esoteric underpinning that supports the essential philosophical teachings concerning our planet and its relationship to the solar system and the sun Sirius. Therefore, when someone below the grade of a seventh degree initiate, with no training in the occult science of sound, changes the Great Invocation, it is no longer the Great Invocation; it is no longer connected to its source vibration. In effect, when the Great Invocation is changed in any way, it is the same as pulling the power cord from a computer or cutting a telephone line to a network—the entire system crashes and cannot operate as intended.

The Seventh Ray–The Fifth Aspect of Mind

The Tibetan recommends we say the Great Invocation mentally rather than emotionally. This means we must use our minds, and consequently the fifth ray. Furthermore, a mantram should be used with ordered rhythm, bringing the seventh ray into activity. Consequently, the fifth and seventh rays are important in the use of the Great Invocation.

This five/seven combination is reflected in the Great Invocation by its composition. First, it is shown by the fact that the 5 stanzas contain 7 sentences, and second, by the middle word position, which is 57, or 5 and 7. Since the fifth mental principle is so important to the Great Invocation, it is significant that the seventh ray can also be viewed as the fifth manasic ray. The Tibetan explains this concept in the following way:

1. Will or Power
2. Love or Wisdom
3. Adaptability or Active Intelligence . . . . .1.
4. Harmony, Beauty or Art . . . . .2.
5. Concrete Knowledge or Science . . . . .3.
6. Abstract Idealism . . . . .4.
7. Ceremonial Magic . . . . .5.[40]

This list is very interesting because it illustrates the five subdivisions of the third ray of Adaptability or Active Intelligence: "*These four Rays with their synthesising Ray make the five rays of Manas or Mind.*"[41] The numbers on the right side of the list are referred to by Djwhal Khul as the manasic aspect. Note that the seventh ray is related to the fifth because the seventh ray is also the fifth manasic aspect within the rays comprising the totality of mind. An example of this close relationship follows:

> The seventh and fifth Rays are occupied with the return of the Son to the Father and are largely centred in pouring forth energising power when it becomes necessary to transfer the life of the Son from an old form into a new, from one kingdom of nature to another on the Path of Return.[42]

In a very real sense this is exactly what the Great Invocation is designed to do. Through its use, humanity is invoking the Christ and certain Members of the Hierarchy into physical appearance in the world. The result of this externalization of the Hierarchy is part of the Plan "to transfer the life of the Son from an old form into a new, from one kingdom of nature to another." Humanity symbolized as the world disciple represents the Son returning to the Father.

This special work of the seventh ray is indicated further in the following:

> This seventh Ray (fifth) ever manifests in a period of transition from one kingdom to another, and this holds hid the mystery of the particular form of service of its planetary Logos. He governs the processes of:
>
> Transmutation
> Incarnation
> Transference
>
> In these three words His life-work is summed up; in these three words is embodied the nature of this great Entity, Who presides over the processes of blending and merging and adaptation; Who, through His knowledge of cosmic Sound, guides the life forces of certain solar and lunar entities from form to form, and is the link between the soul awaiting incarnation, and its body of manifestation.[43]

In these words Djwhal Khul is explaining in technical language what He has said rather clearly elsewhere, which is that the fifth kingdom in nature, that of the Hierarchy, is about to be born into physical manifestation. Conditions on the planet are rapidly reaching a point where this can become possible. Broadly speaking, this will happen in two ways: first, by the externalization of certain ashrams of the Masters onto the physical plane along with the reappearance of the Christ, the World Teacher for the Aquarian Era, and second, by the taking of initiation by many disciples in the near future. The outer activities of the Hierarchy will be greatly facilitated due to greater freedom in the world and the consequent general upliftment of humanity worldwide.

As mentioned in the last section, one of the major ways the seventh ray works is through the power of sound using certain mantrams. The Great Invocation is definitely in this category according to all that Djwhal Khul has said. Speaking about the creative use of sound, Djwhal Khul states:

> The Words of the second aspect concern us closely, but the Words of Brahma are at the present stage more closely connected with our

> work upon the physical plane. These Words, where the three worlds are concerned, very largely fall into a group of mantrams, hidden in the consciousness of the Lords of the fifth and seventh Rays...On the physical plane the words, uttered by the seventh Logos, produce the following results...The transference of the conscious, sentient life from form to form, from group to group, from kingdom to kingdom within the hierarchies.[44]

This quotation shows quite clearly how the fifth and seventh rays are closely related to the use of sound. When DK talks about the Brahma aspect, He is referring to the five manasic ray energies mentioned earlier. The seventh Logos (seventh ray) uses sound to effect change and transference of life forms and entities from kingdom to kingdom. This is happening today with the emerging of the fifth spiritual kingdom, and the transference—through initiation—of many humans from the fourth kingdom into the fifth kingdom of Hierarchy.

Nothing in the universe operates in isolation. All is connected and in dynamic relationship. This principle applies to the seven rays as well. The Great Invocation is a word of power operating on ray seven; however, the various rays work together in order to accomplish the Plan of God. As we enter the next chapter we will find that Sirius influences the Great Invocation through various rays, so we close with the following words concerning ray seven:

> This ray Lord has a peculiar power on earth and on the physical plane of divine manifestation. His usefulness to His six Brothers [the six other rays, JB] is therefore apparent. He makes Their work appear. He is the most active of all the rays in this world period...and His closest relation, symbolically, is to His Brethren of the second and fifth rays *in this world period.*[45]

Notes

1. Budge, *The Gods of the Egyptians*, vol. 1, 407-08
2. G.R.S. Mead, *Thrice Greatest Hermes,* vol. 1, 45.
3. Budge, *The Gods of the Egyptians,* vol. 1, 408-09.
4. Bailey, *A Treatise on Cosmic Fire*, 981.
5. Bailey, *Letters on Occult Meditation,* 302.
6. Antoine Faivre, trans by Joscelyn Godwin, *The Eternal Hermes*, 80.
7. Ibid., 82.
8. Blavatsky, *The Secret Doctrine,* vol. 3, 373.
9. Ibid., 41.
10. Temple, *The Sirius Mystery,* 71.
11. The wording between HPB's "watching over the Earth" and Djwhal Khul's "watch over the destinies" is rather striking. It indicates a continuity of teaching from HPB's *The Secret Doctrine* to Bailey's work as amanuensis for DK. According to the Tibetan, He dictated much of *The Secret Doctrine* to Blavatsky, and this explains why certain details of the ageless wisdom which appear cryptic in *The Secret Doctrine* are revealed in greater detail in the second phase of DK's work with Alice Bailey thirty or forty years later. Evidence of the phased release of esoteric information by Djwhal Khul over several decades spanning the late 19th century and the first half of the 20th century has already appeared in the 10, 6, 5 key word pattern of the Great Invocation. We are now seeing something similar with the identity of Hermes-Mercury (171) at the midpoint of the Great Invocation. It seems a bit beyond coincidence that with all the information connecting Sirius and the Great Invocation, another link involving Mercury and Sirius appears right at the center of this word of power.
12. Bailey, *Esoteric Astrology,* 298.
13. Ibid., 298.
14. Budge, *The Gods of the Egyptians,* vol. 2, 216-17.
15. Sais was the cult center of the ancient Egyptian goddess Net or Neith who was later identified with both Isis and Athena.
16. G.R.S. Mead, *Thrice Greatest Hermes*, vol. 1, 190.
17. The reader is referred to David Fideler's *Jesus Christ, Sun of God* for a fascinating analysis of the gematria surrounding Athena and the dimensions of the Parthenon.
18. Gaskell, *Dictionary of All Scriptures and Myths,* s.v. "Athena."
19. Gustav Schwab, *Gods & Heroes, Myths and Epics of Ancient Greece,* 85.
20. Another version of this story has Hephaistos attempting to rape Athena, but without success.
21. Blavatsky, *Theosophical Glossary,* s.v. "Argha."

22. Bailey, *The Rays and the Initiations,* 418.
23. Ibid., 418.
24. Bailey, *Esoteric Psychology,* vol. II, 217.
25. Ibid., 226.
26. Ibid., 226
27. Although the initiations are numbered the same, they exist at human, solar, and cosmic levels. The fourth initiation for the planetary Logos is actually the second cosmic initiation.
28. Bailey, *A Treatise on Cosmic Fire,* 384.
29. Ibid., 386.
30. Bailey, *Initiation, Human and Solar,* 18.
31. Bailey, *Esoteric Psychology,* vol. I, 155.
32. See chapter 6, "Sixes and Fives."
33. See *A Treatise on Cosmic Fire*. 723-24.
34. Bailey, *Esoteric Astrology,* 259.
35. Bailey, *The Rays and the Initiations,* 130.
36. All the names of the ray seven Lord come from *Esoteric Psychology,* vol. I, 85-86.
37. Bailey, *A Treatise on Cosmic Fire,* 441.
38. Ibid., 451.
39. Ibid., 452.
40. Ibid., 428.
41. Ibid., 361.
42. Ibid., 484.
43. Ibid., 445.
44. Ibid., 449-50.
45. Bailey, *Esoteric Psychology,* vol. I, 86.

11

Sirian Influences and The Great Invocation

Sirius: An Energy Conglomerate

The Great Invocation is all about humanity. The evidence presented so far suggests the Great Invocation is the word of power used by Sanat Kumara and His Shamballa Council to build certain energies into the human kingdom, so humanity can fulfill its destiny when it reaches maturity. Apparently, this cosmic project has continued from the time when Sanat Kumara first came to our planet, up to and including the present time. The Christ, the first Sirian Initiate, is the Wayshower signaling the success of this twenty million year Sirian project of which Sanat Kumara and Shamballa are the Overseers. (Although individualization took place eighteen million years ago, the process leading up to it began approximately twenty million years ago.)

The numeric evidence in the Great Invocation indicates a strong relationship between it and the energies of Sirius. These energies consist of ray and zodiacal influences, along with the qualities of the planets associated with them. In addition, Sirius transmits the energy of the second aspect of the Soul or Cosmic Christ to our solar system. This all presents a staggering array of energy relationships.

The major problem for all esoteric students studying the ray and zodiacal energies affecting our planet is the enormous complexity of the subject. Djwhal Khul gives a myriad of energy combinations at cosmic, systemic, and planetary levels. Added to all of these are relationships involving the various kingdoms of nature, time cycles, nations, groups, and individuals. The scope of possible ray/zodiacal energy combinations is truly staggering and confusing. Further complicating matters, much of the information the Tibetan has made public is only partial; He stated that the final phase of this teaching will not appear until early in the next century. The veil, so to speak, is not fully lifted.

In terms of the cosmic picture we know little about the Great Bear, the Pleiades, and Sirius; however, of these three star systems, the Tibetan refers to and offers more detailed information about Sirius. Generally speaking, this is due to the fact that our solar system is developing the second aspect of Love-Wisdom, which is inherently the Sirian aspect.

The Sirian impact on our Earth and solar system is enormous and complex. The Tibetan offers at least six different and seemingly contradictory energy alignments originating from the Sirian system. It is beyond the scope of this book to examine all these energy pathways. We will concentrate on the obvious alignments which tie into the Great Invocation from the numerological angle, leaving the alternative relationships to be worked out in future research by esoteric students.

Ray Five–The Brother from Sirius

We now know the Great Invocation has a numerological root value of 5. We also know the twenty-one key words have a root value of 5, and they are composed of ninety-five letters which in turn reduce to 5. These ninety-five letters directly correspond to "Sirius," "Hierarchy," "Masters," and "Scorpio" (each term equals 95 AN), all of which have a root value of 5, and moreover are related to one another through Sirius. The title "Christ," as Leader of the Hierarchy equals 77 (AN) and 32 (RAN) which reduces to 5. Leo (which Alice Bailey says has ninety-five stars[1]) has a root value of 5 and is also ruled by Sirius. In addition, the essential fifty-one words of the Great Invocation have a numerological value of 5. What's more, the middle word of these fifty-one is "where," which has five letters and equals 5. Added to all of this is the fact that the middle phrase of the entire Great Invocation—"God is known"—equals the root value 5, and is made up of ten letters (2 x 5).

With the predominance of the number 5, it does not seem unreasonable to contemplate the possibility that the fifth ray has something to do with the Great Invocation and Sirius. The last chapter ended with a quote by the Tibetan stating that the Lord of the seventh ray is symbolically related to rays two and five. Let's discuss ray five first. By scanning the list of names given to this fifth ray Lord, we find many descriptive names, but the most suggestive are "The Precipitator of the Cross" and "The Brother from Sirius." These two names for ray five could not be more clearly articulated in the context of the esoteric numerology of the Great Invocation. The correlation between the Great Invocation and Sirius is significant at this point in our investigation. This fact became abundantly clear in chapter 9 "The Revealing Cross of Sirius," because it is through the Sirian Cross configuration that the esoteric root of the Great Invocation is exposed. Both "The Precipitator of the Cross" (311 AN, 131 RAN) and "The Brother From Sirius" (266 AN, 113 RAN) not only equal 5, but the former name describes the method used to discover the latter in the Great Invocation. Furthermore, "The Precipitator of the Cross" (131) is the identical value of the phrase "God is known" (131 AN) located at the center of the Great Invocation. Chapter 9 makes it abundantly clear that the "God (Who) is known" at the center of the Great Invocation is the "The Precipitator of the Cross."

Keep in mind "the Light of God" (136 AN) infinity loop in the Great Invocation and its numeric equivalent to "the Will of God," and consider the following excerpt by DK:

> The fifth ray is a Being of the intensest spiritual light and in His manifestation on this fifth plane, which is peculiarly His, He symbolises the three aspects in a way achieved by no other ray. Through His quality of higher mind, this ray is a pure channel for the divine will.[2]

This extract is telling us that two expressions found within the Great Invocation, namely "the Light of God" (intensest spiritual light) and "the Will of God" (a pure channel for the divine will) are expressions of the fifth ray Lord.

Next Djwhal Khul states that,

> The fifth ray is one of unique and peculiar potency in relation to the human kingdom. The reason is that the fifth plane of mind is the sphere of His major activity and it is on this plane that we find the triple aspect of mind.[3]

The triple aspect of mind is the abstract mind, the concrete mind, and the Son of Mind or soul. In the context of the mental plane, it is important to remember that the human soul has its primary station on the mental plane. (See diagrams of the seven planes and sub-planes in appendix D.) Our mental plane is, in reality, the fifth sub-plane of the cosmic *physical* plane. The source of mind or *manas*, however, is the fifth level of the cosmic *mental* plane, and emanates from Sirius. Therefore, we as souls or Sons of Mind are micro-cosmic products of the macro-cosmic mind, the "intensest spiritual light."

The truth of this is repeated once more in the aphorisms given by the Tibetan for the fifth ray Lord. Djwhal Khul states that:

> These six aphorisms were chanted by His six Brothers at the momentous crisis wherein the human family came into existence and the solar Angels sacrificed themselves. Esoterically speaking, they "went down into hell, and found their place in prison." On that day souls were born. A new kingdom came into being, and the three higher planes and the three lower were brought into a scintillating interchange.[4]

This extract indicates two things. One, the human kingdom was created with the help of the fifth ray Lord, "The Brother from Sirius." Two, He created the human kingdom by the interchange or exchange of energy between the three higher and the three lower planes. DK, therefore, gives the names "The great Connector" and "The Divine Intermediary" to the Lord of the fifth ray. The Great Invocation reflects this connection and intermediary process through an examination of its structure. By dividing it into a beginning, a middle and an end—three parts—the esoteric secrets of its nature and origin are unveiled.

The revelation of the esoteric aspect of the Great Invocation is symbolized by the seventh ray energy of Hermes Trismegistus, the thrice greatest. Might this title have some correlation with Hermes' relationship to Sirius and ray five? Other names offered by DK for the fifth ray Lord such as "The Threefold Thinker" and "The Ruler of the Third Heaven" hint at this possibility.

More to the point, the structural symbolism of the Great Invocation is unveiled by the middle word "is" which occupies the 57th word position. Referring to the Word Position Index (appendix B), note that the middle word in position 57 is "The great Connector" between the beginning and end of the Great Invocation. More important, perhaps, in the context of the current discussion, is the fact that the word "rose" equals 57 (AN), which is a component in another name for the fifth ray Lord, "The Rose of God."

The Law of Sacrifice and Ray Four

This is suggestive information because the substitution of the word "rose" for "is" at the center of the Sirian Cross is reminiscent of the Rosy cross and the Rosicrucians of seventeenth century Europe. This configuration is the symbol of the Law of Sacrifice. (See discussion in chapter 9, "The Letter 'S.' ") The esoteric name for this law is "The Law of those who choose to die"[5] (321 AN, 132 RAN). Remember the sacrifice of the solar Angels at the time of individualization—"they 'went down into hell, and found their place in prison.' " The Tibetan is describing those who choose to die.

Figure 33. The Rosy Cross of Sirius.

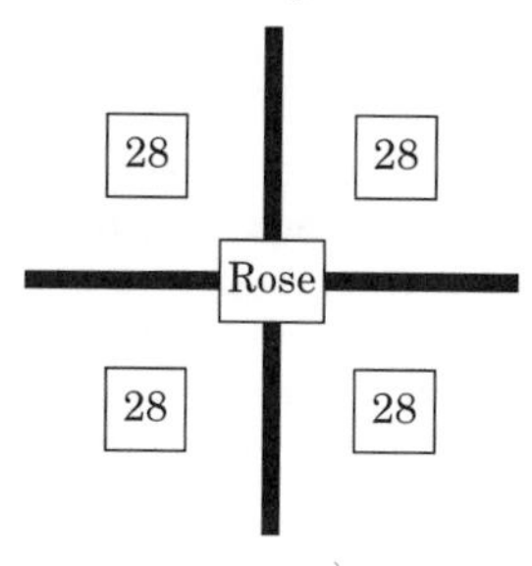

Some thoughts worth reflecting upon involve the symbol described by DK as: "A rosy Cross with a golden bird." Table 48 offers some very interesting esoteric relationships. Note that ray four emerges in the numerology of "golden bird" and "the Moon"

(both 90 AN) because the moon is associated with ray four. The Moon, however, is a dead world with no radiating energy of its own. The presence of the Moon in this table is of true occult significance, because according to the esoteric astrology taught by Djwhal Khul, it veils the three planets Vulcan, Uranus, and Neptune.

Table 48. The Rosy Cross and Golden Bird.

Symbol	AN	Equivalent	Associations
A Golden Bird	91	The Star	Sirius, Second Aspect
A Rosy Cross	152	Tawny Lions	Individualization, Leo, Ray Five
Rosy Cross	151	The Great Work	Alchemy, Hermes, Ray Seven
Golden Bird	90	"Sothis" and "The Moon"	Sirius and Ray Four

Sothis and the Moon both equal 90 (AN). Sothis is also the Egyptian name for Sirius. Therefore, what is the factor that relates Sirius to the Moon? In this case, it is Neptune because its AN value equals 95, the same as Sirius. Neptune is the vehicle in our solar system for the Christ consciousness and Sirius is the Cosmic Christ. Thus, the Moon is veiling Neptune, and Neptune in turn is veiling Sirius. Djwhal Khul gives some further clues to this veiled link in the following passage:

> In this world period and in a peculiar manner, as far as the race (Aryan) to which the Western world belongs, Neptune is known esoterically as the Initiator. In certain ancient formulas, the great Teacher of the West and the present world Initiator, Christ, is spoken of as Neptune, Who rules the ocean, whose trident and astrological symbol signifies the Trinity in manifestation and Who is the ruler of the Piscean Age.[6]

The veiling function of the Moon is present at the center of the Great Invocation through "is" and "s." "Is," valued at 28, represents the complete moon phase cycle. "S," valued at 19, symbolizes the Metonic cycle in which every nineteen years the phases of the moon occur on the exact same day of the week for the entire year.

Now we can complete what was only partially revealed in table 29 (see chapter 7, the section "The Tarot and Ancient Egypt"), which is now expanded as table 49.

Table 49. The One Initiator.

Esoteric Terms	AN	Equivalents	Meaning	AN	RAN
The Sun Sirius	182	The One Initiator	Sanat Kumara	120	30
Isis Veiled	113	The Race of Men	Fourth Kingdom	161	71
Isis Unveiled	148	The Initiator	The Christ	110	47
Total	443	443		391	148

The Sirian process of initiation is being implemented in our solar system on Earth. This can be traced through the Egyptian association of Isis with Sirius, and further by the association of Isis with the ancient Mysteries of Initiation. As you can see in table 49, the planetary equivalent to "the sun Sirius" is "the One Initiator," Sanat Kumara, Who is the Sirian Agent of initiation on Earth. The next term is "Isis veiled," which equals "the race of men." This means that the race of men created by Sanat Kumara, along with help from Sirius, remains hidden until its true work as planetary savior emerges into the light of day. The Moon is the veiling agent in this example because it represents the material forces which block the way to Christ consciousness or initiation into a new life. The beginning of this process is clearly indicated by the Christ Who is "the Initiator" or "Isis Unveiled" (148). The Christ is the first success story of the human kingdom; therefore He is now "the Initiator" or the Wayshower and Forerunner of the human kingdom as the group planetary savior. The synthesis of this fascinating numeric demonstration is indicated by the total value of the terms which equal the total letters of the Great Invocation—443. Notice also the RAN value of Sanat Kumara, the Fourth Kingdom, and the Christ combine to equal 148 or "Isis Unveiled." The numbers 15, 16, 17, 18, 19, 20, 21, and 22 combine to equal 148, and remarkably, the words in the Great Invocation which correspond to these eight number positions are "into the minds of men Let Light descend." These eight words are positioned so that they describe the calling down of Light by the Initiator during the initiatory process. The terms in table 49 clearly indicate this: the *Initiators* expand the consciousness of *the race of Men* by revealing an entirely new dimension of existence into which the liberated human may enter.

We have taken a short (although important) excursion; now let's return to the Law of Sacrifice. Ray four is the energy distributed through the Law of Sacrifice and is, therefore, closely tied to the fourth Creative Hierarchy of human monads. Djwhal Khul states that the aphorisms pronounced by the other six ray Lords occurred "late in the creative period and at the time when the fourth Creative Hierarchy came into incarnation."[7] This statement by DK indicates once again the bond between the solar Angels associated with the number 4 and the manasic principle associated with the number 5, because the fourth Creative Hierarchy incarnated as the fourth kingdom in nature via the fifth plane of mind in order to develop the fifth principle of manas. The Agent for this stupendous effort was Sanat Kumara, the Great Sacrifice. None of this could have happened without the "blessing" of the Lord of Sirius, the source of manas.

The Law of Those Who Choose to Die

The esoteric name for the Law of Sacrifice is the Law of those who choose to die. Sanat Kumara epitomizes this esoteric phrase in terms of His entry onto the cross of substance during this fourth round of our fourth planetary scheme, chain, and globe. The phrase "the Law of those who choose to die" equals 321 (AN) and 132 (RAN). The value 132 is equivalent to the phrase "the Heart of God," found in the second stanza of the Great Invocation. This stanza is related to love and the sacrifice of the world savior, Christ, as it calls for His return to Earth.

The AN value 321 is significant in terms of its deep esoteric meaning and connection to the Great Invocation and Sirius. As table 50 shows, a significant group of terms related to our theme all possess the same values, 321 and 114.

From the standpoint of the Great Invocation, Sirius, Leo, Jupiter, and Hierarchy are the most obscure and abstract of all the entries in table 50. They form an energy alignment which, according to the Tibetan, has a powerful effect on our solar system, and has a special relation to humanity. Other than these few remarks which appear in the book *Esoteric Astrology* on pages 416-17 DK offers little more. I have included them here because of the presence of Sirius in the group, as well as the obvious numerological correspondence with the other items in table 50.

Table 50. The Esoteric Law of Sacrifice.

Description	AN	RAN
The Law of Those Who Choose To Die	321	132
Pallas Athena Parthenos, Sirius	321	114
Osiris, Isis, Horus, Sirius	321	114
Cosmic Christ the Sun Sirius	321	114
Sirius, Leo, Jupiter, Hierarchy	321	141

In general, they deal with the energies of rays two, five, and one. Sirius, as you may recall governs Leo, which was discussed at length in chapter 9 in relation to the first Creative Hierarchy. Jupiter is a ray two planet which we will discuss later in this chapter; and of course, the Hierarchy is a ray two or second aspect center on our planet. The common theme running through each of these items is the Cosmic Christ energy of Love, the Law of Sacrifice, the coming of Sanat Kumara as the first planetary Avatar, and the process of individualization via Leo and the "tawny lions."

In the last chapter we showed how Athena and the Egyptian trinity corresponded numerically (226 AN) to the letters in the fifty-one word version of the Great Invocation. We also indicated the correspondence to "the Plan of Love and Light," which also equals 226 (AN). When Sirius is combined with Athena and the Egyptian trinity, they reflect the value of "the Law of those who choose to die."

In the case of Pallas Athena Parthenos, the Greek goddess represents the feminine counterpart of Hermes and the link with the number 7. She is intimately woven into the fabric of the Great Invocation, as we saw in chapter 10.

Osiris, Isis, and Horus are also deeply connected to the Great Invocation through the Sirian Cross motif explored in chapter 9. We will have more to say about this important Egyptian trinity in the next chapter.

When we attempt to fathom the "Cosmic Christ the Sun Sirius," we enter into "the Heart of God" 132 (RAN) and deal directly with "the Law of those who choose to die," also 132 (RAN). This esoteric term, "Cosmic Christ the Sun Sirius" encompasses the entire subject of "the Law of those who choose to die." In fact, we find that when 321 is divided by 3 it equals 107. The number 107 is the AN value of the "green emerald" at the center of the orange cross symbol of the Path to Sirius.

The Tibetan explains the deep profundity of the highest level of sacrifice of which all others, from the solar Logos to the planetary Logos, and from the world saviors to the solar Angels, are mere reflections:

> Those who thus sacrifice are: *The solar Deity who gave His life to the universe*, to the solar system, to the planet, and the manifested worlds consequently appeared. The cosmic Deity has likewise done the same. But what does this mean to us? Naught, except a symbol...The Cosmic Christ was crucified upon the cross of matter, and by that great sacrifice opportunity was offered to all evolving lives in all kingdoms of nature and in all created worlds. Thus they could progress. The work, in space and time, and the stupendous march of living beings towards an at present unrealised goal, began. We can give no reason for the choice made by Deity thus to act. We do not know His ultimate purpose or plan; and only aspects of His technique and method begin to appear to the illuminated mind.[8]

The Cosmic Christ

If Sirius represents the second aspect of the One About Whom Naught May Be Said, then as mentioned in chapter 9, Sirius may possibly represent the Cosmic Christ. There is some evidence of this in the Tibetan's description of ray two: "The Word is issuing from the heart of God, emerging from a central point of love. That Word is love itself."[9] Djwhal Khul then gives various names for the Lord of the second ray, the last of which is "The Cosmic Christ."

This term, "the Cosmic Christ" equals 172 (AN), which does not at first glance appear to be a significant number compared to the other numbers in our investigation. In reality, however, this number dramatically illustrates the crucifixion of the Cosmic Christ at cosmic and planetary levels of existence. In fact, that crucifixion occurs at the exact midpoint of the 343 rounds which comprise our Earth Scheme—the 172nd round. This translates to the fourth round of the fourth Earth Chain. Symbolically, therefore, our current round—this very time we are living—represents the middle of the cosmic cross upon which the Cosmic Christ is transfixed. This is at least one reason why the current life expression of Sanat Kumara is so important at this time; He is mirroring, in a planetary sense, the same conditions existing in the cosmic sense—that of the Cosmic Christ crucified on the cross of matter. This is illustrated in the diagram of Sanat Kumara "mounting" the cross in the fourth round of the fourth chain at the exact middle of the fourth Earth Scheme. (See figure 25 in chapter 9.) Perhaps even more descriptive of this central theme is figure 28 in chapter 9. This diagram depicts the Great Work of planetary redemption using the words derived from the middle letter "s" of the Great Invocation. The sum of all these words equals 172, which refers to the middle round of the Earth Scheme, but we now see that the number also symbolizes the Great Work of "the Cosmic Christ" (172). Thus, the Great Work of redemption is *central to the Will* of the Cosmic Christ. Referring back to table 44A in chapter 9, note the AN total of all the words in the Great Invocation derived from the *central* letter "s" equal 252—"central spiritual Sun." The Great Invocation thus literally demonstrates the central primacy of the Cosmic Christ and the central spiritual Sun in relation to the Great Work of planetary redemption on Earth at this time.

Now we come to the most profound aspect of this number 172 in terms of the human kingdom, Sanat Kumara, and the Great Invocation. We illustrated in chapter 9 that the 113 words of the Great Invocation symbolize the 113 stages of Sanat Kumara's descent to physical incarnation in the Lemurian root-race. As explained earlier, the Lemurian root-race was the 171st life impulse of the planetary Logos during the fourth Earth Chain and marked His entry into physical incarnation in preparation for His fourth cosmic initiation, the Crucifixion.

At the same time, and as a result of this sacrificial incarnation, the human kingdom was created. Symbolically, at least (and perhaps literally, in a way we cannot comprehend), the 113 energy impulses representing the words of the Great Invocation were completed. This meant that during the very next life impulse or root-race, the Great Invocation could be sounded by Sanat Kumara and the other 104 Kumaras in Shamballa. The time of this first sounding of the Great Invocation may very well have been during the Atlantean root-race, which was the 114th root-race since the arrival of Sanat Kumara from the Venus chain. Just as important, however, is the fact that the Atlantean root-race was the *172nd root-race*, or life impulse of the entire Earth Chain. (See figure 26 in chapter 9.) The incarnation of the planetary Logos of the Earth took 113 life impulses to complete, and the Personality we call Sanat Kumara finally took form in the 171st life impulse of the Earth Chain. Not only was the Atlantean root-race the 172nd life impulse of the Earth Chain, but it was also the midpoint of the 172nd round of the greater cycle of the Earth Scheme. This 172nd round of the scheme and 172nd root-race of the chain marked the exact midpoint and lowest descent of spirit into matter. In the larger picture of the total Earth Scheme of 343 rounds, the planetary Logos took incarnation as Sanat Kumara and began the work of "the Cosmic Christ" (172) on Earth in the 172nd Atlantean root-race, during the 172nd round.

The possibility that the first "sounding" of the Great Invocation by Sanat Kumara and His Disciples coincided with the Atlantean root-race is of tremendous significance because during that time the door of initiation was first opened to humanity.[10] This possibility bolsters the theory that the Great Invocation is a Sirian word of power entrusted to Sanat Kumara for the purposes of assisting the Sirian process of initiation on Earth. The esoteric fact that this coincides with the numeric midpoint of 172 equating it with "the Cosmic Christ" represents a perfect meshing of number, symbolism, and esoteric planetary history.

The fact that during the 114th Atlantean root-race the door of initiation was opened for humanity makes the number 114 significant in relation to initiation. Note in table 50 the "Cosmic Christ the Sun Sirius" equals 114 (RAN). This is a direct numerical correspondence to the time of the opening of the door of initiation in the 114th Atlantean period. This phrase numerologically connects the Cosmic Christ and the sun Sirius to the inauguration of the initiatory process on Earth during the time of Atlantis. Table 51 is a list of terms related in some way to Sirius. Each of the values of 82 are RAN values. When the RAN value for Sirius (32) is added to any of the items in table 51 they equal 114.

The items in table 51 are all related to Sirius and to the Great Invocation. There are several layers of meaning involved with these various elements. First, the Tibetan calls Sirius the star of initiation. Initiation produces adepts using energy. The Egyptian trinity (Osiris, Isis, and Horus), Athena, and the three Egyptian goddesses symbolize adepts using energy. Yet, they represent more than this because they were also Sons of God Who worked under the Law of Sacrifice to lead humanity into greater spiritual Light.

Table 51. Sirius and Related Terms.

Description	RAN
Osiris Isis Horus	82
Pallas Athena Parthenos	82
Star of Initiation	82
The Throne of Isis	82
The Law of Sacrifice	82
Adept Using Energy	82
Isis-Sothis Anukis Satis	82
Father Mother God	82

Whether these gods and goddesses really existed in the actual forms we have inherited from the past is unimportant. The fact remains, the ageless wisdom recognizes that advanced Beings once walked openly amongst the human beings of ancient times. These Initiates were adept at using energy and they taught humanity much about the nature of life and death, the world and the universe. The Throne of Isis symbolizes the "Seat" of the Mysteries on Earth, but it should be pointed out that the ultimate and originating source of the Mysteries was, and still is, Sirius—the star of initiation. Thus, the Initiate-Priests Who administered the secrets of Initiation to their human students were actually the terrestrial Agents of the Sirian Mysteries.

Osiris, Isis, and Horus may predate Egypt and be of Atlantean origin. They symbolize the universal trinity. As Father Mother God, Osiris and Isis bring forth the Son, Horus, the divine manifestation of God living through the Form of the Mother and containing the Life of the Father.

Second, all the elements of this story, excluding Sirius, equal 82, thus demonstrating a numerical, as well as, conceptual consistency describing the coming of higher Beings to Earth in order to stimulate our planet's evolution as part of a greater Plan. The missing element of Sirius, when added to any one of the other elements yields the number 114. When this is done, every item in table 51 is numerically related to the Great Invocation via Sirius (82 + 32 = 114) because the final two words in positions three and eight of the Great Invocation equal 114. (Remember that 3 and 8 are the root values of the Sirian Cross. See figure 20 and table 37 in chapter 9.) Therefore, when these elements are related to Sirius, the Great Invocation is automatically included in the story.

And finally, when the elements are combined with Sirius, not only is the Great Invocation involved via the number 114, but the time period of Atlantis as the 114th root-race is added to the overall story. The entire scenario describes the instituting of initiation by Sirius on Earth through various Initiate "gods and goddesses." These Sons of God used energies beyond the comprehension of early humanity and established the Mystery schools. The Law of Sacrifice was one of the fundamental laws governing the coming of Sanat Kumara and all the other Sons of God to our planet. Somehow the Great Invocation is interlocked with this Sirian initiative which now spans twenty million years.

The other aspect of this fascinating esoteric relationship involves the AN values of "Osiris, Isis, and Horus" and "Pallas Athena Parthenos." Recall that these two sets of terms have a value of 226 (AN), which equal "the Plan of Love and Light," and at the same time correspond to the number of letters in the fifty-one word version of the Great Invocation.

We have already related these terms to Sirius as the star of initiation and to the 114th Atlantean root-race. This was the period in planetary history when the door of initiation was first opened to the human kingdom. This represented the first real achievement of the Sirian Plan of Love and Light. The remarkable numerological aspect of all this is that "the door of initiation" equals 226! Thus, the letters constituting the essential words needed to construct the Great Invocation represent "the door of initiation."

When we realize the door of initiation is of Sirian origin and under Sirian supervision throughout our solar system, we find ourselves face to face with the ultimate recognition that the primary cosmic impulse of our solar system and planetary life on Earth at this time is the "Cosmic Christ the sun Sirius" (321). Then we truly realize the path of initiation is "the Law of those who choose to die" (321)—we truly know that our future liberation is through the lighted threshold of "Sirius, the door of initiation" (321). This phrase can now be added to table 50.

Summary of Ray Influences

Purely from the standpoint of the energies related to our study of the Great Invocation and its relation to Sirius, rays two, seven, five, and four are influential. Ray two governs the overarching framework within which the Sirian process of initiation functions on our planet. The Great Invocation plays a central role in this Plan because it is the primary instrument for invoking the Christ into physical presence on Earth. The Christ is the first human being to manifest the Love-Wisdom energy of the Sirian system, and therefore, was the first human being to use the Great Invocation to carry the Sirian process of evolution to the next stage. As pointed out earlier, this Plan, when carried to completion, will make the Earth a power station of Light and Love in this and surrounding solar systems.

The Great Invocation is a word of power and a sound formula, therefore, relating it to ray seven. This involves the esoteric use of sound and various words of power. At this point in the Earth's evolution, the most potent word of power which humanity is permitted to use is the Great Invocation. According to Djwhal Khul, the proper use of this mantram will produce transformative effects in the lives of individuals and humanity in general.

The Great Invocation must be used with mental focus in order to be effective. Therefore, ray five and the mind are of prime importance to the successful use of the Great Invocation. Current humanity is the fifth root-race and, therefore, a mentally polarized quality of consciousness is under development at this time. The Christ and the Masters invoked by the Great Invocation belong to the fifth kingdom, which is the goal of human evolution. Thus, ray five is very much involved in the Plan at this time. A symbolic point regarding rays 5 and 7 is that the middle word of the Great Invocation occupies the 57th position. From a ray energy perspective, the midpoint highlights the interchange of these two rays in which ray 7 is the 5th manasic ray.

Last but not least is ray four, which governs the fourth human kingdom and fourth Creative Hierarchy. The energy of ray four is subtly present in the Great Invocation via the Egyptian theme since, according to the Tibetan, the Egyptian religion developed under fourth ray influence. We are also told the fourth ray will emerge in the first half of the next century and lead humanity to a renaissance of the arts. Additionally, ray four in the cosmic sense is the buddhic plane of cosmic love-wisdom, the originating source of the Cosmic Christ. According to Djwhal Khul, the Great Invocation is essentially Christ's own mantram. It is, therefore, the word of power for the Son of the Son, the planetary Christ Who is the terrestrial counterpart of the Cosmic Christ crucified on the fixed cross of heavenly matter—primal star substance. The following table summarizes the major energies involved in this complex interchange, reaching from cosmic levels of being to the physical planes of human life. Although three signs are associated with each of the seven rays, table 52 indicates only the sign which is the most active in relation to the particular ray shown. The planets in table 52 are related to the rays, and not to the rulerships of the signs.

Table 52. Ray Energies and Sirius.

Ray	Planet	Associations	Sign	Ray Lord
Two	Jupiter	Isis/Athena (Virgin)	Virgo	The Cosmic Christ
Four	Mercury	Thoth	Scorpio	The Hidden One
Five	Venus	The Lion	Leo	The Brother From Sirius
Seven	Uranus	Hermes Trismegistus	Capricorn	The Unveiled Magician

A review of the ray energies relating Sirius and the Great Invocation indicates two streams of influence. They follow the line of buddhi-manas polarized on the second aspect. Ray four is buddhi and ray five is manas. It is the will of the Lord of Sirius that the Cosmic Christ energy of Love-Wisdom be anchored in our solar system (one of the fourth order[11]), on the fourth Earth Scheme, chain, globe, and round via the fourth human kingdom, equipped with the fifth principle of mind and aided by the fifth kingdom of Hierarchy.

This Plan is being implemented by the seventh ray, which relates spirit to matter and which "governs the processes of Transmutation, Incarnation and Transference." The Great Invocation is a major seventh ray tool in the implementation of this Plan.

The numeric energy arrangement brought about by these ray alignments is 2—4—7 and 2—5—7. The AN value of 247 equals "Hermes Trismegistus" and the AN value of 257 equals "restore the Plan on Earth," the final five words of the Great Invocation. Could Hermes Trismegistus be "the Brother from Sirius" who rules over the sacred science of esoteric philosophy and magic?

Jupiter and Uranus

The ray energies prominent in the Great Invocation—2, 4, 5, and 7—are represented in our solar system by the planets Jupiter, Mercury, Venus, and Uranus. In order to describe the ray influences of Sirius, the planets related to those rays need to be discussed.

Our Earth is part of a fourth order, buddhic, love-wisdom oriented solar system governed by the second aspect parent system of Sirius. As the Tibetan says, "God is Love." The second ray planet Jupiter is of broad importance in relation to the Great Invocation because Jupiter functions as the unifier of mind and heart. Djwhal Khul offers the following remarks about the role of Jupiter in our solar system:

> In connection with a lesser duality found in every human being, that of head and heart, of mind and love, and of will and wisdom, the work of Jupiter is to develop these two qualities and bring them into synthetic interplay. Eventually there has to be the complete fusion of love and mind before a world saviour can manifest and function efficiently.[12]

In the overall context of the Great Invocation, the second ray Jupiter influence is obvious since the mantram calls for the "Plan of Love and Light to work out," and for the Christ, the world savior, to "return to Earth." These are the very factors mentioned by DK in the above extract. In addition, stanzas one and two concern mind and heart respectively, and they each have an identical number of lines, sentences, words, and letters (see table 4), thus reflecting the second ray influence of Jupiter.

The seventh ray planet Uranus is also of special importance to our subject, because it produces real change at the physical level of human existence. This is plain enough when we read the final words of the Great Invocation: "restore the Plan *on Earth*." The information about ray seven in the last chapter applies to Uranus because it is the concentrated energy of the seventh ray in our solar system. Describing Uranus, Djwhal Khul offers these thoughts:

> Uranus...is today the transmitter of Sirian force via Pisces to the Hierarchy.[13]
>
> Uranus [confers, JB] Occult consciousness or that intelligent, fusing condition which produces the scientific at-one-ment of the two factors, higher and lower self, through the intelligent use of the mind.[14]
>
> *Uranus* is the planet whose characteristics are the scientific mind, which, at this stage of the disciple's career, means that he can begin to live the occult life and the way of divine knowledge can take the place of the mystic way of feeling...Uranus, therefore, initiates a new order of life and conditions and this—when developed in the life of the disciple—in its turn produces an understanding of the causes of things as they are, and the desire to change the old order and the old orientation into the new. This produces the reversal of the wheel. This can be seen happening today most clearly in connection with humanity and with world processes...Uranus is exalted in this sign [Scorpio, JB].[15]

These three extracts tie Uranus to Sirius and Scorpio, while at the same time they describe how the energy of Uranus confers the scientific or objective use of the mind on students moving from the mystical stage of spirituality to the psychospiritual approach. The Great Invocation is a seventh ray sound formula. Therefore, it is most effective in its results when used with a scientific mind and an occult consciousness. Then the power of the Great Invocation can be set free to "restore the Plan on Earth."

In chapter 9, the importance of the fourth and fifth Creative Hierarchies was discussed. This numerical correspondence has an affinity to rays four and five. These two ray energies govern the human kingdom. (The two ray lines illustrated in the last section reduce to 4 and 5 respectively. Rays 2—4—7 reduce to 13/4 and rays 2—5—7 reduce to 14/5.) Ray four governs the soul of humanity, while ray five rules the personality. One interpretation suggested by this ray alignment is that the human kingdom is to become the bridge that links the higher and lower kingdoms. This is the function of ray four as it seeks to resolve the conflict between such dualities as good and evil, spirit and matter, and peace and war, to name a few. The instrument our current fourth kingdom is using to help fulfill its soul purpose is the fifth principle of mind, which as we know, comes under ray five.

Mercury and Venus

In terms of the planets in our solar system which express the seven different ray energies, Mercury embodies ray four and Venus embodies ray five. Mercury and Venus are the two most advanced planets in our solar system according to the Tibetan. The Moon is also a fourth ray planet, but it is not a sacred planet. Because we are working with the energies of Sirius, Mercury is the more appropriate focal point for ray four because Mercury is one of the sacred planets. More importantly, Mercury is the hierarchical ruler of Scorpio which, as already discussed, is governed by Sirius.

Ray five comes through the planet Venus. You may recall that Venus was the first planet to undergo the Sirian process of initiation in our solar system. In fact, this brings up some more symbolism regarding the numbers 5 and 7. Djwhal Khul states that the experiment of initiation was so successful on Venus that it completed its evolution in five rounds rather than seven. Once again we see the numbers 5 and 7 emerge in the context of Sirius and initiation. And again, the 57th or middle position of the Great Invocation signals the fundamental centrality of initiation as the prime method of evolutionary advance on our planet.

Mercury and Venus (especially Venus) play an important part in our planet's evolution because they both share a common bond with the sign Gemini. Mercury is the exoteric ruler of Gemini;

Venus is the esoteric ruler, and Earth is the hierarchical ruler. These three types of rulership can be thought of as three levels of energy distribution. The energy is distributed into human consciousness according to soul development or the ability to receive, integrate, and utilize the particular energy. The exoteric ruler delivers energy at the beginners level, the esoteric ruler at the intermediate level, and the hierarchical at the advanced level. The particular sign which a planet represents or rules determines the kind of zodiacal energy it transmits. This is an oversimplification of a very complex topic, but the important point for our discussion is that the Earth, Venus, and Mercury share a common energy connection with the sign of Gemini.

In the book *Esoteric Astrology*, the Tibetan states that "Gemini—forms a point of entrance for cosmic energy from Sirius."[16] The second ray of Love-Wisdom pours through Gemini and into our solar system via Sirius.[17] These two esoteric facts alone reiterate the vast importance of Sirius to our solar system. Djwhal Khul goes on to say:

> Gemini is preeminently the sign of the messenger, and this sign produces many of the messengers of God as they appear down the ages, the revealers of new divine truths and the intermediaries between the fourth and fifth kingdoms.
>
> It is for this reason that you have the exoteric ruler given as Mercury and the esoteric ruler as Venus for they embody between them the energies of the fourth Ray of Harmony through Conflict and the fifth Ray of Concrete Knowledge or Science.[18]

The Tibetan continues:

> Again you find the note of duality in the relationship (established by the activity of these two rulers) between the third kingdom of nature, the animal kingdom and the kingdom of God or of souls, the fifth kingdom in nature, thus producing the fourth or human kingdom...It was the activity of Venus—under the influence of Gemini—which produced the great crisis of the individualisation when the two kingdoms "approached" each other. Venus, Mercury and the Earth then set up a magnetic field which made the intervention of the Great Lodge on Sirius and the dual stimulation of Gemini effective in producing significant results of which the fourth kingdom in nature is the expression.[19]

Now we get a tiny glimpse of the esoteric importance of Mercury and Venus in relation to Earth, Sirius, and the creation of humanity. We already know Sanat Kumara made the Great Sacrifice which resulted in the creation of the human family, but this extract clearly adds the all-important esoteric fact that it was the *intervention* of the Great Lodge on Sirius which set the entire process in motion.

The numbers 4 and 5 are now supported by the number 3, because the animal or third kingdom became the vehicle for the souls of the fifth kingdom in nature. Humanity is thus a dual kingdom, being the product of two others. Symbolically, humanity is the offspring of two other "parent" kingdoms of nature. That is why we humans are the fourth ray bridge between the higher and lower kingdoms of Earth. We as a kingdom are the Mercurial Messenger to the animal, vegetable, and mineral kingdoms of nature. At the same time we incorporate and develop the fifth ray principle of manas, thus linking us to the fifth kingdom of Hierarchy. We are higher abstract spiritual mind, individualized mind, and lower concrete mind embedded in physical flesh and blood donated by the third kingdom in nature.

The duality which DK mentions is depicted by the glyph for Gemini which represents the two pillars of Boaz and Jachin.[20] These are found on each side of The High Priestess on Tarot card II. Since The High Priestess, as we now know, is really Isis veiled or Sirius, the duality of the two pillars indicates that Sirius distributes Love and Wisdom through the dualism of Gemini. Mercury and Venus distribute rays four and five to the fourth ray soul and the fifth ray personality of the human kingdom.

One curious numerological feature of the planets Mercury and Venus involves magic squares which were discussed in the section "The Christ, the Six, and the Five" in chapter 6. The subject of magic squares has little to do with the esoteric subjects of the ageless wisdom presented by DK, but the magic squares of these two planets relate to the Great Invocation. The magic square of Venus consists of a 7 x 7 grid of 49 cells, and the square of Mercury is composed of an 8 x 8 grid of 64 cells. When the magic squares of these two planets are combined their total cells equal 113—the number of words in the Great Invocation. None of the other planetary magic squares combine to equal this total. In light of the importance ascribed to Mercury and Venus in the creation of the human kingdom, this is a correlation with symbolic meaning.

The Three Ray Aspects of the Sirian System

Referring back to table 51 notice the last term—"Father Mother God." This is the only term in table 51 not discussed to this point. This phrase helps clarify the recurring theme of Osiris, Isis, and Horus. We have said much about Isis but little to this point about Osiris and Horus. As you know, Isis and Athena each play a role in the Great Invocation. The role of Isis relates more to the mysteries of initiation associated with Sirius and the establishment of those Mysteries on Earth.

The goddess Athena, on the other hand, is very much involved in the structure of the Great Invocation. This involvement is based on the number 7. Athena, therefore, is associated with ray seven, the energy of structure, order, and form. In line with the grounding energy of ray seven, Athena plays a more open role for the masses as the wise and loving defender of hearth and home.

These two goddesses appear more prominent, perhaps because they personify the inherent natural intelligence of the third aspect of the trinity. The third aspect, or ray of Active Intelligence, was brought to perfection in the first solar system, as mentioned earlier. The goddesses represent the third cosmic intelligence aspect associated with the Pleiades. Isis and Athena, however, are the Pleiadian aspect contained within the Sirian system. Every triplicity contains aspects of the other two.

The time of the Mother aspect has passed. This occurred in the first solar system. Now is the time of the Son. We are currently living in the second solar system and to paraphrase DK, Vishnu, the Son is in manifestation. Therefore, the Mother is also present to bear and nurture the Son. As the Egyptian story goes, Isis keeps Horus from danger until he is mature and ready to fulfill his life task of redemption. Let's look a little closer at the dynamic relationship between these three aspects.

Sirius is the "Father" aspect (ray one) in terms of the Sirian governance of our solar system in general, and the Law of Karma in particular. Sirius certainly represents the Mother aspect in all we have discussed about the goddesses Isis and Athena. We are under the guidance and protection of Sirius through the Shamballa center. The role of the Father-Mother polarity is authoritative, both Law giving and nurturing to all the kingdoms of nature on our planet.

As the Custodian of the will of the Lord of Sirius, Sanat Kumara is the agent of the Father aspect of the trinity. Osiris symbolizes Sanat Kumara. From the human perspective, Sanat Kumara is the Osirian Father, the first aspect of the trinity. In reality, Sanat Kumara is actually the incarnated personality form of the planetary Logos of Earth. The entry of the planetary Logos into the substance of the fourth chain of globes is the coming together of Spirit, first aspect with Substance, third aspect. The former is Osiris and the latter is Isis. Prior to manifestation they are ONE as Osiris-Isis but *appear* separately in the form worlds after manifestation. Therefore, Isis is the feminine substance aspect of the planetary Logos. Without Mother/Substance, the incarnation of the planetary Logos cannot be achieved. Without Father/Energy, Substance is barren.

The entire manifested universe reflects this fundamental principle of polar union. The result of this union is everything existing in the current manifested universe. Christ, Vishnu, and Horus are products of the interaction between Father/Mother God no matter what the trinity is called. Christianity calls them Father, Son, Holy Spirit; Hinduism calls them Shiva, Vishnu, Brahma, and the Egyptian religion calls them Osiris, Isis, Horus.[21]

All three aspects are present simultaneously, but they are not all equal in strength. Only one out of three aspects is predominant at a given time. This is the most important concept we need to understand. Using the human analogy, a woman can be a mother and a father to a child, and yet still be the child of her parents. The same of course holds true for a man. He can be both father and mother to a child, but this does not negate the fact that he is the child of his parents. We are all father, mother, and son/daughter. Everything has the potential to manifest the three primary aspects of the original divine Triad, which is essentially ONE.

In terms of the primary cosmic triad that governs our solar system, the Great Bear, the Pleiades, and Sirius represent the first, third, and second aspects. Theoretically, each of these three mysterious cosmic centers possesses counterparts of the other two aspects. In other words, each of these three celestial systems can be thought of as a triangle of cosmic energy. The Great Bear is a triangle of the first aspect with the second and third aspects less dominant; the Pleiades is a third aspect center with the first and second aspects less dominant; and Sirius is a second aspect triangle with the first and third aspects less dominant.

Therefore, just as sons and daughters are ideally subordinate to their own parents, but superior to their own offspring, Sirius can be thought of as subordinate to its parents (Great Bear and the Pleiades), but superior to its own offspring, which is our solar system. Therefore, Sirius is our Father-Mother God, but is still a second aspect center of cosmic influence relative to the Great Bear and the Pleiades. Furthermore, to complete this analogy, even though a daughter or son is subordinate to its parents, the child is a product of those parents and contains their genetic and social imprint. However, these traits are subordinate to the will and desire of the child. Even though the influences of the parents are present within a child, the universal law of free will holds sway, and the individual subordinates those parental influences to their own life purposes.

Figure 34. Three Aspects of the Sirian System.

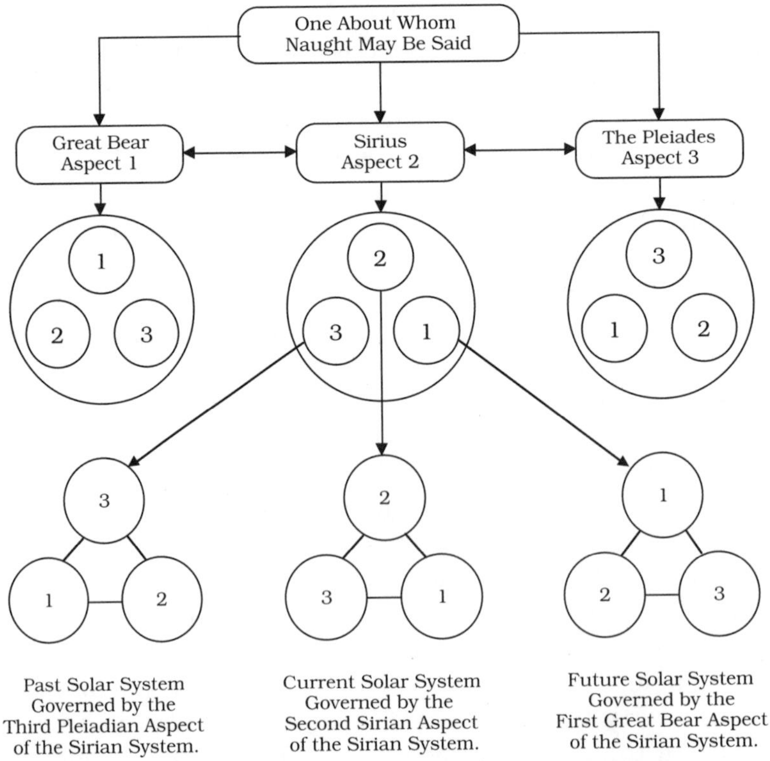

One About Whom Naught May Be Said

Great Bear Aspect 1

Sirius Aspect 2

The Pleiades Aspect 3

Past Solar System Governed by the Third Pleiadian Aspect of the Sirian System.

Current Solar System Governed by the Second Sirian Aspect of the Sirian System.

Future Solar System Governed by the First Great Bear Aspect of the Sirian System.

It is possible the first solar system, governed by the Pleiadian aspect, was directly connected with ours rather than coming through the Sirian system. The same holds true for the future solar system which will be governed by the first aspect of the Great Bear.

Having said all that we will turn to Djwhal Khul's words on this matter:

> There is, in truth a multiplicity of triangles. For the triangle is the basic geometric form of all manifestation and it is to be seen (by those who have eyes to see) underlying the entire fabric of manifestation, whether it is the manifestation of a solar system, the manifestation of the zodiacal round, the cosmic triplicities or the tiny reflection of this divine triple whole which we call man. When the human being is manifest but is not yet truly manifested, the triangles which symbolize this manifestation are the two eyes and the third eye:
> 1. The right eye—the eye of buddhi, of wisdom and of vision.
> 2. The left eye—the eye of mind, of the commonsense and of sight.
> 3. The eye of Shiva—the all-seeing eye, the eye which directs the will and purposes of Deity.
>
> These three are, in reality,
>
> 1. The eye of the Father—carrying light from the Great Bear.
> 2. The eye of the Son—carrying light from Sirius.
> 3. The eye of the Mother—carrying light from the Pleiades.[22]

DK's remarks make it clear that Sirius is indeed the middle aspect, the Son. The middle or second aspect, as we know, is that of Love-Wisdom. It is the energy of the second ray, the Cosmic Christ. This is also the energy of buddhi and wisdom, therefore, it corresponds with the right eye. The paradox is that Sirius is also the source of manas or mind, and so one would think it also corresponds to the left eye of mind. The answer to these paradoxical esoteric problems may be that Sirius is a second aspect center transmitting all three types of energy. Although Sirius contains both third aspect (the mother) and first aspect (the father) characteristics, the second aspect is primary and the first and third aspects are secondary. Sirius is Osiris, Isis, and Horus, but its primary expression at this time is that of Horus, the Son, the Cosmic Christ, the second ray of Love-Wisdom relative to our system and planet.

Notes

1. AAB wrote this over fifty years ago, so it should be noted that this may not be literally true in terms of modern astronomical observations. Beyond this idea, however, is the *symbolism* of the number ninety-five and not the literal quantity of stars in Leo.
2. Bailey, *Esoteric Psychology,* vol. I, 76.
3. Ibid., 76.
4. Ibid., 77-78.
5. Bailey, *Esoteric Psychology,* vol. II, 87.
6. Bailey, *Esoteric Astrology,* 219-20.
7. Bailey, *Esoteric Psychology,* vol. II, 71-72.
8. Ibid., 89-90.
9. Bailey, *Esoteric Psychology,* vol. I, 65.
10. See Bailey, *Esoteric Psychology,* vol. II, 209.
11. This means our solar system is centered on our buddhic plane or the fourth cosmic etheric plane.
12. Bailey, *Esoteric Astrology,* 126.
13. Ibid., 444-45.
14. Ibid., 306.
15. Ibid., 224-25.
16. Ibid., 349.
17. See Bailey *Esoteric Astrology*, 348. It should be pointed out that Gemini forms a cosmic triangle with the Great Bear and the Pleiades which DK calls the "triangle of the Cosmic Christ and is the esoteric symbol lying behind the cosmic cross." *Esoteric Astrology*, 348. It is possible that Sirius, as the Cosmic Christ, is the point within this cosmic triangle distributing divine Love into surrounding space, including our solar system. This speculative idea could be reflected in the triangle now formed on our own planet by the Buddha, the Spirit of Peace, and the Avatar of Synthesis, with the Christ at the center distributing Love to our Earth. See *Reappearance of the Christ.*
18. Ibid., 354.
19. Ibid., 354-55.
20. Two pillars from the temple of Solomon.
21. The Egyptians have various dual gods and goddesses which represent the masculine and feminine aspects of One particular divine quality. Osiris, Isis, and Horus are the most well known, due to the popularity of the Egyptian Book of the Dead.
22. Bailey, *Esoteric Astrology,* 429-30.

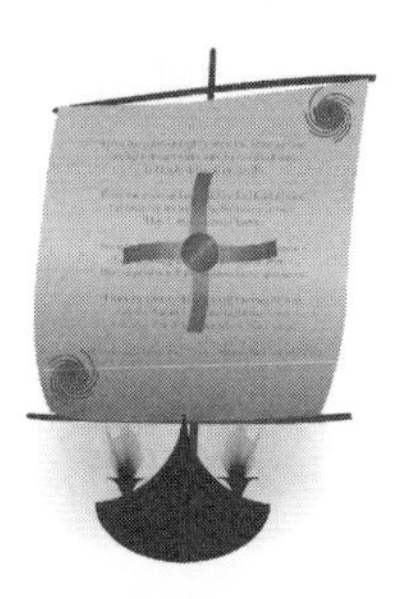

12

The Great Pyramid of Words

This chapter continues our discussion of the Egyptian trinity and its relation to Sirius. In chapter 9, "The Revealing Cross of Sirius," recall that the original numbers obtained from the twenty-eight words in each quadrant of the cross led us to the value 321 which equals "Sirius, Osiris, Isis, Horus." Since that chapter, we have discovered that 321 also relates to the goddess Athena, "the law of those who choose to die," and "Cosmic Christ the Sun Sirius." (See table 50, chapter 11.) The common theme of these phrases is sacrifice and redemption by the Sons of God, Initiates, and Saviors Who appear in the world in times of crisis and need—the Gemini messengers of chapter 11. This story is repeated in some form by every religion and tradition in the world. (Christianity calls this the gospel of the New Testament.) The focus of this universal story is the savior God Who appears in the world as a man or woman in order to establish a new law, teach a new divine quality, or bring some gift to humanity in order to relieve human suffering; such were Christ, Buddha, and Krishna. Athena, Osiris, Isis, and Horus were of lesser direct influence, in terms of our current civilization, but nonetheless they powerfully affected the ancient Greek and Egyptian civilizations.

We will now shift our focus to Horus as the symbol of the primal

Cosmic Christ manifesting in our world at different times and places, but always representing the middle principle, the Son. Extracts from Djwhal Khul and H. P. Blavatsky set the stage for what is to follow in this chapter:

> This is the system of the SON, whose name is Love. This is the divine incarnation of Vishnu. The Dragon of Wisdom is in manifestation, and He brings into incarnation those cosmic Entities who are in essence identical with Himself.[1]

> The Pyramids are closely connected with the ideas of both the constellation of the Great Dragon, and "the Dragons of Wisdom," or the great Initiates of the Third and Fourth Races, and the floods of the Nile, regarded as a divine reminder of the great Atlantic Flood.[2]

The first passage by DK establishes the primary role of the second divine aspect in our solar system and consequently our world. The second quotation by HPB connects the "Dragons of Wisdom" to the line of Initiates Who stretch from the Lemurian third root-race through the Atlantean fourth to the present Aryan fifth race. We are interested in the Egyptian period, when the Initiates of Atlantis left the doomed continent, and entered the Nile valley. It was here they established the esoteric schools to which the later Greek philosophers and others traveled to learn the sacred science and be initiated into the Mysteries.

The symbols, numbers, sounds, colors, rituals, gods, goddesses, myths, monuments, and sacred geometry of the Mysteries are scattered throughout the world. They exist in the form of sacred writings, religions, myths, legends, literature, architecture, art, and music. The works of H. P. Blavatsky and Bailey/Djwhal Khul testify to this fact. The writings of DK especially contain hints and clues to the Mysteries in obvious and subtle forms. Some of these clues are easy to detect while others appear to be within reach yet remain elusive and just beyond comprehension. We are about to deal with both categories.

The Sacred Geometry of Osiris and Isis

The Great Invocation is a word of power, mantram, or world prayer constructed of words. Is it possible these words reflect sacred geometry and physical structure? It appears that this is the case.

The Egyptian trinity is a model of the universal creative process. In human terms Osiris is the Father, Isis is the Mother, and Horus is the Son. Esoterically speaking, Horus, like Christ, is the middle principle of the divine Egyptian trinity. It does not matter whether we are referring to the Christ within the human being, the Christ as Leader of the Hierarchy, the role of Sanat Kumara as the prototypal Avatar/Christ of our planet, the solar Logos in Its second manifestation in which Love or the middle principle is being perfected, or the celestial Cosmic Christ represented by Sirius, the second aspect of the One About Whom Naught May Be Said.

Consider the numbers of these three deities. (We will be using all RAN values unless otherwise stated.) Osiris has a value of 35. This number can also be expressed as 5 x 7; it can be reduced to 8. It is also a tetrahedral number—one that is the sum of a series of triangular numbers. In the case of Osiris, this number series is 1, 3, 6, 10, and 15 (1 + 3 + 6 + 10 + 15 = 35). (See table 10 in chapter 3.) These triangular numbers are usually depicted as triangles in the form of dots. Imagine these dots as oranges. If you stack each triangular group on top of the other, in effect you create a tetrahedron. A tetrahedron is a geometric solid with four sides. It is like a pyramid in the sense that it has a wide base that eventually comes to a singular point at the apex. The only difference between a pyramid and a tetrahedron is that the pyramid has a square base with four triangular sides, while a tetrahedron has a triangular base and three triangular sides.

In the example of Osiris, if we wanted to depict the value of his name (35) geometrically we would put 15 oranges together in the form of a triangle. Then we would place 10 oranges on top of this layer, 6 on top of the second layer, 3 on top of the third layer and one on top of the fourth layer. When we were finished we would have a tetrahedron five tiers high consisting of 35 oranges.

Significantly, Isis has value of 20 which is also a tetrahedral number. The stack of oranges needed to represent Isis would be four tiers high, one less than Osiris. This is all well and good if we work in a fruit market, but what does this have to do with esoteric principles?

In this instance, it is not so much what these two deities mean separately, but what they create as a result of their dynamic interaction. The tetrahedron is the first Platonic solid, and Plato related it to the element of fire. In esoteric terms, fire represents electricity.

The book often quoted here, *A Treatise on Cosmic Fire*, is about the three fundamental fires or forms of electricity in the universe. Djwhal Khul calls them "Fire by Friction," "Solar Fire," and "Electric Fire." These three fires are the divine trinity in terms of pure energy. They are the first, second, and third aspects respectively.

Figure 35. Osiris and Isis Tetrahedrons.

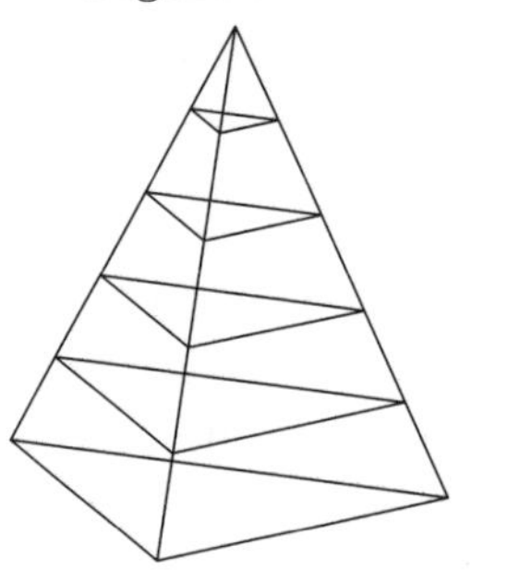

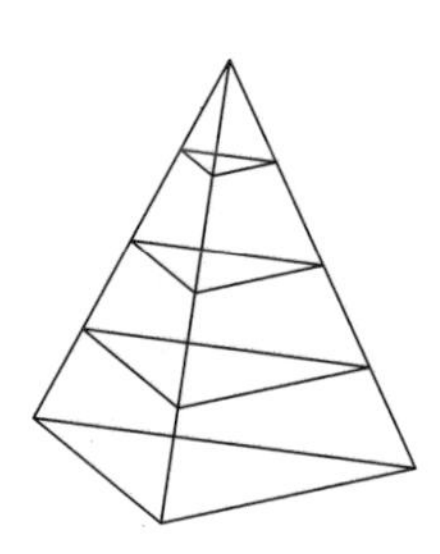

To summarize, Osiris is a five tier tetrahedron composed of 35 parts and Isis is a four tier tetrahedron of 20 parts. The joining of these two will produce the middle aspect of the trinity known as the soul, consciousness, and the Christ principle, which in the Egyptian trinity is named Horus. Symbolically, we might say that Isis (four tiers) and Osiris (five tiers) are the fourth and fifth Creative Hierarchies joined to produce the human kingdom, Horus. As tetrahedrons, therefore, Osiris and Isis symbolize the fires of creation, described by Plato and Djwhal Khul. They bring Horus into being and he shares attributes of both, but is a third and distinct entity in his own right.

The Numbers of Horus

Horus has a value of 27. This number is the cube (3 x 3 x 3 = 27) of 3. The cube is the Platonic solid related to the element of earth. Horus is the god-man who avenges the death of his father by slaying Set, his uncle. Horus thus plays the part of all world saviors by restoring Light and Life (Osiris) where chaos and darkness reign (Set). Horus represents the cube of space, or the manifested son universe containing both father-spirit and mother-matter. For our purposes, it is enough to know that Horus is the Son in manifestation as described by DK in the passage at the beginning of this chapter.

In terms of activity in the physical world of time and space, Horus as the cube corresponds to the energy of Saturn.[3]

If we say that Horus is the mean or average between Osiris and Isis then Horus equals 27.5 (35 + 20 = 55 ÷ 2 = 27.5). In this case, Horus either equals 27 or 28 (if 27.5 is rounded up to the next whole number). The decimal .5 symbolizes Horus or the middle principle as distinct, yet bridging two worlds. Horus is "the relation between" the two opposite poles of spirit (Osiris) and matter (Isis). In this sense Horus truly is the soul, the middle principle, the product of spirit and substance.[4] As the number 27, Horus is still the cube, Vishnu, Cosmic Christ, or Son in manifestation. As the number 28, Horus resides at the center of the Great Invocation as the numeric value of the 57th word "is." Incidently, the term "the cube of space" has a RAN value of 57 thus offering a symbolic representation of Horus, the cube as the middle principle of the trinity and the middle word of the Great Invocation. Figuratively speaking, the Word Position Index provides a graphic depiction of Horus in the form of the word "is" at the middle position between Osiris and Isis, the first and last halves of the Great Invocation.

The Great Invocation provides further evidence of the symbolic creative act which produces Horus. This is substantiated by referring to the Word Position Index. Using the value of each person, we find Osiris represented in word position 35 by "Let" (37 AN); Isis represented at position 20 which is also "Let" (37 AN); and Horus is at position 27 where we find the word "point" with a value of 74 (AN). This is quite remarkable since 37 + 37 = 74, or Let + Let = point, or Osiris + Isis = Horus.

Symbolically speaking, Osiris (35) and Isis (20) combine to create Horus (55). The "Esoteric Numerology Lists" (appendix E) contain two terms equal to 55 (AN) which are Sanat and Heaven. These both pertain to the middle principle when seen from the universal angle, because Sanat is, like the Son (aspect), in incarnation. Sanat most definitely exemplifies the state of heaven since He is the God of our planet, and traditionally God resides in heaven. Esoterically speaking, heaven corresponds to Shamballa.

The Creation of the Horus Pyramid

The tetrahedrons shown in figure 35 represent Osiris with five tiers and Isis with four tiers. When combined (35 + 20), they equal

55; this number represents Horus. The geometric shape produced from the marriage of Osiris and Isis does not result in a tetrahedron, however. Instead, the number 55 is a pyramidal number, which is a number that can be depicted as a pyramid.

If we were stacking wooden blocks in the form of cubes in the shape of a pyramid we would have, for example, a base of 25 blocks, or a 5 by 5 square. On top of this we would build a second layer of 4 by 4, or 16 blocks and so on until we placed one block at the apex. When we finished we would have a five tier pyramid composed of 55 blocks. Therefore, if we built a 5 tier tetrahedron and a 4 tier tetrahedron (35 and 20) out of blocks we would need 55 blocks in all to accomplish our task. We could then take these two tetrahedrons apart and reuse the same 55 blocks to rebuild them in the form of a 5 tier pyramid.

Figure 36. The Horus Pyramid.

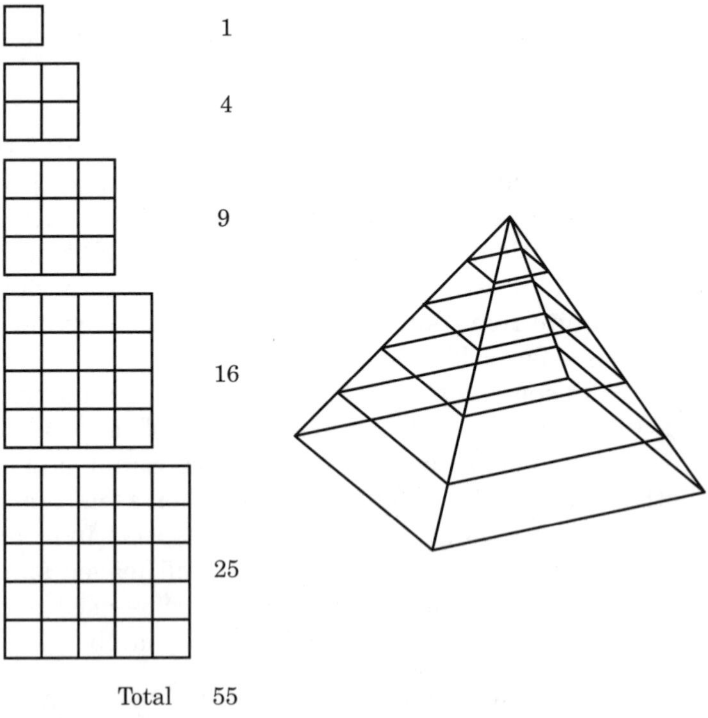

We might say the interaction of Osiris and Isis produces Horus or creates Horus in the form of a pyramid with five tiers. At the end of the section on the "Sacred Geometry of Osiris and Isis," we pointed out that Osiris and Isis are personifications of the fires of creation, or Electric Fire, and Fire by Friction respectively. Their united action (in the form of fiery tetrahedrons) brings Horus or Solar Fire into manifestation. This process is intriguing because the word origin of pyramid may be related to the Latin word *pyramis* or fire.

From what we already know about the Egyptian trinity (and others), we know that Horus symbolizes the soul or middle principle. Therefore, we can speculate somewhat by extending this idea into the nature of the soul as it manifests in various ways, such as individually and cosmically. In the *Dictionary of All Scriptures and Myths*, Gaskell has this to say about the pyramid:

> A symbol of the causal body,—the seat of the spiritual Triad, Atma-buddhi-manas,—resting upon the foundation of the four planes of the lower quaternary (four sides).[5]

Let's define, in brief, the terms Gaskell uses in the above reference.

- The causal body (often called the egoic lotus) is the vehicle of the soul or consciousness. The causal body, according to DK, is normally situated on the third subplane of the mental plane and after initiation, it moves up to the second subplane of the mental.[6]
- The primary energies of the spiritual triad are contained in the causal body. Atma is spiritual will, buddhi is spiritual love-wisdom, manas is spiritual mind.
- The causal body creates vehicles out of the substance of the lower planes in order to gain experience in the world of form. The world of form is usually referred to as "the three worlds" because a human being garners its experience through the physical, emotional (astral), and mental faculties.
- The lower quaternary is actually "the three worlds" but the physical body is constituted of a dense fleshy part, and a vital or etheric part called the etheric body. Therefore, the causal body or soul "rests on the foundation of the four planes of the lower quaternary."

This definition of the pyramid in terms of the human constitution of energy, consciousness, and vehicles is a near perfect metaphor for the human being. This image takes us back to chapter 4 where the seven principles were listed. These are:

1. The etheric energy body
2. Vitality, Prana
3. Desire
4. Concrete mind, lower manas
5. Abstract mind, higher manas
6. Wisdom, Buddhi, Christ force
7. Spiritual Will, Atma

The key to understanding the seven principles in terms of the pyramid is that of the triangle and the square. These are the two geometric polygons upon which a pyramid is based. The solidity of the pyramid as a three-dimensional object symbolizes the world of form. The pyramid is the soul in incarnation, comprised of the spiritual triad of the higher worlds and manifesting through the four types of substance in the lower worlds. The primary key here is that man evolves in the five worlds of the cosmic physical plane. (See appendix D2, planes three through seven.) The seven principles listed above are all contained within the five planes of consciousness. The seven are contained in the five. This is a direct link to the structure of the Great Invocation which DK composed in the form of *five stanzas containing seven sentences*.

Following through on the Hermetic maxim "As above so below," the esoteric teachings indicate that the human egoic lotus or causal body is an individualized, microcosmic model based on a macrocosmic causal body or egoic lotus. If the Law of Correspondences is consistent, our planetary Logos Who is now incarnated as Sanat Kumara has an egoic lotus on cosmic levels. (The same holds true for the solar Logos; "...the Sirian Logos is to our solar Logos what the human Ego is to the personality."[7]) Symbolically speaking, He (Sanat Kumara) is the planetary Horus, a planetary pyramid manifesting in the physical dimension.

The Five Tier Pyramid, Sanat Kumara, and the Manasic Rays

A pyramid with its 5 sides, 5 tiers, and 55 parts offers a symbolic model of the five manasic rays. Our planetary Logos is currently using the third ray and the other four manasic rays as a means of expression through the personality of Sanat Kumara. The subject of the five manasic rays was discussed in chapter 10 in the section, "The Seventh Ray—The Fifth Aspect of Mind." As pointed out in chapter 5, the Kumaras are the builders and creators of the universe on cosmic levels and they exist in various grades, from cosmic, to solar, to planetary. In relation to our planet Earth, there are five Kumaras and they represent the sumtotal of the principle of manas or mind, which is the fifth principle. Quoting DK:

> The planetary Logos of this scheme is one of the four minor Logoi, or Lords of the Rays, and is specially concerned therefore with the development of one attribute of manas. Each of the four minor Rays is, as we know, eventually synthesised, or absorbed into that Ray which is represented on our earth by the Mahachohan. He is the Lord of the third major Ray or Aspect, and synthesises the four. *These four Rays with their synthesising Ray make the five rays of Manas or Mind. We can consider them as:*
>
> a. The fivefold Brahma Aspect.
> b. They were the five Rays of prime importance in the first solar system, and were the five individualised Heavenly Men, called the Mind-born Sons of Brahma...
> c. They are represented on our earth by the five Kumaras Who obeyed the Law, and took human form, as H.P.B. hints in several passages in the *Secret Doctrine*.[8]

The main points to grasp in the above quotation are the following:

- The four lesser rays of manas are absorbed by the synthesizing third ray.
- The planetary Logos of our Earth is developing one aspect of manas out of five.
- There are five Kumaras Who incarnated in human form.
- The five Kumaras represent the five manasic rays—four minor rays and one synthesizing.
- The Mahachohan is a Being Who represents the third ray within the Hierarchy, and this Being has four ray representatives under His supervision.

The symbolism of the "1" and the "4" is obvious in this extract. (Recall the five rivulets on The Star card.) In order to illustrate this more clearly, the list of the seven and five rays is repeated here.

Rays of Aspect	1. Will or Power	
	2. Love or Wisdom	
	3. Adaptability or active intelligence	1.
Rays of Attribute	4. Harmony, Beauty or Art	2.
	5. Concrete Knowledge or Science	3.
	6. Abstract Idealism	4.
	7. Ceremonial Magic	5.[9]

The third ray of Active Intelligence and Adaptability is the synthesizing energy of the rays of Attribute, namely, the fourth ray of Harmony, the fifth ray of Science, the sixth ray of Devotion, and the seventh ray of Organization. From a purely ray viewpoint, the number 5 is that of mind or manas.

The number and ray identities of the Kumaras can be very confusing since they are referred to by so many different names, according to the particular function they perform in the creative process. Therefore, it is not our intention to go into detail on this complex subject, except to point out the relationship between Sanat Kumara, the number 5, and the Horus symbolism in the pyramid. For instance, in the above quotation, Djwhal Khul states that the planetary Logos of our Earth Scheme is "one of the four minor Logoi," and yet Djwhal Khul states elsewhere that the planetary Logos of the Earth possesses a third ray personality:

> The magnetic pull of that which is desired is modified on our planet by the personality ray of our particular planetary Logos. This is the Ray of Active Intelligence, and of selective Adaptability.[10]

It can be assumed from this remark that the soul ray of the planetary Logos is one of the minor rays of attribute, but the personality ray is one of the major rays of aspect, namely, the third.

If you examine the final totals of the Great Invocation in the "Master List of the Great Invocation" in appendix A, you will notice the intermediate number before the final reduction to 5 is 14. This symbolizes the one and the four of the pyramid with its base and four sides, and of the five Kumaras, Sanat—the First Kumara, and the remaining four. It is important to remember here that we are now discussing the Kumaras in terms of the five manasic rays. This does not negate the esoteric fact that 105 Kumaras came to the Earth, but simply describes how these Beings are organized according to ray energies.

This same one and four pattern extends to the five manasic rays themselves. This symbolism does not address rays one through five but simply the presence of five rays; four rays of attribute and one ray of aspect. Referring to point c on page 337, these five rays are represented on our Earth by the five Kumaras Who "took human form." This indicates the taking of form by Sanat Kumara along the line of a third ray personality, with the other four Kumaras representing the four rays of attribute.

The Followers of Horus

Horus personified as Sirius is the second aspect of the One About Whom Naught May Be Said. In terms of scale or grade, Horus at this level is the cosmic Horus. In terms of our own solar system, which is the Son in manifestation, we have the solar Horus. At the planetary level, Sanat Kumara as the incarnation of the planetary Logos represents the planetary Horus. The Christ as the first Sirian Initiate of humanity is the human Horus. All human beings who find their way onto the path of initiation become the individual Horus.

In the book *A Treatise on Cosmic Fire*, DK mentions the three Rods of Initiation. These are:

- The Rod of Initiation used for the first two initiations and wielded by the Great Lord, the Christ...
- The Rod of Initiation known as the "Flaming Diamond" and used by Sanat Kumara, the One Initiator...This Rod was brought by the Lord of the World when He took form and came to our planet eighteen million years ago...
- The Rod of Initiation, wielded by the Logos of the solar system, is called among other things, the "Sevenfold Flaming Fire." It was confided to our Logos by the Lord of Sirius and sent to our system from that radiant sun.[11]

The many wall and temple paintings of ancient Egypt depict the Gods with Their staffs, suggesting the Sirian Rods of Initiation. The Egyptians were one of the last remnants of the Atlantean Mystery schools of initiation. The details of initiation were not revealed, but the culture and civilization resulting from initiation with all its symbols, knowledge, science, and art remained as a testimony to the power and wisdom of the Initiates of that day. They all followed the way of Horus, which is the way of Sirian inspired initiation.

In fact, all Initiates are Followers of Horus and are of different grades, whether they are human, solar, or planetary. Sanat Kumara, as we now know, is currently in physical form in order to prepare for the fourth cosmic initiation. In terms of what we have discussed, Sanat Kumara is a Follower of Horus.

Discussing the various Egyptian gods of heaven, Budge offers the following comments about Horus and his Followers:

> But this heaven also contained several classes of beings, first and foremost among whom may be mentioned the SHESU-HERU, or SHEMSU-HERU, a name which appears in the Pyramid Texts...translated "Followers of Horus." They are, in fact, beings who followed Horus, the son of Isis, in heaven, where they waited upon him and performed his behests, and when necessary defended and protected him. They occupied a position of great importance among the celestial hosts, and are mentioned in such a way as to suggest that they were almost equal to the gods.[12]

This passage indicates the importance of the Followers of Horus who appear here as demi-gods and spiritual Beings of various grades, including, perhaps, the Kumaras.

In this next passage Budge describes Horus in the role of mediator or intercessor for the dead.

> We find, however, that Horus was believed to help the dead generally, even as he helped Osiris, and all men hoped that he would come to their assistance after death, and act as a mediator between the judge of the Underworld and themselves. In the Judgement Scene in the *Book of the Dead* (Papyrus of Ani, plates 3 and 4), Horus, the son of Isis, leads the deceased, after his heart has been weighed, into the presence of Osiris, and he says to his father, "I have come to thee, O Un-nefer, and I have brought unto thee Osiris Ani," and then goes on to say that Thoth has weighed Ani's heart in the Balance according to the decree of the gods, and has found it right and true. He also asks Osiris that Ani may be allowed to appear in his presence, and that cakes and ale may be given to him, and that he may be among the followers of Horus for ever. In none of the variants of the Judgement Scene do we find that the place of Horus as introducer of the dead is taken by any other god, and there is no doubt that this duty was assigned to him because it was believed that Osiris would favourably receive those who were led into his presence by the son who had done so much for him.[13]

This second passage is suggestive of an initiation in which the candidate is taken before the Initiator by his or her sponsor in order to introduce the would-be initiate to the hierophant. The initiation process is very much the same as the experience of death because the candidate is dying to the old life of materialism and being reborn in the life of the spirit. In the hall of judgement, Horus goes before Osiris to plead the case for Ani's safe passage into the afterworld. This is not much different than the initiate's passage into the expanded world of the higher dimensions of consciousness after initiation. And it is not very different than Christ's prayer to His Father in heaven on behalf of his disciples and followers (John 17).

A similar process in which Members of the Hierarchy assemble to initiate an aspirant into the mysteries of our planetary life is described by the Tibetan:

> For the first two initiations the Hierophant is the Christ, the World Teacher, the Firstborn among many brethren, one of the earliest of our humanity to take initiation...But when the initiate has made still further progress, and has taken two initiations, a change comes. The Lord of the World, the Ancient of Days, the ineffable Ruler Himself administers the third initiation.[14]

> In the case of the first two initiations, two Masters stand, one on each side of the applicant, within the triangle; at the third, fourth and fifth initiations, the Mahachohan and the Bodhisattva perform the function of sponsor...The work of the sponsors is to pass through Their bodies the force or electrical energy emanating from the Rod of Initiation.[15]

These passages show the general similarities between the assembled gods of the *Egyptian Book of the Dead* and the various Members of the Hierarchy Who assemble to initiate a candidate into the Mysteries. The point is that all who enter upon the way of initiation can be called the Followers of Horus. DK describes nine levels of initiation, and all of these expansions of consciousness eventually admit the Initiate into the Great White Lodge on Sirius.

Sanat Kumara is the One Initiator on our planet. He wields the Rod of Initiation and is an Agent of the Great White Lodge on Sirius. We might say Sanat Kumara is a Follower of Horus at the planetary level, and He initiates human beings who in turn become Followers of Horus at the human level. Not only does the Initiate become a Follower of Horus, but more importantly he or she *becomes Horus*.

Although we are using the name "Horus" for its numerological significance in relation to the Great Invocation, we are also concerned with the Christ principle as it manifests at the cosmic, solar, planetary, and individual level. Thus, Horus and Christ both represent the second aspect of the trinity. We are dealing with a spiritual chain of being extending from the human phase of existence out and beyond our planet and solar system to the sun Sirius. Within this chain of being, Sanat Kumara has a special relationship with the Lord of Sirius. Djwhal Khul tells us this relationship is one of the secrets of initiation, but maybe a small hint about the nature of this relationship can be revealed by following through on the symbolism of the five tier pyramid of Horus.

Building the House of Horus - Stage One

If Sanat Kumara as a Follower of Horus corresponds to the five tier pyramid at the planetary scale, then following the Hermetic maxim "As above, so below" means that a correspondence to Horus at the cosmic scale may also be evident. This theme addresses several relationships simultaneously: Sanat Kumara and the Lord of Sirius; Sanat Kumara, our solar Logos, and the Lord of Sirius; and all three as a unit and the Great Invocation.

In order to demonstrate this, we must go back to the beginning of chapter 9, "The Revealing Cross of Sirius." That chapter began by stating the great importance of the cross in the Lives of Sirius. By following the theory that the Great Invocation is of Sirian origin, we placed the words of the Great Invocation around the equal-armed cross, leaving the middle word "is" at the intersecting point of the two arms. This exercise produced a wealth of esoteric information linking the Great Invocation to Sirius and related subjects. Now we will put the finishing touches on this theory.

Let's start with our now well-known trinity of Osiris, Isis, and Horus. Their mythological and metaphorical symbolism are the keys to understanding the relationship between Sirius and our planet. It should now be understood that these three Egyptian gods are more than religious icons, for they are numeric templates which serve to delineate an esoteric truth about the mystery of Sirius and our tiny world. The Egyptian trinity is a signpost, a key for unlocking a door to a greater reality concerning our world. When it is said that Osiris, Isis, and Horus are central to the Great

Invocation this is literally true.

AN values:

- Osiris (89) reduced to its root value equals 8 (8 + 9 = 17, 1 + 7 = 8).
- Isis (56) reduced to its root value equals 11 (5 + 6 = 11).
- Horus (81) reduced to its root value equals 9 (8 + 1 = 9).
- Adding the three together yields 28 (8 + 11 + 9 = 28).
- 28 is the AN value of the middle word "is."

RAN values:

- Osiris (35) reduced to its root value equals 8 (3 + 5 = 8).
- Isis (20) reduced to its root value equals 2 (2 + 0 = 2).
- Horus (27) reduced to its root value equals 9 (2 + 7 = 9).
- Adding the three together yields 19 (8 + 2 + 9 = 19).
- 19 is the AN value of the middle letter "s."

This is an impressive demonstration of the consistent integrity of the numeric symbolism built into the core of the Great Invocation. The essential and synthesized numeric energy of the Egyptian trinity, calculated using both techniques of letter/number conversion, is found to match the exact number values located at the very center of the Great Invocation as represented by "is" and "s."

At an even deeper level, the Great Invocation demonstrates the symbolic relationship existing between the Egyptian trinity and Sirius. To illustrate this, we return once again to the Word Position Index in appendix B. Earlier it was explained how the RAN values of the Egyptian trinity were mirrored in the word positions and values contained in the Great Invocation. These values follow:

- Osiris (35) equals "Let" with an AN value of 37.
- Isis (20) equals "Let" with an AN value of 37.
- 37 + 37 = 74.

- Horus (27) equals "point" with an AN value of 74.
- Horus (74) = Osiris + Isis (74)
- The "Dragons of Wisdom," "The Sirian Lodge," "The Hierarchy," and the "Great Invocation" all equal 74 (RAN).

Earlier, we also added the RAN values of Osiris and Isis together in a symbolic union in order to produce Horus. This exercise produced the number 55 and the five tier pyramid. We also viewed Horus as the average between Osiris and Isis which is 27.5. Referring to the Word Position Index, the number 55 takes us to the 55th word "of," with a value of 21. This number refers to the key words, but it also leads us immediately back to the infinity loop signifying "the Great White Lodge on Sirius." If, instead we view the resultant joining of Osiris and Isis as the number 27.5, we are led to a neutral position between words 27 and 28. Word position 27 is "point" equaling 74, and word position 28 is "of" equaling 21. As we now know, both of these numbers are significant. Horus with its value of 27.5 is part Osiris and Isis. Therefore, Horus is both 27 and 28 or 74 and 21. The combined value of the words in these two positions equals 95—the AN value of Sirius. This esoteric numerological exercise demonstrates that the Great Invocation, Sirius, and the Egyptian trinity are intimately connected. Now that we have established a stronger esoteric link between these three elements, we can proceed to the first stage of building the House of Horus.

Figure 37. The 28 Triangulation.

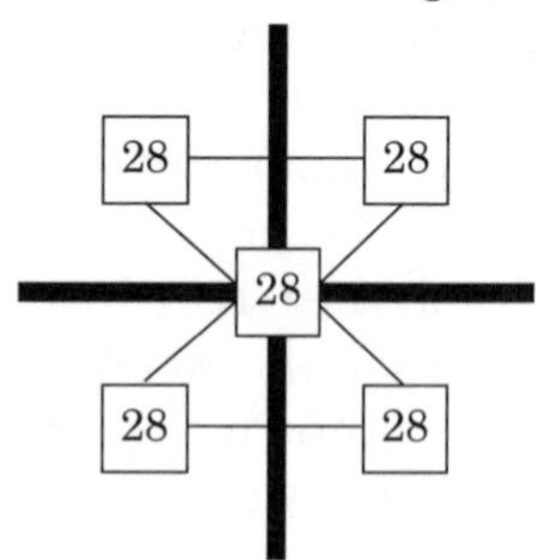

When the Great Invocation is divided into four sections based on the number 28, we are actually dividing it by the resonating number frequency of the combined root values of Osiris, Isis, and Horus. (See page 343, "AN values.") This configuration is displayed on the previous page (figure 37) by the two triangles relating the first and second halves of the Great Invocation to each other. Recall that the total of each triangle equals 84 (3 x 28 = 84), which corresponds to "Dog Star."

It should be obvious by now that beneath its 113 words, the Great Invocation is fundamentally an energy field of tremendous potency. We use it in the physical world in a linear fashion, but from the angle of the inner dimensions, linearity as we know it (time and space) are non-existent. Applying this concept to the Great Invocation allows us to create four triangular relationships in the cross configuration. Therefore, we can depict a schematic of the Great Invocation as seen in figure 38. In effect, we have created a pyramid design viewed from an angle directly above the apex.

Figure 38. The 28 Pyramid.

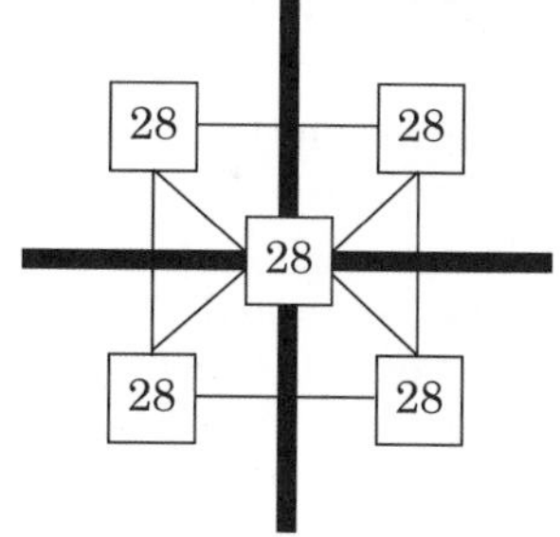

The next step in our process of building the House of Horus is to recognize that all the numbers in the schematic are the triangular number 28. This means they are the result of combining the numbers 1 through 7 (1 + 2 + 3 + 4 + 5 + 6 + 7 = 28). Since they are triangular numbers they can be arranged in the form of a triangle, substituting a dot for each word. Since there are four sets of twenty-eight words surrounding the cross, four triangles of twenty-eight dots each are necessary to depict each word group.

Noting figure 39 on the next page, we can say that symbolically speaking, each triangle is an outer or exoteric expression of the monadic point at the center of the cross which is the AN number frequency (28) of the middle word "is." This middle word is the root seed of the divine trinity, and each triangle born from it is the manifested triplicity of Osiris, Isis, and Horus whose combined root values are 28.

Figure 39. The Cross of Septenary Perfection.

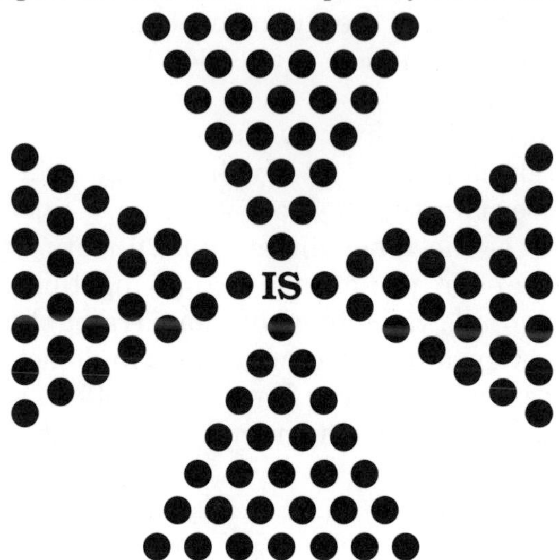

Djwhal Khul says this about the trinity:

> Spirit is *One*, but within that essential unity the "points of fire" or "the divine sparks" can be seen and noted. These unities, within the unity, are coloured by, and react qualitatively to, three types of energy, for it is scientifically true, and a spiritual fact in nature, that God is the Three in One and the One in Three. The spirit of man came into incarnation along a line of force emanation from one or other of these three streams, which form one stream, emanating from the Most High.
>
> These streams of energy differentiate into a major three, yet remain one stream. This is an occult fact worthy of the deepest meditation. In their turn they differentiate into seven streams which "carry into the light," as it is called, the seven types of souls.[16]

This configuration (figure 39) of the Great Invocation tells the fundamental story which DK succinctly explains in the passage above. From the one word (28) emerges the fundamental trinity, the triangular number 28. This number contains the seven rays since it is the result of adding the numbers 1 through 7 together. Djwhal Khul continues:

> The energies into which the three distribute themselves thus becoming seven, in their turn produce the forty-nine types of force which express themselves through all the forms in the three worlds and the four kingdoms in nature.[17]

This paragraph describes in further detail what is evident in the schematic of the Great Invocation depicted in figure 39. In that diagram we see the three worlds and the four kingdoms symbolized as 4 three-sided polygons (triangles). The three aspects of will, love, and intelligence are reflected in the three worlds of human living by the lower mind, the emotions, and the physical body; the four kingdoms are indicated by the four triangles.

Within each triangle every dot represents a ray. The single dot at the apex is ray one, the two dots below it represent ray two, and so on. The entire triangle represents the three aspects which are expressed through each of the seven rays. As figure 40 clearly shows, the seven rays combine to yield the perfect number 28.

Figure 40. The Seven Rays Equal 28.

The only item mentioned by DK which is not readily visible concerns the forty-nine types of force expressing themselves in the three worlds and four kingdoms. This is a bit more esoteric, and in order to see the significance of these forty-nine types of force we need to use the Word Position Index in appendix B. Since the number in question is 49, we will return to the fundamental exercise of using the trinity concept with the Great Invocation. If the Great Invocation is a sacred vessel of esoteric principles, it should yield some information about the forty-nine types of force.

Therefore, let's divide the Great Invocation into three parts as we have already done with the middle letter, the middle word, and the middle phrase. By dividing the Great Invocation into forty-nine words in the first and last halves, a total of fifteen words remains in the middle position. In the Word Position Index these fifteen words are in positions 50 through 64.

When the AN values of the fifteen middle words are combined they total 777. At this point we must recall that Athena represents the structure of the Great Invocation as the number 7. Here she is overwhelmingly present as two 7 x 7 grids of words surrounding fifteen words whose AN values are 777! Once more the Great Invocation exhibits a structure based on the number 7.

Figure 41. Athena.

7 x 7
777
7 x 7

The emergence of the number 7 is remarkable, but perhaps even more striking is the appearance of the number 777 between the two sets of forty-nine words. This is very symbolic and esoteric. It not only indicates the three divine qualities or aspects expressing themselves through the seven rays (3 x 7 = 21), but of even greater esoteric significance is the fact that 777 is the number associated with the planetary Logos incarnated in the form of Sanat Kumara.

We might imagine the Word Position Index as a symbolic depiction of the Assembled Council of Sanat Kumara at Shamballa. At the center are fifteen words totaling 777. The value of the fifteen words symbolizes Sanat Kumara, and the words themselves represent the fifteen Kumaras mentioned by DK in *A Treatise on Cosmic Fire*.

> Fifteen, therefore, of these Entities (again the ten and the five) form a centre in the body of the planetary Logos, and the three Kumaras about Whom we are told (Who in Themselves are fivefold, making the fifteen) are the entifying Lives of the particular centre which is involved in the coming Initiation of the Heavenly Man, and to which the human units at this time, and during this greater cycle, belong.[18]

These fifteen words contain sixty-two letters, the value of which equals the phrase “House of Horus” (RAN). In order to find a synthesis of this particular configuration of the Great Invocation, we will combine the three elements involved. These are the fifteen words with a total value of 777 and the two sets of forty-nine words each. Adding 49 + 777 + 49 results in 875. The number 875 is significant in terms of the House of Horus. This number is created by multiplying 5 x 5 x 5 x 7. These factors reveal what was said earlier about Sanat Kumara and the Horus pyramid. These numbers signify the 5 sides of the pyramid, the 5 tiers (of 55 elements), and the 5 manasic rays. The special relationship Sanat Kumara has with the Lord of Sirius is revealed by multiplying 5 x 5 x 5. The result of 125 is the RAN value of "Sirius the Great White Lodge." The seven rays emanating from the Great Bear via Sirius generate the number 875 (125 x 7), which is esoterically present within the Great Invocation.

Building the House of Horus - Stage Two

Let's proceed with the construction of the House of Horus. Up to this point, we have created a configuration of dots in the form of a triangular-armed cross. This shape symbolizes the four sets of twenty-eight words surrounding the original Sirian Cross shown in the preceding pages.

Although we are depicting the words in each section of the cross as a series of four triangular patterns of dots, in reality the words of the Great Invocation themselves can be laid out in such a way as to form the same cross with the middle word at the intersection of the horizontal and vertical arms. Such a cross is depicted in figure 42.

Figure 42. The Triangular-armed Cross of the Great Invocation.

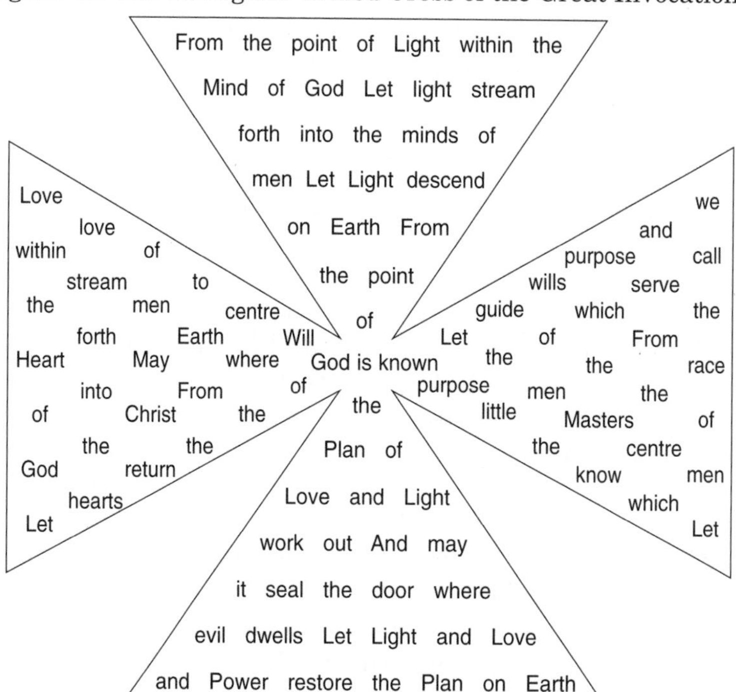

Of particular interest is the relationship between the AN values of the total words in each arm of the cross. The numeric value of the horizontal arm is 2751. The numeric value of the vertical arm is 2545. The difference between these values is 206 (2751 - 2545 = 206). The title of "the Great Invocation" equals 206. The upper and left arms have a total value of 2648 and the bottom and right arms also have a value of 2648. The middle word has a value of 28. Taking these in the order in which they appear:

- 2 + 6 + 4 + 8 = 20, 2 + 0 = 2
- 2 + 8 = 10, 1 + 0 = 1
- 2 + 6 + 4 + 8 = 20, 2 + 0 = 2
- The root values read in order are 2, 1, 2 or 212—"The Dog Star Sirius."

The final phase in the construction of the House of Horus involves a little imagination. Looking at the four triangular arms of the cross, imagine that they can be folded downward so the arms come together. When this is done the arms form themselves into a pyramid. Because each arm of the cross is comprised of the triangular number 28, it must have seven tiers of dots or words as shown in figure 42. When the four arms are folded into a pyramid shape, the result is a pyramid with seven tiers. This is clearly illustrated in figure 43 which is a view of the seven tier pyramid looking directly down over the apex. The truly amazing feature of this transformation of the Great Invocation into a pyramid is that all of the words fit on its surface. As you can see, every one of the 113 words of the Great Invocation has a place on each block. Each cornerstone contains two words; the capstone holds five words, one on each of the four sides, with the fifth and final word "Earth" on the top. This is the House of Horus, a three dimensional representational image of the Great Invocation viewed from above.

In terms of the Mysteries, the Great Pyramid is, perhaps, the most famous symbol known today of the temple of initiation in the ancient world. Within the sacred vessel of the pyramid the candidate for initiation took a journey of spiritual transformation, renewal, and redemption. By the symbolic placement of its words over the entire face of a seven tier pyramid, the Great Invocation is revealed as a sacred vessel of the Mysteries in the form of words—words of renewal and redemption—accessible to people everywhere.

Figure 43. The House of Horus.

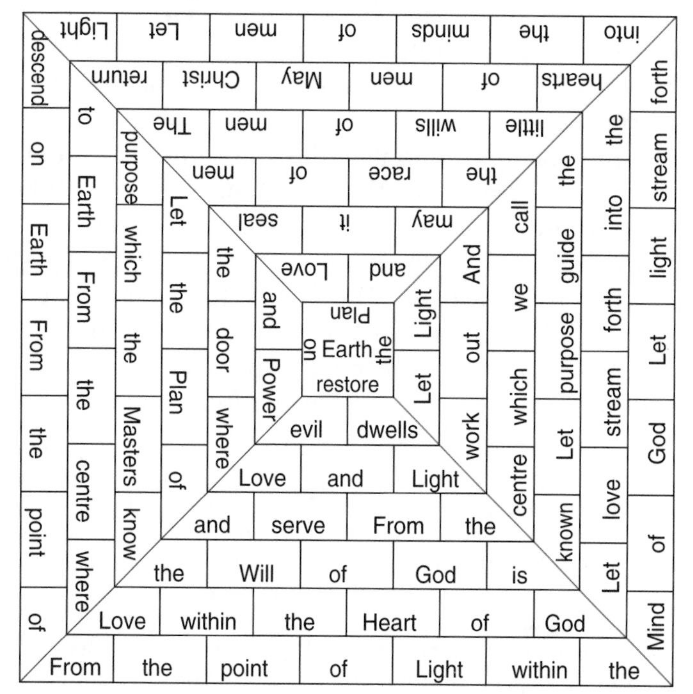

In chapter 6, the hidden pattern of the twenty-one key words was shown to be a code for the numerological value of Sanat (55) Kumara (65) or 5565. The manner in which the key words are spread throughout the five stanzas of the Great Invocation brings to mind the idea that Sanat Kumara is hidden within the Word of Power. This is literally true because the five tier pyramid of 55 parts (blocks) is actually inside the seven tier pyramid formed from the words of the Great Invocation.

Figure 44. Sanat Kumara in the House of Horus.

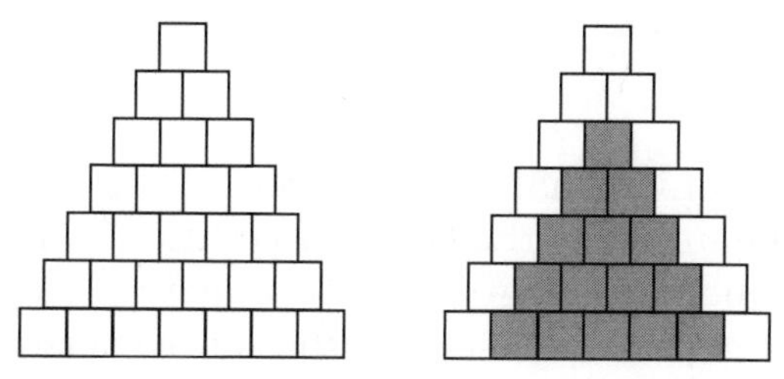

This pyramid is called the House of Horus because Sanat Kumara is located within it. The pyramid with seven tiers completely encases the pyramid with five tiers, so the larger pyramid includes the smaller one within its radius (indicated by the gray area in the right pyramid).

Imagine that each pyramid is built from stones cut into the shape of cubes. The pyramid with five tiers contains 55 stones and the pyramid with seven tiers contains 140 stones. The larger pyramid contains 85 more stones than the smaller one. Symbolically speaking, Sanat (55 AN) is living within "the Earth" (85 AN) thus paralleling the incarnation of Sanat Kumara some eighteen million years ago.

In 1994, this author wrote the following words in the conclusion to a Master's thesis on the esoteric numerology of the Great Invocation:

> The evidence suggests that the Master Djwhal Khul may have intentionally created and structured this powerful mantram in order to place a message within the message. This conclusion is analogous to that of the Great Pyramid of Giza. This ancient structure once served as a place of sacred religious rites and initiation into the mysteries—a place of transformation. Yet built into its very structure is a vast storehouse of mathematical information about the dimensions of our planet and our relation to the stars and seasons, along with the symbolic depiction of the spiritual journey of the aspirant to the mysteries and the destiny of humanity. At the risk of stretching an analogy too far, the Great Invocation represents, perhaps, a "Great Pyramid of Words and Sound Vibration."[19]

At the time this was written, the author had no concrete evidence or idea that such a possibility remotely existed; now it seems as if this was an intuition of a truth waiting to be discovered. What is the message within the message of the Great Invocation? That will have to wait for the concluding chapter, for we must first attend to other matters.

The Light from Sirius

It cannot be denied that we are faced with a "great pyramid of words" when the image of the Great Invocation confronts us in the form of a pyramid. One begins to think more seriously about the identity of the Egyptian priests and the source of their knowledge.

Recent books by Robert Bauval and Adrian Gilbert, *The Orion*

Mystery, and Graham Hancock and Robert Bauval, *The Message of the Sphinx*, contain powerful arguments in favor of an Egyptian science far exceeding anything accepted by mainstream Egyptologists. Some of the information uncovered by their investigations has a connection with the esoteric ideas presented in this book. Most of these connections are still too abstract and unclear to be presented at this time, except for one bit of information related to the Great Pyramid.

Bauval points out in his book that the so-called air shafts of the Great Pyramid point to four stars in the northern hemisphere. Egyptologists have always assumed these shafts were built into the pyramid for ventilation because they did not appear to have any other logical function. There are two shafts in the King's Chamber and two in the lower Queen's Chamber. Within each chamber, one shaft points north and the other south.

Bauval explains, however, that these shafts actually point to specific stars when corrections are made for the positions of the stars as they appeared in the sky at the time when the pyramid was believed to have been built. Correlating his work with others (Sir Flinders Petrie in 1880 and more recently Rudolf Gautenbrink in 1992 and 1993), Bauval shows that between 2425 BCE and 2475 BCE or 2450 BCE, the shafts in the Great Pyramid were pointing to the following stars:

- King's Chamber northern shaft—*Thuban*, the ancient pole star in the constellation Alpha Draconis.
- King's Chamber southern shaft—*Al Nitak*, the lowest and brightest star in the belt of Orion.
- Queen's Chamber northern shaft—*Kochab*, in the constellation of Ursa Minor, the Little Bear.
- Queen's Chamber southern shaft—*Sirius*, in the constellation of Canis Major, the Great Dog.[20]

Although there is much of interest here for esoteric astrologers and students of Djwhal Khul's teachings, we are primarily concerned with Sirius and the shaft in the southern part of the Queen's Chamber. The fascinating part of the story is this: the shaft in the Queen's chamber pointing to Sirius has no opening to the outside of the pyramid. Still more intriguing, Rudolf Gautenbrink sent a tractor driven robot (named Upuaut II) rigged with a video camera into this shaft in 1993, and the robot was stopped by a door after traveling 200 feet up the passage. What lies beyond this door is anyone's guess, but this is a most significant discovery that many researchers are anxiously waiting to explore more fully.

For our purposes, this connection between the Queen's Chamber and the shaft pointing to Sirius is enough to continue our investigation. If the original builders' intent was for the outer end of the shaft to be closed, then obviously Sirius could not be seen through the shaft with the physical eye at the time of alignment. Perhaps the message of the ancient Egyptian priests is that the real light from Sirius can only be seen with the inner eye, the eye of Horus. "The central light of Sirius shone through the eye of the Son; the vision came."[21] (This quotation by DK is part of an elaboration of the three eyes mentioned at the end of chapter 11.)

Three types of light enter our world from three cosmic centers. Light from the Great Bear comes from the "eye of the Father," light from the Pleiades comes from "the eye of the Mother," and light from Sirius comes from "the eye of the Son." The southern shaft in the Queen's Chamber of the Great Pyramid is somehow connected to the light from Sirius and the eye of the Son.

Remarkably, from a numerological standpoint, "the eye of the Son," "the eye of Horus," "the Great Pyramid," and "House of Horus" each equal 170 (AN). From a visual standpoint, the middle word "is" lies by itself at the middle of the Word Position Index like "the eye of the Son." When the cross of the Great Invocation is folded into the shape of a pyramid (figure 42), the apex position is occupied by the middle word "is." In other words, "the eye of Horus" or the eye of the Son occupies the highest level of "the Great Pyramid of words—the capstone." Remember it is "the eye of the Son" which carries the light from Sirius. Recall that the AN value of "is" equals 28, which is the equivalent of "the star" in RAN format. Of particular note, the words "heaven," "goddess," and "Egypt" also equal 28 RAN. The *heaven goddess* of *Egypt* was *the star*, Isis-Sothis or Sirius.

The inherent relationship between the total number of words in the Great Invocation and the middle word position is evident when these two numbers are combined (113 + 57 = 170 House of Horus), because this indicates the paramount importance of the midpoint unit or *soul* in relation to the whole. Man (28 AN) "the star" (28 RAN) is central to the Great Invocation. Recall DK's statement, "This mantram is peculiarly and essentially Christ's Own mantram."[22] The fact that DK says the Christ is the first true Sirian Initiate born from the human family identifies Him as "Man," "the Star" of perfection—28 the perfect number. By viewing the Great Invocation as a sacred vessel holding the pattern of our spiritual evolution, we might say that when the human kingdom reaches maturity and stands at the midpoint bridging the higher worlds of spirit to the lower worlds of matter, the eye of the Son opens and the Light from Sirius penetrates the darkness of the world, restoring the Plan on Earth. The fact that all the words of the Great Invocation fit onto a seven tier pyramid simply reinforces the idea that the numbers related to the Egyptian trinity are being used in concert with the Great Invocation in order to communicate an esoteric idea about the destiny of the human kingdom in our solar system.

The 140 Blocks of the Great Pyramid of Words

Another important number that must be addressed is 140 because this is the quantity of blocks required to build a pyramid of seven tiers. If we can place all the words of the Great Invocation on such a pyramid, then we must assume the possibility that the number 140 is meaningful to our study. For example, one interpretation of this number relates directly to Sirius because 140 is the AN value of "eastern star," a term often applied to Sirius.

However, we are going to interpret this number in another way which entails the intriguing possibility that the 140 components of the pyramid formed from the Great Invocation reveal its originating point. Earlier we quoted Gaskell, who defined the pyramid as the causal body or egoic lotus. We then discussed the fact that since humans are a microcosm within the macrocosm and have causal bodies, then greater entities such as planetary, solar, and cosmic Beings also have causal bodies. In order to understand the real significance of this, we need to illustrate how the cosmic planes of consciousness relate to the systemic planes. (See appendix D1.)

According to the esoteric philosophy, the seven planes of consciousness in which the myriad life forms in our solar system are living and evolving are actually the physical level of seven greater planes of consciousness. These are called the seven cosmic planes. The seven planes of the solar system in which we find ourselves are called the cosmic physical plane. Beings such as our planetary Logos and our solar Logos are evolving on cosmic levels of consciousness.

Following the Hermetic rule, "As above, so below," the names and associations we are familiar with on the cosmic physical plane are lower reflections of the cosmic planes. The best analogy is probably that in which the various notes of the musical scale exist at higher and lower octaves. Therefore, when we speak of the astral plane we are really talking about the *systemic* astral plane within the confines of our solar system because there is a corresponding *cosmic* astral plane at a higher level. In turn, when we talk about the mental plane there is a corresponding cosmic mental plane at a higher level, and so on. The fact that there are correspondences between these planes is probably the most practical information we have about them. Djwhal Khul himself admits to knowing little about these higher worlds of cosmic consciousness (if that's the correct word to describe them); nevertheless, relative to our knowledge of these higher dimensions He is an expert. Most of the information provided on these planes is mainly about how they relate to our corresponding lower planes, or how a lower plane vibrates or corresponds to its higher counterpart.

In a human being, the causal body is normally found on the third subplane of the mental plane (See appendix D2.) As a person advances in their spiritual evolution, the causal body becomes more refined, and therefore, moves up a subplane and occupies a position on the second subplane (technically speaking, the sub-atomic subplane) of the mental plane. Counting the planes from below upward, this means the causal body of an advanced soul can be found on the twentieth subplane out of the forty-nine which constitute the cosmic physical plane.

> The causal body of the average man is on the third subplane [of the mental, JB], and as a man becomes fit for the merging into the Triad, that causal body has to be discarded and done away with. Under the Law of Sacrifice and Death, the disintegration is begun on the third level and is consummated on the second, when the man merges with the Triad, preparatory to the final merging with the Monad.[23]

Now we will expand our reference point from the systemic mental plane to the cosmic mental plane. In order to do this we must multiply our reference point by 7 because the cosmic planes are 7 times greater than ours. (We are only one seventh of the greater whole.) Since the human causal body can be found on the 20th subplane of the cosmic physical plane, following the Law of Correspondences, the causal body of the solar Logos *should* be located on the sub-atomic plane of the cosmic mental plane, which is the 140th level (7 times higher than the 20th level of the human causal body—7 x 20). This is not the case, however, since according to Djwhal Khul:

> The causal body of the Heavenly Men [planetary Logoi, JB] is upon the third subplane of the cosmic mental plane, while that of the solar Logos and those of the three Persons of the logoic Trinity are upon the first subplane.[24]

Therefore, the symbolism of the 140 blocks is not directly referring to the causal body of the solar Logos. This number 140 may simply be indicating the level of cosmic consciousness at which the Great Invocation was created. The numerological evidence suggests this is quite possibly the case. Considering the close relationship existing between Sirius and our solar Logos and the fact that both are connected to the cosmic mental plane, it is not unreasonable to explore the possibility that somehow the Lord of Sirius is closely involved with the creation and establishment of this all-important Word of Power in our solar system, with the full cooperation of our solar Logos.

Here are some statements describing the relationship between our solar Logos and Sirius. Some of these statements may have appeared earlier, but are repeated here for continuity. I have italicized those portions which specifically refer to Sirius.

> This fire of mind has its source in a constellation until recently unrecognized by exoteric science as having any relation of an intimate nature to our solar system, owing to its tremendous distance away. *The sun "Sirius" is the source of logoic manas.*[25]

> We need always to remember that the consciousness of the cosmic mental plane is the logoic [solar, JB] goal of attainment, and that *the Sirian Logos is to our solar Logos what the human Ego is to the personality.* The Law of Karma, or cosmic Fixation, is the law of the cosmic mental plane, and controls the corresponding law in our system.[26]

> *There is also an intermediate law, which is the synthetic law of the system of Sirius. This law is called by the generic term, the Law of Karma, and really predicates the effect the Sirian system has on our solar system....*We have practically no effect on *our parent system*, the reflex action is so slight as to be negligible, but *very definite effects are felt in our system through causes arising in Sirius.* These causes, when experienced as effects, are called by us the Law of Karma...

> *The Lipika Lords of our system, the systemic Lords of Karma, are under the rule of a greater corresponding Lord on Sirius...*
>
> *Our Logos Himself* [solar, JB], *the heart of His system, is on the cosmic astral plane...*
>
> *The system of the Sirian Logos is on the cosmic mental plane....*the Law of Karma, on the third subplane of the cosmic mental plane, which law really controls our Logos [solar, JB], and His actions, in the same way as the ego—in due course of evolution—controls the human personality....
>
> Each one of us, in due process of evolution, forms part of one of the Heavenly Men, Who Themselves form the seven centres in that greater Heavenly Man, the Logos. Yet, though we are merged with the whole, we do not lose our identity, but forever remain separated units of consciousness, though one with all that lives or is. *In like manner our Logos loses not His identity, even though He forms part of the Consciousness of the Logos of Sirius.* In His turn, the Sirian Logos forms one of the seven Grand Heavenly Men, who are the centres in the body of ONE OF WHOM NOUGHT MAY BE SAID.[27]
>
> The activity of the second aspect has been called *spiral-cyclic*, which in itself involves the concept of duality....It is that which brings about the periodical appearing and disappearing of all existences, great or small. It is intimately linked with the will aspect of Divinity, and with the Lipika Lords of the highest degree and its origin is, therefore, difficult for us to comprehend. *Perhaps all that can be said about it is that it is largely due to certain impulses which (as far as our solar system is concerned) can be traced to the sun Sirius.* These impulses find their analogy in the impulses emanating in cyclic fashion from the causal body of man, which impulses bring about his appearance upon the plane of maya for a temporary period....*In the threefold Ego* [causal body or soul body, JB]...*is seen a correspondence to the three groups of Lipika Lords who are the karmic cause of solar manifestation, and who control its periodic manifestation. These three groups are related to Their guiding Intelligences on Sirius.*[28]

The main thrust of all these extracts indicates that—

- the cosmic mental plane is especially important in relation to Sirius.
- Sirius is especially important in relation to our solar system.
- the fifth principle of manas in our solar system has its source on Sirius.
- Sirius controls the manifestation of our solar Logos in a manner analogous to the way the causal body or egoic lotus controls the birth or incarnation of a human being.

Djwhal Khul warns us about being overly liberal in the use of analogies when it comes to detailed comparisons between the lives of human beings and the Lives of cosmic Beings, but at the same time He also tells us to rely on the Law of Correspondences. Therefore, since the information gathered about the Great Invocation has led us this far, it is reasonable to propose the theory that the pyramid of 140 parts with all the words of the Great Invocation covering it identifies the second subplane of the cosmic mental plane as the originating point of the Great Invocation.

The information which Djwhal Khul provides about Sirius and its relation to our solar system is unclear and perhaps deliberately contradictory. In one sense, it appears that our solar Logos forms part of the causal body of the Sirian Logos. In another sense, the Sirian Logos and our Logos are described in terms which lead to the belief that they are separate Identities or Entities, but that they are connected in consciousness. Maybe the Lord of Sirius (a more advanced Being than our solar Logos) is training Him for a cosmic initiation. Nevertheless, one thing is clear—the numbers provide pertinent information relating the Great Invocation to Sirius.

What then is the House of Horus and the meaning of the seven tier 140 part pyramid of the Great Invocation? The House of Horus is the entire field of evolution of our solar Logos. This field of consciousness contains 140 distinct grades of consciousness below the level of His causal body, BUT our solar Logos is not yet fully aware nor in control of all of them. Remember the earlier quote by DK: "Our Logos Himself, the heart of His system, is on the cosmic astral plane." At the same time our solar Logos is in incarnation and just as a human student of meditation must learn to contact his or her Higher Self or causal body on the second or third subplane of the mental plane, so too does our solar Logos need to stay aligned with His causal body on the cosmic mental plane, which is at the 141st level of consciousness from the human standpoint.

Theoretically, if the Lord of Sirius is training our solar Logos for a cosmic initiation, then maybe a cosmic Word of Power was created by the Sirian Lord and given to our solar Logos in order to help Him attain the goal. The solar Logos eventually transferred this Word of Power to Sanat Kumara, Who voluntarily incarnated on Earth where this Word of Power has been kept and used by the Lords of Shamballa; a Word of Power we call the Great Invocation.

The House of Horus is the field of evolution of the solar Logos represented by the seven tier pyramid containing the 140 blocks (the 140 sub-subplanes). Sanat (55) Kumara is the 55 block, 5 tier pyramid contained within the House of Horus. This is consistent with the teaching of the ageless wisdom because Sanat Kumara, as a planetary Being, lives within the House of Horus or within the planes of consciousness of the solar Logos. Sanat Kumara forms part of the consciousness of the solar Logos, yet is a separate Existence in that Greater Life, just as the solar Logos forms part of the consciousness of the Sirian Logos, yet remains a separate Entity.

Figure 45. The 140 Units of the House of Horus.

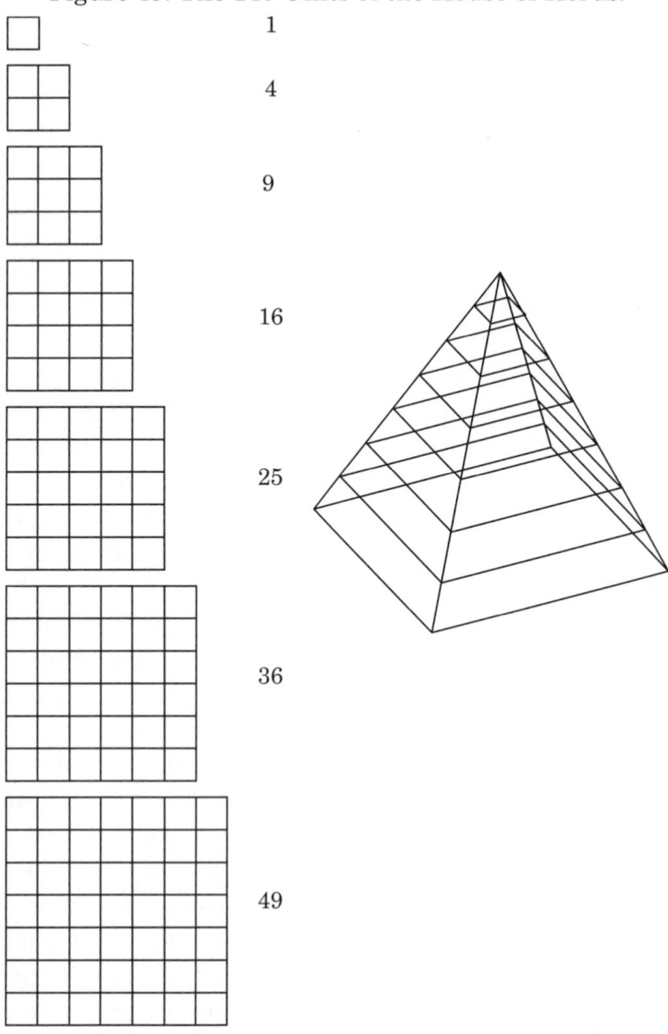

Notes

1. Bailey, *A Treatise on Cosmic Fire,* 176.
2. Blavatsky, *The Secret Doctrine,* vol. 3, 352.
3. For those interested in the cabala, *The Cube of Space,* by Kevin Townley describes much of this in great detail.
4. There is a relationship to ray four here. While discussing the fourth ray, DK states that the positive resolution of conflict by the fourth ray individual results in "the 'Birth of Horus,' of the Christ, born from the throes of constant pain and suffering." Bailey, *Esoteric Psychology,* vol. I, 206.
5. Gaskell, *Dictionary of All Scriptures and Myths*, s.v. "Pyramid."
6. See Bailey, *A Treatise on Cosmic Fire,* 714, 840.
7. Bailey, *A Treatise on Cosmic Fire,* 592.
8. Ibid., 361.
9. Ibid., 428.
10. Bailey, *Esoteric Psychology,* vol. I, 337.
11. Bailey, *A Treatise on Cosmic Fire,* 210-212.
12. Budge, *The Gods of the Egyptians,* vol. 1, 158-59.
13. Ibid., 490.
14. Bailey, *Initiation, Human and Solar,* 88.
15. Ibid., 111.
16. Bailey, *Esoteric Psychology,* vol. I, 6-7.
17. Ibid., 7.
18. Bailey, *A Treatise on Cosmic Fire,* 388.
19. John Berges, "A Study and Analysis of The Great Invocation Using Esoteric Numerology," 72-73.
20. Reference can be made to Robert Bauval and Adrian Gilbert, *The Orion Mystery,* (Crown Publishers, New York, 1994), 98-104. Also see Hancock and Bauval, *The Message of the Sphinx*, 65.
21. Bailey, *Esoteric Astrology,* 431.
22. Bailey, *Discipleship in the New Age,* vol. II, 173.
23. Bailey, *A Treatise On Cosmic Fire,* 582.
24. Ibid., 532.
25. Ibid., 347.
26. Ibid., 592.
27. Ibid., 569-70, 570, 571, 571-72.
28. Ibid., 1033.

13

The Capstone

The capstone of the Great Pyramid of Giza has never been found, perhaps, because there never was one. Dozens of researchers and thousands of the curious have speculated about the true meaning of the Great Pyramid. Was it a tomb for one of the pharaohs? If so, then why is the sarcophagus in the King's Chamber empty? And why is there no evidence of personal treasures and other paraphernalia usually found buried with the deceased? Why is nothing written on the walls of the Great Pyramid when all the other pyramids and temples of ancient Egypt are overflowing with hieroglyphics?

These questions are meant to draw attention to the idea that the Great Pyramid was built by initiates of the Mysteries in order to preserve the wisdom of the ages in stone. The mathematical wonders of this mysterious structure are beyond the scope of this book, nevertheless, for those who are open minded enough to study the Great Pyramid, it soon becomes evident that great minds designed and built it. The Great Pyramid symbolizes the height of esoteric symbolism. It is a testimony to the Mysteries.

This all becomes even more amazing when one discovers there is some connection between the Great Pyramid and the Great Invocation in terms of symbolism. It is abundantly clear that the number 5 is the underlying numeric vibration of the Great Invocation. The fact that its words can be laid out on the surface of a pyramid is beautifully symbolic and remarkable. In his fascinating book *The Great Pyramid Decoded*, Peter Lemesurier comments on the work of pyramid researcher Adam Rutherford:

> Again, Rutherford notes that the number 5 is the Pyramid number *par excellence*. After all, the full design has five points and five sides (i.e. four faces and a base), each of its faces contains a one-fifth scale inset triangle, and a factor of five constantly recurs in its interior measurements...Nevertheless, it should be noted that the Pyramid's exterior will be truly five-based only when it is finally completed to that full design, and when the capstone—itself a five-sided pyramid—is finally added. Thus the significance of the number 5 seems to be intimately linked up with the function of the Pyramid itself, and in particular with the *birth of enlightenment* apparently associated with the final addition of its capstone. The tentative reading *initiation*, *initiate* or *bringer of enlightenment* for the number 5 would therefore seem justified initially. Meanwhile the symbolism of the five-pointed and five-sided capstone suggest that it is the specific function of this light-bringer to bring an imperfect world to perfection through the power of that enlightenment.[1]

Lemesurier's comments are insightful and right on the mark, and can almost be equally applied to the Great Invocation in terms of our own investigation. Let's see what the capstone of the Great Invocation tells us.

Restore the Plan on Earth

The words at the head of this section are those on the capstone of the House of Horus in figure 43 of chapter 12. "Restore the Plan on Earth" is a proclamation from the Great White Lodge on Sirius. In his books, Djwhal Khul speaks considerably about the Plan, but as with the many grades of consciousness there are various levels to the Plan. The Hierarchy has an immediate Plan which is being implemented right now. This Plan is based on a larger Purpose known only in Shamballa, "where the will of God is known."

The immediate Plan of the Hierarchy involves the creation of a global civilization of international cooperation and goodwill based on right human relations and freedom in all countries. This Plan is part of a larger Plan, and when the Great Invocation ends with the words "restore the Plan on Earth," this edict comes ultimately from the Lord of Sirius and it is directed to our solar Logos and Sanat Kumara.

The Plan has various levels of meaning depending on one's perspective. In the Sirian sense, restoring the Plan on Earth means making up the time lost when the Atlantean catastrophe occurred and humanity fell victim to the forces of darkness. Then the Hierarchy withdrew, leaving mankind to struggle with its own maturing process with only occasional guidance from the Messengers of the Hierarchy (Krishna, Buddha, Moses, Christ, Mohammed and others). This Plan is cosmic in scope. Its long range goals encompass much more than our planet alone, but as pointed out in chapter 10 (in the section "The Work of the Sirian Lodge"), the human kingdom is to serve as "an outpost of Consciousness of God in the solar system" and is destined to be "a factor in the solar system, bringing about changes...in the planetary life and lives...and inducing an interstellar activity."

From the planetary perspective, "Restore the Plan on Earth" means implementing the immediate Plan of the Hierarchy by creating a world of peace and brotherhood, resulting in the reappearance of the Christ, the externalisation of the Hierarchy and the restoration of the Mysteries. Then the Earth and its inhabitants can begin to fulfill their true purpose as a station of Light within the solar system. Restoring the Plan on Earth involves much more than the affairs of our own planet. The Earth is a vital part of a larger cosmic purpose, and until our tiny planet restores the Plan on Earth, the larger cosmic Plan is unattainable.

In the last chapter, the House of Horus was shown to be the 140 planes of consciousness below that of the causal body of the solar Logos. There is a deeper meaning here however, that relates to the Lives Who live in the House of Horus. The term "house" not only means structure, but more importantly it signifies a line of Enlightened Beings stretching from the Hierarchy of our planet to the Great White Lodge on Sirius. We can all become members of this House. The House of Horus is a House of Initiates living within the body of the Logos—planetary, solar, and cosmic. It is the work of the Sirian Lodge to train the initiates who reside in the House of Horus—and the Hierarchy of our planet is an integral part of this training process. This is all part of the effort to restore the Plan on Earth.

So, the "House" is not only where we dwell, but an Order,

Brotherhood, or Lodge of Enlightened Beings Who have attained Mastery over the human dimension of living. All traditions worldwide have produced such Liberated Souls through the ages. Membership in this House of Horus is not limited by race, religion, or ethnic background, but only by selfishness, hatred, and bigotry.

The phrase "restore the Plan on Earth" contains five words. This may come as no surprise to us at this point of our study. As the previous passage says, "a factor of five constantly recurs in its interior measurements." So the Great Pyramid of words continues along the same theme. This phrase contains twenty-one letters. Again, the symbolism is consistent (and persistent) in that it points directly to the twenty-one key words and their relationship to Sanat Kumara. This is reinforced further by the fact that 5 words x 21 letters = 105, or the number of Kumaras Who came to Earth from the Venus chain.

The numerology of this five word phrase demonstrates beyond doubt the consummating beauty of this entire Word of Power.

"Restore the Plan on Earth" equals
- 257 (AN) or 2 + 5 + 7 = 14, 1 + 4 = FIVE
- 104 (RAN) 1 + 0 + 4 = FIVE

The capstone of the Great Invocation *equals 5, contains five words, and twenty-one letters*. What could be more appropriate for the summit of this profound invocation of Light, Love, and Power?

Let's examine these numbers a bit more closely. The RAN value of the five word phrase is 104. This number corresponds to the phrase "the lifting of the veil." This is exactly what the symbolism of the missing capstone on the Great Pyramid means. When the Plan is restored on Earth (thus activating the next phase of the greater Plan), "the lifting of the veil" will occur. This implies some sort of revelation for the world. Here is an intriguing quotation from Djwhal Khul:

> The consensus of opinion in the religious and spiritualistic fields and in the field of biblical prophecy, and likewise a study of the symbolism of the Pyramid, lead students to believe that the immediate future will see some great event and some unforeseen spiritual happening. This should be duly anticipated, and careful preparation should be made for it. I refer not to any coming of any individual. I refer to a natural process with far-reaching effects.[2]

The veil that will be lifted may refer to some new ability of the human eye to see onto the etheric plane. Humanity will then be aware of an entirely new world of reality existing right in its midst. Etheric vision would forever change our materialistic concept of the universe and life after death. The Tibetan continues:

> We only need more light, in the esoteric sense, in order to see the soul, and that light will shortly be available and we shall understand the meaning of the words, "And in Thy light shall we see light."[3]

The Tibetan explains that the quality of light is currently changing, and these changes have occurred several times through the ages. He mentions three kinds of light which affect life on our planet: "The light of the sun...light in the planet itself...A light seeping in...from the astral plane."[4] He then tells of a fourth type of light:

> A light which is beginning to merge itself with the other three types and which comes from that state of matter which we call the mental plane—a light in its turn reflected from the realm of the soul.[5]

DK goes on to say that these four qualities of light will continue to intensify until the year 2025, at which point their radiation will level off and become steady. The intensification of these lights are breaking down the barrier between the astral and physical planes.

> The light from the astral plane (a starry radiance) and the light of the planet itself will be more closely blended, and the result upon humanity and upon the three kingdoms in nature cannot be over-emphasized. It will, for one thing, profoundly affect the human eye and make the present sporadic etheric vision a universal asset. It will bring within the radius of our range of contact the infra-red and ultra-violet gamut of colours, and we shall see what at present is hidden.[6]

The Tibetan gave this information in the 1930's, and we are certainly seeing this process working out in the world. The development of lasers, microwaves, radio telescopes, and astronomical instruments which detect many forms of light radiation in space are examples of this intensification. The dramatic change in the ozone layer above the north and south poles may also be an indication of these changes. Finally, the overall increase in psychic phenomena, angel sightings, religious visions, UFO activity, and close encounters with alien life forms may indicate the development of etheric vision. These all represent humanity's increasing ability to see what was once hidden but living in our midst at another level of consciousness. The edict from on High, "restore the Plan on Earth" (104), thus equates and coincides with "the lifting of the veil" (104).

The AN value of "restore the Plan on Earth" equals 257. There is only one other phrase in the Esoteric Numerology Lists (appendix E) which corresponds to 257; however, it is not an AN value, but a RAN value. Esoterically present in the final five words of the Great Invocation, culminating at the apex of the seven tier pyramid, is the phrase *"Sirius—the Star of Sensitivity—governing the Hierarchy"*[7] (257 RAN). This phrase consists of 47 letters. The two phrases in the Esoteric Numerology Lists with RAN values of 47 are "Isis-Sothis" and "The Christ." Indeed, Sirius (Isis-Sothis) is the Christ—it is the Cosmic Christ, the Second Aspect of the One About Whom Naught May Be Said.

Placement of the Capstone

If the missing capstone of the Great Pyramid of Giza was ever found and set in place on the topmost stonework, it would rest on the 203rd tier. A diagram depicting this appears in the book *The Great Pyramid Decoded*. The 203rd tier is a curious feature relating to the esoteric numerology of the star Sirius.

The last chapter contained the phrase "The eye of the Son—carrying light from Sirius." The last three words of this phrase, "light from Sirius," equals 203 (AN). Therefore, light from Sirius (203) is esoterically connected to the Great Pyramid at the 203rd level, the planned location for the missing capstone. Curiously, "the House of Horus" also equals 203 (AN). Putting these three elements together creates the idea that the light from Sirius meets the House of Horus at the 203rd level where the capstone should be located. What might all this indicate?

We have established the symbolic meaning of the House of Horus to be that of the solar Logos. In terms of numbers, this may signify the 140 distinct planes of awareness located below the causal body or soul body of the solar Logos. Let's expand our thinking to include the idea that the unfinished Great Pyramid symbolizes the current situation of the solar Logos Who is polarized on the cosmic astral plane but seeking mental polarization. The 203rd level of the Great Pyramid is where the capstone will be placed in order to complete the pyramid and bring about perfection. The 203 tiers of stonework are analogous to the 140 planes of the solar Logos. When the Logos is able to establish causal consciousness or fusion with the 141st plane of consciousness, the capstone will be symbolically placed, and the 204th tier will crown the pyramid and establish perfection. Then the House of Horus will be fully functional, and light from Sirius will pour into our entire solar system and irradiate every world and plane of existence within it.

This number symbolism is literally mapped onto the 343 planes of consciousness shown in figure 46. (Also note appendix D3.) Each plane actually contains two values, depending on which way the planes are counted. Therefore, the 141st sub-subplane is also the 203rd level. This suggests, symbolically at least, that the causal body of the solar Logos is immersed in the "light from Sirius" (203).

Figure 46. Plane of the Great Invocation.

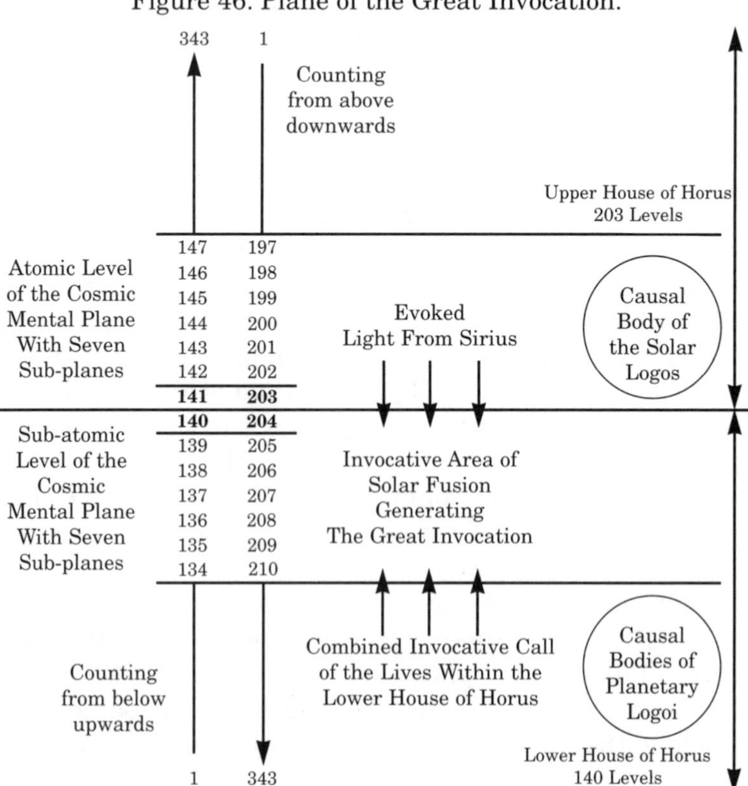

In addition, the 140th sub-subplane is also the 204th level. So when the light from Sirius (203) penetrates the 140th plane, it also enters, the 204th plane, symbolizing the placement of the capstone or the 204th tier of stonework on the Great Pyramid. The Great Invocation is a prototypal cosmic seed representing the future completed House of Horus with the capstone already in place. Its seven tiers and 140 components are crowned with the command "restore the Plan on Earth."

We can say that the House of Horus has a dual existence. First, it is the 140 planes below the level of the causal body of the solar Logos. This represents the personality vehicle of the solar Logos and is symbolically indicated by the 7 tier pyramid of 140 blocks. Second, "the House of Horus" (203) is the higher spiritual aspect of the lower form (140 planes). In actuality, since the ageless wisdom posits the existence of 343 levels of consciousness within the One About Whom Naught May Be Said, then the causal body of the solar Logos is located within the 203 levels above the 140 lower sub-subplanes (140 + 203 = 343). Again, "as above, so below"—the lower worlds comprising the 140 planes are the lower reflection of the 203 causal and spiritual planes above them. Thus, "the House of Horus" (203) reflects itself in the 140 sub-subplanes below it, encompassing the totality of 343 planes.

The solar Logos is building a cosmic bridge of light between levels 134 and 140 or 210 and 204, depending on which direction the sub-subplanes are counted. In order to accomplish this task, the solar Logos must contact the "light from Sirius" (203), which immerses "the House of Horus" (203) at the 203rd tier or 141st sub-subplane. Remember, just as the human personality in incarnation must invoke its own spiritual soul at the causal level (appendix D2), so too, the personality of the solar Logos must penetrate and fuse with Its spiritual soul on Its own high cosmic plane (appendix D3 and figure 46). This cosmic invocation process may be in operation at the second subplane of the cosmic mental plane. (We have broken this down further to sub-subplanes 134-140.) As light from across the "divide" is invoked from Sirius by the incarnated solar Logos, cosmic and solar fusion occur, and the bridge of Light is built between the manifested aspect of the solar Logos, His causal body, and the cosmic mental permanent atom, which may be Sirius. This three part bridging is the cosmic antahkarana.

Theoretically, this sub-atomic level of the cosmic mental plane (levels 140-134) is where the Great Invocation was placed by the Lord of Sirius when it was constructed as a Word of Power for this bridging process. In its original form, the Great Invocation is an energy sound of incomprehensible proportions. It is Fire, Electricity, Sound, Color, and Number all in one Cosmic Package. Perhaps this Sound was used by the solar Logos and the solar Hierarchy for millions of years before it was adapted to the needs of the Earth Scheme, where it was entrusted to Sanat Kumara over eighteen million years ago.

The original Word of Power has never been altered, but only reduced in potency as it descended the dimensions from cosmic to solar, planetary, Hierarchical, and individual human use. Perhaps this is why DK said, "The wonder of these mantric stanzas is that they are comprehensible to members of the human family and to members of the Kingdom of God."[8]

Some may wonder why the Great Invocation does not emanate directly from the causal body of the solar Logos, given the importance of the soul aspect in esoteric philosophy. The answer to this question relates to the composition of the energies required to make the Great Invocation effective. This energy formula was deliberately created at the cosmic level so it would vibrate at a sound frequency that would be most effective in fostering the future evolution of human consciousness on Earth. Stepping this energy concentration down to the corresponding plane within our solar system reduces it to the human scale of evolution. This is borne out by the following statement by the Tibetan which provides the key to understanding the importance of the 140th level: "After initiation, the causal body is found on the second subplane of the mental plane, and monadic control then commences."[9] This level of consciousness encompasses the lowest one-seventh of the entire House of Horus, because the second mental subplane is the 20th subplane of the cosmic physical plane, or to use a musical analogy, seven octaves below the level of the solar Logoic causal body.

The initiation to which Djwhal Khul refers is the third, because it is at this expansion of consciousness that the initiate first comes under the influence of the monad. The important point to grasp, however, is the relationship between the second and fifth planes and rays.

> I would have you remember with still greater emphasis the relation of rays II and V and of the second plane, the monadic plane, and the

> fifth plane, the mental plane; it is the relation of these major energies which makes the initiation of the Transfiguration possible.[10]

The cosmic correspondence to these energies is found on the 140th level of the House of Horus. This is why the Great Invocation is so powerful and so effective. It is designed specifically to work with a mentally focused point of concentration (ray five) while holding an attitude of selfless love (ray two). These ray numbers correspond to the second subplane of the fifth mental plane.

It is significant that the Great Invocation has a basic numerical energy of 5, and that it was first used by the fifth root-race during a period of history when the fifth ray of knowledge, science, and technology began to powerfully affect our entire planet. The following comments by DK are of special significance in respect to the originating level and energy composition of the Great Invocation. He is discussing the tremendous effect ray five is having on our planet:

> The effect of these influences is very great and of supreme importance in this fifth root-race, the Aryan race, in this second solar system. Again you can see the clarity of the correspondences which are emerging. I would have you note them again.
>
> 1. Ray II, the Ray of Love-Wisdom; and Ray V, the Ray of Concrete Knowledge or Science.
> 2. The second plane, the monadic plane; and the fifth plane, the mental plane.
> 3. The second solar system of love; and the fifth root-race, the Aryan race, of active intelligence.[11]

The next section will further clarify why the Great Invocation is a Word of Power specifically charged with and composed of cosmic energy found on the second subplane of the fifth cosmic mental plane, or at the highest level of the House of Horus just below the plane of the solar causal body.

Supremacy of the Second Aspect of Love

> In all these basic relationships, that which is the fifth in order is destined to be the instrument, the vehicle or the implementing factor for the second. The Universal Mind, as it works through all the planes of our conscious planetary life, is the creative agent, and form-building factor which makes the revelation of love possible.[12]

This statement by Djwhal Khul is of profound significance to the Great Invocation and its fundamental energy composition on the second subplane of the fifth cosmic plane. This passage follows directly after the last extract in the previous section. The Tibetan is talking about rays five and two.

The Great Invocation is a powerful "instrument...vehicle or...implementing factor" for the second ray of love. The conclusion that the Great Invocation was designed at the level of Universal Mind, the cosmic mental plane, suggests two important clues for understanding its true power. 1) The second subplane of the cosmic mental plane is the higher correspondence to the plane in our solar system on which the human causal body is found when a human being becomes an initiate and true member of the Great White Lodge on Earth—a lower reflection of the Great White Lodge on Sirius. This implies that the Great Invocation is an instrument for consciousness expansion or initiation. 2) The second subplane of every plane resonates to the second plane of the Monad. The second plane is governed by the second Ray of Love-Wisdom.

> The second aspect of the Logos (that of love or the manifestation of the love nature of the Logos, through the medium of the Son) is the one demonstrating in this system. This system is:
>
> - A Son of Necessity, or of desire
> - Vibrant to the key of the cosmic Ray of Love
> - The form through which this ray of cosmic Love...is expressing itself
> - Governed by the cosmic Law of Attraction. The monads of love are the dominating quality.[13]

There are three fundamental laws of the cosmos:

- The Law of Synthesis, Will, The First Aspect
- The Law of Attraction, Love, The Second Aspect
- The Law of Economy, Activity, The Third Aspect

Because our solar Logos is manifesting as the second aspect, the Law of Attraction is the most important law at this time.

Numerical affinity runs throughout all the planes of consciousness; therefore, the second aspect and the second plane are of significant importance to all life in our solar system. The second plane is called the Monadic plane because it is the level at which the essential units of life—the Monads are located. The human Monads exist on the upper three subplanes of the Monadic plane. The Monads of power are located on the first subplane, the Monads of love are found on the second subplane, and the Monads of activity are on the third subplane. Note that all these Monads correspond to the three cosmic laws listed previously. According to the Tibetan, "the majority of the Monads are on the second subplane and they are the Monads of love."[14]

The cosmic Law of Attraction dominates our second aspect solar system. Within our system are seven systemic laws which correspond to each of the seven planes. These laws are:

1. The Law of Vibration
2. The Law of Cohesion
3. The Law of Disintegration
4. The Law of Magnetic Control
5. The Law of Fixation
6. The Law of Love
7. The Law of Sacrifice and Death

These laws also correspond to the seven rays. Because the second cosmic Law of Attraction is dominant in our system, the second Law of Cohesion and the second ray of Love-Wisdom are also significant factors in the life of the entire solar system. Now comes something very subtle but meaningful in relation to the Great Invocation. Djwhal Khul states:

> We might now briefly trace the correspondence in the second round and the second root-race, showing how the Law of Cohesion was specially active at these periods....in the second round, and also in the second race, a definite cohesion is noticeable, and form is more clearly recognisable in outline.[15]

While this passage may not seem very significant, this is the time period when Sanat Kumara entered our fourth chain by transferring from the second chain to the second globe during the second round. At the end of chapter 9 in the section "The Words Made Flesh," we theorized that the 222nd letter of the Great Invocation was a clue to the exact round, globe, and root-race when Sanat Kumara entered our fourth Earth chain. Now in this passage, DK is stating that the second systemic Law of Cohesion was very active during this time period. The following passage reinforces the importance of the second subplane of the cosmic mental plane (the fifth) in relation to the energy comprising the Great Invocation.

> There is a direct channel, as we know, between the atomic subplane on each plane. This is more or less true of each subplane and its corresponding higher subplane numerically, and there is, therefore, a direct and quite expansive channel between the second subplane on all planes, enabling the Monads of love to link up with peculiar facility with all their vehicles when composed of second subplane matter.[16]

This passage makes it quite clear that the energy composition of the Great Invocation on the second subplane of the cosmic mental plane was designed to make it accessible to the Monads of Love on the second Monadic plane of our system, and especially accessible to initiates with causal bodies on the second subplane of our mental plane, or those souls working toward that level of development: as above, so below.

Because the causal body is located on the mental plane, the fifth systemic Law of Fixation is directly related to this entire issue. According to the Tibetan:

> This is the governing law of the mental plane, finding its greater correspondence in the Law of Karma on cosmic mental levels....
>
> This law of the fifth, or mental plane is one of the most important laws with which we have to do at any time...
>
> It is the law under which the evolving personality builds up, during the course of many lives, the causal body...
>
> Each of the seven subsidiary laws is linked to one of the cosmic laws or with the Sirian Law of Karma.[17]

This extract indicates the correlation of the Law of Fixation with the cosmic mental plane and the Law of Karma. Sirius represents the second or soul aspect at cosmic levels, and therefore Sirius governs the Law of Attraction which is the law of the second aspect. Since our solar system is manifesting as the Son or second aspect, the Law of Attraction is the most important of the cosmic laws in our system.

Some time has been spent on explaining the importance of the second Monadic plane, the mental plane, and its second subplane in order to substantiate the reasoning behind the theory that the Great Invocation is a Word of Power specifically charged with the energy of the second subplane of the cosmic mental plane or 140th level of the House of Horus.

From all the foregoing extracts, we see that the cosmic mental plane involves our own solar Logos and the Lord of Sirius. The causal body of the solar Logos is on the cosmic mental plane, and the Law of Karma which governs our entire solar system originates at the cosmic mental level. Since this Law of Karma emanates from the cosmic mental plane and Sirius is polarized at the same level, it is clear that Sirius has a tremendous effect on the life of our solar Logos and the manifestation of this Logos as our solar system on the cosmic physical plane.

We must ask ourselves whether it is a coincidence that the 113 words of the Great Invocation just happen to fit onto a pyramid of seven tiers requiring 140 components to construct. Is it a coincidence that 113 reduces to 5, or that 140 reduces to 5, or that the last 5 words on the capstone reduce to 5 and that their RAN value equals 104, a numeric anagram of 140, that also reduces to 5? Is it a chance occurrence that the AN value of these last 5 words equal 257, and that the numbers 2-5-7 correspond to the all-important cosmic and systemic second Monadic plane, the fifth mental plane, and the seventh physical plane where the Plan must be restored?

We must ask ourselves whether it is a coincidence that the capstone at the summit of the pyramid contains the words "restore the Plan on Earth," which equal 104 (RAN), "the lifting of the veil." And is it a further coincidence when we find the AN value of the same five words equals 257, which corresponds to "Sirius—the Star of Sensitivity—governing the Hierarchy?" Is this not the lifting of the veil of a mystery involving "those advanced Beings Who, from the distant sun, Sirius, the seat of the true Great White Lodge, watch over the destinies of our solar system, but Who pay particular attention (why They do so is not yet revealed) to our relatively little and apparently unimportant planet, the Earth"?

Notes

1. Peter Lemesurier, *The Great Pyramid Decoded,* 26-27.
2. Bailey, *Esoteric Psychology*, vol. I, 103.
3. Ibid., 103.
4. Ibid., 102.
5. Ibid., 102.
6. Ibid., 102-3.
7. Bailey, *Esoteric Astrology,* 198.
8. Bailey, *Discipleship in the New Age,* vol. II, 156.
9. Bailey, *A Treatise on Cosmic Fire,* 578.
10. Bailey, *The Rays and the Initiations,* 593.
11. Ibid., 593.
12. Ibid., 593.
13. Bailey, *A Treatise on Cosmic Fire*, 511.
14. Ibid., 578.
15. Ibid., 579.
16. Ibid., 578.
17. Ibid., 591-92.

14

Conclusion

"In receiving this Invocation, in its use and distribution, you have been participating in a cosmic event of tremendous importance."[1]

These words by Djwhal Khul appeared at the beginning of this book. The impact of these words, after all that has been discovered about the Great Invocation, now has a totally different effect on consciousness. The vision offered us by this glimpse into the energy field of the Great Invocation drives home the esoteric fact that we are fully engaged and immersed in a Plan of cosmic proportions. This Plan encompasses Beings Whose Lives are lived at levels of consciousness beyond our human comprehension. We literally live within the Body of God. To paraphrase St. Paul, God is the One in Whom we live and move and have our being. Our planetary Logos lives within the solar Logos, and He in turn lives within the consciousness of the Lord of Sirius. And all of These, including humanity, are living conscious aspects of the One About Whom Naught May Be Said.

Despite the overwhelming enormity of this grand design and the sense of smallness we feel when faced with the immensity of the cosmic Life, today is the day of opportunity for Humanity. The cosmic cycle, the great wheel has turned, and Man is now central to the Plan of God. The fourth human kingdom, the fourth Creative Hierarchy of Human Monads on the fourth Earth Scheme, in the fourth Earth chain, on the fourth dense globe, in the fourth round of a solar system of the fourth order is now of primary importance in the Life of the solar Logos, because the human kingdom is rapidly achieving mental polarization and its advanced members are taking initiation. This indicates the human kingdom is reaching maturity and becoming useful in the service of the planetary Logos of Earth, and consequently in the solar system itself. It also means the human kingdom is responding to the special Sirian method of evolution called initiation.

The opening of the door to initiation during the fourth root-race was a major achievement for the entire Earth Scheme because the fourth Atlantean root-race represented the exact midpoint of evolution in the overall cycle of manifestation for our planetary Logos. The fourth root-race was the 172nd cyclic impulse out of the possible 343 cycles for our Earth chain. The esoteric fact that the fourth human kingdom in nature produced initiates during the fourth root-race is highly significant and symbolic.

> It might be of interest to here note that Christ was the first of earth humanity to achieve the goal...so rapid was the development of the Christ that in Atlantean days He found Himself upon the Path of Probation...From the angle of evolution the rapid unfoldment of the evolution of Christ was, and has been, *totally unparalleled.* It has never been duplicated.[2]

This event signaled the readiness of the human kingdom to enter into the Sirian evolutionary process of initiation. The fact that one particular human being was developing at such a rapid pace was to have great implications for the future.

> The Sirian influence was not recognised, and little of it was definitely focussed in the Hierarchy, until Christ came and revealed the love of God to humanity. He is the expression, par excellence, of a Sirian initiation, and it is to that high place He will eventually go.[3]

We are told that the Christ became the head of Hierarchy during the period when He overshadowed the Master Jesus 2,000 years ago. Apparently since the time the Christ became the leader of Hierarchy, He, as the first human Sirian Initiate, has been "learning" and "in training" for communication with the Beings on Sirius. We must assume that sometime in the 1940's when the Tibetan was dictating the book *Esoteric Astrology* to Alice Bailey, the Christ made a breakthrough and was able to communicate with the Great White Lodge on Sirius.

> For the first time in the history of both mankind and disciples the energy of Sirius, pouring into the seven groups which form our planetary Hierarchy evokes response.[4]

From the information given, it appears that the Christ was finally able to respond to the Sirian energy inflow, or He had already achieved this goal but was finally able to train the seven groups (ashrams) within the Hierarchy to respond in turn.

After the Second World War, the Christ decided to reappear physically in the world, and therefore, Sanat Kumara gave the Christ permission to use the ancient undated (from the Hierarchy's standpoint) Word of Power called the Invocation for Power and Light.

> If one may venture to speak in such terms (reverent and symbolical), the reward accorded to the Christ, as He announced His decision [to reappear in the world, JB] as final and irrevocable, was the permission or rather the right to use a certain great Invocation—never before granted....The right to use certain great Words of Power or "Stanzas of Direction" is never lightly accorded. The decision of Christ to appear again among men, bringing His disciples with Him, drew forth this permission from the Lord of the World, the Ancient of Days.[5]

Following this momentous event, the Great Invocation was pronounced by the Christ at the time of the full moon of June in 1945, and this was the first time any being outside of Shamballa had ever used this ancient mantram.

> This mantram is peculiarly and essentially Christ's Own mantram and its "*sound* has gone forth" to the entire world through the medium of His enunciation of it and through its use by the Hierarchy.[6]

Why is the Great Invocation Christ's Own mantram? The Great Invocation is Sirian in origin. Therefore, it symbolically belongs to the first human being of the Earth's evolution to reach the level of a

Sirian Initiate—that human being is the One we call the Christ.

What evidence exists to support this theory other than the logic of it as presented in these extracts from Djwhal Khul's books? Such evidence presented by the numbers and structure of the Great Invocation strongly supports such an idea. Following are many of the key points supporting this theory, along with a few new ones.

1. The Great Invocation is composed of five stanzas, seven sentences, thirteen lines, 113 words, and 443 letters. Each one of these is a prime number. This means no other numbers can produce these numbers. The Great Invocation contains energy which is unique unto itself—nothing else can produce such energy.

2. The divine trinity forms the basis of most religions and philosophies, and is a major aspect of the teachings of DK. The Great Invocation yields valuable esoteric information when divided into three parts.

3. The Tetraktys is the Pythagorean name for the first ten numbers (1 - 10). The decad was sacred to many ancient Greek philosophers; they considered it God. When the first ten numbers are added together they equal 55.

4. When the first fifty-five words and the last fifty-five words of the Great Invocation are separated from each other, three words remain in the middle. They are "God is known." This phrase equals 5.

5. The incarnation of our planetary Logos is called Sanat Kumara. The name "Sanat" equals 55.

6. The middle aspect of the trinity is the soul or Christ principle. Therefore, the middle phrase "God is known" implies that God is the middle principle. Esoterically this is true in one sense, because Sanat Kumara is the "Great Sacrifice" Who incarnated as the original savior of our planet, thus exemplifying the middle soul principle that mediates between Spirit and Matter.

7. The middle word of the Great Invocation is "is" which equals 28 (AN), a perfect number. "The star" (RAN) and "Man" (AN) both equal 28. The human kingdom is Man, and symbolically it is meant to become the star of perfection.

8. When the Great Invocation is viewed from the angle of the middle word, there are fifty-six words before and after this middle word. These two sets of fifty-six words have an identical numerological value of 2648. The number 2648 has an intermediate reduction value of 20 (2 + 6 + 4 + 8 = 20), which is the RAN value of Isis.

9. When 2648, 28, and 2648 are reduced to single digits they read 2, 1, 2. The number 212 equals the title "The Dog Star Sirius."

10. The number 56 equals Isis (AN), who was the Egyptian goddess personified as the star Sirius. The number 56 also equals "the sun Sirius" (RAN). Therefore, if these two phrases are superimposed over the two sets of fifty-six words, the Great Invocation reads "Isis is the sun Sirius." This is a statement of fact in relation to the ancient Egyptians.

11. The Great Invocation can also be divided into five parts. These form two sets of twenty-eight words at the beginning, the middle word "is" with a value of 28 at the center, and two more sets of twenty-eight words at the end. If any two sets of twenty-eight words are added to the value of the middle word, the result is 84 (3 x 28 = 84). The number 84 equals "Dog Star."

12. The Great Invocation contains twenty-one key words consisting of ninety-five letters. The arrangement of these twenty-one key words forms a pattern in which there are five key words in stanza one, five in stanza two, three in stanza three, three in stanza four, and five in stanza five or 55335. When the will of God (in stanza three) works out as the Plan of Love and Light in the centre called the "race of men" (in stanza four), the three key words in each of these two stanzas are combined to form 6, or the perfection of form. Then the key

word pattern is fulfilled, and 55335 becomes the number series 5565, or the name Sanat (55) Kumara (65).

13. The number 5565 is a triangular number, the result of adding the first 105 numbers together. DK states that 105 Kumaras came to Earth in order to stimulate the lagging evolution of the human kingdom in the Earth Scheme.

14. The numbers 5 and 6 within the Great Invocation, such as word position combinations (5, 6, 56, and 65), numerological values, words with five and six letters, combinations of 10 and 11 all relate to the theme of Sanat Kumara, the number 21, and the number of the planetary Logos 777. The twenty-one key words link Sanat Kumara to Sirius (95) through the ninety-five letters composing these words.

15. The Venus Scheme and the Earth Scheme are the only two planetary schemes in our solar system as yet which have undergone the process of initiation as a form of evolutionary acceleration. This process of initiation originates on Sirius. When the numerological values of Venus Scheme (134), Earth Scheme (105), Sirius (95), and the total letters in the Great Invocation (443) are added together, they equal 777.

16. The essential words needed to create the Great Invocation total 51; the remaining sixty-two words are simply duplicates of the originals. The number 51 is the number of whole degrees by which a circle can be divided into seven parts. The Greek goddess, Pallas Athena Parthenos is the personification of the number 7 in the Pythagorean school of philosophy. Her name equals 226, and there are 226 letters in the fifty-one essential words of the Great Invocation. The Egyptian trinity of Osiris, Isis, and Horus also equals 226. This septenary theme is extended to the entire Great Invocation when the first forty-nine words (7 x 7) and the last forty-nine words (7 x 7) are separated from the fifteen words remaining at the center. These fifteen words have an AN value of 777. Moreover, when the middle word position (57) is divided into the total letters (443) the result is 7.77. Furthermore, the Great Invocation can be divided into four

units of twenty-eight words each, or 4 x 7 quadrants. The middle word "is" at the center of this cross has a value of 28 or 4 x 7, thus mirroring the surrounding septenary groups. See figure 30 in chapter 10.

17. The middle letter (222nd), the total letters (443), and the total words (113) of the Great Invocation are time markers. The middle letter of the Great Invocation is "s," and it is located at the 222nd position. Sanat Kumara left the 2nd Venus chain and entered the 2nd globe of the Earth chain in the 2nd round. This momentous planetary event is highlighted by the fact that the middle letter of the Great Invocation is located at the 222nd position.
    Sanat Kumara did not physically incarnate until later. He eventually incarnated on the 4th globe (our dense Earth) in the 4th round during the 3rd root-race (Lemurian)—thus 443. The number of cycles between the time of Sanat Kumara's arrival in our fourth Earth chain and His actual physical incarnation on the Earth is exactly 113. This strongly suggests the possibility that He actually entered our fourth chain on the 2nd globe in the 2nd round during the 2nd root-race. DK offers a clue about this when He mentions that the *2nd* Law of Cohesion was particularly active during the *2nd* round and *2nd* root-race.

18. The Great Invocation has a root numerological value of 5; the fifty-one word version has a root value of 5; the twenty-one key words have a root value of 5, and the middle phrase has a root value of 5. When the three crucial middle elements are factored with the root number 5, the following results appear. The middle letter equals 19; 5 x 19 = 95—Sirius. The middle word equals 28; 5 x 28 = 140—all the subplanes of consciousness below the atomic cosmic mental plane of our solar Logos and Sirius. The middle phrase equals 131; 5 x 131 = 655. The 6 and 5s relate to Sanat Kumara and the Great Work of redemption. Sanat Kumara mounted the Fixed Cross (of Cosmic Discipleship) when He entered the fourth Earth chain. The middle phrase "God is known" is Sanat Kumara on the Fixed Cross. Numerologically this results in 655 ("God is known" x 5) + 122 (fixed cross) = 777

(the number symbolizing the redemptive mission of Sanat Kumara).

19. The three words that form the middle phrase are located in word positions 56, 57, and 58. These combined word position numbers equal 171, "The Queen of Heaven," who was Isis-Sothis or Sirius. "Isis-Nephthys," "Hermes-Mercury," and "the Celestial Ship" are related to Sirius, and also equal 171. The following three terms are RAN values:
The Sun Sirius = 56, Initiation = 57, and Cosmic Christ = 58.

20. There are no words in the Great Invocation with a numerological value (AN) greater than 110 (that word is "purpose"). By using a word position number in the Great Invocation, the numerological value of that word can be used to find another word. Since the Great Invocation has only 113 words, this indicates there is no way to reference a word with a value that lies "outside" the Great Invocation. This process of jumping from word to word eventually leads to an infinity loop. That loop contains the words "the," "of," "Light," and "God." These words can form the phrase "The Light of God" or "The God of Light." The AN value of these four words is 136. This number is the RAN value of "The Great White Lodge on Sirius."

21. The words of the Great Invocation can literally be placed onto the blocks of a pyramid. In order to include all the words, a pyramid must have seven tiers. A pyramid composed of cubical blocks seven tiers high contains 140 blocks, the House of Horus. These blocks symbolize the number of subplanes in which the solar Logos is manifesting at this time. If the words of the Great Invocation were inscribed on the faces of the blocks of a seven tier pyramid from the bottom to the apex, the capstone would hold the final five words of the Great Invocation. Those words are "restore the Plan on Earth." There are twenty-one letters in this phrase. The value of this phrase is 104 (RAN) and 257 (AN), with its root value equaling 5—the same as the other major elements of the Great Invocation. The RAN correspondence to the number 257 is "Sirius—the Star of Sensitivity—governing the Hierarchy."

These twenty-one points speak for themselves. There is no doubt that all of this information can be mined from the depths of this Word of Power. The question remains as to whether this Great Invocation was ingeniously constructed in such a way in order to convey powerful esoteric facts about the origin and nature of the world. After spending over three years and many hundreds of hours of meditation, reflection, and analysis, I believe the Master Djwhal Khul deliberately constructed and coded a message within the message called the Great Invocation. After discovering all the magical, profound, and subtle weavings, the intricate connections and layered meanings of number and structure, symbology and correspondence, analogy and metaphor, the Great Invocation suddenly extends beyond the surface of its words to new heights of meaning and significance. These words by the Tibetan now convey new meaning:

> The meaning of this Invocation has been expressed in terms which are understandable, in a measure, to the average person because of its familiar wording, based on many Scriptural terms. *But the true inner implications and significances are of very deep import and are not superficially apparent.* I challenge you to penetrate, through meditation, more deeply into the vital meaning of these words, these amazing words.[7] [My emphasis, JB.]

The actual Great Invocation is energy. When DK speaks of the "vital meaning of these words," He means the etheric energy field of this Word of Power. The words which DK used to construct this Great Invocation are based upon the essential and vital etheric waveform or sound of the Mantram as it exists on the inner planes. Whether that plane is the fourth cosmic etheric, the buddhic plane where the Hierarchy is now located, or some other level is not as important as the fact that this Word of Power possesses an essential energy signature composed of vibration, sound, color, and number. The words constituting the Great Invocation are points of anchorage and definition for use on the physical plane. Once the "gravity" of the words is overcome, we are free to escape into the sacred space of the Mantram Itself. At that level we are able to contact the internal channels that connect this sacred sound to its root energy sources.

In order for the Great Invocation to retain its potency, DK had to translate it into English words and phrases which would be meaningful to people from different regions and religious backgrounds of the world (even when translated into other languages). But the resonating frequencies of the seven original etheric word forms had to remain intact, otherwise the Great Invocation would not be effective as a true Word of Power. Therefore, the English words Djwhal Khul chose to construct this mantram directly reflect the underlying esoteric energy pattern. By applying numbers to these words we have stepped inside the Great Invocation; we have penetrated below the surface of the words and sought the internal vibrational frequencies relating the words to their essential source.

If the Great Invocation is the most powerful tool we have for invoking the reappearance of the Christ and restoring the Plan on Earth, then it should contain information that is foundational, fundamental, and essential to the purposes of Those Who originally created it. People who change the Great Invocation should not delude themselves into thinking they have merely altered a few words. What they have done, in fact, is destroyed the esoteric and vital energy framework that makes it a true Word of Power. In reality, they are no longer contacting or bringing through the energy which is meant to be released when the Great Invocation is used. They have removed all the esoteric underpinnings that make it truly effective according to the intent of its Creators. In fact, according to Djwhal Khul: "...it embodies the divine intent and summarizes the conclusions of the planetary Logos."[8] Once the Great Invocation is changed, it is simply a different prayer or mantram and should not be referred to as the Great Invocation because the vital etheric energy pattern of the original is not present.[9]

By accepting the hypothesis that the Great Invocation is older than humanity and was created far beyond our own planet, we are faced with a profound challenge to our standard frame of reference. Our evolution as a species was planned, and at the hour of birth when individualization occurred through the sacrifice of Sanat Kumara, the energy formula, the sacred Word of Power we know as the Great Invocation was also born. Sanat Kumara and the 104 Exalted Beings of Shamballa used this Sirian Mantram to stabilize and nurture the newborn human kingdom with the sacred milk, the nectar, the soma of Sirius. The vibratory sound of the Great Invocation, the primordial energy of Sirius, was fed into the pristine causal bodies (the egoic buds) of the newborn human family. The heart of every permanent atom of each human soul was saturated with the SOUND of the Sacred Word of Power entrusted to

Sanat Kumara for the fostering of the new kingdom of humanity.

We are thus forced to think in terms which shatter the boundaries of ordinary thinking. We must think as the soul thinks. We must expand the horizons of our minds to include worlds and dimensions beyond the familiar and mundane. To grasp the magnitude of this expanded vision, we are forced to experience the entire concept of the Great Invocation four dimensionally, that is, beyond the three worlds of conventional activity, emotion, and number-crunching analytical thinking. We are being asked to think synthetically, intuitively, abstractly, beyond space and time, beyond the nuts and bolts world of mechanical computation. Only the open eye of the soul, the eye of the Son, the eye of Horus, the eye of Christ can respond to the Light of Love. This is a Light of all-encompassing inclusiveness irradiating that which has always remained hidden to the eyes of humanity, prior to the emergence of the Light and Love of Sirius, realized and anchored on Earth by the Christ 2,000 years ago.

The implications of everything presented in this book demand that we think at the level of the Spiritual Soul, free of the fetters of linear thought. The beautiful and magnificent pattern of Light woven into this Great Invocation invites us to see with the eye of Horus, for this Great Word of Power carries light from Sirius, the Light of Liberation through Initiation, "the Light which ever shineth in the East."

Notes

1. Bailey, *Discipleship in the New Age,* vol. II, 187-88.
2. Bailey, *Esoteric Psychology,* vol. II, 210.
3. Bailey, *The Rays and the Initiations,* 415.
4. Bailey, *Esoteric Astrology,* 198.
5. Bailey, *The Reappearance of the Christ,* 72-73.
6. Bailey, *Discipleship in the New Age,* vol. II, 173.
7. Ibid., 156.
8. Ibid., 156.
9. In fact, shortly after Djwhal Khul gave Alice Bailey the Great Invocation, He suggested that Christians might find it easier to use if the third verse said "The Purpose which the Master knows and serves" or "which disciples know and serve." By making these modifications, the potency of the mantram is altered somewhat but it is still effective to some degree. This alternative wording also changes the final root value total of the Great Invocation to 6 rather than 5, and the entire meaning of the key words is disrupted. See Bailey, *Discipleship in the New Age*, vol. II, 157.

Afterword

I had a friend who was a joy to be with; comforting and kind, wise and inspiring, with traits and qualities as human as myself. Yet unknown to me all the while, my companion was an Emissary from beyond my world. I had been in the presence of One Who carried the true story of my past, the blueprint of my future. I had taken this friend into my heart and soul and never realized the tremendous majesty and power I had absorbed into the fiber of my human frame and mind. I never realized the transforming power of our relationship.

Now I see with eyes which cannot be closed again. My friend who is so much like me, is a Power from on high in human guise. Unknowingly, I traveled with a Messenger from the stars. I never quite knew why, but in times of trouble the words of my friend brought Light where only darkness reigned. Like magic this voice produced a Sound so pure, yet I never heard more than my own small voice repeating its words as they echoed in my mind. What a patient friend indeed, for this great Visitor from on High stayed in my presence till I was ready to hear the message held tight within that sacred heart—a message for us all.

Like so many others, I have spent many hours with the Great Invocation, and never knew the enormity of its meaning; the capacity of its words; the extent of its influence until I applied number and symbol to its structure. The pages of this book speak for themselves. Now we know the enormous power hidden within this Sacred Vessel. The Great Invocation is "wired" to the cosmos. This dynamo, powered by the electric waters of Life, generates and delivers transformative energy wherever it finds an outlet.

Knowing the conduits of spiritual transmission hidden within this simple prayer should inspire us all to use this Great Invocation with renewed strength and clear intent. Now we know when we sound the Great Invocation we are linking ourselves to a network of profound proportions extending far beyond anything we ever imagined. May the energy of the Great Invocation transform our world with the Light, Love, and Power it brings into our midst.

Appendices

Master List of the Great Invocation

Word Pos.	Word	No. Ltrs.	AN Val.	RAN Val.	Root Val.
1	From	4	52	25	7
2	the	3	33	15	6
3	point	5	74	29	11
4	of	2	21	12	3
5	Light	5	56	29	11
6	within	6	83	38	11
7	the	3	33	15	6
8	Mind	4	40	22	22
9	of	2	21	12	3
10	God	3	26	17	8
11	Let	3	37	10	1
12	light	5	56	29	11
13	stream	6	76	22	22
14	forth	5	67	31	4
15	into	4	58	22	22
16	the	3	33	15	6
17	minds	5	59	23	5
18	of	2	21	12	3
19	men	3	32	14	5
20	Let	3	37	10	1
21	Light	5	56	29	11
22	descend	7	54	27	9
23	on	2	29	11	11
24	Earth	5	52	25	7
25	From	4	52	25	7
26	the	3	33	15	6
27	point	5	74	29	11
28	of	2	21	12	3
29	Love	4	54	18	9
30	within	6	83	38	11
31	the	3	33	15	6
32	Heart	5	52	25	7
33	of	2	21	12	3
34	God	3	26	17	8
35	Let	3	37	10	1
36	love	4	54	18	9
37	stream	6	76	22	22
38	forth	5	67	31	4
39	into	4	58	22	22
40	the	3	33	15	6
41	hearts	6	71	26	8
42	of	2	21	12	3
43	men	3	32	14	5
44	May	3	39	12	3
45	Christ	6	77	32	5
46	return	6	96	33	6
47	to	2	35	8	8
48	Earth	5	52	25	7
49	From	4	52	25	7
50	the	3	33	15	6
51	centre	6	65	29	11
52	where	5	59	32	5
53	the	3	33	15	6
54	Will	4	56	20	2
55	of	2	21	12	3
56	God	3	26	17	8
57	is	2	28	10	1
58	known	5	77	23	5

Word Pos.	Word	No. Ltrs.	AN Val.	RAN Val.	Root Val.
59	Let	3	37	10	1
60	purpose	7	110	38	11
61	guide	5	46	28	1
62	the	3	33	15	6
63	little	6	78	24	6
64	wills	5	75	21	3
65	of	2	21	12	3
66	men	3	32	14	5
67	The	3	33	15	6
68	purpose	7	110	38	11
69	which	5	51	33	6
70	the	3	33	15	6
71	Masters	7	95	23	5
72	know	4	63	18	9
73	and	3	19	10	1
74	serve	5	69	24	6
75	From	4	52	25	7
76	the	3	33	15	6
77	centre	6	65	29	11
78	which	5	51	33	6
79	we	2	28	10	1
80	call	4	28	10	1
81	the	3	33	15	6
82	race	4	27	18	9
83	of	2	21	12	3
84	men	3	32	14	5
85	Let	3	37	10	1
86	the	3	33	15	6
87	Plan	4	43	16	7
88	of	2	21	12	3
89	Love	4	54	18	9
90	and	3	19	10	1
91	Light	5	56	29	11
92	work	4	67	22	22
93	out	3	56	11	11
94	And	3	19	10	1
95	may	3	39	12	3
96	it	2	29	11	11
97	seal	4	37	10	1
98	the	3	33	15	6
99	door	4	52	25	7
100	where	5	59	32	5
101	evil	4	48	21	3
102	dwells	6	75	21	3
103	Let	3	37	10	1
104	Light	5	56	29	11
105	and	3	19	10	1
106	Love	4	54	18	9
107	and	3	19	10	1
108	Power	5	77	32	5
109	restore	7	100	37	1
110	the	3	33	15	6
111	Plan	4	43	16	7
112	on	2	29	11	11
113	Earth	5	52	25	7
TOTALS	113	443	5324	2210	752
	5	11	14	5	14
	5	11	5	5	5

Word Position Index

1 From 52	2 the 33	3 point 74	4 of 21	5 Light 56	6 within 83	7 the 33
8 Mind 40	9 of 21	10 God 26	11 Let 37	12 light 56	13 stream 76	14 forth 67
15 into 58	16 the 33	17 minds 59	18 of 21	19 men 32	20 Let 37	21 Light 56
22 descend 54	23 on 29	24 Earth 52	25 From 52	26 the 33	27 point 74	28 of 21
29 Love 54	30 within 83	31 the 33	32 Heart 52	33 of 21	34 God 26	35 Let 37
36 love 54	37 stream 76	38 forth 67	39 into 58	40 the 33	41 hearts 71	42 of 21
43 men 32	44 May 39	45 Christ 77	46 return 96	47 to 35	48 Earth 52	49 From 52
50 the 33	51 centre 65	52 where 59	53 the 33	54 will 56	55 of 21	56 God 26
			57 is 28			
58 known 77	59 Let 37	60 purpose 110	61 guide 46	62 the 33	63 little 78	64 wills 75
65 of 21	66 men 32	67 The 33	68 purpose 110	69 which 51	70 the 33	71 Masters 95
72 know 63	73 and 19	74 serve 69	75 From 52	76 the 33	77 centre 65	78 which 51
79 we 28	80 call 28	81 the 33	82 race 27	83 of 21	84 men 32	85 Let 37
86 the 33	87 Plan 43	88 of 21	89 Love 54	90 and 19	91 Light 56	92 work 67
93 out 56	94 And 19	95 may 39	96 it 29	97 seal 37	98 the 33	99 door 52
100 where 59	101 evil 48	102 dwells 75	103 Let 37	104 Light 56	105 and 19	106 Love 54
107 and 19	108 Power 77	109 restore 100	110 the 33	111 Plan 43	112 on 29	113 Earth 52

113 Steps of Sanat Kumara

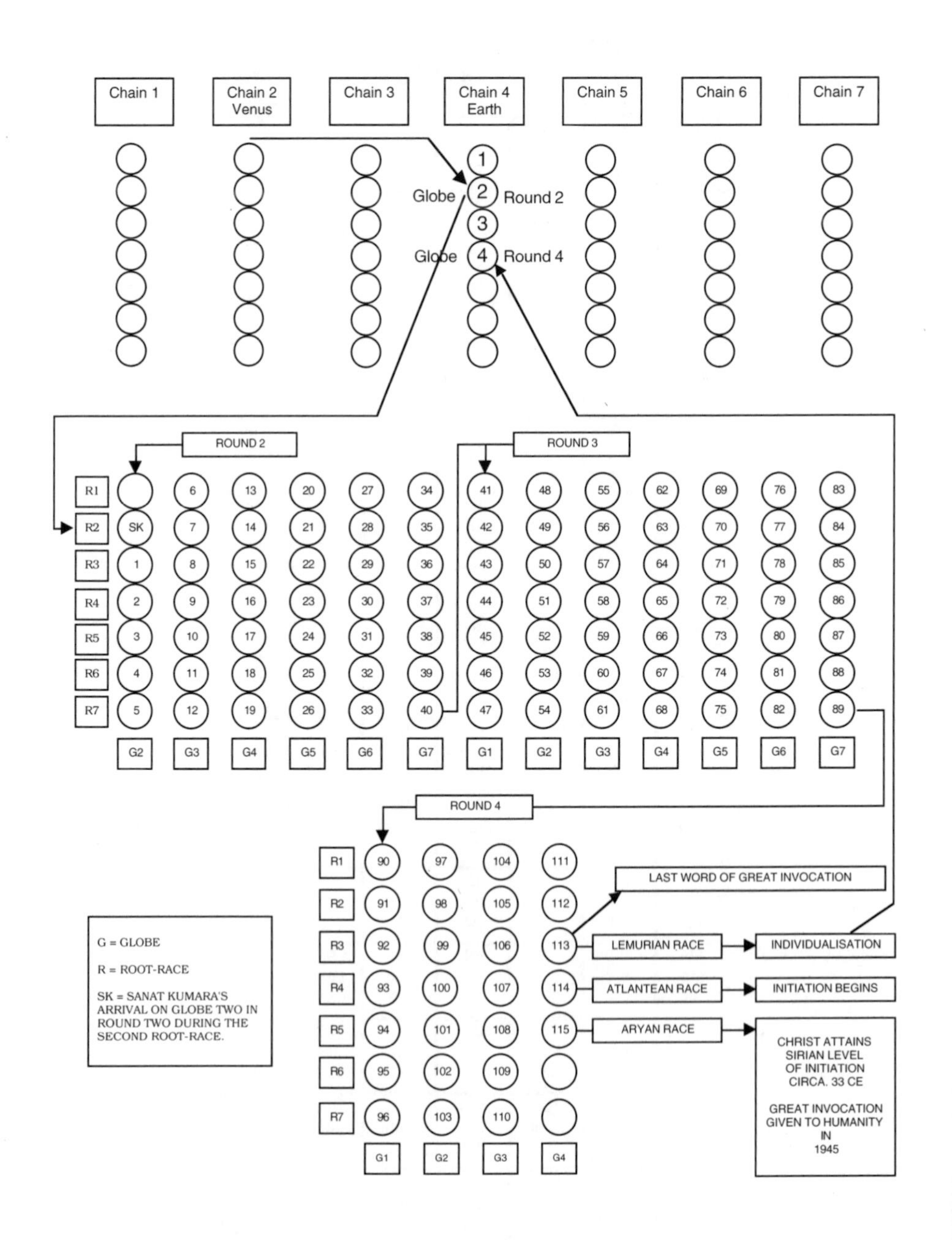

The Seven Cosmic Planes of Life

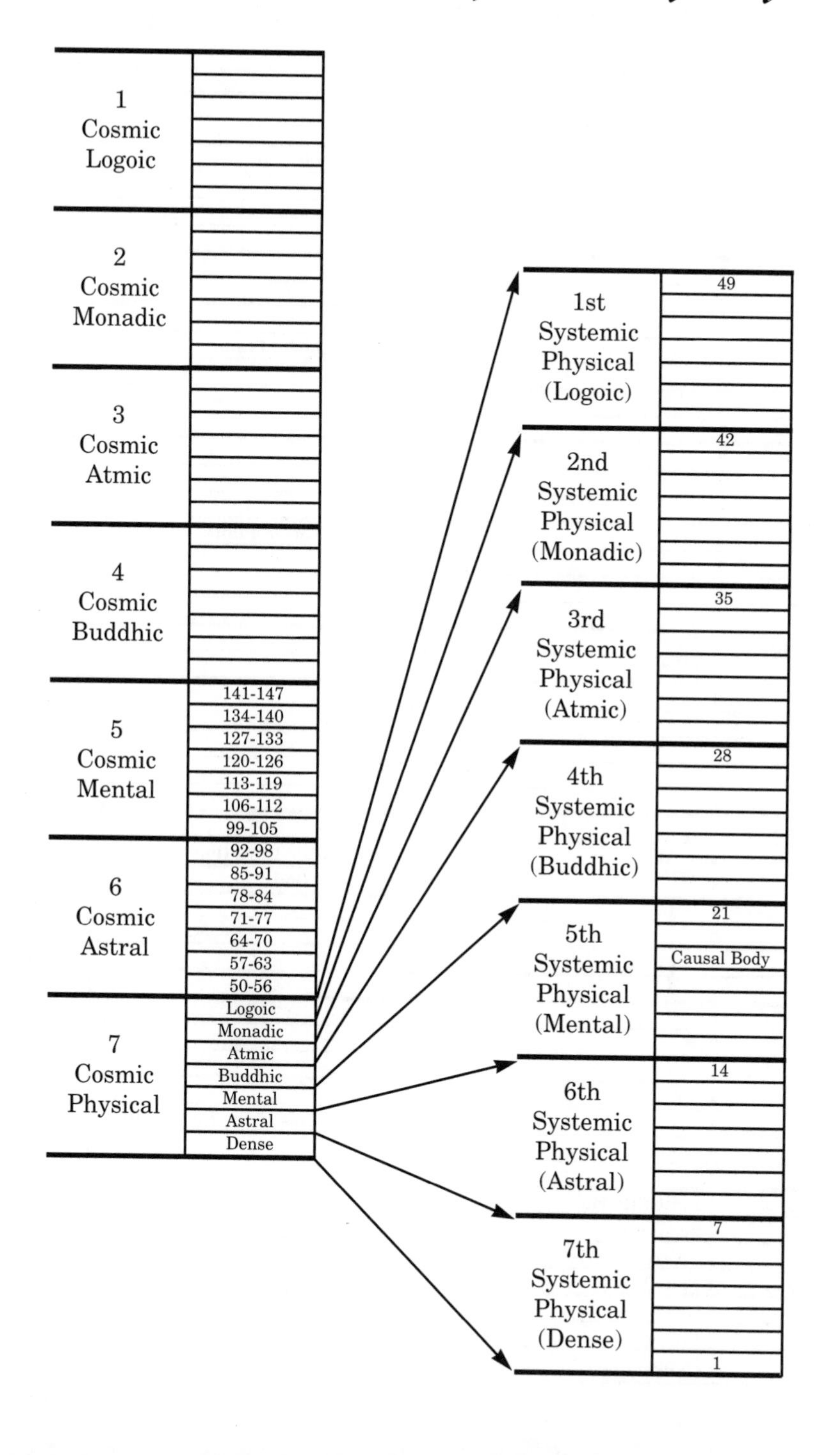

The Seven Subplanes of the Cosmic Physical Plane

Plane	Subplane		No.
Logoic	1 Atomic Subplane	First Cosmic Etheric Plane	49
	2 Sub-Atomic		48
	3 Subplane		47
1	4 Subplane		46
	5 Subplane		45
	6 Subplane		44
	7 Subplane		43
Monadic	1	Second Cosmic Etheric Plane	42
	2		41
	3		40
2	4		39
	5		38
	6		37
	7		36
Atmic	1	Third Cosmic Etheric Plane	35
	2		34
	3		33
3	4		32
	5		31
	6		30
	7		29
Buddhic	1	Fourth Cosmic Etheric Plane	28
	2		27
	3		26
4	4		25
	5		24
	6		23
	7		22
Mental	1	Abstract	21
Gaseous	2	▲ Causal after Initiation	20
	3	▲ Causal Body	19
5	4	Concrete / 18 Subplanes of the Personality	18
	5		17
	6		16
	7		15
Astral	1		14
Liquid	2		13
	3		12
6	4		11
	5		10
	6		9
	7		8
Physical	1 First Etheric		7
Dense	2 Second Etheric		6
	3 Third Etheric		5
7	4 Fourth Etheric		4
	5 Gaseous		3
	6 Liquid		2
	7 Dense		1

Planes of the Solar Logos

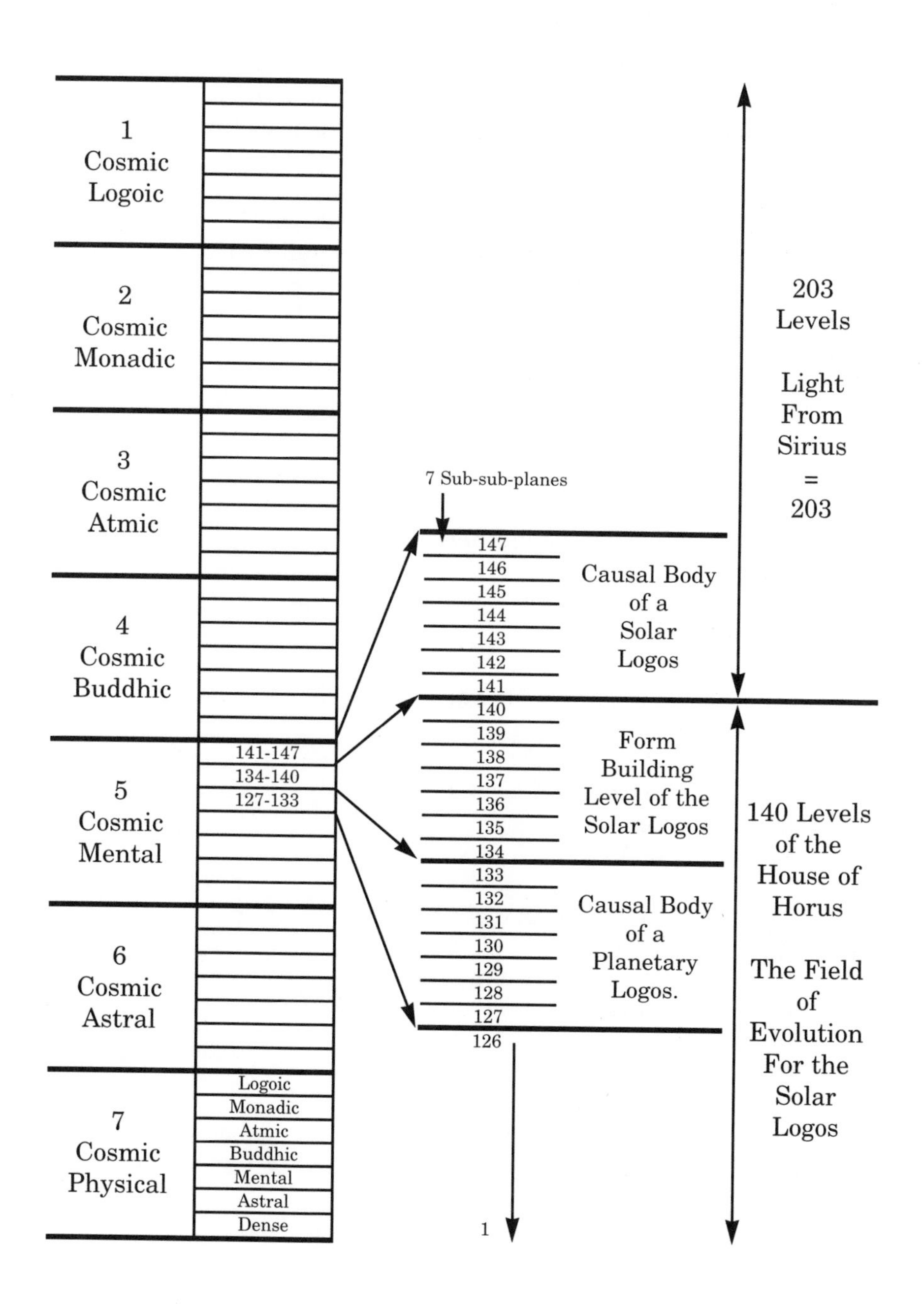

Esoteric Numerology Lists

The following list of esoteric words and phrases is arranged in four different categories—alphabetical, AN values, RAN values, and Root values. I have included a number of terms which do not appear in the main text. These entries suggest some connection to the Great Invocation, but not enough to warrant detailed discussion at the expense of more important terms. I am including them, however, in the interests of continuing research.

NOTE: Terms with asterisks indicate items which are not master numbers by *both* methods of calculation, i.e. AN and RAN.

Alphabetical

AN	RAN	Root	Terms
212	95	5	A New Heaven and A New Earth
46	19	1	Adept
190	82	1	Adept Using Energy
39	21	3	Angel
66	21	3	Anubis
75	21	3	Anukis
69	42	6	Archangel
120	75	3	Archangel Michael
35	26	8	Argha
41	23	5	Argo
212	95	5	Argo The Celestial Ship
66	21	3	Argus
30	12	3	Ark
98	35	8	Aspirant
262	118	1	Aspirant Disciple Initiate
49	22	22	Athena*
240	114	6	Athena The Virgin Mother
53	26	8	Athene
63	18	9	Avatar
159	69	6	Birth of Horus
83	38	11	Blue Lodge
252	81	9	Central Spiritual Sun
77	32	5	Christ
139	58	4	Cosmic Christ
321	114	6	Cosmic Christ The Sun Sirius
74	20	11	Cross*
73	28	1	Crown

AN	RAN	Root	Terms
95	41	5	Curtained
41	23	5	Dagon
77	41	5	Disciple
203	113	5	Divine Hermaphrodite
84	30	3	Dog Star
59	32	5	Dragon
163	73	1	Dragon of Wisdom
182	74	11	Dragons of Wisdom
52	25	7	Earth
105	51	6	Earth Scheme
140	41	5	Eastern Star
58	31	4	Emerald
192	84	3	Emerald Orange Cross
95	32	5	Empress
74	38	11	Energy
120	57	3	Energy Adept
48	21	3	Evil
42	24	6	Five
183	93	3	Fourth Hierarchy
161	71	8	Fourth Kingdom
57	39	3	Gemini
26	17	8	God
131	50	5	God Is Known
73	28	1	Goddess
51	24	6	Great
77	41	5	Great Bear
173	74	11	Great Invocation
107	62	8	Green Emerald
70	34	7	Hathor
52	25	7	Heart
99	54	9	Heart of God
160	61	7	Heart of the Sun
55	28	1	Heaven
196	70	7	Heavenly Jerusalem
120	48	3	Heavenly Man
91	37	1	Hercules
140	77	5	Hermaphrodite
68	32	5	Hermes
171	72	9	Hermes Mercury
139	58	4	Hermes Thoth
247	85	4	Hermes Trismegistus
95	59	5	Hierarchy

AN	RAN	Root	Terms
114	60	6	Hierophant
81	27	9	Horus
170	62	8	House of Horus
57	21	3	Human
111	39	3	Humanity
95	41	5	I am That I am
192	84	3	Individualisation
87	42	6	Initiate
120	57	3	Initiation
313	142	7	Invocation for Power and Light
56	20	11	Isis*
171	63	9	Isis Nephthys
146	47	11	Isis-Sothis
289	82	1	Isis Sothis Anukis Satis
384	114	6	Isis-Sothis Anukis Satis Sirius
148	58	4	Isis Unveiled
113	50	5	Isis Veiled
104	32	5	Jerusalem
74	11	11	Jesus
151	43	7	Jesus Christ
65	20	11	Kumara*
84	21	3	Kumaras
189	126	9	Kumaras 105
32	14	5	Leo
56	29	11	Light
343	127	1	Light From Eastern Star Sirius
203	86	5	Light From Sirius
353	146	11	Light Love And Power From Sirius
50	23	5	Lion
189	81	9	Lion of Cosmic Will
383	158	5	Lions The Divine And Tawny Orange Flames
43	25	7	Lodge
68	23	5	Logos
49	22	22	Lord*
165	66	3	Lord of Sirius
175	76	4	Lord of The World
133	52	7	Lords of Karma
159	69	6	Lords of The Flame
54	18	9	Love
74	38	11	Lucifer
45	18	9	Makara
28	10	1	Man

AN	RAN	Root	Terms
48	12	3	Manas
76	22	22	Master*
95	23	5	Masters
103	40	4	Mercury
74	29	11	Messiah
51	33	6	Michael
40	22	22	Mind*
87	51	6	Mind of God
289	154	1	Mind of God Heart of God Will of God
47	20	11	Monad*
79	34	7	Mother
56	29	11	Neith
115	43	7	Nephthys
95	32	5	Neptune
70	25	7	Nommo
68	23	5	Oannes
60	33	6	Orange
134	53	8	Orange Cross
89	35	8	Osiris
226	82	1	Osiris Isis Horus
321	114	6	Osiris Isis Horus Sirius
262	118	1	Our God Is A Consuming Fire
61	16	7	Pallas
226	82	1	Pallas Athena Parthenos
116	44	8	Parthenos
147	48	3	Physical Sun
43	16	7	Plan
112	40	4	Planetary
180	63	9	Planetary Logos
71	35	8	Pleiades
77	32	5	Power
111	39	3	Prajapatis
86	41	5	Pyramid
140	50	5	Quaternary
62	26	8	Queen
119	56	11	Redemption
103	31	4	Regulus
257	104	5	Restore The Plan On Earth
57	21	3	Rose
151	43	7	Rosy Cross
73	46	1	Sacrifice
55	10	1	Sanat

AN	RAN	Root	Terms
120	30	3	Sanat Kumara
68	14	5	Satis
84	30	3	Savior
105	33	6	Saviour
53	26	8	Scheme
95	41	5	Scorpio
183	84	3	Secret of The Dragon
81	27	9	Sekhmet
60	15	6	Sept
171	72	9	Serpent Energy
220	76	4	Serpents of Wisdom
65	20	11	Seven*
202	103	4	Sevenfold Flaming Fire
69	24	6	Shamballa
75	39	3	Shekinah
113	59	5	Sirian Lodge
95	32	5	Sirius
267	105	6	Sirius The Cosmic Christ
287	125	8	Sirius The Great White Lodge
617	257	5	Sirius The Star of Sensitivity Governing The Hierarchy
133	43	7	Solar Logos
48	12	3	Son
192	84	3	Son of the Morning
114	42	6	Sons of God
68	32	5	Sophia
151	61	7	Sophia Wisdom
90	27	9	Sothis
67	13	4	Soul
125	44	8	Spiritual
192	57	3	Spiritual Soul
177	69	6	Spiritual Triad
199	82	1	Star of Initiation
202	85	4	Star of the Morning
83	20	11	Tawny*
152	44	8	Tawny Lions
71	26	8	Temple
166	58	4	Tetragrammaton
169	70	7	The Ancient of Days
217	73	1	The Boat of Mystery
437	176	5	The Boat of Mystery Which Ploughs The Ocean
245	110	11	The Bright Morning Star*

AN	RAN	Root	Terms
266	113	5	The Brother From Sirius
266	113	5	The Burning Sons of Desire
157	58	4	The Celestial Boat
171	72	9	The Celestial Ship
380	128	11	The Central Spiritual Sun Sirius
398	173	11	The Centre Where The Will of God Is Known*
110	47	11	The Christ*
357	114	6	The City That Stands Foursquare
172	73	1	The Cosmic Christ
390	192	3	The Council Chamber of The Three Divinities
212	77	5	The Dog Star Sirius
226	109	1	The Door of Initiation
85	40	4	The Earth
173	56	11	The Eastern Star
170	71	8	The Eye of Horus
170	71	8	The Eye of The Son
87	42	6	The God Man
110	56	11	The Great Bear*
157	67	4	The Great Goddess
206	89	8	The Great Invocation
353	146	11	The Great Invocation From Sirius
163	73	1	The Great Mother
170	80	8	The Great Pyramid
157	85	4	The Great Sacrifice
192	93	3	The Great White Lodge
316	136	1	The Great White Lodge on Sirius
151	61	7	The Great Work
132	69	6	The Heart of God
189	90	9	The Heart of The Lion
128	74	11	The Hierarchy
195	87	6	The High Priestess
182	83	11	The Holy of Holies
203	77	5	The House of Horus
157	49	4	The Human Soul
148	67	4	The Initiator
346	157	4	The Invocation for Power and Light
163	82	1	The Law of Sacrifice
321	132	6	The Law of Those Who Choose To Die
212	104	5	The Lifting of The Veil
136	73	1	The Light of God
374	176	5	The Light Which Ever Shineth In The East
111	48	3	The Lion Man

AN	RAN	Root	Terms
137	83	11	The Lodge On High
200	83	11	The Lodge On Sirius*
101	38	11	The Logos*
198	81	9	The Lord of Sirius
166	67	4	The Lords of Karma
134	62	8	The Love of God
282	129	3	The Messenger At The Eighth Gate
120	66	3	The Mind of God
90	36	9	The Moon
179	62	8	The New Jerusalem
182	83	11	The One Initiator*
121	67	4	The Place of Peace
123	60	6	The Plan of God
151	61	7	The Plan of Love
226	100	1	The Plan of Love and Light
213	78	6	The Planetary Logos
333	108	9	The Planetary Logos Sanat Kumara
104	50	5	The Pleiades
95	41	5	The Queen
171	81	9	The Queen of Heaven
113	59	5	The Race of Men
300	111	3	The Seat of Power On Sirius
190	73	1	The Silent Watcher
146	74	11	The Sirian Lodge
123	51	6	The Sphinx
210	84	3	The Spiritual Triad
91	28	1	The Star
192	66	3	The Star In The East
383	149	5	The Star Regulus The Heart of The Lion
373	139	4	The Star, The Sun, The High Priestess
87	24	6	The Sun
182	56	11	The Sun Sirius
190	82	1	The Throne of Isis
81	36	9	The Veil
191	92	11	The Virgin Mother
136	64	1	The Will of God
105	42	6	The World
71	26	8	Thoth
242	98	8	Thoth Hermes Mercury
182	74	11	Throne of Horus
157	67	4	Throne of Isis
190	82	1	Throne of Osiris

AN	RAN	Root	Terms
105	51	6	Tiphareth
121	58	4	Triadal Light
92	38	11	Unveiled
48	21	3	Veil
57	30	3	Veiled
81	18	9	Venus
134	44	8	Venus Scheme
56	20	11	Will*
103	49	4	Will of God
83	29	11	Wisdom
390	147	3	Within The Sunshine of The Major Sun
158	68	5	Word of Power

AN Values

AN	RAN	Root	Terms
26	17	8	God
28	10	1	Man
30	12	3	Ark
32	14	5	Leo
35	26	8	Argha
39	21	3	Angel
40	22	22	Mind*
41	23	5	Argo
41	23	5	Dagon
42	24	6	Five
43	16	7	Plan
43	25	7	Lodge
45	18	9	Makara
46	19	1	Adept
47	20	11	Monad*
48	12	3	Manas
48	12	3	Son
48	21	3	Evil
48	21	3	Veil
49	22	22	Athena*
49	22	22	Lord*
50	23	5	Lion
51	24	6	Great
51	33	6	Michael
52	25	7	Earth
52	25	7	Heart
53	26	8	Athene
53	26	8	Scheme
54	18	9	Love
55	10	1	Sanat
55	28	1	Heaven
56	20	11	Isis*
56	20	11	Will*
56	29	11	Light
56	29	11	Neith
57	21	3	Human
57	21	3	Rose
57	30	3	Veiled
57	39	3	Gemini
58	31	4	Emerald

AN	RAN	Root	Terms
59	32	5	Dragon
60	15	6	Sept
60	33	6	Orange
61	16	7	Pallas
62	26	8	Queen
63	18	9	Avatar
65	20	11	Kumara*
65	20	11	Seven*
66	21	3	Anubis
66	21	3	Argus
67	13	4	Soul
68	14	5	Satis
68	23	5	Logos
68	23	5	Oannes
68	32	5	Hermes
68	32	5	Sophia
69	24	6	Shamballa
69	42	6	Archangel
70	25	7	Nommo
70	34	7	Hathor
71	26	8	Temple
71	26	8	Thoth
71	35	8	Pleiades
73	28	1	Crown
73	28	1	Goddess
73	46	1	Sacrifice
74	11	11	Jesus
74	20	11	Cross*
74	29	11	Messiah
74	38	11	Energy
74	38	11	Lucifer
75	21	3	Anukis
75	39	3	Shekinah
76	22	22	Master*
77	32	5	Christ
77	32	5	Power
77	41	5	Disciple
77	41	5	Great Bear
79	34	7	Mother
81	18	9	Venus
81	27	9	Horus
81	27	9	Sekhmet

AN	RAN	Root	Terms
81	36	9	The Veil
83	20	11	Tawny*
83	29	11	Wisdom
83	38	11	Blue Lodge
84	21	3	Kumaras
84	30	3	Dog Star
84	30	3	Savior
85	40	4	The Earth
86	41	5	Pyramid
87	24	6	The Sun
87	42	6	Initiate
87	42	6	The God Man
87	51	6	Mind of God
89	35	8	Osiris
90	27	9	Sothis
90	36	9	The Moon
91	28	1	The Star
91	37	1	Hercules
92	38	11	Unveiled
95	23	5	Masters
95	32	5	Empress
95	32	5	Neptune
95	32	5	Sirius
95	41	5	Curtained
95	41	5	I am That I am
95	41	5	Scorpio
95	41	5	The Queen
95	59	5	Hierarchy
98	35	8	Aspirant
99	54	9	Heart of God
101	38	11	The Logos*
103	31	4	Regulus
103	40	4	Mercury
103	49	4	Will of God
104	32	5	Jerusalem
104	50	5	The Pleiades
105	33	6	Saviour
105	42	6	The World
105	51	6	Earth Scheme
105	51	6	Tiphareth
107	62	8	Green Emerald
110	47	11	The Christ*

AN	RAN	Root	Terms
110	56	11	The Great Bear*
111	48	3	The Lion Man
111	39	3	Humanity
111	39	3	Prajapatis
112	40	4	Planetary
113	50	5	Isis Veiled
113	59	5	Sirian Lodge
113	59	5	The Race of Men
114	42	6	Sons of God
114	60	6	Hierophant
115	43	7	Nephthys
116	44	8	Parthenos
119	56	11	Redemption
120	30	3	Sanat Kumara
120	48	3	Heavenly Man
120	57	3	Energy Adept
120	57	3	Initiation
120	66	3	The Mind of God
120	75	3	Archangel Michael
121	58	4	Triadal Light
121	67	4	The Place of Peace
123	51	6	The Sphinx
123	60	6	The Plan of God
125	44	8	Spiritual
128	74	11	The Hierarchy
131	50	5	God Is Known
132	69	6	The Heart of God
133	43	7	Solar Logos
133	52	7	Lords of Karma
134	44	8	Venus Scheme
134	53	8	Orange Cross
134	62	8	The Love of God
136	64	1	The Will of God
136	73	1	The Light of God
137	83	11	The Lodge On High
139	58	4	Cosmic Christ
139	58	4	Hermes Thoth
140	41	5	Eastern Star
140	50	5	Quaternary
140	77	5	Hermaphrodite
146	47	11	Isis-Sothis
146	74	11	The Sirian Lodge

AN	RAN	Root	Terms
147	48	3	Physical Sun
148	58	4	Isis Unveiled
148	67	4	The Initiator
151	43	7	Jesus Christ
151	43	7	Rosy Cross
151	61	7	Sophia Wisdom
151	61	7	The Great Work
151	61	7	The Plan of Love
152	44	8	Tawny Lions
157	49	4	The Human Soul
157	58	4	The Celestial Boat
157	67	4	The Great Goddess
157	67	4	Throne of Isis
157	85	4	The Great Sacrifice
158	68	5	Word of Power
159	69	6	Birth of Horus
159	69	6	Lords of The Flame
160	61	7	Heart of the Sun
161	71	8	Fourth Kingdom
163	73	1	Dragon of Wisdom
163	73	1	The Great Mother
163	82	1	The Law of Sacrifice
165	66	3	Lord of Sirius
166	58	4	Tetragrammaton
166	67	4	The Lords of Karma
169	70	7	The Ancient of Days
170	62	8	House of Horus
170	71	8	The Eye of Horus
170	71	8	The Eye of The Son
170	80	8	The Great Pyramid
171	63	9	Isis Nephthys
171	72	9	Hermes Mercury
171	72	9	Serpent Energy
171	72	9	The Celestial Ship
171	81	9	The Queen of Heaven
172	73	1	The Cosmic Christ
173	56	11	The Eastern Star
173	74	11	Great Invocation
175	76	4	Lord of The World
177	69	6	Spiritual Triad
179	62	8	The New Jerusalem
180	63	9	Planetary Logos

AN	RAN	Root	Terms
182	56	11	The Sun Sirius
182	74	11	Dragons of Wisdom
182	74	11	Throne of Horus
182	83	11	The Holy of Holies
182	83	11	The One Initiator
183	84	3	Secret of The Dragon
183	93	3	Fourth Hierarchy
189	81	9	Lion of Cosmic Will
189	90	9	The Heart of The Lion
189	126	9	Kumaras 105
190	73	1	The Silent Watcher
190	82	1	Adept Using Energy
190	82	1	The Throne of Isis
190	82	1	Throne of Osiris
191	92	11	The Virgin Mother
192	57	3	Spiritual Soul
192	66	3	The Star In The East
192	84	3	Emerald Orange Cross
192	84	3	Individualisation
192	84	3	Son of the Morning
192	93	3	The Great White Lodge
195	87	6	The High Priestess
196	70	7	Heavenly Jerusalem
198	81	9	The Lord of Sirius
199	82	1	Star of Initiation
200	83	11	The Lodge On Sirius*
202	85	4	Star of the Morning
202	103	4	Sevenfold Flaming Fire
203	77	5	The House of Horus
203	86	5	Light From Sirius
203	113	5	Divine Hermaphrodite
206	89	8	The Great Invocation
210	84	3	The Spiritual Triad
212	77	5	The Dog Star Sirius
212	95	5	A New Heaven And A New Earth
212	95	5	Argo The Celestial Ship
212	104	5	The Lifting of The Veil
213	78	6	The Planetary Logos
217	73	1	The Boat of Mystery
220	76	4	Serpents of Wisdom
226	82	1	Osiris Isis Horus
226	82	1	Pallas Athena Parthenos

AN	RAN	Root	Terms
226	100	1	The Plan of Love and Light
226	109	1	The Door of Initiation
240	114	6	Athena The Virgin Mother
242	98	8	Thoth Hermes Mercury
245	110	11	The Bright Morning Star*
247	85	4	Hermes Trismegistus
252	81	9	Central Spiritual Sun
257	104	5	Restore The Plan On Earth
262	118	1	Aspirant Disciple Initiate
262	118	1	Our God Is A Consuming Fire
266	113	5	The Brother From Sirius
266	113	5	The Burning Sons of Desire
267	105	6	Sirius The Cosmic Christ
282	129	3	The Messenger At The Eighth Gate
287	125	8	Sirius The Great White Lodge
289	82	1	Isis-Sothis Anukis Satis
289	154	1	Mind of God Heart of God Will of God
300	111	3	The Seat of Power On Sirius
313	142	7	Invocation for Power and Light
316	136	1	The Great White Lodge on Sirius
321	114	6	Cosmic Christ The Sun Sirius
321	114	6	Osiris Isis Horus Sirius
321	132	6	The Law of Those Who Choose To Die
333	108	9	The Planetary Logos Sanat Kumara
343	127	1	Light From Eastern Star Sirius
346	157	4	The Invocation for Power and Light
353	146	11	Light Love And Power From Sirius
353	146	11	The Great Invocation From Sirius
357	114	6	The City That Stands Foursquare
373	139	4	The Star, The Sun, The High Priestess
374	176	5	The Light Which Ever Shineth In The East
380	128	11	The Central Spiritual Sun Sirius
383	149	5	The Star Regulus The Heart of The Lion
383	158	5	Lions The Divine And Tawny Orange Flames
384	114	6	Isis-Sothis Anukis Satis Sirius
390	147	3	Within The Sunshine of The Major Sun
390	192	3	The Council Chamber of The Three Divinities
398	173	11	The Centre Where The Will of God Is Known*
437	176	5	The Boat of Mystery Which Ploughs The Ocean
617	257	5	Sirius The Star of Sensitivity Governing The Hierarchy

RAN Values

AN	RAN	Root	Terms
28	10	1	Man
55	10	1	Sanat
74	11	11	Jesus
30	12	3	Ark
48	12	3	Manas
48	12	3	Son
111	48	3	The Lion Man
67	13	4	Soul
32	14	5	Leo
68	14	5	Satis
60	15	6	Sept
43	16	7	Plan
61	16	7	Pallas
26	17	8	God
45	18	9	Makara
54	18	9	Love
63	18	9	Avatar
81	18	9	Venus
46	19	1	Adept
47	20	11	Monad*
56	20	11	Isis*
56	20	11	Will*
65	20	11	Kumara*
65	20	11	Seven*
74	20	11	Cross*
83	20	11	Tawny*
39	21	3	Angel
48	21	3	Evil
48	21	3	Veil
57	21	3	Human
57	21	3	Rose
66	21	3	Anubis
66	21	3	Argus
75	21	3	Anukis
84	21	3	Kumaras
40	22	22	Mind*
49	22	22	Athena*
49	22	22	Lord*
76	22	22	Master*
41	23	5	Argo

AN	RAN	Root	Terms
41	23	5	Dagon
50	23	5	Lion
68	23	5	Logos
68	23	5	Oannes
95	23	5	Masters
42	24	6	Five
51	24	6	Great
69	24	6	Shamballa
87	24	6	The Sun
43	25	7	Lodge
52	25	7	Earth
52	25	7	Heart
70	25	7	Nommo
35	26	8	Argha
53	26	8	Athene
53	26	8	Scheme
62	26	8	Queen
71	26	8	Temple
71	26	8	Thoth
81	27	9	Horus
81	27	9	Sekhmet
90	27	9	Sothis
55	28	1	Heaven
73	28	1	Crown
73	28	1	Goddess
91	28	1	The Star
56	29	11	Light
56	29	11	Neith
74	29	11	Messiah
83	29	11	Wisdom
57	30	3	Veiled
84	30	3	Dog Star
84	30	3	Savior
120	30	3	Sanat Kumara
58	31	4	Emerald
103	31	4	Regulus
59	32	5	Dragon
68	32	5	Hermes
68	32	5	Sophia
77	32	5	Christ
77	32	5	Power
95	32	5	Empress

AN	RAN	Root	Terms
95	32	5	Neptune
95	32	5	Sirius
104	32	5	Jerusalem
51	33	6	Michael
60	33	6	Orange
105	33	6	Saviour
70	34	7	Hathor
79	34	7	Mother
71	35	8	Pleiades
89	35	8	Osiris
98	35	8	Aspirant
81	36	9	The Veil
90	36	9	The Moon
91	37	1	Hercules
74	38	11	Energy
74	38	11	Lucifer
83	38	11	Blue Lodge
92	38	11	Unveiled
101	38	11	The Logos*
57	39	3	Gemini
75	39	3	Shekinah
111	39	3	Humanity
111	39	3	Prajapatis
85	40	4	The Earth
103	40	4	Mercury
112	40	4	Planetary
77	41	5	Disciple
77	41	5	Great Bear
86	41	5	Pyramid
95	41	5	Curtained
95	41	5	I am That I am
95	41	5	Scorpio
95	41	5	The Queen
140	41	5	Eastern Star
69	42	6	Archangel
87	42	6	Initiate
87	42	6	The God Man
105	42	6	The World
114	42	6	Sons of God
115	43	7	Nephthys
133	43	7	Solar Logos
151	43	7	Jesus Christ

AN	RAN	Root	Terms
151	43	7	Rosy Cross
116	44	8	Parthenos
125	44	8	Spiritual
134	44	8	Venus Scheme
152	44	8	Tawny Lions
73	46	1	Sacrifice
110	47	11	The Christ*
146	47	11	Isis-Sothis
120	48	3	Heavenly Man
147	48	3	Physical Sun
103	49	4	Will of God
157	49	4	The Human Soul
104	50	5	The Pleiades
113	50	5	Isis Veiled
131	50	5	God Is Known
140	50	5	Quaternary
87	51	6	Mind of God
105	51	6	Earth Scheme
105	51	6	Tiphareth
123	51	6	The Sphinx
133	52	7	Lords of Karma
134	53	8	Orange Cross
99	54	9	Heart of God
110	56	11	The Great Bear*
119	56	11	Redemption
173	56	11	The Eastern Star
182	56	11	The Sun Sirius
120	57	3	Energy Adept
120	57	3	Initiation
192	57	3	Spiritual Soul
121	58	4	Triadal Light
139	58	4	Cosmic Christ
139	58	4	Hermes Thoth
148	58	4	Isis Unveiled
157	58	4	The Celestial Boat
166	58	4	Tetragrammaton
95	59	5	Hierarchy
113	59	5	Sirian Lodge
113	59	5	The Race of Men
114	60	6	Hierophant
123	60	6	The Plan of God
151	61	7	Sophia Wisdom

AN	RAN	Root	Terms
151	61	7	The Great Work
151	61	7	The Plan of Love
160	61	7	Heart of the Sun
107	62	8	Green Emerald
134	62	8	The Love of God
170	62	8	House of Horus
179	62	8	The New Jerusalem
171	63	9	Isis Nephthys
180	63	9	Planetary Logos
136	64	1	The Will of God
120	66	3	The Mind of God
165	66	3	Lord of Sirius
192	66	3	The Star In The East
121	67	4	The Place of Peace
148	67	4	The Initiator
157	67	4	The Great Goddess
157	67	4	Throne of Isis
166	67	4	The Lords of Karma
158	68	5	Word of Power
132	69	6	The Heart of God
159	69	6	Birth of Horus
159	69	6	Lords of The Flame
177	69	6	Spiritual Triad
169	70	7	The Ancient of Days
196	70	7	Heavenly Jerusalem
161	71	8	Fourth Kingdom
170	71	8	The Eye of Horus
170	71	8	The Eye of The Son
171	72	9	Hermes Mercury
171	72	9	Serpent Energy
171	72	9	The Celestial Ship
136	73	1	The Light of God
163	73	1	Dragon of Wisdom
163	73	1	The Great Mother
172	73	1	The Cosmic Christ
190	73	1	The Silent Watcher
217	73	1	The Boat of Mystery
128	74	11	The Hierarchy
146	74	11	The Sirian Lodge
173	74	11	Great Invocation
182	74	11	Dragons of Wisdom
182	74	11	Throne of Horus

AN	RAN	Root	Terms
120	75	3	Archangel Michael
175	76	4	Lord of The World
220	76	4	Serpents of Wisdom
140	77	5	Hermaphrodite
203	77	5	The House of Horus
212	77	5	The Dog Star Sirius
213	78	6	The Planetary Logos
170	80	8	The Great Pyramid
171	81	9	The Queen of Heaven
189	81	9	Lion of Cosmic Will
198	81	9	The Lord of Sirius
252	81	9	Central Spiritual Sun
163	82	1	The Law of Sacrifice
190	82	1	Adept Using Energy
190	82	1	The Throne of Isis
190	82	1	Throne of Osiris
199	82	1	Star of Initiation
226	82	1	Osiris Isis Horus
226	82	1	Pallas Athena Parthenos
289	82	1	Isis-Sothis Anukis Satis
137	83	11	The Lodge On High
182	83	11	The Holy of Holies
182	83	11	The One Initiator
200	83	11	The Lodge On Sirius*
183	84	3	Secret of The Dragon
192	84	3	Emerald Orange Cross
192	84	3	Individualisation
192	84	3	Son of the Morning
210	84	3	The Spiritual Triad
157	85	4	The Great Sacrifice
202	85	4	Star of the Morning
247	85	4	Hermes Trismegistus
203	86	5	Light From Sirius
195	87	6	The High Priestess
206	89	8	The Great Invocation
189	90	9	The Heart of The Lion
191	92	11	The Virgin Mother
183	93	3	Fourth Hierarchy
192	93	3	The Great White Lodge
212	95	5	A New Heaven And A New Earth
212	95	5	Argo The Celestial Ship
242	98	8	Thoth Hermes Mercury

AN	RAN	Root	Terms
226	100	1	The Plan of Love and Light
202	103	4	Sevenfold Flaming Fire
212	104	5	The Lifting of The Veil
257	104	5	Restore The Plan On Earth
267	105	6	Sirius The Cosmic Christ
333	108	9	The Planetary Logos Sanat Kumara
226	109	1	The Door of Initiation
245	110	11	The Bright Morning Star*
300	111	3	The Seat of Power On Sirius
203	113	5	Divine Hermaphrodite
266	113	5	The Brother From Sirius
266	113	5	The Burning Sons of Desire
240	114	6	Athena The Virgin Mother
321	114	6	Cosmic Christ The Sun Sirius
321	114	6	Osiris Isis Horus Sirius
357	114	6	The City That Stands Foursquare
384	114	6	Isis-Sothis Anukis Satis Sirius
262	118	1	Aspirant Disciple Initiate
262	118	1	Our God Is A Consuming Fire
287	125	8	Sirius The Great White Lodge
189	126	9	Kumaras 105
343	127	1	Light From Eastern Star Sirius
380	128	11	The Central Spiritual Sun Sirius
282	129	3	The Messenger At The Eighth Gate
321	132	6	The Law of Those Who Choose To Die
316	136	1	The Great White Lodge on Sirius
373	139	4	The Star, The Sun, The High Priestess
313	142	7	Invocation for Power and Light
353	146	11	Light Love And Power From Sirius
353	146	11	The Great Invocation From Sirius
390	147	3	Within The Sunshine of The Major Sun
383	149	5	The Star Regulus The Heart of The Lion
289	154	1	Mind of God Heart of God Will of God
346	157	4	The Invocation for Power and Light
383	158	5	Lions The Divine And Tawny Orange Flames
398	173	11	The Centre Where The Will of God Is Known*
374	176	5	The Light Which Ever Shineth In The East
437	176	5	The Boat of Mystery Which Ploughs The Ocean
390	192	3	The Council Chamber of The Three Divinities
617	257	5	Sirius The Star of Sensitivity Governing The Hierarchy

Appendix E

Root Values

AN	RAN	Root	Terms
28	10	1	Man
46	19	1	Adept
55	10	1	Sanat
55	28	1	Heaven
73	28	1	Crown
73	28	1	Goddess
73	46	1	Sacrifice
91	28	1	The Star
91	37	1	Hercules
136	64	1	The Will of God
136	73	1	The Light of God
163	73	1	Dragon of Wisdom
163	73	1	The Great Mother
163	82	1	The Law of Sacrifice
172	73	1	The Cosmic Christ
190	73	1	The Silent Watcher
190	82	1	Adept Using Energy
190	82	1	The Throne of Isis
190	82	1	Throne of Osiris
199	82	1	Star of Initiation
217	73	1	The Boat of Mystery
226	82	1	Osiris Isis Horus
226	82	1	Pallas Athena Parthenos
226	100	1	The Plan of Love and Light
226	109	1	The Door of Initiation
262	118	1	Aspirant Disciple Initiate
262	118	1	Our God Is A Consuming Fire
289	82	1	Isis-Sothis Anukis Satis
289	154	1	Mind of God Heart of God Will of God
316	136	1	The Great White Lodge on Sirius
343	127	1	Light From Eastern Star Sirius
30	12	3	Ark
39	21	3	Angel
48	12	3	Manas
48	12	3	Son
48	21	3	Evil
48	21	3	Veil
57	21	3	Human
57	21	3	Rose
57	30	3	Veiled

AN	RAN	Root	Terms
57	39	3	Gemini
66	21	3	Anubis
66	21	3	Argus
75	21	3	Anukis
75	39	3	Shekinah
84	21	3	Kumaras
84	30	3	Dog Star
84	30	3	Savior
111	48	3	The Lion Man
111	39	3	Humanity
111	39	3	Prajapatis
120	30	3	Sanat Kumara
120	48	3	Heavenly Man
120	57	3	Energy Adept
120	57	3	Initiation
120	66	3	The Mind of God
120	75	3	Archangel Michael
147	48	3	Physical Sun
165	66	3	Lord of Sirius
183	84	3	Secret of The Dragon
183	93	3	Fourth Hierarchy
192	57	3	Spiritual Soul
192	66	3	The Star In The East
192	84	3	Emerald Orange Cross
192	84	3	Individualisation
192	84	3	Son of the Morning
192	93	3	The Great White Lodge
210	84	3	The Spiritual Triad
282	129	3	The Messenger At The Eighth Gate
300	111	3	The Seat of Power On Sirius
390	147	3	Within The Sunshine of The Major Sun
390	192	3	The Council Chamber of The Three Divinities
58	31	4	Emerald
67	13	4	Soul
85	40	4	The Earth
103	31	4	Regulus
103	40	4	Mercury
103	49	4	Will of God
112	40	4	Planetary
121	58	4	Triadal Light
121	67	4	The Place of Peace
139	58	4	Cosmic Christ

AN	RAN	Root	Terms
139	58	4	Hermes Thoth
148	58	4	Isis Unveiled
148	67	4	The Initiator
157	49	4	The Human Soul
157	58	4	The Celestial Boat
157	67	4	The Great Goddess
157	67	4	Throne of Isis
157	85	4	The Great Sacrifice
166	58	4	Tetragrammaton
166	67	4	The Lords of Karma
175	76	4	Lord of The World
202	85	4	Star of the Morning
202	103	4	Sevenfold Flaming Fire
220	76	4	Serpents of Wisdom
247	85	4	Hermes Trismegistus
346	157	4	The Invocation for Power and Light
373	139	4	The Star, The Sun, The High Priestess
32	14	5	Leo
41	23	5	Argo
41	23	5	Dagon
50	23	5	Lion
59	32	5	Dragon
68	14	5	Satis
68	23	5	Logos
68	23	5	Oannes
68	32	5	Hermes
68	32	5	Sophia
77	32	5	Christ
77	32	5	Power
77	41	5	Disciple
77	41	5	Great Bear
86	41	5	Pyramid
95	23	5	Masters
95	32	5	Empress
95	32	5	Neptune
95	32	5	Sirius
95	41	5	Curtained
95	41	5	I am That I am
95	41	5	Scorpio
95	41	5	The Queen
95	59	5	Hierarchy
104	32	5	Jerusalem

AN	RAN	Root	Terms
104	50	5	The Pleiades
113	50	5	Isis Veiled
113	59	5	Sirian Lodge
113	59	5	The Race of Men
131	50	5	God Is Known
140	41	5	Eastern Star
140	50	5	Quaternary
140	77	5	Hermaphrodite
158	68	5	Word of Power
203	77	5	The House of Horus
203	86	5	Light From Sirius
203	113	5	Divine Hermaphrodite
212	77	5	The Dog Star Sirius
212	95	5	A New Heaven And A New Earth
212	95	5	Argo The Celestial Ship
212	104	5	The Lifting of The Veil
257	104	5	Restore The Plan On Earth
266	113	5	The Brother From Sirius
266	113	5	The Burning Sons of Desire
374	176	5	The Light Which Ever Shineth In The East
383	149	5	The Star Regulus The Heart of The Lion
383	158	5	Lions The Divine And Tawny Orange Flames
437	176	5	The Boat of Mystery Which Ploughs The Ocean
617	257	5	Sirius The Star of Sensitivity Governing The Hierarchy
42	24	6	Five
51	24	6	Great
51	33	6	Michael
60	15	6	Sept
60	33	6	Orange
69	24	6	Shamballa
69	42	6	Archangel
87	24	6	The Sun
87	42	6	Initiate
87	42	6	The God Man
87	51	6	Mind of God
105	33	6	Saviour
105	42	6	The World
105	51	6	Earth Scheme
105	51	6	Tiphareth
114	42	6	Sons of God
114	60	6	Hierophant

AN	RAN	Root	Terms
123	51	6	The Sphinx
123	60	6	The Plan of God
132	69	6	The Heart of God
159	69	6	Birth of Horus
159	69	6	Lords of The Flame
177	69	6	Spiritual Triad
195	87	6	The High Priestess
213	78	6	The Planetary Logos
240	114	6	Athena The Virgin Mother
267	105	6	Sirius The Cosmic Christ
321	114	6	Cosmic Christ The Sun Sirius
321	114	6	Osiris Isis Horus Sirius
321	132	6	The Law of Those Who Choose To Die
357	114	6	The City That Stands Foursquare
384	114	6	Isis-Sothis Anukis Satis Sirius
43	16	7	Plan
43	25	7	Lodge
52	25	7	Earth
52	25	7	Heart
61	16	7	Pallas
70	25	7	Nommo
70	34	7	Hathor
79	34	7	Mother
115	43	7	Nephthys
133	43	7	Solar Logos
133	52	7	Lords of Karma
151	43	7	Jesus Christ
151	43	7	Rosy Cross
151	61	7	Sophia Wisdom
151	61	7	The Great Work
151	61	7	The Plan of Love
160	61	7	Heart of the Sun
169	70	7	The Ancient of Days
196	70	7	Heavenly Jerusalem
313	142	7	Invocation for Power and Light
26	17	8	God
35	26	8	Argha
53	26	8	Athene
53	26	8	Scheme
62	26	8	Queen
71	26	8	Temple
71	26	8	Thoth

AN	RAN	Root	Terms
71	35	8	Pleiades
89	35	8	Osiris
98	35	8	Aspirant
107	62	8	Green Emerald
116	44	8	Parthenos
125	44	8	Spiritual
134	44	8	Venus Scheme
134	53	8	Orange Cross
134	62	8	The Love of God
152	44	8	Tawny Lions
161	71	8	Fourth Kingdom
170	62	8	House of Horus
170	71	8	The Eye of Horus
170	71	8	The Eye of The Son
170	80	8	The Great Pyramid
179	62	8	The New Jerusalem
206	89	8	The Great Invocation
242	98	8	Thoth Hermes Mercury
287	125	8	Sirius The Great White Lodge
45	18	9	Makara
54	18	9	Love
63	18	9	Avatar
81	18	9	Venus
81	27	9	Horus
81	27	9	Sekhmet
81	36	9	The Veil
90	27	9	Sothis
90	36	9	The Moon
99	54	9	Heart of God
171	63	9	Isis Nephthys
171	72	9	Hermes Mercury
171	72	9	Serpent Energy
171	72	9	The Celestial Ship
171	81	9	The Queen of Heaven
180	63	9	Planetary Logos
189	81	9	Lion of Cosmic Will
189	90	9	The Heart of The Lion
189	126	9	Kumaras 105
198	81	9	The Lord of Sirius
252	81	9	Central Spiritual Sun
333	108	9	The Planetary Logos Sanat Kumara
47	20	11	Monad*

AN	RAN	Root	Terms
56	20	11	Isis*
56	20	11	Will*
56	29	11	Light
56	29	11	Neith
65	20	11	Kumara*
65	20	11	Seven*
74	11	11	Jesus
74	20	11	Cross*
74	29	11	Messiah
74	38	11	Energy
74	38	11	Lucifer
83	20	11	Tawny*
83	29	11	Wisdom
83	38	11	Blue Lodge
92	38	11	Unveiled
101	38	11	The Logos*
110	47	11	The Christ*
110	56	11	The Great Bear*
119	56	11	Redemption
128	74	11	The Hierarchy
137	83	11	The Lodge On High
146	47	11	Isis-Sothis
146	74	11	The Sirian Lodge
173	56	11	The Eastern Star
173	74	11	Great Invocation
182	56	11	The Sun Sirius
182	74	11	Dragons of Wisdom
182	74	11	Throne of Horus
182	83	11	The Holy of Holies
182	83	11	The One Initiator
191	92	11	The Virgin Mother
200	83	11	The Lodge On Sirius*
245	110	11	The Bright Morning Star*
353	146	11	Light Love And Power From Sirius
353	146	11	The Great Invocation From Sirius
380	128	11	The Central Spiritual Sun Sirius
398	173	11	The Centre Where The Will of God Is Known*
40	22	22	Mind*
49	22	22	Athena*
49	22	22	Lord*
76	22	22	Master*

Symbolic Number Glossary

2 Second major Tarot card, The High Priestess; she corresponds to Isis.

3 Root value of the five key words in stanza five of the Great Invocation.

4 Root value of all the words in stanza four of the Great Invocation.

5 Root value of the Great Invocation.

Root value of the twenty-one key words of the Great Invocation.

Number of stanzas in the Great Invocation.

Root value of the fifty-one essential words of the Great Invocation.

Root value of the five key words in stanza one of the Great Invocation.

Root value of stanza three of the Great Invocation.

Number of times the word "light" appears in the Great Invocation.

Other terms related to five. Fifth principle of manas. The fifth root-race. The fifth kingdom of nature—Hierarchy. The fifth ray. The five senses. The five pointed star of initiation, symbol of the perfected human. Leo, the fifth sign of the zodiac.

6 A perfect number because its factors—1, 2 and 3 total 6.

A triangular number resulting from the addition of the first three numbers—1 + 2 + 3 = 6.

Number of the perfection of form through initiation.

Number of "The Great Work."

The cube.

Root value of stanza five of the Great Invocation and the key words in stanza three.

Number of Tiphareth—the Christ consciousness—relative to the Cabalistic Tree of Life.

Symbolizes the perfected Master in relation to 66 and 666.

Related to 66 and 666 in terms of perfecting form.

7 Number of sentences in the Great Invocation.

Structural pattern of the Great Invocation.

The divisions of the planes and subplanes of consciousness in the cosmos.

The seven rays. The seven root-races, rounds, globes, and chains within a planetary scheme.

The relative perfection of man before attaining Christ consciousness. Relates to 28, 51, 226, and 777.

8 Root value of stanza one of the Great Invocation.

The number of the Christ consciousness and of the Hierarchy.

9 Root value of stanza two of the Great Invocation.

Root value of the key words in stanzas two and four of the Great Invocation.

The symbolic number of initiation and of Shamballa.

10 The number of divine perfection—God.

A triangular number resulting from the addition of the first four numbers—1 + 2 + 3 + 4 = 10.

The number of key words repeated beyond the original eleven.

The divine Tetraktys of the Pythagoreans.

The tenth sign of the zodiac, Capricorn.

11 Number of words in stanza five of the Great Invocation.

Number of essential key words in the Great Invocation.

Number of words in the Great Invocation that have a root value of 5—11 x 5 = 55; related to 55.

Aquarius, the eleventh sign.

The number symbolizing the adept using energy.

13 Number of lines in the Great Invocation.

14 Code number given by Djwhal Khul for one of the Creative Hierarchies associated with the Path to Sirius.

Relates to Leo and Hierarchy One; related to table 40.

The Tarot card Temperance.

17 Code number given by Djwhal Khul for one of the Creative Hierarchies associated with the Path to Sirius.

Relates to Scorpio and Hierarchy Four; related to table 40.

The date in Scorpio when Osiris was slain.

The Tarot card The Star.

19 AN value of the letter "s"—the middle letter of the Great Invocation.

The Tarot card The Sun.

The 19 expressions of God through the seven rays and the twelve constellations of the zodiac.

20 Sum of the first four triangular numbers—1 + 3 + 6 + 10 = 20.

A tetrahedral number represented as a triangular-based solid with four distinct tiers.

The RAN value of Isis.

21 The total number of key words in the Great Invocation.

The RAN value of the word "kumaras."

The result of 7 + 7 + 7.

The result of the addition of the three Hebrew letters for God—Yod = 10, Vau = 6, He = 5 (10 + 6 + 5 = 21).

Related to 95, 105, 5565, and 1065.

24 Number of words each in stanzas one and two of the Great Invocation.

26 Number of words in stanza three of the Great Invocation.

28 Number of words in stanza four of the Great Invocation.

AN value of the middle word of the Great Invocation— "is."

The number of words in each quadrant of the Sirian Cross when the Great Invocation is divided by 4, excluding the middle word "is."

The age of Osiris when he was slain, or the year of his reign when he was slain.

Number of digits (one finger width) in one Egyptian cubit.

Alice Bailey notes in *The Labors of Hercules* that the constellation Capricorn contains twenty-eight stars.

A triangular number resulting from the addition of the first seven numbers—1 + 2 + 3 + 4 + 5 + 6 + 7 = 28.

Symbolically, 28 represents a synthesis of all seven rays and seven planes of consciousness.

A perfect number through the addition of all its own factors— 1 + 2 + 4 + 7 + 14 = 28.

The value of the combined numbers of the fourth and fifth Creative Hierarchies from which humanity is made. The fourth and fifth Creative Hierarchies are also the ninth and tenth depending on which way they are counted. Therefore, 4 + 5 + 9 + 10 = 28. Related to 57.

Schematic pattern of the Great Invocation is based on twenty-eight words in each quadrant of the Sirian Cross resonating with the AN value of the middle word "is" (28).

Related to 7, 51, 226, and 777.

Total combined value of each stanza in the Great Invocation before its reduction to root value of 5.

32 Total combined value of the key words in each stanza in the Great Invocation before their reduction to a root value of 5.

33 The total root value of the 4 words found in positions 5, 6, 56, and 65 of the Great Invocation. These words form the phrase "God of Light within;" related to 132.

RAN value of "saviour" and "Master Jesus"—22 + 11 = 33.

35 Sum of the first five triangular numbers—
1 + 3 + 6 + 10 + 15 = 35.

A tetrahedral number represented as a triangular based solid with five distinct tiers.

The RAN value of Osiris.

38 Value of the combined Creative Hierarchies found in table 40.

The two digits (3 and 8) left in the Sirian Cross Level Three as the root values for each of the four sets of twenty-eight words of the Great Invocation excluding "is." Related to 8338.

41 AN value of "Argo" which is symbolically associated with Sirius. Related to 21, 287, and 861.

44 Number of letters in stanza five of the Great Invocation.

45 A triangular number resulting from the addition of the first nine numbers—1-9.

The word "Christ" is the 45th word in the Great Invocation.

50 RAN value of the three middle words of the Great Invocation, "God is known."

AN value of the words located in the 12th, 17th, and 21st positions of the Great Invocation based on the Sirian Cross Level Two. See figure 22.

Value of the Hebrew name "Dagh Gadhol," translated as "Great Fish." Dagon was the Chaldean god "Oannes" who was both man and fish.

The approximate number of years necessary for Sirius B to complete one orbit of Sirius A.

51 Number of different words contained in the Great Invocation; the remaining sixty-two words are duplicates.

Number of whole degrees in one-seventh of a circle. This number is symbolically linked to the Greek goddess, Athena.

Related to 7, 28, 226, and 777.

55 A pyramidal number. The sum of the first five square numbers—1, 4, 9, 16, and 25.

The number of units in a pyramid five tiers high. A seven tier pyramid completely envelops this one.

Related to 85 and 140.

The AN value of “Sanat.”

The total root value of “Light” (11) which appears five times in the Great Invocation—5 x 11 = 55.

56 Number of words in the Great Invocation before and following the middle word “is.”

AN value of “Isis.”

RAN value of “the sun Sirius.”

The position of the first word in the middle phrase of the Great Invocation— “God.”

57 The position of the middle word “is” (28 AN) of the Great Invocation.

The position of the second word in the middle phrase of the Great Invocation— “is.”

Symbolizes the “veiled” (57) nature of the middle word “is” or half of “Isis.”

Related to 28 and 1995.

58 The position of the third word in the middle phrase of the Great Invocation— “known.”

64 The total RAN value of the four words in the twenty-eighth position of the four quadrants of the Great Invocation laid out around the Sirian Cross.

The RAN value of “the Will of God.” Related to 136.

66 The AN value of the four letters found on The High Priestess Tarot card—B, J, T, O, R, A. This card is Isis veiled.

AN value of “Anubis,” the dog-headed Egyptian god who was the devoted aide and guardian of Isis.

Symbolizes the state of consciousness of the third degree initiate.

Related to 6 and 666.

77 A special number in relation to the Great Invocation and especially the middle letter "s." Since "s" is the 19th letter of the alphabet it can be numerologically manipulated to produce various other values which refer to specific word positions within the Great Invocation. One value produced results from adding the numbers 1-19 yielding the triangular number 190. Since this number is greater than the amount of words in the Great Invocation, the number of words (113) is subtracted from 190 in order to find the reference word within it. This produces the number 77. The 77th word of the Great Invocation is "centre" which refers back to the centre letter "s." Related to 252.

84 The result of combining any two 28 word quadrants in the Great Invocation with the AN value of the middle word "is" which also equals 28. The quadrant design is based on the symbolic cross of Sirius. 28 + 28 + 28 = 84. "Dog Star" equals 84.

85 Amount of outside facing blocks on a pyramid of seven tiers. All 113 words of the Great Invocation fit onto these 85 blocks. Related to 55 and 140.

91 AN value of "The Star." Relates to the middle word "is" where the letter "i" has a RAN value of 9 and "s" has a RAN value of 1. Thus, "is" substitutes for 91 and veils The Star.

95 Number of letters in each of stanzas one and two of the Great Invocation.

Number of letters forming the twenty-one key words.

Number of stars in Leo, according to Alice Bailey. (This may be an occult hint.)

AN value of "Sirius," which according to DK, governs Leo.

101 Number of letters in stanza four of the Great Invocation.

105 Number of Kumaras Who came to Earth from the Venus chain. (Sanat Kumara plus 104 Assistants.)

Kumaras are saviors and the word “saviour” equals 105 (AN).

Related to 21 and 5565.

108 Number of letters in the third stanza of the Great Invocation.

113 Number of words in the Great Invocation.

Amount of root-races between the incarnation of Sanat Kumara on the second globe, the second root-race of that globe during the second round and His densest point of manifestation during the fourth round on the fourth globe (our Earth) during the third root-race, the Lemurian. Related to 222 and 443. See appendix C.

AN value of “Isis veiled” and “Sirian Lodge.” These terms are intimately connected to Venus and Mercury because these two planets along with Earth formed a triangle which resulted in the intervention of the Sirian Lodge and the creation of humanity through Sanat Kumara.

Combined total of the number of cells comprising the magic squares of Venus (7 x 7) and Mercury (8 x 8). Both these planets played a close role with the Earth at the time of the coming of the Kumaras, the founding of the Hierarchy, and the creation of the human kingdom eighteen million years ago.

114 Total AN value of the two referenced words of the Great Invocation in the Sirian Cross Level Three (see figure 20 and table 37).

The number of the first root-race following the incarnation of Sanat Kumara, the Atlantean (the 114th race of the Earth chain). It was the first human root-race to experience the opening of the door of initiation.

121 The square of 11, the number of the adept using energy.

131 The total value of the factors necessary to yield 30, which is the RAN value of the word "savior."

The AN value of "God is known," the three middle words of the Great Invocation.

A number line of 1, 3, and 1 referring to the root values of each word in the phrase "Goddess of Heaven." This phrase refers to Isis-Sothis or Sirius.

132 Total value of the words located in the positions of the Great Invocation involving the numbers 5 and 6 (5 + 6 + 56 + 65 = 132). These words form the phrase "God of Light within." Related to 5, 6, 56, and 5565.

136 The total AN value of the twenty-eighth word in each quadrant of the Sirian cross added together.

Value of the words and word positions forming the infinity loop in the Great Invocation. The words are "the God of Light." This number is also equal to the phrase "the Great White Lodge on Sirius" (RAN). Related to 28.

AN value of "the Will of God."

140 A pyramid number. The sum of the first 7 square numbers. (1 + 4 + 9 + 16 + 25 + 36 + 49 = 140.)

Total number of elements needed to construct a pyramid with seven tiers. Related to 55 and 85.

The number of the first level of consciousness below the causal body of our solar Logos. The form or personality domain of the solar Logos. Thus, the term, "the House of Horus." See appendix D3.

171 The total of the word positions (56 + 57 + 58) of the three middle words "God is known."

The result of multiplying the AN values of the two letters forming the middle word of the Great Invocation, "is." 9 = i, 19 = s (9 x 19).

AN value of related phrases, "The Queen of Heaven,"

"Hermes Mercury," and "The Celestial Ship."

Page number in the book *Initiation: Human and Solar* on which is found the phrase "The Boat of Mystery which Ploughs the Ocean." Related to 176.

172 The midpoint of the 343 cosmic planes of consciousness.

The midpoint in the 343 rounds in a planetary scheme.

The midpoint in the 343 root-races in a planetary chain.

The AN value of Sirius (95) + Christ (77).

The AN value of "the Cosmic Christ." According to DK, Sirius is the Cosmic Christ.

176 Total root value of the twenty-one key words in the Great Invocation. Related to 482 and 1103.

RAN value of "The light which ever shineth in the East" and "The Boat of Mystery which Ploughs the Ocean." Related to 437.

189 A number symbolizing the 105 Kumaras Who came to Earth. 105 + 84 (Kumara).

190 A triangular number resulting from the addition of the first nineteen numbers. (See 6.)

AN value of "The Throne of Isis," "Throne of Osiris," "Adept using Energy," and "The Silent Watcher."

Twice the value of "Sirius" (2 x 95).

192 Number equaling "emerald" and "orange cross" (58 + 134) which are parts of the symbol of the Path to Sirius.

203 The AN value of "the Great White Lodge."

The number of cosmic planes of consciousness beyond the lower 140 levels of manifestation of the solar Logos. 140 + 203 = 343. Related to 140.

The total number of stone tiers in the Great Pyramid of Gizeh minus the missing capstone.

The AN value of "the House of Horus" and "light from Sirius."

206 The difference in AN values between the horizontal and vertical arms of the triangular cross arrangement of the Great Invocation. This number equals the title "the Great Invocation."

212 A number line composed of 2, 1, 2. The first 2 is the root value of the first 56 words of the Great Invocation. The number 1 is the root value of "is," the middle word of the Great Invocation. The second 2 is the root value of the 56 words following "is."

AN value of the terms "the lifting of the veil" and "the Dog Star Sirius."

AN value of "Argo the celestial ship." Related to 437.

222 The number position of the middle letter "s" in the Great Invocation.

A number indicating the coming of Sanat Kumara to our fourth chain, the Earth. He came from chain 2 (Venus chain) to globe 2 (of our chain) during round 2.

A detailed computation based on the 113 words of the Great Invocation indicates the real possibility Sanat Kumara actually arrived in our fourth chain on globe 2, in root-race 2 during round 2.

Related to 113 and 443. See chapter 9, "The Words Made Flesh."

226 The amount of letters in the essential fifty-one word version of the Great Invocation.

The AN value of "Pallas Athena Parthenos."

Related to 7, 28, 51, and 777.

231 Total AN value of the five key words that appear more than once in the Great Invocation—Light, God, Earth, Love, and Power.

A triangular number resulting from the addition of the first twenty-one numbers.

242 The result of multiplying 11 by 22. Eleven is the number of the adept using energy and 22 is the number of the adept.

This number is the AN value of "Thoth Hermes Mercury."

247 A number line referring to rays 2, 4, and 7 which relate to Hermes Trismegistus.

The AN value of "Hermes Trismegistus."

252 The number produced by the addition of the AN values of the words located in positions 1, 10, 19, 45, and 77 of the Great Invocation. These numbers are based on all the possible numerological combinations of the central letter "s."

The letter "s" symbolizes the central spiritual sun located at the very center of the Great Invocation. The term "central spiritual sun" equals 252. Related to 77.

257 A number line referring to rays 2, 5, and 7.

AN value of "restore the Plan on Earth," the last five words of the Great Invocation.

280 The total AN value of "Light" when multiplied by 5—the number of times it appears in the Great Invocation. (5 x 56.)

The total AN value of "Isis" when multiplied by 5—the number of times it appears on The Sun Tarot card.

285 The total value of the word positions in the Great Invocation which are multiples of nineteen. The letter "s" is the central letter of the Great Invocation and has a value of 19 and the phrase "central spiritual Sun" equals 285 AN or 15 x 19.

287 The total of all possible number combinations derived from the code numbers 14 and 17 veiling the Creative Hierarchies associated with the Path to Sirius. Related to 14 and 17.

AN value of "Sirius the Great White Lodge."

289 The square of 17. Number of The Star Tarot card.

Total value of the rays emanating from the sun on The Sun Tarot card. The straight lines symbolize the letter "i" and the wavy lines signify the letter "s." These spell "is" ten times or "Isis" five times (280) with one "i" equaling 9 remaining (280 + 9).

Combined AN value of the three phrases in the Great Invocation, "Mind of God," "Heart of God," and "Will of God."

Combined AN value of the three Egyptian goddesses, Isis-Sothis, Satis, and Anukis who are associated with Sirius, Sirius B, and Sirius C (if C exists).

Combined AN value of Osiris, Isis, Horus, and Sirius.

Combined AN value of the words found in the positions derived from the twenty-eight words in each quadrant of the Sirian Cross Level One (see figure 18 and table 35).

Related to 14, 17, 280, and 287.

321 Total value of the word positions derived from the twenty-eight words in each quadrant of the Sirian Cross Level One (see figure 18 and table 35). Related to 289.

AN value of "the law of those who choose to die," the esoteric name for the Law of Sacrifice. Also equals the Egyptian trinity, the goddess Athena, the Cosmic Christ, and "Leo, Jupiter, Hierarchy, Sirius." See table 50.

383 A value formed from the core root numbers 3 and 8 in each quadrant of the Sirian cross.

AN value of "Lions the divine and tawny orange Flames," a reference to the human souls created at the time of individualization.

AN value of the phrases “the star Regulus, the heart of the Lion” and “the Dog Star Sirius the Queen of Heaven,” which controls Leo and consequently Regulus.

Other related phrases are “Sirius, Heart of the Sun, the Hierarchy” and “Our God is a consuming Fire, Triadal Light.” These phrases all relate ultimately to the controlling influence of Sirius over Leo, Regulus, our solar system, Earth, the Hierarchy, individualization, initiation, and the Great Invocation because these numbers (3 and 8) are found at its core. See chapter 9.

390 AN value of “within the sunshine of the major Sun,” a reference to Sirius. Related to 485.

397 Total AN value of the six key words not repeated—Mind, Heart, Christ, Will, Masters, and Power.

437 The result of 19 x 23; 19 refers to the value of the middle letter “s” of the Great Invocation, and 23 refers to the RAN value of “Argo.” Related to 212.

AN value of “The Boat of Mystery which Ploughs the Ocean.” Related to 176.

441 21 x 21 or the amount of key words squared.

Combined AN value of the three related terms, “the sun Sirius,” “Cosmic Christ,” and “initiation.”

443 Amount of letters in the Great Invocation.

Total AN value of the three phrases, “Isis Veiled,” “Isis Unveiled,” and “the sun Sirius.”

Code number for fourth round, fourth globe and third root-race.

Related to 113 and 222.

482 Total RAN value of the twenty-one key words. Related to 176 and 1103.

485 Result of squaring the two code numbers (14 and 17) connected with the Path to Sirius and adding them together.

AN value of "within the sunshine of the major Sun Sirius."

AN value of "I Hermes Trismegistus am the Light of the World."

531 9 x 59; 59 equals the RAN value of "Sirian Lodge," "Hierarchy," and "the race of men." Each of these three is made up of three parts, thus yielding 9. The Hierarchy and the race of men will eventually work together in order to work out the larger Plan of the Sirian Lodge. This is indicated in the Great Invocation by the phrase "the Plan of Love and Light." This phrase occupies word positions 86 through 91 (86 + 87 + 88 + 89 + 90 + 91 = 531).

539 Total AN value of the words located in the positions derived from all the combinations of the code numbers 14 and 17 which relate to the Path to Sirius. Related to 14, 17, and 287.

AN value of "Sanat Kumara the Planetary Logos" plus "the Great Invocation."

AN value of "The Plan of Love and Light" plus "Invocation for Power and Light."

666 The material form side of life. Symbolizes the state of consciousness of the "newborn" aspirant at the time of the first initiation. Related to 66 and 6.

695 A highly significant number in relation to the Great Invocation. It is the total of all the possible numerological values (AN, RAN and root) of all the three midpoint elements—the middle phrase, word, and letter. This number is a synthesis of the soul or middle aspect of the Great Invocation.

5 x 139; 5 is the total value of the Great Invocation and 139 is the AN value of "Cosmic Christ" and "Thoth Hermes." Also the combined RAN value of the major Tarot cards The High Priestess, The Star, and The Sun.

698 The total value of all the elements which form the Great

Invocation. This number reduces to a root value of 5. 6 + 9 + 8 = 23, 2 + 3 = 5.

777 The number related to the planetary Logos of our Earth.

Relates to the twenty-one key words. 7 + 7 + 7 = 21.

Result of the addition of "Earth Scheme," "Venus Scheme," "Sirius," and 443 (the number of letters in the Great Invocation).

The total AN value of the middle fifteen words of the Great Invocation. Based on the symbolism of forty-nine words before and forty-nine words after the middle fifteen words. Thus there are 7 x 7 words, followed by fifteen words valued at 777, followed by the final 7 x 7 words—7 x 7 777 7 x 7. This underlying septenary structure is associated with the goddess Athena. Related to 7, 28, 51, and 226.

861 A triangular number resulting from the addition of the first 41 numbers. Related to 41.

3 x 287; 287 equals "Sirius the Great White Lodge" and 3 refers to the number of influences flowing from Sirius into our planet. Related to 287 and 531.

The total of the word positions in the Great Invocation from 86-91 (the Plan of Love and Light) plus 81-84 (the race of men). The greater Plan involves Sirius and Humanity.

862 The value of the description given by DK of the Path to Sirius. "Two wheels of electric fire, revolving around an orange Cross with an emerald at the centre."

875 The total of the AN value of the middle fifteen words of the Great Invocation (777) plus the forty-nine (7 x 7) words before and the forty-nine (7 x 7) words after the middle group.

7 x 125; 7 symbolizes the seven original "word forms" of the Great Invocation before DK translated them into English, and 125 equals the RAN value of "Sirius the Great White Lodge." Seven also symbolizes the seven rays emanating from Sirius.

888 The value of "Jesus" in Greek gematria. 12 x 74. Related to 1480.

1065 The unified number formed from 10, 6, and 5.

A coded form of "Sanat" (10 RAN) "Kumara" (65 AN).

Related to 10, 6, 5.

1103 The AN value of all twenty-one key words found in the Great Invocation. Related to 176 and 482.

1110 A unified number formed from 11 and 10, the respective amount of original key words and duplicated key words in the Great Invocation.

The number of petals in the chakras excepting the spleen and the "three lower organs of creation." See *Letters on Occult Meditation,* pp. 80-81.

1259 The AN value of the twenty-eight words of the Great Invocation located in the fourth quadrant of the Sirian Cross.

1286 The AN value of the twenty-eight words of the Great Invocation located in the first quadrant of the Sirian Cross.

1362 The AN value of the twenty-eight words of the Great Invocation located in the second quadrant of the Sirian Cross.

1389 The AN value of the twenty-eight words of the Great Invocation located in the third quadrant of the Sirian Cross.

1480 The value of "Christos" in Greek gematria. 20 x 74. Related to 888.

1995 The result of multiplying the twenty-one key words by their 95 letters. Related to 95 and 21.

The result of 5 x 7 x 57; 5 equates with the five stanzas of the Great Invocation, 7 equates with the seven sentences, and 57 equates with the middle word position of the Great Invocation.

The year 1995, the fiftieth anniversary of the use of the Great Invocation by the Christ, Hierarchy, and Humanity. Related to 50.

Related to 5, 7, and 57.

2545 The AN value of the vertical arm of the triangular cross arrangement of the Great Invocation. Related to 206 and 2751.

2648 The AN value of the fifty-six words of the Great Invocation before the middle word "is" and the AN value of the fifty-six words following the middle word.

2751 The AN value of the horizontal arm of the triangular cross arrangement of the Great Invocation. Related to 206 and 2545.

5565 A triangular number resulting from the addition of the first 105 numbers.

A multi-faceted number in relation to the Great Invocation. It relates to the positions of the twenty-one key words within the stanzas (S): 5 in S1, 5 in S2, 6 in S3 and 4 combined, and 5 in S5.

A code number for "Sanat" (55 AN) "Kumara" (65 AN). Counting Sanat Kumara, 105 Kumaras came to Earth as part of a great cosmic Plan of redemption. Related to 21, 105, and 1065.

8338 The value of The Star (91 AN) squared (8281) added to "veiled" (57 AN).

Multiple numbers

3.8

The two different root number values of the twenty-eight words located in each quadrant of the Sirian cross. Related to 38.

8.3.3.8

The four root number values of the twenty-eight words located in each quadrant of the Sirian Cross Level Three. (See figure 20 and table 37.) Related to 17.12.21.12, and 1259, 1286, 1362, and 1389. Related to 38.

10.5.6.5

The values of the Hebrew letters which spell Jehovah.

Yod (10) He (5) Vau (6) He (5). A code number for 105 (10, 5) Kumara(s) (65 AN).

10.6.5

The number referred to by HPB in the *The Secret Doctrine* which is most sacred and related to the twenty-one Kumaras (10 + 6 + 5 = 21).

Arrangement of the twenty-one key words of the Great Invocation by combining stanzas: S1 and S2 (5 + 5), S3 and S4 (3 + 3) and S5 (5).

12, 13, 59, 62, 86, 89

The six different word positions in the Great Invocation created from pairing the AN values of the twenty-eight words located in each quadrant of the Sirian Cross Level One. (See figure 18 and table 35.) Related to 1259, 1286, 1362, and 1389.

17.12.21.17

The four word positions in the Great Invocation created from reducing the AN values of the twenty-eight words located in each quadrant of the Sirian Cross Level Two. (See figure 19 and table 36.) Related to 8.3.3.8.

27.5

The only decimal number in the index. This is the symbolic number of Horus, the offspring of Osiris (35 RAN) plus Isis (20 RAN). Thus 35 + 20 = 55 ÷ 2 = 27.5.

Ageless Wisdom. The name given to a transcendent teaching which forms the basis of all religion, science, art, and philosophy. It is a secret science of life purportedly given to humanity by divine Instructors and taught in the ancient mystery schools of initiation.

AN Method. A numerological method of converting letters to numbers using the natural order of the alphabet wherein A = 1 and Z = 26. For instance, the letter J equals 10 or has an AN value of 10 using this numerological method because it is the tenth letter of the alphabet.

Antahkarana. Sanskrit for "intermediate method." Specifically referred to in the ageless wisdom as a bridge in consciousness linking the lower logical mind with the higher abstract mind.

AN Value. Alpha Number Value. The sum of a word or phrase derived from the AN method. For instance, the AN value of the word "Isis" equals 56 (9 + 19 + 9 + 19).

Aquarian Age. Sometimes referred to as the New Age. This is a cycle of approximately 2,150 years in which the Sun appears in the constellation of Aquarius due to the precession of the equinox. The Aquarian Age is characterized by group activities, brotherhood, humanitarianism, and the use of the mind.

Ashram. A Sanskrit term for a group of spiritual students gathered around a teacher or guru. In the ageless wisdom, a specific type of group consciousness comprised of spiritual aspirants and disciples dedicated to a common goal. There are various levels and kinds of ashrams but they all have an advanced spiritual teacher as a leader. Ashrams are places of activity and work for the betterment of the world, not places of guru worship.

Astral. Emotional or desire nature. A quality of consciousness or plane of existence in which most souls find themselves after death. Usually considered a plane of glamour and illusion.

Atlantis. An ancient civilization of advanced technology that was destroyed through greed, ignorance, and the misuse of science.

In the ageless wisdom this is the generic term applied to the fourth root-race.

Atma. The first or will aspect of the spiritual triad. Related to purpose and the first ray.

Buddhi. The second or love-wisdom aspect of the spiritual triad. Related to intuition and the second ray.

Causal Body. Also called the egoic lotus. Symbolically the "command center" of the incarnating soul from lifetime to lifetime. When a human being incarnates on the physical plane, it is from the causal body on the higher mental plane from which they emerge. Following death, the human soul ultimately returns to the causal body after various experiences on the astral and lower mental planes. The causal body houses or stores the thousands of experiences of a human being over many lifetimes. Thus, it is a vessel of the accumulated wisdom of the ages.

Central Spiritual Sun. That aspect of any solar Logos which relates to the Monad or life of that cosmic Entity. The first aspect of a solar Logos is associated with the highest Will and Purpose.

Chain. That part of a planetary scheme which comprises a series of seven globes. Each globe is a specific dimensional "locale" in which a planetary Logos experiences evolutionary life and works out some particular purpose which can generally be called God's Plan. Since the seven globes are connected in a series they are referred to as a chain. Seven chains equal one planetary scheme.

Chakra. A focal point on the etheric, astral, or mental plane of consciousness which receives and transmits energy of a specific quality. The ageless wisdom recognizes seven primary chakras in a human being, although there are lesser chakras throughout the body. Chakras are like energy portals which regulate the flow of forces within and between life systems. Chakras exist in many forms, including animals, humans, regions of the Earth (sacred sites), planets, and entire solar systems.

Christ. The supreme Teacher of Humanity, and Leader of the spiritual Hierarchy. The Christ is a title for the One Who holds that high position of leadership in the Hierarchy. Through the ages there existed various advanced souls Who headed the Hierarchy. In the ageless wisdom, the Christ is not limited to the role of a religious figure, but is the supreme spiritual Leader and Teacher Who transcends all religions and philosophies.

Christ Principle. 1. Associated with the soul and the second aspect of the basic triplicity of the ageless wisdom. 2. Consciousness, the product of spirit and substance. 3. The evolutionary force which propels consciousness growth.

Creative Hierarchy. A life stream interacting with the various planes of consciousness for purposes of furthering the evolutionary development of entire planets and solar systems. There are twelve Creative Hierarchies, each associated with a particular constellation of the zodiac. Only seven Creative Hierarchies are actively manifesting in our solar system. One of these is the human Hierarchy of which the human kingdom is a lower reflection.

Disciple. Any person who is committed to spiritual growth regardless of religious affiliation. The ageless wisdom extends the definition of disciple to include any person who is working for the betterment of the human condition and not just for one's own personal gain.

Ego. A term the ageless wisdom originally applied to the soul in contrast to the personality. This term does not apply to the ego of mainstream psychology.

Esoteric Astrology. Astrology of the soul rather than the personality. This form of astrology is developed by Djwhal Khul in the book by the same title, in which emphasis is placed on spiritual development rather than the mundane events of the outer life such as career, money, relationships, etc.

Esoteric Numerology. The specific conversion of letters to numbers in order to penetrate into the inner meaning and correspondences between terms, names, and phrases. As in esoteric astrology, this form of numerology focuses on spiritual qualities and subjective relationships rather than on outer mundane affairs.

Etheric. A specific type of substance lying just beyond the range of the five physical senses. Etheric matter is still considered part of the world of form despite its invisibility to ordinary sense perception. The ethers are divided into four distinct types. All physical objects have an etheric counterpart which is the underlying structural network carrying life and consciousness to the outer world.

Factor. Two or more numbers associated through the product of their multiplication. For instance, 2 and 3 are factors of 6. In esoteric numerology a word or phrase is subjectively linked to the factors which interact to give it birth.

First Aspect. That part of the basic triplicity of the ageless wisdom relating to pure Spirit, Non-duality, Will, the Christian Father of the trinity, and the Monad.

Globe. A specific world located in a particular dimension or plane of consciousness. For instance, the Earth globe is located on the dense physical plane. A globe exists as one unit in a series of seven globes called a chain.

Heart of the Sun. That aspect of a solar Logos which relates to the Soul or quality of that cosmic Entity. The second aspect of a solar Logos is associated with the divine quality of Love.

Hierarchy. 1. In general, the great chain of being found throughout the universe in which life systems contain lesser systems and are themselves contained within greater systems. All systems are alive, conscious, and intelligent, pursuing their own growth as part of some greater whole system. 2. The spiritual Hierarchy of the Earth is a second aspect center of activity led by the Christ and comprised of Beings Who have evolved through the human stage of consciousness. All the Members of the Hierarchy were once human beings. The purpose of the

Hierarchy is to oversee planetary evolution in all the kingdoms of nature including the human. The Hierarchy never interferes with humanity's free will. It guides and teaches, leaving humanity the freedom to make its choices based on the spiritual principles expressed through the various religions and philosophies made available throughout the ages.

Individualization. The evolutionary method of creating individual and distinct souls with the free will to pursue life in relative freedom. This planetary event occurred about eighteen million years ago and resulted in the creation of the human kingdom. This initiative by Sanat Kumara and 104 other Kumaras began about twenty million years ago but took two million years to achieve success. Sirius was involved in the crisis of individualization because it involved the initiation of our planetary Logos.

Initiation. A special form of consciousness expansion employed on Earth in order to accelerate evolution. There are nine possible initiations available on our planet. Completion of the first five initiations liberate a person from the human kingdom and allow full entry into the Hierarchy. Initiation originates on Sirius, and the Christ is the most advanced Sirian Initiate Whose soul originated on Earth.

Invocation. 1. A prayer or mantram. 2. The act of calling forth some higher power to intervene in a time of crisis.

Karma. The result of cause and effect. Karma can be positive or negative. Karma exists at many levels: cosmic, systemic, planetary, racial, national, familial, and individual. All karma in our solar system is governed by Sirius.

Key Word. A term created for the specific analysis of the Great Invocation. The number of words in the Great Invocation which are capitalized, excluding the words which begin each line. There are twenty-one key words in the Great Invocation.

Law of Correspondences. Also called the Law of Analogy. A method for investigating the possible relationships existing between apparently unconnected objects, people, energies, ideas, or events. The ageless wisdom teaches that objective forms including thoughtforms are actually connected at a deeper subjective, archetypal level. This law helps penetrate and interpret the concepts and energy patterns found at these abstract and intuitive planes of consciousness.

Lemuria. The third root-race. The first race of human beings created after the process of individualization was completed.

Lords of Karma. Advanced Entities Who control the law of cause and effect in our solar system. These Beings are also called the Lipika Lords or the Recorders of all acts, events, thoughts, and experiences. These Lords have the responsibility of maintaining balance through the meting out of those experiences (good and bad) which will either offset the misuse of spiritual and physical laws by teaching the consequences of ignorance, or provide more knowledge and guidance as an incentive for the better use of spiritual and physical laws.

Lords of the Flame. Another name for that class of Beings Who brought manas or mind to animal man. Generally speaking, these are also called the Kumaras.

Manas. Sanskrit for the "mind principle." This is divided into two aspects: higher mind, producing abstract thought and wisdom, and lower mind, producing concrete thought and knowledge. It was the principle of manas which the Lords of the Flame or the Kumaras instilled in the Lemurian race. The manasic principle was successfully "individualized" resulting in the self-conscious human soul or individual. These individualized units of consciousness resulted in the human kingdom.

Mantram. Sanskrit for prayer; also called mantra. More specifically, the ageless wisdom teaches that mantrams produce powerful effects when sounded according to a particular rhythm. The Great Invocation is a mantram of high potency when sounded with complete mental concentration and focused intent.

Master. A Member of the spiritual Hierarchy Who was formerly a human being. These advanced souls are called Masters because they have learned all the lessons which the human experience can teach. They have transcended the human level of living by mastering every aspect of the human condition. They now work toward mastering higher levels of existence.

Master Jesus. A Member of the Hierarchy Who leads the Christian religion in all its aspects. This Master was overshadowed by the Christ in Palestine 2,000 years ago. Jesus and the One Who is known as the Christ are two separate and distinct Beings.

Master Number. 1. In traditional numerology, 11 and 22 are considered master numbers, although some numerologists use 11, 22, 33, 44, 55, 66, 77, 88, and 99 as master numbers. This book uses only the numbers 11 and 22. 2. Master numbers are not reduced to single digits (1 + 1 = 2 or 2 + 2 = 4) in esoteric numerology (or traditional numerology, in most cases); as root values they symbolize the use and control of energy. For instance, the word "light" equals 56 or 29 depending on whether the AN or RAN method is used to determine its numeric value. However, its root value is 11 by either method (5 + 6 or 2 + 9). Thus, the word "light" is not reduced to 2 (1 + 1) because it is a master number. Note that not every word reduces to a master number when it is subjected to both the AN and RAN methods. For instance, the word "Isis" equals 56 (AN) and 20 (RAN). Therefore, its root value for the AN method is the master number 11; but its root value for the RAN method is 2 because 2 + 0 = 2.

Monad. The divine spark of a human being. It corresponds to the first aspect of the basic triplicity of the ageless wisdom. The monad also corresponds to the Father aspect of the trinity.

Non-sacred Planet. A term used to differentiate the spiritual evolution of the planetary Logoi in our solar system; a planetary Logos Who has not yet taken one of the higher cosmic initiations. The Earth is a non-sacred planet, but our planetary Logos, through the incarnation of Sanat Kumara, is currently undergoing that particular initiatory process which will make our planet sacred. Technically, the Earth is already a sacred planet, but until this can be practically expressed at the physical level through the manifesting kingdoms (especially the human), the Earth is still considered a non-sacred planet. The other non-sacred planets in our solar system are the Sun, the Moon, Mars, and Pluto.

Perfect Number. Any number which equals the sum of its factors, not counting itself. For instance, 6 is a perfect number. Its factors are 1, 2, and 3 (1 x 6 and 2 x 3). Thus 1 + 2 + 3 = 6. The first three perfect numbers are 6, 28 and 496.

Permanent Atom. A term used in the ageless wisdom for a unit of substance which stores the experiences of consciousness during the manifestation of a soul or spiritual entity. There are permanent atoms for each level of consciousness an entity is potentially able to experience. Thus, the average human being possesses a physical, an astral, and a mental permanent atom. Each of these stores the experiences and knowledge gained during the soul's cycle of manifestation. There are manasic, buddhic, and atmic permanent atoms, but for all practical purposes these do not concern us. Entities such as planetary and solar Logoi also have permanent atoms.

Personality. 1. The form manifestation of the soul. The personality is the instrument used by the soul to contact the lower mental, astral, and physical planes of consciousness. 2. The personality is a type of consciousness which is self-ish. It represents a stage of consciousness growth wherein individuality is developed.

Piscean Age. The 2,150 year zodiacal cycle which is now ending as the Sun precesses into the constellation of Aquarius. The Piscean era was characterized by faith, devotion, idealism, sacrifice, individual effort, and emotions.

Plane. 1. A level or dimension of consciousness. Each plane has its own characteristics. For instance, the astral plane is based on emotions and feelings; the mental plane is a world of thoughts and thoughtforms. 2. The ageless wisdom describes 343 possible planes of consciousness. There are seven cosmic planes. Each cosmic plane is divided into seven subplanes, called systemic planes. Each one of the seven systemic planes is divided once more into seven subplanes. Thus, there are 7 x 7 x 7 planes of consciousness (343) recognized at this time by the ageless wisdom. Thus, the densest level of substance in which consciousness can express itself can be notated as the 343rd sub-subplane of the entire known spectrum of consciousness.

Precession. The apparent backward motion of the sun through the twelve signs of the zodiac due to the wobble of the Earth's axis. This wobble shifts the apparent position of the sun backward, relative to the zodiacal signs about one degree every seventy years. It takes approximately 25,880 years for the sun to complete one revolution through all the constellations of the zodiac. The beginning of an age, such as the age of Aquarius, is measured by the year when the sun enters the first degree of a sign on the vernal equinox or first day of spring.

Planetary Logos. A cosmic Entity Who ensouls or manifests through a planet. Such a planetary Logos manifests through a planetary scheme of worlds. The planetary Logos of the Earth Scheme is currently incarnated as Sanat Kumara.

Planetary Scheme. The entire series of worlds through which a planetary Logos creates and manifests during the cyclic activity of a solar system.

Pyramidal Number. A number which is the sum of a series of square numbers. For instance, 14 is a pyramidal number because it is the sum of 1 x 1, 2 x 2 and 3 x 3 or 1 + 4 + 9. Fourteen wooden cubes are arranged in the form of a pyramid by placing 9 cubes in a square (3 x 3) at the base, 4 cubes on top of these (2 x 2), and 1 cube at the apex (1 x 1).

RAN Method. A numerological method of converting letters to numbers using the reduced values of the alphabet. For instance, the letter J is the 10th letter of the alphabet, but instead of counting J as 10 it is reduced to 1 by adding 1 + 0. Thus the letter J = 1 or has a RAN value of 1 as opposed to its AN value which equals 10.

RAN Value. Reduced Alpha Number Value. The sum of a word or phrase derived from the RAN method. For instance, the RAN value of the word "Isis" equals 20 (9 + 1 + 9 + 1).

Ring-pass-not. A boundary or limitation of influence and conscious awareness beyond which an entity cannot go. This term applies to humans, planetary Logoi, and solar Logoi as well as to other life forms defined by the ageless wisdom.

Root Value. A numerological term applied to the lowest number to which any word or phrase can be reduced. For instance, the word "god" has an AN value of 26 (7 (g) + 15 (o) + 4 (d)), a RAN value of 17 (7 (g) + 6 (o) + 4 (d)) and a root value of 8 (2 + 6 or 1 + 7). No matter what the AN or RAN value of any word or phrase is, it can always be reduced to a root number.

Root-race. 1. A distinct type of consciousness development seeded into a particular group of souls living in human form. The physical race in which a particular quality of consciousness develops is irrelevant because a root-race has no relation to racial body type. For instance, the current fifth root-race is developing lower manas or the ability to use the concrete, logical, reasoning faculty. The ability to integrate doing, feeling, and thinking (manas) into a smoothly operating personality is the present goal for the humanity of the modern world. This is fifth root-race consciousness. Each root-race is the means by which a planetary Logos experiences, develops, and synthesizes a particular principle or quality of consciousness. The collective psychological fruit of a root-race is absorbed by the planetary Logos as part of His own growth experience in the cosmos. 2. Each globe produces seven root-races. On the Earth globe the first two root-races were etheric. The first physical plane root-race was the Lemurian, but technically it is referred to as the third root-race. This group of humans developed the ability to integrate basic survival instincts and physical plane activity. The Atlantean root-race, the fourth, developed and integrated the emotional and feeling principle with that already developed by the Lemurian race. Our current humanity is the Aryan fifth root-race. It is combining the physical, emotional, and mental principles into one integrated unit of consciousness, called the personality. This is being accomplished through the rapid spread of education and technology throughout the world. Hitler used the Aryan idea to spread his insanely distorted and evil philosophy of the superman. This was and still is a complete misuse and distortion of the root-race concept. To repeat, root-race has nothing to do with the color of a person's skin or their ethnic background; it is simply a term used to describe the overall development of human consciousness.

Round. A cycle of experience which encompasses the passage of seven root-races through seven globes of a chain. Ideally, since there are seven rounds in every chain this means each globe will eventually host forty-nine root-races. Taken as a whole, one chain of seven rounds will host 343 root-races, or 7 root-races x 7 globes x 7 rounds = one chain.

Sacred Planet. The definition of a planetary Logos Who has taken a particular cosmic initiation resulting in His liberation from lower cosmic planes of consciousness, and His consequential expansion into higher cosmic levels of experience and life.

Sanat Kumara. 1. The incarnated planetary Logos of the Earth. In terms analogous to the human experience, Sanat Kumara is the personality incarnation of the soul of the planetary Logos. 2. Loosely translated from Sanskrit, Sanat means "first" and Kumara means "eternal youth" or "born with difficulty." Sanat Kumara is also called Melchizedek, The Lord of the World, The Great Sacrifice, and The Ancient of Days.

Second Aspect. A term referring to the soul or middle aspect of the basic triplicity of the ageless wisdom. It is the Christ principle and the Cosmic Christ. In terms of the Christian trinity, it is the Son. It also corresponds to Love-Wisdom and Universal Consciousness.

Seven Rays. The seven distinct cosmic energies which constitute all life and planes of consciousness as we know it in our solar system and in the One About Whom Naught May Be Said. The seven rays are: (1) Will and Purpose, (2) Love-Wisdom, (3) Intelligent Activity, (4) Harmony Through Conflict or Beauty, (5) Science and Concrete Knowledge, (6) Devotion and Idealism, (7)

Ritual and Order.

Shamballa. The highest spiritual center of our planet, the focal point of Sanat Kumara, and the supreme ruling spiritual Council for all the kingdoms of our planet. This is the center where the Will of God is known. According to the ageless wisdom, Shamballa is located on the highest physical etheric plane somewhere in central Asia. Shamballa is related to the First Aspect of the basic triplicity.

Shekinah. A Hebrew term generally translated as divine Intelligence, Sophia, Wisdom, and spiritual Light. This is the divine feminine principle and is related to the third aspect of the basic triplicity.

Sirian Cross. 1. An equal-armed cross related to the star system of Sirius. 2. A graphic symbol used to decode specific sections of the Great Invocation using esoteric numerology.

Sirius. 1. The most influential cosmic source of spiritual energy in our solar system. 2. The fifth closest known star to our solar system, 8.7 light years from Earth. There are at least two, maybe three stars in the Sirian system; Sirius A, the main star and Sirius B, a white dwarf which orbits the much larger Sirius A approximately once every fifty years. There is some evidence that a third star is part of the Sirian system but this has not yet been proven.

Solar Logos. A cosmic Entity that ensouls an entire solar system when in physical manifestation. The ageless wisdom teaches that our solar Logos will manifest three times. During each manifestation one aspect of the basic triplicity will be perfected. Our solar logos has already manifested in an earlier cycle. That first solar system perfected the third aspect of Intelligence. Our present solar system is the second manifestation of the solar Logos in which the second aspect of Love-Wisdom is being brought to perfection. The third solar system will perfect the first aspect of the basic triplicity, that of Will.

Soul. The second aspect of the basic triplicity of the ageless wisdom. The soul is consciousness itself. The chief characteristic of the soul is group relationship. Soul consciousness corresponds to the Christ principle, the Son, the product of divine spirit, and divine substance.

Spiritual Triad. 1. The manifestation of the monad on the three planes of atma—spiritual will, buddhi—spiritual love-wisdom and manas—spiritual mind. The spiritual triad is the human correspondence to the three aspects of the basic triplicity of the ageless wisdom. As far as is known this triplicity is universal. 2. The human personality, constituted of mind, emotion, and physical body is the lower reflection of the spiritual triad. The lower concrete mind corresponds to higher spiritual, abstract mind, emotions correspond to spiritual love-wisdom, and physical/etheric activities correspond to spiritual will. 3. The soul is the middle principle partaking of both spirit and personality qualities.

Square Number. Any number which is the result of multiplication with itself. For instance 9 is a square number, being the product of the factors 3 x 3.

Tetrahedral Number. The sum of a series of triangular numbers. For instance, 20 is a tetrahedral number because it is the sum of the first four triangular numbers 1, 3, 6, and 10 (1 + 3 + 6 + 10 = 20). For instance twenty oranges are arranged in the form of a tetrahedron by placing 10 in a triangular pattern at the base, a triangular pattern of 6 on top of these, 3 on top of these, and 1 at the apex. The resultant pile of fruit is a tetrahedron or a four-sided object consisting of 20 oranges.

The Great Work. 1. Traditionally, the alchemical process of transmuting lead into gold. 2. Symbolically, it is a transformative process applied to any situation requiring release from unnecessary limitations into an expanded state where new growth can proceed. 3. The spiritual path of redemption. The release of the soul that is identified with material form and thus trapped on the wheel of rebirth or what Christianity considers sin. The Great Work of redemption is transmuting, transforming, and ultimately transfiguring. It involves the process of initiation and consequent release and spiritual evolution of the individual into a greater life, which cannot be accurately described, but only experienced. The Great Work is individual, group, planetary, and cosmic in scope.

Third Aspect. That part of the basic triplicity relating to divine Substance, Intelligence, the divine Feminine, and the Christian Holy Spirit of the trinity. In the human being it corresponds to the spiritualized personality.

Triangular Number. Any number which is the result of the addition of the numbers one through x. For instance, 10 is a triangular number because it is the result of the addition of the numbers 1 through 4 (1 + 2 + 3 + 4 = 10). Thus, the numbers 10 and 4 have a numeric relationship. The number 14 is not a triangular number because 1 through 4 equals 10 and 1 through 5 equals 15 (1 + 2 + 3 + 4 + 5 = 15). Thus 10 and 15 are triangular numbers, but 14 is not. Triangular numbers are inherently related to the number which produces them.

Word of Power. A mantram or sound formula capable of effecting spiritual, psychological, and physical change when used with the correct note and rhythm. The Great Invocation is a word of power specifically designed to be effective when used with mental concentration and spiritual intent.

Works Cited

Agni Yoga Society. *New Era Community*. Agni Yoga Society, Inc., 1951.

Bailey, Alice A. *A Treatise on Cosmic Fire*. 1925. Reprint, New York: Lucis Publishing Co., 1964.

———. *A Treatise on the Seven Rays*. Vol. I. *Esoteric Psychology*. 1936. Reprint, New York: Lucis Publishing Co., 1967.

———. *A Treatise on the Seven Rays*. Vol. II. *Esoteric Psychology*. 1942. Reprint, New York: Lucis Publishing Co., 1966.

———. *A Treatise on the Seven Rays*. Vol. III. *Esoteric Astrology*. 1951. Reprint, New York: Lucis Publishing Co., 1970.

———. *A Treatise on the Seven Rays*. Vol. IV. *Esoteric Healing*. 1953. Reprint, New York: Lucis Publishing Co., 1970.

———. *A Treatise on the Seven Rays*. Vol. V. *The Rays and the Initiations*. 1960. Reprint, New York: Lucis Publishing Co., 1970.

———. *A Treatise on White Magic*. 1934. Reprint, New York: Lucis Publishing Co., 1979.

———. *Discipleship in the New Age*. Vol. II. 1955. Reprint, New York: Lucis Publishing Co., 1968.

———. *From Bethlehem to Calvary*. 1937. Revised ed., New York: Lucis Publishing Co., 1968.

———. *Initiation, Human and Solar*. 1922. Reprint, New York: Lucis Publishing Co., 1970.

———. *Letters on Occult Meditation*. 1922. Reprint, New York: Lucis Publishing Co., 1970.

———. *The Externalisation of the Hierarchy*. 1957. Reprint, New York: Lucis Publishing Co., 1968.

———. *The Labours of Hercules*. 1957-58. Reprint. New York: Lucis Publishing Co., 1977.

———. *The Reappearance of the Christ*. 1948. Reprint, New York: Lucis Publishing Co., 1969.

———. *The Unfinished Autobiography*. 1951. Reprint, New York: Lucis Publishing Co., 1951.

Bailey, Foster. *Reflections*. New York: Lucis Publishing Co., 1979.

———. *Things To Come*. New York: Lucis Publishing Co., 1974.

———. "The Great Invocation." *The Beacon* XXX, No., 3-4 (June-July, 1951).

Bailey, Mary. *A Learning Experience*. New York: Lucis Publishing Co., 1990.

———. *Bridge To the Future,* video. New York: Lucis Productions Co., 1984.

Barborka, Geoffrey A. *The Divine Plan*. Adyar, India: The Theosophical Publishing House, 1980.

Berges, John. "A Study and Analysis of the Great Invocation Using Esoteric Numerology." Master's thesis, Tahlequah, OK: Sancta Sophia Seminary, 1994.

Blavatsky, Helena P. *The Secret Doctrine*. Adyar ed. 6 vols. Adyar, India: Theosophical Publishing House, 1962.

———. *The Theosophical Glossary*. 1892. Reprint, Los Angeles: The Theosophical Company, 1973.

Budge, E. A. Wallis. *The Gods of the Egyptians* in 2 vols. 1904. Reprint, New York: Dover Publications, Inc., 1969.

Burnham, Robert, Jr. *Burnham's Celestial Handbook*. Vol. 3. New York: Dover Publications, Inc., 1978.

Case, Paul Foster, *The Tarot: A Key to the Wisdom of the Ages*. 1947. Revised ed., Los Angeles: Builders of the Adytum, Ltd., 1990.

Eisen, William. *The English Cabalah*. Vol. 2: The Mysteries of Phi. Marina del Rey, CA: DeVors & Co., 1982.

Eisler, Robert, *Orpheus—The Fisher: Comparative Studies in Orphic and Early Christian Symbolism*. Reprint, Kila, MT: Kessenger Publishing Co., 1991.

Faivre, Antoine. *The Eternal Hermes*, trans. Joscelyn Godwin. Grand Rapids, MI: Phanes Press, 1995.

Fideler, David. *Jesus Christ, Sun of God: Ancient Cosmology and Early Christian Symbolism*. Wheaton, IL: Quest Books, 1993

Gaskell, G. A. *Dictionary of All Scriptures and Myths*. 1960 by The Julian Press. Reprint, New York: Avenel Books, 1981.

Godwin, David. *Godwin's Cabalistic Encyclopedia*. 1979. Third ed., St. Paul, MN: Llewellyn Publications, 1994.

Hall, Manly P. *The Initiates of Greece and Rome*. Los Angeles: The Philosophical Research Society, Inc., 1981.

———. *The Secret Teachings of All Ages*. Reprint black and white facsimile of Golden Ann. ed. Los Angeles: The Philosophical Research Society, Inc., 1977.

Higgins, Godfrey. *Anacalypsis* in 2 vols. 1833. Reprint Kila, MT: Kessenger Publishing Co. n.d.

Iamblichus. *The Theology of Arithmetic*. Trans. Robin Waterfield. Grand Rapids, MI: Phanes Press, 1988.

Integral Yoga Institute. *Dictionary of Sanskrit Names*. Yogaville, VA: Integral Yoga Publications, 1989.

Lemesurier, Peter. *The Great Pyramid Decoded*. Dorset, Great Britain: Element Books Ltd., 1993.

Lotterhand, Jason C. *The Thursday Night Tarot*. North Hollywood, CA: Newcastle Publishing Co., Inc., 1989.

Mead, G. R. S. *Thrice Greatest Hermes*. Reprint, Kila, MT: Kessenger Publishing Co., n.d.

Meyer, Marvin W., ed. *The Ancient Mysteries, A Sourcebook*. New York: Harper Collins, 1987.

Pike, Albert. *Morals and Dogma of the Ancient and Accepted Scottish Rite of Freemasonry*. Reprint, Kila, MT: Kessenger Publishing Co. n.d.

Plato. Phaedrus. In *Plato: Collected Dialogues*, trans. R. Hackforth, et. al. Princeton: Princeton University Press, 1961.

Reese, W. L. *Dictionary of Philosophy and Religion*. Atlantic Highlands, NJ: Humanities Press Inc., 1980.

Schuhmacher, Stephen, and Gert Woerner, eds. *The Encyclopedia of Eastern Philosophy and Religion*. Boston: Shambhala. 1989.

Schwab, Gustav. *Gods & Heroes, Myths and Epics of Ancient Greece*. New York: Fawcett World Library, 1965.

Scott, Walter, ed. and trans. *Hermetica*. Boulder, CO: Hermes House, 1982.

Taylor, Thomas. *The Theoretic Arithmetic of the Pythagoreans*. York Beach, ME: Samuel Weiser, Inc., 1983.

Temple, Robert K. G. *The Sirius Mystery*. Rochester, VT: Destiny Books, 1976.

Waite, Arthur Edward. *The Pictorial Key to the Tarot*. 1910. Reprint, New Hyde Park, NY: University Books, Inc., 1959.

West, John Anthony. *Serpent in the Sky*. Wheaton, IL: Theosophical Publishing House, 1993.